COMMUNICATION ACTIVISM

Volume 2
Media and Performance Activism

Edited by

Lawrence R. Frey
University of Colorado at Boulder

Kevin M. Carragee
Suffolk University

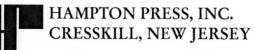

HAMPTON PRESS, INC.
CRESSKILL, NEW JERSEY

Printed in the United States of America

Library of Congress Cataloging-in-Publication Data

Communication activism/edited by Lawrence R. Frey, Kevin M. Carragee.
   v. cm.
  Includes bibliograhpical references and index.
  Contents: V. 2. Media and performance activism.
  ISBN 1-57273-698-4 (casebound) -- ISBN 1-57273-699-2 (paperbound)
  1. Communication in social action. 2. Communication--Social aspects. 3.
Communication--Political aspects. I. Frey, Lawrence R. II. Carragee,
Kevin M.
  HM1206.C6475 2007
  361.201`4--dc22
          2006035764

Hampton Press, Inc.
23 Broadway
Cresskill, NJ 07626

CONTENTS

Introduction

COMMUNICATION ACTIVISM AS ENGAGED SCHOLARSHIP

Lawrence R. Frey

University of Colorado at Boulder

Kevin M. Carragee

Suffolk University

There certainly is no shortage of controversial issues confronting contemporary U.S. society. Consider, for instance, the highly contested Iraq War, with, as of October 3, 2006, 2,721 U.S. soldiers dead and 19,910 wounded (Iraq Coalition Casualty Count, 2006); the concerns raised about the continued use of capital punishment, with, since 1973, 123 people from 25 states released from death row because of evidence of factual innocence (Death Penalty Information Center, 2006); the arguments raging across the country in courtrooms, state legislatures, and at ballot boxes over same-sex marriage, with nearly half the states having outlawed or poised to ban such marriages in their constitution (Peterson, 2006); or the controversy surrounding immigration, with hundreds of thousands of immigrants and advocates taking to U.S. city streets on May 1, 2006, to protest proposed immigration laws ("Thousands March," 2006), as U.S. President George W. Bush tries to balance sending the National Guard to help patrol the U.S. border with Mexico with offering a temporary guest worker program and paths to citizenship for long-term illegal immigrants.

One might think that the members of the academy would be at the forefront of confronting these and other important social issues. After all, as Crabtree and Ford point out in their chapter in Volume 1 of these texts, many U.S. colleges and universities were established, as part of their mission, to generate knowledge to better their communities (see, e.g., C. W. Anderson, 1993; Barber, 1992; Checkoway, 2001; Kennedy, 1997). Unfortunately, however, over the years, higher educational institutions tended to abandon this civic mission (see, e.g., Boyer, 1987; Butler, 2000; Sandmann & Lewis, 1991; Sirianni & Friedland, 1997) in favor of research directed toward a relatively small, insular group of fellow scholars, with the number of scholarly journals now estimated to be between 80,000-100,000 (Tenopir & King, 2000). This focus on research directed toward other scholars rather than toward helping communities to solve societal problems probably was related to the privileging of "theory" over "application" in the academy, for if one follows the etymology of the word *theory*, derived from the Greek words *theoria* ("contemplation, speculation, a looking at, things looked at"), *theorein* ("to consider, speculate, look at"), *theoros* ("spectator"), and *thea* ("a view") (Online Etymology Dictionary, 2006), scholars are supposed to be spectators whose work is best done by looking at and contemplating what occurs without trying to affect it.

One might think that communication scholars, in particular, would be confronting societal issues. After all, communication inherently is a "practical discipline" (Craig, 1989, 1995; Craig & Tracy, 1995) concerned with cultivating communicative *praxis* that yields useful knowledge. The historical roots of the formal discipline of communication (with the study of communication dating back at least to antiquity) certainly were grounded in producing useful knowledge, such as teaching people to become better speakers in their everyday interactions and in the public sphere (e.g., W. H. Davis, 1915, on debating as related to nonacademic life) and engage in effective communicative practices (e.g., Dewey's, 1910, reflective thinking process) for democratic group decision making (see, e.g., A. C. Baird, 1927; Elliott, 1927; McBurney & Hance, 1939; Sheffield, 1926; for a review, see Frey, 1996), as well as mass communication research directed toward understanding and, hopefully, improving media practices and people's ability to process mediated messages (such as not being easily persuaded by propaganda; for historical overviews of such research, see, e.g., Delia, 1987; Rogers, 1994;

Schramm, 1997). Unfortunately, however, communication scholars, like their counterparts in the other social sciences and humanities, and perhaps, in part, because of their desire to obtain disciplinary legitimacy in the eyes of those colleagues, all too frequently, over the course of time, shied away from addressing important societal issues to focus, instead, on disciplinary theoretical concerns, such as the great metatheoretical debates, starting during the 1970s and continuing for quite some time, about what theories should be employed in communication research (see, e.g., Benson & Pearce, 1977) and what criteria should be used to judge the admissibility of evidence to support theoretical propositions in communication scholarship (see, e.g., Cronkhite & Liska, 1977).

This failure to confront salient social issues is unfortunate, for given the sheer volume and significance of these issues and the potential contributions that communication knowledge can make to managing them, the exigency for communication scholars to engage in direct vigorous action in support of needed social change has never been more apparent and important. In short, communication scholars need to engage in "communication activism."

COMMUNICATION ACTIVISM

Ac·tiv·ism: A doctrine or practice that emphasizes direct vigorous action especially in support of or opposition to one side of a controversial issue

—Merriam-Webster Online (2006)

"Activism" has a long and distinguished history (see, e.g., Downs & Manion, 2004; Eno, 1920; Reed, 2005; Santiago, 1972; Wigginton, 1991). Literally thousands of books have been written about activism theory and practice (e.g., W. Clark, 2000; Falconer, 2001; Schragge, 2003; Weissberg, 2005), activism art and performance (e.g., Bass, 1999; Gómez-Peña, 2005), and activist individuals (e.g., Avakian, 2000; DeLeon, 1994) and networks (e.g., Ferree & Tripp, 2006; Keck & Sikkink, 1999), as well as particular contexts/forms of activism—including abortion (e.g., Seaton, 1996; Staggenborg, 1991), AIDS (e.g., R. A. Smith & Siplon, 2006; Stockdill, 2003), animal rights (e.g., Beers, 2006; Guither, 1998), antinuclear (e.g., Dawson, 1996; Holsworth, 1989), corporate (e.g., Eisenhofer & Barry, 2006; Monks, 1999); environmental (e.g., DeLuca, 1999; Mauch, Stolzfus, & Weiner, 2006), gay and lesbian (e.g., Leyland, 2002; Stevenson & Cogan, 2003), legal (e.g., Fisher, 1997; Wolfe, 1997), Native American (e.g., T. R. Johnson, 1996; T. Johnson, Nagel, & Champagne, 1997), race (Alleyne, 2002; Jennings, 1997), religious/spiritual (e.g., Lampert, 2005; Weiss, 2002), student/youth (e.g., Ginwright, Noguera, & Cammarota, 2006; Rhoads, 1998), women/feminism (e.g., Baumgadner & Richards, 2005; Hawkesworth, 2006b), and worker activism (e.g., de Witte, 2005; Markowitz, 2000)—and specific countries and regions of the world, in addition to the United States, where activism has been documented—such as China (Chan, 1985), Eastern Europe (e.g., Bugajski & Pollack, 1989), Guatemala (e.g., Warren, 1998), India (Bharucha, 1998), and Yemen (Carapico, 1998).

To this literature, we add the concept of communication activism, which has a number of historical roots and related branches. Rhetoricians, for instance, especially during the turbulent decade of the 1960s, examined the communicative practices of social protest by activist individuals, groups, organizations, and movements (see, e.g., Andrews, 1969; J. E. Baird, 1970; Benson & Johnson, 1968; Bowen, 1963a, 1963b, 1967; Fernandez, 1968; Gregg, 1971; Haiman, 1967; Kerr, 1959; Kosokoff & Carlmichael, 1970; Lawton, 1968; Lomas, 1960, 1963; Martin, 1966; McEdwards, 1968; Rude, 1969; Scott & Smith, 1969; D. H. Smith, 1967; Toch, Deutsch, & Wilkins, 1960; Yoder, 1969).

Historical and contemporary analyses of activist communicative practices are alive and well today (recent examples include Chvasta, 2006; DeLuca & Peeples, 2002; Grano, 2002; Hasian, 2001; Hung, 2003; Knight & Greenberg, 2002; Kowal, 2000; McChesney, 2004a; McGee, 2003; Peeples, 2003; Pezzullo, 2001, 2003; Reber & Berger, 2005; Sanchez & Stuckey, 2000; Sender, 2001; Shi, 2005; Sowards & Renegar, 2004; Theodore, 2002; West & Gastil, 2004). Many contemporary studies focus on media activism, such as activists' use of media (especially the internet) and efforts by social movement organizations to influence news media coverage of societal issues (recent examples include Atkinson & Dougherty, 2006; Bennett, 2003; Bullert, 2000; Carroll & Hackett, 2006; Coopman, 2000; de Jong, Shaw, & Stammers, 2005; Diani, 2000; Dichter, 2004; Garrett, 2006; Gibson, 2003; Gillett, 2003; Greenberg & Knight, 2004; Harold, 2004; Kahn & Kellner, 2004; McCaughey & Ayers, 2003; Meikle, 2002; Palczewski, 2001; Palmeri, 2006; Pickerill, 2003; Pini, Brown, & Previte, 2004; Ryan, 1991; Ryan, Carragee, & Meinhofer, 2001; Ryan, Carragee, & Schwerner, 1998; Stengrim, 2005; Van de Donk, Loader, Nixon, & Rucht 2004).

These studies of activists' communicative practices are part of the larger grounding of communication activism in *applied communication scholarship*. As Cissna (1982) explained:

> *Applied* research sets out to contribute to knowledge by answering a real, pragmatic, social question or by solving a real pragmatic, social problem. Applied *communication* research involves such a question or problem of human communication or examines human communication

in order to provide an answer or solution to the question or problem. The intent or goal of the inquiry (as manifest in the research report itself) is the hallmark of applied communication research. Applied communication research involves the development of knowledge regarding a real human communication problem or question. (p. ii)

This applied view of communication scholarship grew out of the 1968 New Orleans Conference on Research and Instructional Development, which encouraged research on the communication dimensions of current social problems (see Kibler & Barker, 1969, especially the essay in that text by Cronkhite, 1969). (The concept of "applied research" in the social sciences dates back to Lazarsfeld's sociological research during the 1940s and his creation in 1944 of the Bureau of Applied Social Research at Columbia University; see, e.g., Delia, 1987; Rogers, 1994; Schramm, 1997.) Five years later, in 1973, the *Journal of Applied Communications Research* was created (see Hickson, 1973), which subsequently became the *Journal of Applied Communication Research*, which now is sponsored (along with an Applied Communication Division) by the National Communication Association (NCA; for a historical overview of applied communication scholarship, see Cissna, Eadie, & Hickson, in press). Although applied communication research, as compared with *basic communication research* (designed to test communication theory), certainly was a hotly contested issue for many years (see, e.g., Eadie, 1982; Ellis, 1982, 1991; Kreps, Frey, & O'Hair, 1991; Miller, 1995; Miller & Sunnafrank, 1984; O'Hair, Kreps, & Frey, 1990; Seibold, 1995; Wood, 1995), today, applied scholarship is an integral part of the communication discipline and its focal areas (see, e.g., Frey & Cissna, in press).

Applied communication scholars have contributed substantially to understanding the communicative practices of activist individuals, groups, and organizations. One of the best examples is the communication research on *health activism*, which Zoller (2005) defined as "a challenge to the existing order and power relationships that are perceived to influence some aspects of health negatively or to impede health promotion" (p. 344; see also Geist-Martin, Ray, & Sharf, 2003). Brashers, Haas, and Neidig (1999), for instance, created the Patient Self-Advocacy Scale to measure people's involvement in their healthcare decision-making interactions with physicians. Brashers, Haas, Klingle, and Neidig (2000) later showed that those engaged in AIDS activism at the collective level (by participating in the AIDS activist organization ACT UP) exhibited a number of self-advocacy behaviors that affected their interactions with physicians, including increased education about illness and treatment options, which allowed activist patients to challenge physicians' expertise; assertiveness toward their healthcare, which led them to confront physicians who communicated using a paternalistic or authoritarian style; and a willingness to be mindfully non-adherent, which resulted in them sometimes rejecting treatments recommended by physicians and articulating reasons for doing so. Brashers, Haas, Neidig, and Rintamaki (2002) also found important differences in the healthcare practices of activist and nonactivist individuals with HIV or AIDS, with activists employing more problem-focused and less emotion-focused coping, possessing greater knowledge of HIV-treatment information sources, and having greater HIV social network integration. (Regarding the communication tactics of ACT UP and other AIDS activist individuals, groups, and organizations, see Brashers & Jackson, 1991; Brouwer, 1998, 2001; Christiansen & Hanson, 1996; Dow, 1994; Fabj & Sobnowsky, 1993, 1995; McGee, 2003; Melcher, 1995; Meyers & Brashers, 2002; Sobnowsky & Hauser, 1998.)

Although the scholarship cited here has contributed substantially to understanding activist communication, most of it constitutes *third-person-perspective studies* in which researchers study individuals, groups, and organizations engaging in communication activism. Third-person-perspective researchers, thus, stand outside the stream of human events and observe, describe, interpret, explain, and (in rhetorical criticism) critique what occurs, as well as (in applied communication scholarship) offer suggestions for what could or should occur. These studies stand in sharp contrast to *first-person-perspective studies* in which researchers want to get in the stream and affect it in some significant ways (e.g., build a dam or change its flow).

The call for first-person-perspective communication research directed toward solving significant social issues (what we call *communication activism scholarship*) emanated from a number of directions in the communication discipline. One source was communication scholars, especially in rhetoric and organizational communication, who employed critical theory to not just understand or explain society but to critique and change it (in communication scholarship, see, e.g., Carey, 1982; Farrell & Aune, 1979; Hardt, 1986, 1992, 1993; Held, 1982; Real, 1984; Strine, 1991), and/or engaged in cultural studies to analyze cultural practices in relation to social and political issues such as power, ideology, race, social class, and gender (in communication scholarship, see, e.g., Artz & Murphy, 2000; Carey, 1983, 1989; Carragee, 1990; Carragee & Roefs, 2004; Grossberg, 1993a, 1993b, 1997; Grossberg, Nelson, & Treichler, 1992). Rhetoricians working from these perspectives argued for "ideological criticism" (see, e.g., Rushing & Frentz, 1991; Wander, 1983, 1984; Wander & Jenkins, 1972), "critical rhetoric" (see, e.g., N. Clark, 1996; McGuire & Slembeck, 1987; McKerrow, 1989, 1991, 1993; Ono & Sloop, 1992), and, most recently, "partisan criticism" (Swartz, 2004, 2005)—forms of rhetorical theory and criticism that certainly represent an "activist" turn (see Andersen, 1993; for critical responses to this rhetorical turn, see, e.g., Charland, 1991; Condit, 1993; Hariman, 1991;

Hill, 1983; Kuypers, 2000; Rosenfield, 1983). Organizational communication scholars who advocated these perspectives questioned the traditional privileging of management's interests and argued that research should root out normative systems of control to represent all stakeholders' voices and, thereby, promote democracy in the workplace (see, e.g., Carlone & Taylor, 1998; Cheney, 1995; Deetz, 1982, 1988, 1992; Deetz & Mumby, 1990; Mumby, 1993).

Another impetus for communication activism scholarship (albeit one that stressed the need for first-person-perspective activism research rather than demonstrated activism per se) came from applied communication scholars. Frey (2000), for instance, argued that given the common dictionary definition of the term *applied* as meaning "to put into practice," the most pressing question facing applied communication scholars was not whether to put communication into practice (which is what is done in a "practical discipline" like communication) or what to put into practice (communication knowledge and skills), but *who* should put communication into practice. As Frey (2000) argued:

> We should start from the premise that in research, "to put into practice" applies to *researchers*, as opposed to simply anyone who puts communication into practice (e.g., the research participants studied). Accordingly *applied communication scholarship* might be defined as "the study of researchers putting their communication knowledge and skills into practice." (p. 179; for a critique of this position, see Seibold, 2000)

Although all this work certainly helped to set the stage for communication activism scholarship, it constituted calls for such research, not activism research per se. The work done from critical theory and cultural studies perspectives remained, for the most part, theoretical and abstract, with scholars staying in the realm of discourse rather than intervening into discourses (see, e.g., Cloud, 1994; Frey, 2006a; Rakow, 2005), and much of the applied communication research that did adopt a first-person perspective was directed toward serving the interests of the powerful and well resourced (such as communication consulting work with for-profit organizations that serves corporate interests; see, e.g., Eadie, 1994; Phillips, 1992; C. K. Stewart, 1991), often at the expense of marginalized and underresourced populations (see, e.g., Frey, Pearce, Pollock, Artz, & Murphy, 1996).

One perspective that both articulated and resulted in some communication activism research was the "communication and social justice approach" advanced by Frey et al. (1996; see also W. B. Pearce, 1998; Pollock, Artz, Frey, Pearce, & Murphy, 1996; Swan, 2002; the essays in Swartz, 2006; for critiques of this perspective, see Makau, 1996; Olson & Olson, 2003; Wood,

1996). Frey et al. described *social justice* as "the engagement with and advocacy for those in our society who are economically, socially, politically,
and/or culturally underresourced" (p. 110), and called on communication
scholars to conduct research that "identifies and foregrounds the grammars
that oppress or underwrite relationships of domination and then recon-
structs those grammars" (p. 112). Frey et al. maintained that this "social justice sensibility" meant adopting, among other things, an activist orientation,
claiming:

> It is not enough merely to demonstrate or bemoan the fact that some
> people lack the minimal necessities of life, that others are used regularly
> against their will and against their interest by others for their pleasure or
> profit, and that some are defined as "outside" the economic, political, or
> social system because of race, creed, lifestyle, or medical condition, or
> simply because they are in the way of someone else's project. A social
> justice sensibility entails a moral imperative to *act* as effectively as we
> can to do something about structurally sustained inequalities. To con-
> tinue to pursue justice, it is perhaps necessary that we who act be per-
> sonally ethical, but that is not sufficient. Our actions must engage and
> transform social structures. (p. 111)

Frey (1998a) subsequently edited a special issue of the *Journal of
Applied Communication Research* on "Communication and Social Justice
Research" that featured "original, empirically grounded case studies that
demonstrated ways in which applied communication researchers have made
a difference in the lives of those who are disadvantaged by prevalent social
structures" (Frey, 1998b, p. 158). Ryan et al. (1998) showed how their work
as members of the Media Research and Action Project (MRAP), an organization that assists marginalized groups in employing news as a social
resource, had a significant impact on Boston-area newspaper coverage of
workplace reproductive rights stemming from a U.S. Supreme Court case
alleging discrimination against a battery-producing company because it
excluded fertile women from working in high-lead areas, and how the
Court's finding of discrimination against that company stressed media
frames that MRAP highlighted. Crabtree (1998) documented two case studies in El Salvador and Nicaragua of a mutual empowerment approach to
cross-cultural participatory development communication projects that
employed service learning with her university students and was directed
toward social change and social justice. Artz (1998) examined a campaign by
his undergraduate rhetoric students to increase the number of African
American students at the university where he taught. Hartnett (1998)
explained a project from one of his communication classes taught in a prison
that combined progressive pedagogical practices with traditional public

speaking skills—with students/prisoners restaging the 1858 Lincoln/ Douglas debates as a 3-way debate that included the Black abolitionist, David Walker—to create a "heuristic social space" in which these marginalized individuals could engage in serious and thoughtful political debate about the complicated political, economic, and cultural systems that supported and contested slavery, many of which still exist today in the fight for racial equality and social justice. Varallo, Ray, and Ellis (1998) reported on follow-up interviews conducted with adult survivors of incest whom they had interviewed in previous research to reveal how those survivors had benefited from participating in that research. Subsequent communication studies by T. S. Jones and Bodtker (1998), Novek (2005), and Palmeri (2006) adopted this social justice perspective as well.

The study by Varallo et al. (1998) points to another important influence driving communication activism scholarship: the articulation of various research methods that promote "research as an empowering act, as a way of uniting people working for social change, disrupting restrictive ways of thinking, and transforming the social world" (Ristock & Pennell, 1996, p. 113; see also M. Fine, 2006; Sanford & Angel-Ajani, 2006; Swartz, 1997). Such methods include, among others, (a) (social/participatory) action research (see, e.g., the journal *Action Research*; Costello, 2003; Greenwood & Levin, 2000; Kemmis & McTaggart, 2005; McNiff & Whitehead, 2002, 2006; Reason & Bradbury, 2001; Stringer, 1999; in communication scholarship, see Anyaegbunam, Karnell, Cheah, & Youngblood, 2005; Clift & Freimuth, 1997; Gatenby & Humphries, 1996; Jensen, 1990; Pilotta et al., 2001; Quigley, Sanchez, Handy, Goble, & George, 2000; Schoening & Anderson, 1995); (b) critical ethnography (see, e.g., Foley & Valenzula, 2005; Madison, 2005a, 2005b; Thomas, 1993; in communication, see Artz, 2001; Carbaugh, 1989/1990; Carragee, 1996; Conquergood, 1991b; Cushman, 1989/1990; Gibson, 2000); (c) feminist methods (see, e.g., Gaternby & Humphries, 1996; Hawkesworth, 2006a; Hesse-Biber, 2006; Nielsen, 1990; Oleson, 2005; Reinharz, 1992; Sprague, 2005; in communication, see Carter & Spitzack, 1989; Condit, 1988; M. G. Fine, 1990; Lemish, 2002; Lengel, 1998); and (d) performance ethnography (see, e.g., Denzin, 2003; McCall, 2000; Mienczakowski, 1995; Turner & Turner, 1982, 1988; in communication, see Alexander, 2005; Conquergood, 1985, 1991b, 2002b; J. L. Jones, 2002a; Olomo, 2006).

One of the best examples in the communication discipline of employing such methods to promote social change and social justice are the critical ethnographic studies of gang communication by Conquergood (1991a, 1992a, 1994; see also the communication studies of the Hmong by Conquergood, 1988, 1992b; Conquergood & Siegel, 1985). To understand gang communication, Conquergood lived for 20 months in Big Red, a dilapidated tenement building located in northwest Chicago's "Little

Beirut" area, a territory controlled by Latin King gang members. He slowly developed a relationship with these gang members and was allowed to observe and interview them and participate in their activities. Conquergood showed in his published work how gang communication (e.g., graffiti and reppin' practices) is a complex system of signification that creates a sense of place and security for these marginalized members of U.S. society. By offering a compassionate, alternative reading of gangs and their communication, his work contests dominant descriptions (e.g., by the media and government officials) of gang members as vicious animals, descriptions that, Conquergood (1994) contended, "help redirect material resources away from educational and employment programs that could help these youngsters and toward the much more costly buildup of a state apparatus of surveillance, control, and punishment—gang squads, jails, and prisons" (pp. 54-55). Conquergood, however, did not just describe, interpret, and explain gang communication or critique dominant rhetoric about gangs; he spent countless hours teaching these youth to read and write, and taught them marketable skills as camera operators in the making of his award-winning documentary about gang communication (Conquergood & Siegel, 1990). He also raised bail money for gang members who had been arrested, and he testified on their behalf in court trials. Conquergood's studies, therefore, demonstrated some of the promises, possibilities, and practices of communication activism scholarship.

Communication activism scholarship, thus, emerges from this confluence of scholarly streams. Such scholarship is grounded in communication scholars immersing themselves in the stream of human life, taking direct vigorous action in support of or opposition to a controversial issue for the purpose of promoting social change and justice. The purpose of this 2-volume text, therefore, is to showcase communication scholars who have engaged in activism and, thereby, promote activism as a significant form of communication scholarship.

OVERVIEW OF THE TEXTS

To select the chapters for these texts, an open call was issued through various print and online sources seeking proposals for original research studies that documented communication activism. All domains of communication scholarship (e.g., interpersonal, group, organizational, and media studies), theoretical perspectives, and methodological approaches (e.g., qualitative, quantitative, and rhetorical) were welcome, as long as the proposed chapter focused on an intervention conducted by the *researcher* (as opposed to someone else) that was designed to assist groups and communities to secure social reform. We, thus, sought to showcase original studies of how communication scholars have employed their resources (e.g., theories, methods, and other practices) to promote social change. We were especially interested in studies that assisted marginalized groups and communities to secure political and social reform in the quest for social justice. Chapter proposals explained the nature of the communication activism, including the groups and communities involved, the interventions designed to secure needed change/reform, the theories and methods that informed the projects, and what lessons might be learned from the study about engaging in communication activism scholarship.

This call resulted in more than 70 chapter proposals being submitted, a large number considering that only about 15 manuscripts were submitted for the special issue of the *Journal of Applied Communication Research* on "Communication and Social Justice Research" that Frey (1998a) edited about 10 years earlier, which suggests that such scholarship has substantially increased over that time period. We were so impressed with the number and high quality of the proposals that we asked Barbara Bernstein of Hampton Press, who had contracted with us for this text, whether it might be possible to produce a 2-volume set, and she immediately saw the advantages of doing so. We thank Barbara for her enthusiastic support of this project (and for the other texts that Frey, 1995, 2006b, has published with Hampton Press). We also thank the contributors to these texts for their excellent chapters (and for their receptivity to our editing suggestions). In addition, we are grateful for a grant that was awarded by Dr. Michele Jackson, chair of the Department of Communication at the University of Colorado at Boulder, that helped to cover the cost of the subject indexes for these volumes, and we thank Jane Callahan and Fran Penner for their initial subject index of Volume 2.

In discussing the commissioned chapters, we let authors know that there was no one way to write them and that we were open to whatever worked best for each chapter. There were, however, some things that we asked authors to consider. First, we asked them to provide a thorough explanation of the situation, problem/issue, and activities that comprised their communication activism. Second, to the extent possible, we wanted them to situate the analysis of their communication activism within relevant theory, research, and practice. Third, we encouraged them to reflect on the dialectical tensions/paradoxes they experienced in performing their communication activism. Fourth, we suggested that they share salient lessons learned about communication activism that might benefit others who either are engaged in or wish to engage in this form of scholarship.

As explained next, Volume 1, subtitled *Communication for Social Change*, showcases original research studies on "Promoting Public Dialogue, Debate, and Discussion" and "Communication Consulting for

Social Change"; Volume 2, subtitled *Media and Performance Activism*, presents original studies on "Managing the Media" and "Performing Social Change." Together, these texts provide needed empirical research on communication activism and offer important insights about engaging in such scholarship.

Volume 1, Part I: Promoting Public Dialogue, Debate, and Discussion

Since at least the time of ancient Greece, rhetoricians have stressed the relationship between public communicative practices and civic processes and outcomes—most notably, democracy. Today, communication (and other) scholars talk about "deliberative democracy" (e.g., Asen, 2005; Gastil, 2006; Gastil & Levine, 2005; Hauser & Benoit-Barne, 2002; Hicks, 2002; Ishikawa, 2002; Ivie, 1998; Kim, Wyatt, & Katz, 1999; Kurpius & Mendelson, 2002; Mattson, 2002; Murphy, 2004; Pingree, 2006; Ryfe, 2002, 2005; Salter, 2004; Welsh, 2002), "rhetorical democracy" (e.g., Hauser & Grim, 2004; Whedbee, 2003, 2004), and a "discourse theory of democracy" (e.g., Habermas, 1996) and "citizenship" (e.g., Asen, 2004). This communication approach to democracy, and its attendant commitments and practices (e.g., the quest for justice) rests, of course, on people employing appropriate and effective public communicative practices, from the everyday "vernacular rhetoric" that occurs between interactants on street corners and other public places (see Hauser, 1998, 2002) to group deliberation and discussion (see, e.g., Burkhalter, Gastil, & Kelshaw, 2002; Gastil, 2004; Gastil & Dillard, 1999; Gastil & Levine, 2005; Levine, Fung, & Gastil, 2005) to civic argumentation and debate (see, e.g., Auer, 1939; Fleming, 1998; Hicks, 1998; Hicks & Greene, 2000; Hicks & Langsdorf, 1998; Hitchcock, 2002; Jørgensen, 1998; Shotter, 1997; D. C. Williams, Ishiyama, Young, & Launer, 1997) to public/community dialogue (see, e.g., R. Anderson, Cissna, & Arnett, 1994; R. Anderson, Cissna, & Clune, 2003; Arnett, 2001; Barge, 2002; Hyde & Bineham, 2000; K. A. Pearce & Pearce, 2001; W. B. Pearce & Pearce, 2000a, 2000b; K. A. Pearce, Spano, & Pearce, in press; Spano, 2001, 2006) to social protest rhetoric (see previous citations). The chapters in this section document communication scholars' collaborations with individuals, groups, organizations, and communities to develop their repertoire of public communicative practices that promote social change.

In Chapter 1, Spoma Jovanovic, Carol Steger, Sarah Symonds, and Donata Nelson document their efforts as communication scholars teaching and learning at the University of North Carolina at Greensboro and as residents of the Greensboro community to assist the Greensboro Truth and Community Reconciliation Project (GTCRP). The GTCRP's mission is to help the citizens of that city engage in dialogue about what had been an "undiscussable" event for nearly 25 years: the killing of 5 people and the wounding of 10 others by members of the Klu Klux Klan (KKK) and neo-Nazis during a social protest on November 3, 1979, against the growing influence of the KKK. Jovanovic et al. first describe their involvement with the GTCRP, which arose from a graduate course on "Communication and Social Change" taught by Jovanovic, and their social action research plan for this project, which was grounded in a dialogic partnership with community members and included participating and observing, examining historical records and news media representations of the 1979 event, interviewing task force members and others, surveying community members, raising funds, designing a web site, and creating many documents to share the project's process with the community. They then explain two theoretical influences on their communication activism: Young's (2000) political theory of inclusion, community, and democracy; and Levinas's (1961/1969) philosophy of ethics. They subsequently describe how the GTCRP promoted dialogue about this critical incident, and analyze that social change effort through the lens of social justice communication scholarship and the conceptual connection between communication and community development, to show how new, more socially just community narratives were and can be constructed. They conclude the chapter by talking about some important challenges to their communication activism, including overcoming opposition to dialogue—in this case, in large measure because of norms of Southern U.S. civility—dialectical tensions they experienced in performing this community action—such as balancing being intimately involved and remaining outsiders to the social change process—and some lessons learned about communication activism—including, most importantly, how to help communities dialogue about difficult issues.

Following up on the importance of public dialogue about difficult issues, Chapter 2, by Carey Adams, Charlene Berquist, Randy Dillon, and Gloria Galanes, details three public dialogue projects with which these scholars have been involved as members of the Department of Communication at Missouri State University. They first explicate public dialogue as a form of "practical theory" designed to "improve the lives of people and have applicability for enhancing their capacity for action" (Barge, 2001, p. 6; see also Barge & Craig, in press), and their particular approach to dialogue, promoted by the Public Dialogue Consortium (PDC), which is based on the coordinated management of meaning (CMM) theory and action research principles. They then describe the three public dialogue projects, all based in the state of Missouri: (a) the Every Kid Counts Initiative, designed to confront disturbing trends about the quality of life for youth in Springfield, Missouri; (b) the Older Adults Project, to improve the life of older adults; and (c) the Raise Your Voice—Student

Action for Change Campaign, an initiative by Campus Compact (a national coalition of more than 950 college and university presidents dedicated to promoting community service, civic engagement, and service learning in higher education; see http://www.compact.org/) to promote students' participation in public life—in this case, by engaging them in conversations about civic engagement and social and political issues important to them. Adams et al. conclude the chapter by discussing some lessons learned about communication activism from these public dialogue projects—most importantly, the significance of talk for promoting social change.

Mark P. Orbe, in Chapter 3, confronts the important question of civil rights in U.S. communities. Offering leadership to a team of researchers from Western Michigan University, where he teaches, Orbe worked with the Michigan Department of Civil Rights and local communities across that state on the Civil Rights Health (CRH) Project to develop a community-based assessment instrument for systematically describing the state of civil rights health in communities, a first step in facilitating needed social change. After describing the history and goals of the CRH Project, Orbe explains how co-cultural theory, derived from the lived experiences of a variety of "nondominant" or "co-cultural" groups, served as the theoretical foundation for the civil rights health assessment, and how phenomenological inquiry—a 3-step methodology used to gather, thematize, and analyze descriptions of lived experiences—was employed in the project in three pilot communities. He explains how this research resulted in the creation of a CRH Resource Manual that serves as a guide for groups interested in facilitating a civil rights health assessment in their communities, and how that manual was used in Kalamazoo, Michigan. He concludes the chapter by exploring some important challenges confronted in this project, and lessons learned from those challenges, including (a) managing individual, oftentimes competing, agendas; (b) sustaining community participation; (c) negotiating tensions between processes and outcomes; (d) creating meaningful processes and outcomes with long-term impact; and (e) facilitating social change.

Chapter 4 explains the work of Donald C. Shields and C. Thomas Preston, Jr. with urban debate leagues (UDLs), which provide training in argumentation and debate for disadvantaged inner-city high school students and their faculty. Shields and Preston start by examining the inherent relationship between public policy debate and the promotion of democracy and democratic values, as well as empirical evidence showing the value of educational training in debate, but they point out that within most major U.S. cities, until the formation of the UDLs, such training had not been available to at-risk, underserved students attending public schools. As co-principal investigators on a 3-year grant (1998-2001), Shields and Preston formed the Urban Debate League–St. Louis (SLUDL), with Preston as the primary administrator of the project and Shields an unpaid advisor on project activities and research studies about the project. To explain the history and purpose of the UDLs across the nation and the SLUDL, in particular, Shields and Preston use symbolic convergence theory to articulate the UDL rhetorical vision (and accompanying plot lines) of sharing debate with traditionally underserved student populations and communities as an educational tool of empowerment (in line with the vision of Brazilian educator Paulo Freire, 1970, 1994, 1997, 1998) for changing inequitable conditions in U.S. society. They also document research studies and participants' narratives showing the benefits of and reactions to the UDL movement nationally. The authors then present their case study of the SLUDL, including its structure and student and teacher participation, and the extent to which its activities over that 3-year period, as assessed in multiple ways (including research studies conducted), promoted engagement and empowerment for the participants. Shields and Preston conclude the chapter by sharing important lessons learned from this communication activism about perpetuating rhetorical visions concerned with reducing gaps between the "haves" and "have-nots."

Chapter 5, by Stephen John Hartnett, concludes this section of Volume 1 by focusing on antiwar activism—specifically, the war on Iraq. Starting with, and grounding the chapter in Eugene Victor Debs's (1918) plea that "You are fit for something better than slavery and cannon fodder" (p. 26), said publicly in protest against the United States entering World War I and the passing of the Sedition Act and the Espionage Act, Hartnett documents (including visually) antiwar efforts by he and his colleagues in Champaign-Urbana, Illinois. He first politically situates the need for communication activism against the war on Iraq by explicating and showing how President George W. Bush's national security strategy is tied to globalizing capitalism and the quest for empire, and how, historically, the use of military force to champion "free markets" and build empire (such as by the British Empire) has failed. Hartnett then outlines four theses—(a) interweaving the local and the global, (b) defending democratic practices, (c) the mysterious logic of multiplier effects, and (d) the power of delayed impact—that have guided his antiwar activism, along with six thematically organized sets of communication strategies—(a) teach-ins, working groups, and pedagogical communication; (b) political art and startling communication; (c) marches, vigils, rallies, and the public communication of anger and hope; (d) postering, e-mailing, chance communication, and targeted networks; (e) media communication; and (f) picnics, parties, and interpersonal communication—he has employed to protest the war and reclaim democracy from empire. He concludes the chapter by talking, as undoubtedly Debs would, about communication activism as a way of being in the world with others and communicating hope in an age of terror, war, and empire. Following the chapter, Laura Stengrim and Hartnett offer an extensive appendix of 113 online and print resources, organized into 9 themes, that scholars and activists can use to inform and enrich their communication activism.

Volume 1, Part II: Communication Consulting for Social Change

The term *communication consulting* most likely brings to mind the image of an "expert" who is paid to help for-profit organizations (typically large ones, such as IBM) to communicate more effectively for the ultimate purpose of promoting management's bottom line—making money. Indeed, the scholarly communication literature invariably associates consulting with for-profit organizations (see, e.g., Browning, 1982; Browning & Hawes, 1991; B. D. Davis & Krapels, 1999; Gieselman & Philpott, 1969; Goodall, 1989; Hildebrandt, 1978; Kreps, 1989; Lange, 1984; March, 1991; Muir, 1996; Phillips, 1992; Plax, 1991; Poe, 2002; Sussman, 1982). Even scholars concerned with the ethical practice of communication consulting have viewed that activity primarily within the context of business organizations (e.g., Goldberg, 1983; Harrison, 1982; Montgomery, Wiseman, & DeCaro, 2001; J. Stewart, 1983), as have those who teach communication consulting within the educational context (see, e.g., Alderton, 1983; Cronin & Hall, 1990; Dallimore & Souza, 2002; Freeman, 1986; Jarboe, 1989; Redding, 1979).

There is, however, no reason why communication consulting should be tied to for-profit organizations per se, or engaged in for payment. Jarboe (1992), in arguing for a scholar-practitioner approach to communication consulting, asserted that "to have honesty and integrity, consulting should be done for scholarly knowledge and public service" (p. 232). Although some communication scholars have consulted for these purposes (e.g., some political communication consulting; see, e.g., Friedenberg, 1997; Johnson-Cartee & Copeland, 1997; Whillock, 1989), often as part of community service, there is a lack of scholarly literature about communication consulting with nonprofit groups and organizations (or underresourced for-profit organizations that promote social good). The lack of such scholarship is unfortunate, for there are many such groups and organizations in need of the consulting expertise that communication scholars can offer, providing rich sites for shedding light on and hopefully encouraging other scholars to engage in communication activism consulting. The chapters in this section document communication scholarship that has reclaimed consulting to promote social change.

In Chapter 6, Robbin D. Crabtree and Leigh Arden Ford discuss their experiences working with a sexual assault recovery center (SARC). After situating their work within the historical mission of, and contemporary need for, civic engagement by faculty and students at U.S. universities, they examine sexual assault as a social justice issue. They then illustrate how "activist consulting" can emerge organically from a scholar's life in a community by sharing personal narratives of their long-term involvement with SARC. Crabtree's narrative reveals how her work with SARC—which emerged from an MA service-learning course she taught on "Communication and Social Change" and included media relations, promotion, fund-raising, training, and special event planning—was part of her healing process from sexual assault victim to survivor to activist. Ford's narrative documents how her involvement with SARC—including serving first as a board member and later, after the executive director resigned and the agency experienced a financial crisis that threatened to close it, as a grant-writer and supervisor of SARC personnel—evolved from her feminist politics and desire to put her expertise in organizational theory into practice. Interpreting their experiences with SARC using feminist narrative analysis, Crabtree and Ford recast the traditional activist-consultant dichotomy as a dialectical relationship filled with tensions that need to be managed, including tensions that result from (a) participating and observing, (b) balancing dialogic with authoritarian communication, and (c) blending the professional and the personal (especially in situations in which someone has been as deeply affected by an issue as Crabtree was in this case). They conclude the chapter by talking about the benefits of communication activism for (a) groups, agencies, and communities served; (b) activist scholars; and (c) institutions of higher education, as well as some of the risks involved in the activist mode of communication consulting.

Chapter 7 focuses on how Sunwolf, a communication professor and lawyer, helps defense attorneys to create collaborative courtroom conversations with potential jurors to prevent their clients from receiving the death penalty. Sunwolf first examines the controversial topic of capital punishment, including evidence that has led to the release of numerous innocent people from death row but also shows that others have been put to death. She explains the enormous challenges that confront capital defense attorneys, including citizens' preconceived ideas about the jury deliberation task, the death-qualification selection process that dismisses those who are not willing to give the death penalty, the lack of resources available to these lawyers, and the dialectical challenges they confront when engaging in "death talk" with potential jurors. Drawing on her experiences as a capital defense lawyer and her communication scholarship on the dynamics of social influence during group decision making, Sunwolf describes an intervention that she created and uses in national workshops conducted with criminal defense attorneys who have been appointed by the court to represent an indigent client who faces the death penalty to help them dialogue with potential jurors about their views of the death penalty. She explains the workshops, focusing on specific communication challenges facing defense

attorneys in talking about death with potential jurors and new communication tools she has created to cope with these challenges that employ an
"empathic attunement" technique (see Sunwolf, 2006) to shift those interactions from interrogations to collaborative conversations that promote empathy. She ends the chapter by reflecting on lessons learned from these workshops about communication activism, including the challenges of coping
with unsuccessful interventions (in this case, resulting in a person's death)
and being an "itinerate" activist who often never knows the consequences of
his or her activism.

Chapter 8 documents David L. Palmer's involvement as a member of
Meta-, a progressive activist antiglobalization group, and how he collaborated with that group to engage more formally and effectively in consensus
building, as the group planned for and took part in an international trade
summit protest—the Free Trade Area of the Americas (FTAA) protest in
Miami, in November 2003. After explaining the rise of globalization and the
antiglobalization movement that has mobilized in the form of *affinity
groups*, small progressive groups that act together to resist globalization,
Palmer describes how affinity groups rely on consensus building as their
primary means for making democratic decisions, but how those groups,
including Meta-, do not always practice effective consensus building. He,
thus, invited the members of Meta- to analyze and, if necessary, modify their
discussion and decision-making practices as the group prepared for the
FTAA protest. He reviews the methodology that he developed for this project—the emergent-consensus program—which relies on meta-discussion
(discussion about the discussion process; hence, the pseudonym for this
affinity group) and is grounded in the work on consensus models, group
diagnostic models, and inductive models of inquiry. Palmer then walks
through the emergent-consensus program in action, explaining, both in narrative and expository form, how the group analyzed its discussion and decision-making practices and the changes it did (and did not) make prior to the
week of the protest, with the protest week, itself, captured vividly through
photographic evidence. Palmer reflects on the lessons learned from this
communication activism, including the need for scholar-activists to be
involved in projects of popular resistance, helping social movement activists
to build network infrastructures, and how such groups and movements provide rich sites for gaining insights into important communication concerns,
such as group communication and consensus building.

Shelly Campo and M. Somjen Frazer, in Chapter 9, combine participatory action research (PAR) and communication activism to affect community health—in this case, to improve services for women who partner with
women (WPW) at the college healthcare center where the authors taught
and studied, respectively, at the time. They start by explaining the barriers to
effective healthcare for WPW, in general, and the particular healthcare cen-

ter and groups with which they partnered to conduct this research. Campo and Frazer then articulate their methodological and theoretical groundings—PAR, queer theory and feminism, and health communication theories (specifically, the health belief model, the theory of planned behavior, and fear appeals)—followed by an explanation of their research project, which included both qualitative and quantitative components. They describe the process of creating a PAR project (including obtaining financial support and establishing a trusting research relationship), the interviews conducted with and questionnaires completed by WPW students about the healthcare center, and the interviews conducted with key informants and clinicians at the center. Campo and Frazer present the results of the data analysis (which included creating a concept map of barriers to healthcare that WPW experienced at that center) and describe how they used those results as the basis for conducting workshops with students and clinicians. They explain the key institutional changes that were made in the center's practices and space to make healthcare more accessible and friendly to WPW as a result of sharing the research findings and conducting the workshops, the connections made between university units, and the general raising of awareness about the healthcare needs of WPW as a result of the project. They conclude the chapter by sharing lessons learned about communication activism, including the importance of establishing trust between oppositional groups and between those groups and researchers, conducting an effective PAR project, and conducting PAR in the university context.

In Chapter 10, Stuart L. Esrock, Joy L. Hart, and Greg Leichty, from the University of Louisville, report their most recent efforts with Kentucky Health Investment for Kids (KHIK), a coalition working to raise the cigarette excise tax in Kentucky for the first time in 30-plus years, in line with public health advocates' findings that a substantial state tax is the single-best means of reducing smoking. After discussing tobacco use, in general, they focus on the state of Kentucky (ranking second highest in tobacco production, second lowest in cigarette excise tax, and first in death rate from lung cancer) and KHIK's campaign, including their association with this activist group. They then explain how they employed rhetorical theory (on cultural topoi and defensive rhetoric) and the literature on media framing to conceptually understand the culture of tobacco in Kentucky and inform the strategic development of counterarguments that KHIK could use against opponents' arguments. They describe their research, which included rhetorical analysis of three television shows about the proposed tax increase to uncover successful and unsuccessful arguments on both sides, survey questionnaires completed by campaign leaders and interested state representatives about the arguments they used to support the tax increase, and focus groups conducted with KHIK leaders and lawmakers to further refine arguments in favor of and responses to arguments against the tax increase. The presentation of their findings and recommendations to KHIK resulted in the group changing some of its rhetorical strategies. Esrock et al. conclude the chapter by discussing some tensions and paradoxes that arose during their intervention research—including those related to working with savvy and relatively resourced activists and with colleagues who smoke—and some lessons learned about communication activism—including the need for patience when working on issues, such as this one, that have little chance of succeeding in the short run, as well as the effects of activism on scholars' research and their roles as academics and citizens.

Chapter 11 concludes this section and this volume, with Leah Ritchie's case study of being an organizational activist consultant with a nonprofit organization. She begins by pointing out how critical communication scholars have rightfully identified the need for more balanced systems of power that promote democracy in the workplace, but have done little to intervene on behalf of workers. To fill this gap between theory and practice, Ritchie employs Habermas's (1984) concept of the *ideal speech situation*—a discursive space that provides full and equal access to communication for all parties—and a functionalist perspective of social activism—people using persuasive discourse to create new perspectives on their situations—to explain her attempt as a pro bono consultant to decentralize power at the Massachusetts-based neighborhood center (MNC, a pseudonym), a nonprofit, faith-based organization that had recently fallen on hard times. Ritchie and her graduate students first conducted peer-only focus groups, followed by private interviews, with MNC employees to determine the root causes of communication problems in the organization. Their analysis of the interview data showed that the controlling and hierarchical culture at MNC—exercised through pressure for employees to silence themselves and interpersonal distance and lack of trust between organizational groups—had a significant negative effect on employees. Ritchie explains her use of a communication intervention process called "Organizational Fitness Profiling" (Beer & Eisenstat, 1996, 2000; Beer, Eisenstat, & Spector, 1990), which involves lower level employees in organizational strategic planning, to attempt to produce a "quasi-ideal" speech situation at MNC. She concludes the chapter by analyzing her activities at MNC, including her successes and failures, through a functionalist lens that draws parallels between activist strategies and consulting work, and by sharing lessons learned about engaging in communication activism within the constraints of organizational settings.

Volume II, Part I: Managing the Media

Scholars and activists have long viewed the media as crucial political and cultural arenas, shaping definitions of, and policies toward, issues, events, groups, and communities. Although mainstream social-scientific approaches to the media have been faulted for their failure to examine the media's ideological role, multiple perspectives—including the Frankfurt School, cultural studies, political economy approaches, and critical media sociology—have devoted extensive attention to the media's role in sustaining social systems characterized by significant economic and political inequalities. These perspectives have played an essential role in describing, explaining, and critiquing the media's political and cultural roles by exploring significant issues related to power, ideology, hegemony, cultural resistance, and the consequences of economic concentration (see, e.g., Alasuutari, 1999; Artz & Murphy, 2000; Bagdikian, 2004; Carragee, 1993, 1996; Dines & Humez, 2002; Dow, 1996; Durham & Kellner, 2005; Entman, 1989; Gamson, Croteau, Hoynes, & Sasson, 1992; Grossberg, Wartella, Whitney, & Wise, 2005; Hall, 1977, 1997; Hallin, 1987; Herman & Chomsky, 1988; Horkheimer & Adorno, 1972; Kellner, 1990, 1995; Lewis, 1999, 2001; McChesney, 1999, 2004b; Meehan & Riordan, 2001; Morley, 1980, 1992; Mosco, 1996; Schiller 1989, 1996; R. Williams, 1975).

Unfortunately, this longstanding critique of the media has not been accompanied by extensive efforts by scholar-activists to assist marginalized groups and communities in using or influencing the media to secure social and political reform. Thus, there is a striking imbalance between critiques of the media's role in contemporary societies and interventions designed to help disenfranchised groups use the media in their quest for social justice. This imbalance is particularly evident in studies exploring the relationship between social movements and the news media. Extensive scholarship exists on the interaction between news organizations and social movements, with much of this literature documenting the media's support of the status quo by disparaging and delegitimizing movements seeking meaningful social and political change (see, e.g., Ashley & Olson, 1998; Barker-Plummer, 1995; Carragee, 1991, 2003; Carragee & Roefs, 2004; Deluca & Peeples, 2002; Entman & Rojecki, 1993; Gamson, 1992; Gamson & Wolfsfeld, 1993; Gitlin, 1980; Hertog & McLeod, 1995; Kielbowicz & Scherer, 1986; McAdam, 1996; Noakes & Wilkins, 2002; Oliver & Myers, 1999; Rojecki, 1999, 2002; Shoemaker, 1984; J. Smith, McCarthy, McPhail, & Augustyn, 2001; Tuchman, 1978; Zald, 1996). However, only a few scholars have engaged in interventions designed to assist social movement organizations in securing their goals (e.g., Carragee, 2005; Hoynes, 2005; McHale, 2004; Ryan, 1991, 2005; Ryan et al., 1998, 2001). The chapters in this section address this imbalance by documenting the efforts of scholar-activists to help marginalized groups and communities use the media to achieve meaningful social and political change.

In Chapter 1, Eleanor Novek and Rebecca Sanford explore the multilayered paradoxes confronting their teaching of journalism classes and producing a newspaper at a state prison for women. After documenting the rise of prisons (including those for women) in the United States, they explain the specific context for their work, the Clara Barton Correctional Facility for Women (a pseudonym), and the difficulties they encounter there. Their theoretically informed activist research—relying on feminist perspectives (especially given the special impact of prisons on women), Foucault's (1979) work on prisons, and social justice research—and use of methodological triangulation—participant observation, interviewing, and textual analysis—creates a richly documented account of how journalistic writing helped these women to express their cultural understandings of prison life and, thereby, served as a path to empowerment for them. The authors also explore how these prison journalists confronted institutional constraints in researching and writing news stories about, for instance, the harshness of prison life and the incompetent medical care they receive. Novek and Sanford also carefully detail the complexities and challenges of the relationships formed between the women who contributed to the prison newspaper, as well as how they, as authors, try to treat the women fairly in their written and oral representations of them. They conclude the chapter by reflecting on the significant dilemmas confronting their intervention, including the tension between their desire to engage in activist research to improve the life of these women coupled with the simultaneous need to follow prison rules and regulations to have continued access to them.

Sue Ellen Christian, in Chapter 2, also discusses an intervention linked to the production of a newspaper—The Student Newspaper Diversity Project, a high school newspaper community project that Christian spearheads that focuses on issues related to diversity. Supported by the NCA's Communicating Common Ground initiative, the Southern Poverty Law Center, Campus Compact, and the American Association for Higher Education, this 15-week project involves the student newspaper staff of an economically and racially diverse urban public high school in southwest Michigan and journalism and communication students from Western Michigan University who serve as mentors and editors for the high school journalists, and results in the publication of a once-a-year special edition of the student newspaper that focuses on a community issue related to diversity. After describing the project, Christian explains how service-learning and civic journalism traditions shaped her communication activism, for despite their manifest differences and significant shortcomings (e.g., both frequently ignore structural inequalities in U.S. society), they share a common concern with promoting civic responsibility and engagement, activism, and social change. Christian then documents important outcomes of this project, including heightened sensitivity of issues related to diversity and increased journalistic skills among the high school newspaper staff, as well as the impact of the newspaper on readers. At the same time, she notes important limitations of the project, such as the lack of specific school reforms after exposing patterns of segregation and integration in the high school, with the tracking of students of color continuing and the school failing to hire additional minority faculty. Christian also addresses the thorny issue of the censorship of newspaper content by the high school administration and how that affects staff self-censorship to avoid administrative rejection of specific stories, ultimately concluding that the issue provided the student newspaper staff with valuable lessons regarding the limitations of journalism as an agent of social change.

Sharing Christian's commitment to service learning as a means for social change, Leda Cooks and Erica Scharrer, in Chapter 3, explain their media literacy service-learning project focused on violence and conflict resolution. An ongoing university-community collaboration, the Media Literacy and Violence Prevention Program (MLVPP) fosters learning, transformation, and advocacy about mediated and interpersonal violence and conflict resolution strategies for participating sixth graders, their teachers, and their families, as well as for the undergraduate students at the University of Massachusetts at Amherst engaged in service learning. Cooks and Scharrer first articulate their social constructionist perspective, making their intervention very different from traditional media literacy projects because of its focus on "learning-as-change," with learning and change viewed as grounded in the same social processes, such that as people learn, they change, and vice versa. At the same time, their intervention reflects the longstanding interest of media literacy projects in developing a critical understanding of the processes that shape both the production and reception of media texts. Cooks and Scharrer explain the MLVPP and assess, using a pre/postprogram design, the learning that occurs from exposure to it via questionnaires completed by the children, their written responses after viewing a media clip, and videotapes of classroom interactions, with the influence of the service-learning project assessed through university students' journals and response papers. Cooks and Scharrer document the project's multiple influences on the sixth graders, including their more sophisticated understanding of conflict resolution, media violence, and media decision-making processes, as well as how children resisted aspects of the project, such as discounting the influence of media violence on their life and displacing it onto their younger brothers and sisters. They also reveal that some of the undergraduate students redefined their social activism role from educating others to educating themselves. The authors conclude the chapter by examining the implications of the learning-as-change perspective for communication activism.

Van M. Cagle, in Chapter 4, documents his tenure as the first Director of Research & Analysis at the Center for the Study of Media & Society (CSMS) sponsored by the Gay & Lesbian Alliance Against Defamation (GLAAD), an advocacy organization that encourages fair and inclusive representation of gay, lesbian, bisexual, and transgendered (LGBT) people in news and entertainment media. The CSMS was established in 2000 to promote relationships between media scholarship and GLAAD's media activism. Cagle first explains GLAAD's research needs, the CSMS, and his role in commissioning, producing, and promoting multimethodological scholarship focusing on media representations of LGBT people and audience interpretations of these representations that could provide practical benefits for GLAAD's activists. He then focuses on four recurring struggles he experienced in forging connections between media scholarship and LGBT activism. First, he notes that GLAAD activists perceived a disconnect between their work and that of scholars, with activists preferring quantitative data to support their lobbying of media professionals and viewing qualitative studies, mainly driven by cultural studies and queer theory, as "academic theorizing" that was irrelevant to their work. Second, the pace of activist and scholarly work differs considerably, with GLAAD's activists facing pressing deadlines and needing to respond quickly to breaking news events related to LGBT issues, whereas research necessitates considerable time for data collection and reflection. Third, activists demand studies documenting clear causal relationships between, for instance, stereotypical media depictions of gays and lesbians and negative attitudes and behaviors toward those groups, but scholars question such simple causal relationships and believe there are diverse audience interpretations of the same media text. Fourth, Cagle contrasts the commitment of GLAAD's activists to a form of identity politics, which often assumes a gay/straight binary, with queer theorists' critique of this binary and fixed gay and lesbian identities. Cagle concludes the chapter by examining some lessons learned about communication activism from trying to navigate the different assumptions and practices of the academic world and the world of LGBT activism.

In Chapter 5, John P. McHale examines how his video documentary, *Unreasonable Doubt: The Joe Amrine Case* (McHale, Wylie, & Huck, 2002; available from Hampton Press) helped to free a man on death row in Missouri who had been falsely convicted of a murder. McHale first reviews scholarship on media, in general, and video and film documentary, in particular, as tools for social protest, but points out that little work has been done on the use of documentary video/film by activists engaged in social movements, such as those seeking to abolish the death penalty. He provides background on Amrine's case, including how he became involved with Amrine, and the strong relationship that existed between the video documentary and those involved in the antideath penalty movement. McHale describes the creation and distribution of the documentary, from preproduction, production, and postproduction, to its promotion and exhibition, a discussion informed by McHale's (2004) recent ethnographic, grounded theory of activists' use of media. He then addresses the documentary's multiple influences, including educating viewers on the miscarriage of justice in the Amrine case, shaping news media coverage of the case, mobilizing advocates in their campaign against capital punishment, and, most importantly, the significant role the documentary played in influencing the Missouri Supreme Court to release Amrine. McHale's conclusions include the important connection that activist-scholars need to make, when possible, between their communication activism and broader social movements working on an issue. In this case, the considerable connections between McHale's project and the movement against capital punishment in Missouri significantly enhanced the making and influence of the documentary. McHale argues, therefore, that the effectiveness of a film/video documentary as an agent of social reform is largely dependent on the amount of coordination between the producers of the documentary and the broader collective effort by activists to secure social justice.

Like McHale's communication activism, Ted M. Coopman's intervention, detailed in Chapter 6, involved extensive interaction with a social movement. As a scholar-activist in the micro radio movement, which stemmed from pursuing his master's degree in mass communication, Coopman played an essential role in bridging differences in this movement's effort to secure the legalization of low-power FM radio services. After providing a brief history of the micro radio movement, Coopman highlights important characteristics of new social movements such as this one, including their heterogeneity (in this case, anarchists, community groups, and libertarians of the political left and right who had very different visions for micro radio) and how they function as an emergent network (in this case, a *dissent network*, or *dissentwork*, terms Coopman coins to reference a network of individuals opposing entrenched hierarchical systems) that relies to a great extent on communication technology (e.g., the internet, e-mail, and listservs). Coopman narrates how these characteristics made it very difficult to craft a joint statement that could influence the Federal Communication Commission's (FCC) rule-making concerning low-power radio. Coopman, however, succeeded in drafting a document, the Joint Statement on Micro Radio (JSMR), which attracted widespread support within the micro radio movement and influenced the FCC's decision to legalize micro radio in 2000. He details how his scholarly knowledge of First Amendment law, federal regulation, and FCC culture shaped the drafting of the JSMR, and how activists' perceptions of him as an "honest broker" between diverse groups attracted support for the document. Coopman concludes the chapter with suggestions about negotiating the chasm that often exists between simultaneously being a communication scholar and activist.

Following up on Coopman's discussion of technology and social change, Andrew P. Herman and James S. Ettema, in Chapter 7, describe their efforts to reduce the digital divide among groups and organizations in a lower income African American community in Chicago. Their Neighborhood Communication Project, a partnership between Northwestern University (where Herman was a doctoral student at the time and Ettema is a professor) and a community-based organization (CBO) in need of technology expertise, involved creating a community technology coordinator to assist this CBO. Herman and Ettema first explain two theoretical perspectives informing their intervention: (a) the theory of asset-based community development, which recognizes that communities need external assistance but stresses understanding and mapping the resources and capacities that exist within all communities; and (b) the work on social capital highlighting the significance of social networks and relationships in enhancing community life. The authors describe mapping this community's assets and how, in response to the need, the community technology coordinator (an African American raised in Chicago whom Herman and Ettema mentored) brokered relationships between organizations to reduce the digital divide in the community by creating additional social capital (networks of useful relationships) and intellectual capital (problem-solving abilities and leadership). They document the benefits that accrued to the community, including creating a community web site, the dramatic increase in the number of community technology centers, and the sharing of technology information that eventually occurred among 50 community groups and small businesses. Organizational leaders also completed a quantitative questionnaire to assess the project's effectiveness, with the results showing how these groups engaged in communicative behaviors to increase their social capital, although the digital divide among participating organizations did not diminish because of the scarcity of technical expertise in the community and the tendency for assistance to flow to those best positioned to seek and use it. The authors conclude that communication activism addressing the digital divide may well result in one divide closing but other divides opening.

Volume 2, Part II: Performing Social Change

Art, although certainly used at times to maintain the status quo (see Cohen-Cruz, 2006; Glassberg, 1990), has long been employed as a form of activism to communicate community needs and promote social change (see, e.g., Barndt, 2006; Felshin, 1995; Kaplan, 2006; Korza & Bacon, 2005). As Cohen-Cruz (2006) explained, "Activist art is aesthetic production as part of a struggle for social change, such as seeking more rights for people who are being exploited, or resistance to changes that are deemed detrimental" (p. 427). Performance/theater activism, in particular, has a deep history in the United States (see, e.g., Dijkstra, 2003; Lubin, 1994) and elsewhere (see, e.g., Shepherd, 1998; van Erven, 1992), including the workers theater during the 1930s Great Depression (see, e.g., Friedman, 1985), the Black arts movement (see Neal, 1968; regarding Black performance studies, see, e.g., E. P. Johnson, 2006; Ugwu, 1995) and Chicano theater groups (such as El Teatro Campesino; see, e.g., Broyles-González, 1994) during the 1960s, and, later, the global movement of the "Theatre of the Oppressed" started by Brazilian director and Worker Party activist Augusto Boal (e.g., 1979, 1995) and based on the critical pedagogy articulated by Freire (e.g., 1970, 1994, 1998). Today, scholars in communication, literature, performance studies, theater, education, and many other disciplines study performance as a significant form of communication activism (see, e.g., Billingham, 2005; Capo, 1983; Caster, 2004; Cohen-Cruz, 1998, 2006; Conquergood, 1988, 1998, 2002a, 2002b; Denzin, 2003; Dolan, 2001a, 2001b; Elam, 2003; Fuoss, 1997; Gómez-Peña, 2005; Haedicke & Nellhaus, 2001; Inomata & Cohen, 2006; J. L. Jones, 2002b; Kershaw, 1992; Klope, 1994; Madison, 2006; Park-Fuller, 2003; Strine, 1992; Stucky, 2006; Taylor, 2003; Toc, 1971). However, only a few scholars, such as Hartnett's (1998) work on performance in a prison setting (see also Conquergood, 1988), have employed and documented performance as a form of communication activism. The chapters in this section report three such efforts by communication scholars to use performance to promote social change.

In Chapter 8, Lynn Harter, Devendra Sharma, Saumya Pant, Arvind Singhal, and Yogita Sharma discuss their complex integration of an entertainment-education (E-E) project with participatory theater workshops and performances in India's Bihar State. After surveying the social landscape of India and Bihar, Harter et al. historically situate the workshops and performances conducted within a broader E-E project—the Indian radio soap opera, *Taru*, which promoted the values of gender equality, small family size, reproductive health, and communal and caste harmony. The authors' dialogic interventions are informed by the work of Freire and Boal (cited previously), whose vision of social activism is rooted in the lived experience of groups and communities suffering oppression and disenfranchisement coupled with the recognition that marginalized people are active subjects rather than objects. Boal's Theatre of the Oppressed, a participatory form of theater used to challenge and change repressive social practices, directly shaped the design of the workshops and performances facilitated by Harter et al. They explain how 50 members of *Taru* listening groups in four Bihar villages first participated in theater workshops, developing script-writing and performance skills, and then put those skills into practice to produce three plays, with all aspects of the plays and performances created by the participants. Interviews with participants and audience members, along with photographic evidence, document the multiple influences of their interventions. They show, for example, how the content of the plays provided striking counter-narratives to dominant cultural practices in Bihar by criticizing both the caste and dowry systems. The workshops and performances also created enduring social networks among the participants, increasing their social capital and likely setting the stage for future grassroots initiatives for social change. They end the chapter by examining how communication activism is enabled and constrained by structural and cultural forces, noting, for example, the lack of caste diversity among participants, which resulted in their communication activism more effectively challenging gender (by bringing men and women together to perform, a unique occurrence in India) than caste inequalities.

Chapter 9, by Marc D. Rich and José I. Rodríguez, provides a unique and insightful analysis of a participatory theater project focusing on sexual assault. After documenting the pervasiveness of sexual assault and date rape on college campuses and criticizing traditional sexual assault intervention programs for being didactic, they explain a university-based performance troupe, interACT (headed by Rich since 2000), that employs techniques and strategies associated with participatory theater to educate college students about sexual assault. Rich and Rodríguez, like Harter et al., use Boal's Theatre of the Oppressed as the theoretical grounding for their facilitation of social change through participatory theatre. They discuss the interACT performance, which combines two scripted scenes of a potential sexual assault episode with four proactive scenes created by audience members. Their study is methodologically unique and innovative because they employed a quasi-experimental design involving 458 undergraduate students to assess the effects of the performance. Multiple social-scientific models—the elaboration likelihood model, the affective learning model, and the altruistic and egoistic models—shape their research questions and the variables assessed for students in the experimental group (the interACT performance) and those in a control group (a lecture/demonstration on a web-based instructional program related to course content). In comparison to the control group, students exposed to the interACT performance reported higher levels of affective and cognitive learning, value-relevant involvement, and issue-relevant thinking. Rich and Rodríguez's findings, thus, support participatory theater as an influential form of communication activism, and they offer guidelines for engaging in this type of activism, although they are quick to note limitations of their study and the need for additional research that directly compares performance-based projects with more didactic forms of communication activism. They also argue persuasively for how quantitative studies can complement what has heretofore been qualitative evidence (because of performance studies scholars' suspicion of quantitative research) for the effects of performance activism.

In the final chapter in this volume, Deborah Cunningham Walker and Elizabeth A. Curry reflect on their participation (as graduate students) in the

University Community Initiative (UCI) Project, a collaboration between Community Action Stops Abuse (CASA), a nonprofit organization devoted to preventing domestic violence, and the communication and sociology departments of the University of South Florida. They first provide an overview of CASA's range of services for survivors of domestic violence, which include emergency assistance and long-term support, and they explain the UCI Project, a long-term, comprehensive participatory ethnography employing interactive interviews to collect narratives from CASA staff, which has resulted in numerous products, including a booklet of stories that CASA uses as a lobbying, recruiting, and fundraising tool. Walker and Curry then explicate their theoretical and methodological frameworks: social action research, feminist perspectives, and Gergen's (2000) narrative concept of "poetic activism," in which scholar-activists approach social change with an emphasis on both the process of developing research relationships and the products of those relationships. They illustrate this unique form of activism by providing a detailed autoethnographic narrative of a university colloquium that involved them and two CASA staff members sharing the evolution of their research as a process of forging trusting relationships, with the colloquium becoming an enactment of their relationship. Walker and Curry reflect on both the successes and the challenges of their communication activism, paying particular attention to the need to cultivate a dialogic relationship between researchers and activists characterized by trust, empathy, mutual respect, active listening, metacommunication, and collaborative learning.

LESSONS LEARNED
ABOUT COMMUNICATION ACTIVISM

The chapters in these two volumes, as a set, shed significant light on the nature and practice of communication activism scholarship. Here, we share some broad lessons learned from these studies about engaging in communication activism (citing relevant sample chapters in the order they appear in the volumes).

First, communication activism research, like all scholarship, reflects a choice that scholars make about what communication phenomena they will study, how they will study those phenomena, and to what ends they will put the findings from their research. The scholars who contributed to these texts consciously chose to engage in research that potentially could make an important difference in the world. Of course, all communication scholars undoubtedly are interested in making a difference, but the question that needs to be asked is whose interests are being served by their research. As Becker (1995) pointed out, "The major question most of us face in our lives as scholars is not whether our research should be useful; it is, rather, what it should be useful for and for whom it should be useful" (p. 102).

These scholars chose to conduct research that potentially could make an important difference for marginalized and underresourced individuals, groups, organizations, and communities attempting to promote social change and social justice. In that sense, there is a significant difference between, for instance, serving as a pro bono consultant to a struggling non-profit organization (e.g., as Ritchie did) and being a paid consultant to the management of IBM. Although we certainly respect scholars' right to choose how to devote their resources, scholars also need to realize that they are embedded within economic, political, social, and cultural systems, meaning that their research has important implications for maintaining or challenging those systems; consequently, their research choices must be open to being called into question. Conquergood (1995) forcefully explained the choice confronting researchers:

> The choice is no longer between pure and applied research. Instead, we must choose between research that is "engaged" or "complicit." By engaged I mean a clear-eyed, self-critical awareness that research does not proceed in epistemological purity or moral innocence. There is no immaculate perception. Engaged individuals take responsibility for how the knowledge that they produce is used instead of hiding behind pretenses and protestations of innocence. In a post-colonial, late capitalistic world, marked by sexism, racism, homophobia, and class bias, we understand, with Said (1989), that "Innocence is now out of the question of course" (p. 213). As communication scholars who traffic in symbols, images, representations, rhetorical strategies, signifying practices, the media, and the social work of talk, we should understand better than anyone else that our disciplinary practice is *in* the world. As engaged intellectuals we understand that we are entangled within world systems of oppression and exploitation. . . . Our choice is to stand alongside or against domination, but not outside, above, or beyond it. (p. 85)

The communication scholars in these volumes chose to stand against domination, oppression, and other social injustices by using their resources to fight against capital punishment (Sunwolf; McHale), domestic violence (Walker & Curry), globalization (Palmer), homophobia (Campo & Frazer; Cagle), racism (Jovanovic et al.; Orbe), sexism (Harter et al.), sexual assault (Crabtree & Ford; Rich & Rodríguez), and war (Hartnett), among many other things. Their reasons for choosing these particular issues undoubtedly differ, with some scholars, for instance, readily admitting in their chapter that they have experienced the issue personally, such as Crabtree being a victim of sexual assault, or are associated with the group being studied, such as Campo and Frazer's promotion of better healthcare for lesbians, with both of them being women who partner with other women. In other cases, they became involved because the opportunity presented itself. Jovanovic, for example, recently moved to Greensboro, North Carolina, and discovered the grassroots movement there for truth, justice, and reconciliation; Hartnett responded to the exigency of the moment created by the war on Iraq; and McHale, as he reported, found out serendipitously from one of his former students about Joe Amrine, well after Amrine had been on death row but, fortunately, before he had been executed. In these and the other cases, these scholars were particularly well suited and positioned to take advantage of the opportunity presented to them (e.g., because of Jovanovic's deep concern with ethics; Hartnett's scholarly focus on war and empire, as well as his involvement in other protest movements; and McHale's immersion in the antideath penalty movement). In fact, in some of these cases, the activism came first, followed by the documenting of it for research purposes. Ultimately, then, their choice to work for social change and social justice on behalf of those who have been marginalized springs from who they are as people and what they value, showing, as Adelman and Frey (2001) contended in an autoethnographic account of their longitudinal communication activism program on communication and community in a AIDS residential facility (see, e.g., Adelman & Frey, 1997), "that the most meaningful research (to researchers and participants alike) is that which resonates with researchers' personal values and characteristics" (pp. 208-209). Other scholars, of course, will make their own choices based on their personal values and characteristics, but they also must be willing to own those choices and the values those choices represent.

Second, communication activism, as "engaged" scholarship (see also Applegate, 2001, 2002; Cheney, Wilhelmsson, & Zorn, 2002), transforms researchers into citizen-scholars (see, e.g., Grund, Cherwitz, & Darwin, 2001; Pestello, Saxton, Miller, & Donnelly, 1996; Rakow, 2005) connected with their communities and the significant issues that confront them. Most of the projects featured in these volumes involve scholars promoting social change and social justice with/in their local communities. Rakow (2005), in talking about the need for community research in the communication discipline, asserted, in both a joking and serious manner:

> According to the timeworn joke, the chicken crossed the road to get to the other side. So why did the scholar cross the road? To do research on the other side, presumably. Why do scholars go elsewhere to do research, like the proverbial wandering chicken, instead of staying right where we are? Is there nothing of significance in our own communities that is worthy of study? Is there no role for our research in the daily struggles of local citizens to create healthy and just communities? Is a scholar also a citizen? (p. 6)

The scholars spotlighted in these volumes did not, for the most part, cross the road but, instead, stayed in their communities. They engaged in communication activism with/for students in their classes and/or the universities where they taught or went to school (Jovanovic et al.; Crabtree & Ford; Campo & Frazer; Christian; Cooks & Scharrer; Rich & Rodríguez; Walker & Curry); the local organizations and institutions where their fellow citizens worked, went to school, or, in the case of prison, were kept (Crabtree & Ford; Ritchie; Novek & Sanford; Christian; Cooks & Scharrer; Walker & Curry); the neighborhoods, towns, and states where they lived (Jovanovic et al.; Adams et al.; Orbe; Shields & Preston; Esrock et al.; McHale; Herman & Ettema); or, in the case of Harter et al., the home country of some of the authors (India). In some cases, they sought policy changes at the national level (Hartnett campaigning against the war on Iraq in his hometown with local groups; Palmer protesting globalization with a local affinity group where he lives; Coopman promoting the legalization of low-power FM radio, and Cagle seeking fair media coverage of GLBT people), in large measure because those policy changes would have significant effects at the local community level (e.g., preventing men and women from Hartnett's town and state from being killed and wounded, keeping workers' jobs in Palmer's town, allowing "mom and pop" radio stations where Coopman lived, and promoting fair local media coverage of GLBT people in Cagle's city). Sunwolf's case may be the most unique in that she worked with capital defense attorneys who came from afar to attend her workshops, but the goal still was to have substantial effects at the local level (the prevention of state execution).

These studies, thus, reveal that even as broader (e.g., national or global) communication activism needs to be expressed via local activism, the efficacy of local activism is linked to and animated by its engagement with broader social movements seeking to secure social and political change. For example, Jovanovic et al.'s local activism with the citizens of Greensboro to seek truth and reconciliation regarding a racial incident that occurred more than 30 years ago assumes significance given its connection to the civil rights movement and the problems that the U.S. South, in particular, has experienced with civil rights; Palmer showed how his local affinity group's activism could not have happened were it not for the group's connection to and coordination with other affinity groups fighting globalization; Hartnett illustrated how the local actions of peace groups in Champaign-Urbana, Illinois connected to the actions of an international peace movement protesting the war on Iraq, noting how seemingly local actions can have "multiplier effects" that spread through space to reach audiences never imagined by "local" activists; and McHale increased the influence of his video documentary that helped to save an innocent person on death row through his close association and interactions with activists in the antideath penalty movement in Missouri. The chapters, thus, show that communication activism truly is both local and global.

Third, communication activism necessitates citizen-scholars intervening in some way, for this type of scholarship, as explained earlier, involves first-person- rather than third-person-perspective research. The interventions may differ slightly with respect to the degree to which scholars are positioned and participate in the group, organization, or community with which they are connected (e.g., Ford serving as an actual organizational member of a sexual assault recovery services center versus Ritchie consulting for a non-profit neighborhood organization), but all the interventions that communication scholars employ revolve, of course, around some form of communication practice that they facilitate. Hence, the interventions documented in these chapters include, among many others: (a) facilitating public dialogues (Jovanovic et al.; Adams et al.); (b) crafting reports and other documents (Jovanovic et al.; Orbe; Cagle; Coopman; Walker & Curry); (c) providing training in debate and argumentation skills (Shields & Preston; Esrock et al.); (d) leading marches, vigils, protests, and rallies (Hartnett; Palmer); (e) offering workshops (Sunwolf; Campo & Frazer); (f) helping groups to meta-communicate (Palmer); (g) producing newspapers (Novek & Sanford; Christian) and video documentaries (McHale); and (h) performing (Harter et al.; Rich & Rodríguez; Walker & Curry). These interventions and the issues they address span the communication discipline from, for instance, interpersonal and group communication to organizational communication to media studies, demonstrating that all communication scholars can engage in communication activism if they choose to do so.

Fourth, these interventions are informed by and, in turn, inform theory. Wood (1996) cautioned communication scholars interested in pursuing social justice to:

> Bear in mind that passion alone is no guarantee of positive results, nor does the intent to empower oppressed peoples necessarily cohabit with genuine understanding of and respect for others and their interpretations of their lives. Such passion and intents are most effective when they are infused by theoretical understandings. (p. 165)

The chapters in these texts demonstrate how theoretical understandings infuse communication activism. Not surprisingly, given their focus on describing and explaining systems of domination and subordination and their interest in forms/practices of cultural and political resistance, critical theories shaped many of the interventions (especially those directed toward managing the media and performing social change). For example, Ritchie's organizational study relied on Habermas's critical theory, especially his concept of the "ideal speech situation" (Habermas, 1984); Novek and Sanford consulted Foucault's (1979) work on prisons; Campo and Frazer, along with Cagle, employed queer theory; and Harter et al. and Rich and Rodríguez grounded their performance-based interventions in Freire's (1970, 1994, 1997, 1998) critical pedagogy theory and Boal's (1979) application of that theory in the Theatre of the Oppressed. Many of these scholars also based their interventions on feminist theories and perspectives (Crabtree & Ford; Novek & Sanford; Campo & Frazer; Walker & Curry). These chapters extend the scholarship on critical and feminist theory in a significant manner by using these theories to inform practical interventions designed to assist marginalized individuals, groups, organizations, and communities achieve social change and social justice.

Interpretive theories also inform many of these communication activism studies. For example, Jovanovic et al. used ethics theory, Orbe linked his civil rights project to co-cultural theory, Adams et al. and Cooks and Scharrer located their studies firmly within social constructionism, Shields and Preston relied on symbolic convergence theory, Sunwolf employed dialectical theory, Esrock et al. applied rhetorical theory (on cultural topoi and defensive rhetoric) and media framing theory, and Harter et al. and Walker and Curry used narrative theory. These chapters highlight the need for communication activism research to examine the complex processes of meaning making by individuals, groups, organizations, and communities. Together with the chapters employing critical perspectives, these studies underscore that people live in both a symbolic and material world and that they are purposive social actors who define, interpret, critique, and can attempt to change oppressive structures and practices. Indeed, many, if not most, of the chapters stress the tension or clash between the construction and expression of meaning by those who are marginalized and broader hegemonic meanings produced, disseminated, and enforced by elite actors and institutions.

Mainstream social-scientific theories also inform these interventions and research projects, such as Sunwolf's use of group decision-making theory; Palmer's adoption of group consensus and group diagnostic models; the grounding of Campo and Scharrer's study in the health belief model, theory of planned behavior, and fear appeals; the incorporation of media effects theory by Cooks and Scharrer and by McHale; Coopman's review of computer-mediated communication theory and research; Herman and Ettema's application of asset-based community development theory, and Rich and Rodríguez's testing of the elaboration likelihood, affective learning, altruistic, and egoistic models. Importantly, all the studies just mentioned consciously combined critical/interpretive and social-scientific perspectives, such as Cooks and Scharrer's bridging of the gap between the two main camps in media literacy scholarship—the intervention-oriented, media effects-based approach and the cultural studies-based perspective.

Using theory to inform and make sense of communication interventions has the important consequence of contributing to those theories by testing and fleshing them out in practice. Consequently, communication activism research, as Wood (1995) contended about applied communication research, "is practicing theory and theorizing practice" (p. 157). Moreover, an important lesson learned from the theoretical pluralism and integration demonstrated within and across this set of studies is that the distinctions often drawn between the three major social-scientific paradigms—the critical, interpretive, and mainstream social-scientific paradigms—are facile when it comes to communication activism scholarship, for these paradigms can be employed individually or in combination to promote social change and social justice.

Fifth, leading directly from this last point, these studies demonstrate that virtually any research method and technique can be used to guide and document communication activism. Frey, Botan, and Kreps (2000) identified four major methods employed by communication scholars: experimental, survey, textual analysis (e.g., rhetorical criticism, content analysis, and performance studies), and naturalistic inquiry (e.g., ethnography, critical ethnography, and autoethnography). All these studies, given that they are, in one sense, case studies that employ (because they are first-person-perspective research) participant observation at the very least, could be labeled naturalistic inquiry, but some of the studies also use the other three methods, either as part of their communication interventions or to document the nature and effects of their activism: (a) experimental (Cooks & Scharrer; Rich & Rodríguez); (b) survey (Jovanovic et al.; Campo & Frazer; Christian; Cagle); and (c) textual analysis–rhetorical criticism (Jovanovic et al.; Hartnett; Esrock et al.), content analysis (Orbe; Cagle), and performance studies (Harter et al.; Rich & Rodríguez; Walker & Curry). Besides participant observation, these studies also employ numerous research techniques, including: (a) interviews, both individual (Jovanovic et al.; Orbe; Ritchie; Novek & Sanford; Christian; Cooks & Scharrer; McHale; Herman & Ettema; Harter et al.; Walker & Curry) and group (Adams et al.; Orbe; Campo & Frazer; Ritchie; McHale; Harter et al.; Walker and Curry); (b) questionnaires (Shields & Preston; Campo & Frazer; Cooks & Scharrer; Herman & Ettema; Rich & Rodríguez); and (c) document analysis (Jovanovic et al.; Orbe; Hartnett; Esrock et al.; Novek & Sanford; Cooks & Scharrer; Cagle; McHale). Three of the authors also document their intervention efforts via photography (Hartnett; Palmer; Harter et al.). Most of these studies, in fact, enlist multiple research methods and techniques as part of their communication interventions and/or to enrich the insights derived from analyzing those interventions.

The methodological pluralism demonstrated in these studies as a set, like the theoretical pluralism, deeply questions the traditional divide drawn between quantitative, rhetorical, and qualitative research by demonstrating that all the various methods and techniques available can be employed in communication activism scholarship. Moreover, by grounding interventions in and contributing back to theoretical perspectives and using research methods as part of those interventions and/or to document intervention efforts, the chapters realize the elusive goal of *praxis*—no small accomplishment.

Sixth, the *praxis* of communication activism is based, in large measure, on the creation of a trusting, collaborative partnership that produces a reflexive research process shaped by both researchers and the social actors seeking social change. Novek and Sanford, for instance, talked about how they work with the women inmates to produce the prison newspaper, negotiating the content of the paper with these women and learning from them the explicit and implicit constraints of prison life, with the collaborative character of this project extending, as it does in many of the chapters, to inmates' review of drafts of Novek and Sanford's scholarship. Harter et al. explained how the plays and performances that characterized their intervention were the result of collaboration with the participants and their families, and in Walker and Curry's case, they and their collaborators performed the colloquium together and cogenerated the knowledge derived from their interventions. By recognizing that marginalized individuals and groups are purposive social actors and involving them in the research process, these projects democratize research (Greenwood & Levin, 2000) and, thereby, deconstruct the traditional divide drawn between researchers and the impoverished and patronizing view of people as "research subjects." Communication activism scholarship, as Frey (1998b) noted about social justice scholarship, is grounded in "researchers' involvement in the life of 'another,' as opposed to studying 'an other'" (p. 162).

Seventh, we would be remiss if we did not point out that attempting to enact these and other principles of communication activism scholarship presents significant challenges. Some of these challenges are experienced in other forms of communication scholarship (e.g., gaining access to community groups, obtaining informed consent, and collecting data), but many of them spring from the unique nature of communication activism scholarship. Cagle and Coopman, for instance, talked about conflicts that can exist between activists and scholars because of their different backgrounds, needs, interests, and agendas, and Crabtree and Ford, as well as Ritchie, noted significant tensions associated with being both an activist and a consultant. Novek and Sanford discussed how they must negotiate the fine balance between challenging prison authorities and working with them to have continued access to the prison. Esrock et al. stressed tensions that exist between researchers assisting people and, at the same time, critically evaluating their actions, with Harter et al. underscoring the difficulty in deciding when to accept and when to challenge local customs and practices. As "outsiders-within" (Collins, 2000; see Crabtree & Ford), scholar-activists need to identify and engage with those with whom they seek meaningful social and political reforms, but identification and engagement should not blind scholar-activists to weaknesses that hinder people from securing those goals. Moreover, as Jovanovic et al. pointed out, communication activism, if it is to be successful in the long run, demands wide involvement, even by those who are against a social change project, although obtaining and maintaining their involvement is no easy matter. These and the many other challenges discussed in the chapters appear inevitable in communication activism.

Challenges also result from conducting communication activism research within the university context and academia, as well as within the communication discipline. All the scholars here are embedded within and subject to the constraints of the university context, and many of them talked about how they and others who conduct such research are affected by that context. For instance, communication activism scholarship can take a much longer period of time than some other forms of scholarship (e.g., handing out questionnaires in a large lecture class and analyzing the data), making such scholarship vulnerable to the "quantity" argument that often surfaces in tenure and promotion considerations. However, scholars also pointed out that universities can provide enormous resources for communication activism (such as the video equipment and facilities that McHale used), and, in some cases, communication activism resonates with the mission of a university and can bring much prestige to that university and those who conduct such research (such as at the Jesuit university where Crabtree teaches).

There are, unfortunately, those in the academy who argue against the engaged scholarship reflected in communication activism. Fish (2004), for example, on leaving his position as Dean of the College of Liberal Arts and Sciences at the University of Illinois at Chicago, offered the following advice to academics in an op-ed piece titled, "Why We Built the Ivory Tower," published in *The New York Times*:

> Don't confuse your academic obligations with the obligation to save the world; that's not your job as an academic. . . . In short, don't cross the boundary between academic work and partisan advocacy, whether the advocacy is yours or someone else's.
>
> Marx famously said that our job is not to interpret the world, but to change it. In the academy, however, it is exactly the reverse: our job is not to change the world, but to interpret it. (p. A23)

Although the communication discipline probably is one of the better disciplines with respect to supporting communication activism scholarship (having long ago dismissed the "debate" about quantitative versus qualitative research and recognizing the centrality of applied communication scholarship, including the articulation of a social justice communication approach), some members of the discipline do share the anti-activism position preached by Fish (2004). Kuypers (2000), for instance, asked the question, "Must we all be political activists?" and then answered it by arguing that "the leaders of our discipline have gone too far in their attempt to foster social change, both within the discipline and society" and suggesting that "if critics in our discipline wish to engage in such [political partisanship] they should leave the academy. . . . We should be professors, not social activists" ("Conclusion," ¶ 1, 16).

We certainly are not suggesting that all communication scholars should engage in communication activism. We do, however, advocate creating a space for activism in communication scholarship, contest the notion that communication scholars can remain politically neutral in what they study (and how they study and report it), and call on communication scholars to own their choices and be explicit about whose interests they privilege.

Finally, despite the pragmatic and systemic challenges involved, this scholarship can have tremendously important effects. Among the many effects documented in the chapters, communities talked, many for the first time, about the significant problems they faced (Jovanovic et al.; Adams et al.), and they now have an instrument to assess the state of their civil rights health (Orbe); inner-city youth who participated in the urban debate leagues went on to college (Shield & Preston); nonprofit organizations dealing with sexual assault and domestic violence and a neighborhood center now are more stable (Crabtree & Ford; Ritchie; Walker & Curry); women who partner with women have a healthcare center that is more receptive to their needs (Campo & Frazer); women prisoners (Novek & Sanford) and high school students (Christian) learned journalistic skills and practices; 6th-grade children became more critical viewers of the daily mediated violence to which they are exposed (Cooks & Scharrer); fairer media coverage of gay, lesbian, bisexual, and transgendered people was obtained (Cagle); low-power FM radio now is legal (Coopman); needed social capital was created in a lower income community (Herman & Ettema); women were able to perform with men in India to express their outrage with dowry (Harter et al.); college students learned how to respond more appropriately to women who have been sexually assaulted (Rich & Rodríguez); and, in perhaps the most dramatic example of all, an innocent man was saved from being executed because of McHale's documentary and, hopefully, other people will be spared that fate as a result of Sunwolf's workshops.

Communication activism also has important implications for a person's scholarship and teaching. Many of the authors talked about how their activism deepened their understanding of the research topic studied, the theories on which they relied, and the research methods they employed, and how their research inspired them to continue wanting to engage in scholarship that promotes social change and social justice. In six of the cases (Jovanovic; Crabtree; Ritchie; Christian; Cooks & Scharrer; Herman & Ettema), the research projects stemmed from teaching a service-learning course (with Jovanovic and Crabtree each teaching a course titled "Communication and Social Change") and/or working with graduate students (including involving them as coauthors in Jovanovic's case), and the activism by Coopman and by Walker and Curry resulted from being communication graduate students. Although scholars have raised important questions and critiques of service learning, they also agree that service learning can be an important vehicle for promoting social change and social justice (see, e.g., Artz, 2001; Christian, this volume; Crabtree, 1998; Novek, 1999). Most importantly, many of the scholars talked about how their communication activism influenced their teaching, providing them, for instance, with real-life examples to use in their classes and ultimately making them better teachers.

Communication activism, however, is not done simply to achieve the end products, for in many cases, the particular changes being advocated may take a long time to occur (the "power of delayed impact," as Hartnett called it) or they may never occur at all. Hartnett has not stopped the war on Iraq; Palmer has not prevented globalization; Esrock et al. have not been successful getting the Kentucky legislature to discuss an increase in the cigarette excise tax, let alone approve one; and Sunwolf, as an itinerate activist, typically does not know the results of her activism. Scholars engaging in communication activism, thus, have to manage the tensions between processes and outcomes, learning, among many other things, to be patient, sustain passion in the face of significant opposition, tolerate imperfect planning and execution, operate within contextual constraints, develop contingency plans, and cope with unsuccessful interventions. Hopefully, the expertise of communication scholar-activists in being able to talk about such issues will help to manage the inevitable tensions and challenges they will experience.

CONCLUSION

Communication activism is a significant form of communication scholarship that can be engaged in by scholars from across the communication discipline using a wide range of interventions, theories, and methods to promote social change and social justice for marginalized and underresourced individuals, groups, organizations, and communities. In the final analysis, although there are many potential rewards, scholars engage in communication activism because they are engaged citizens, using their knowledge and expertise to promote social change and social justice. They do it because, on so many levels, communication activism is the right thing to do.

REFERENCES

Adelman, M. B., & Frey, L. R. (1997). *The fragile community: Living together with AIDS.* Mahwah, NJ: Erlbaum.

Adelman, M. B., & Frey, L. R. (2001). Untold tales from the field: Living the autoethnographic life in an AIDS residence. In S. L. Herndon & G. L. Kreps (Eds.), *Qualitative research: Applications in organizational life* (2nd ed., pp. 205-226). Cresskill, NJ: Hampton Press.

Alasuutari, P. (Ed.). (1999). *Rethinking the media audience: The new agenda.* Thousand Oaks, CA: Sage.

Alderton, S. M. (1983). Survey course in organizational communication consulting: A processual model. *Communication Education, 32,* 413-420.

Alexander, B. (2005). Performance ethnography: The reenacting and inciting of culture. In N. K. Denzin & Y. S. Lincoln (Eds.), *Handbook of qualitative research* (3rd ed., pp. 411-442). Thousand Oaks, CA: Sage.

Alleyne, B. W. (2002). *Radicals against race: Black activism and cultural politics.* New York: Berg.

Andersen, P. A. (1993). Beyond criticism: The activist turn in the ideological debate. *Western Journal of Communication, 57,* 247-256.

Anderson, C. W. (1993). *Prescribing the life of the mind: An essay on the purpose of the university, the aims of liberal education, the competence of citizens, and the cultivation of practical reason.* Madison: University of Wisconsin Press.

Anderson, R., Cissna, K. N., & Arnett, R. A. (Eds.). (1994). *The reach of dialogue: Confirmation, voice, and community.* Cresskill, NJ: Hampton Press.

Anderson, R., Cissna, K. N., & Clune, M. K. (2003). The rhetoric of public dialogue. *Communication Research Trends, 22,* 1-34.

Andrews, J. R. (1969). Confrontation at Columbia: A case study in coercive rhetoric. *Quarterly Journal of Speech, 55,* 9-16.

Anyaegbunam, C., Karnell, A. P., Cheah, W. H., & Youngblood, J. D. (2005). Designing communication research for empowering marginalized populations: A participatory method. In S. H. Priest (Ed.), *Communication impact: Designing research that matters* (pp. 49-65). Lanham, MD: Rowman & Littefield.

Applegate, J. L. (2001, September). Engaged graduate education: Skating to where the puck will be. *Spectra,* pp. 2-5.

Applegate, J. L. (2002). Skating to where the puck will be: Engaged research as a funding activity. *Journal of Applied Communication Research, 30,* 402-410.

Arnett, R. C. (2001). Dialogic civility as pragmatic ethical praxis: An interpersonal metaphor for the public domain. *Communication Theory, 11,* 315-338.

Artz, L. (1998). African-Americans and higher education: An exigence in need of applied communication. *Journal of Applied Communication Research, 26,* 210-231.

Artz, L. (2001). Critical ethnography for communication studies: Dialogue and social justice in service-learning. *Southern Communication Journal, 66,* 239-250.

Artz, L., & Murphy, B. O. (2000). *Cultural hegemony in the United States.* Thousand Oaks, CA: Sage.

Asen, R. (2004). A discourse theory of citizenship. *Quarterly Journal of Speech, 90*, 189-211.

Asen, R. (2005). Why deliberative democracy? *Argumentation & Advocacy, 42*, 48-49.

Ashley, L., & Olson, B. (1998). Constructing reality: Print media's framing of the women's movement. *Journalism & Mass Communication Quarterly, 75*, 263-277.

Atkinson, J., & Dougherty, D. S. (2006). Alternative media and social justice movements: The development of a resistance performance paradigm of audience analysis. *Western Journal of Communication, 70*, 64-88.

Auer, J. J. (1939). Tools of social inquiry: Argumentation, discussion and debate. *Quarterly Journal of Speech, 25*, 533-539.

Avakian, M. (2000). *Reformers: Activists, educators, religious leaders.* Austin, TX: Raintree Steck-Vaughn.

Bagdikian, B. H. (2004). *The new media monopoly.* Boston: Beacon Press.

Baird, A. C. (1927). *Public discussion and debate.* Boston: Guinn.

Baird, J. E. (1970). The rhetoric of youth in controversy against the religious establishment. *Western Speech, 34*, 53-61.

Barber, B. R. (1992). *An aristocracy of everyone: The politics of education and the future of America.* New York: Ballantine Books.

Barge, J. K. (2001). Practical theory as mapping, engaged reflection, and transformative practice. *Communication Theory, 11*, 5-13.

Barge, J. K. (2002). Enlarging the meaning of group deliberation: From discussion to dialogue. In L. R. Frey (Ed.), *New directions in group communication* (pp. 159-177). Thousand Oaks, CA: Sage.

Barge, J. K., & Craig, R. T. (in press). Practical theory. In L. R. Frey & K. N. Cissna (Eds.), *Handbook of applied communication.* Mahwah, NJ: Erlbaum.

Barker-Plummer, B. (1995). News as a political resource: Media strategies and political identity in the U.S. women's movement, 1966-1975. *Critical Studies in Mass Communication, 12*, 306-324.

Barndt, D. (Ed.). (2006). *Wild fire: Art as activism.* Toronto, Canada: Sumach Press.

Bass, R. (1999). *Brown dog of the Yaak: Essays on art and activism.* Minneapolis, MN: Milkweed.

Baumgardner, J., & Richards, A. (2005). *Grassroots: A field guide for feminist activism.* New York: Farrar, Strauss and Giroux.

Becker, S. L. (1995). Response to Conquergood: Don Quixotes in the academy—Are we tilting at windmills? In K. N. Cissna (Ed.), *Applied communication in the 21st century* (pp. 1-19). Mahwah, NJ: Erlbaum.

Beer, M., & Eisenstat, R. A. (1996). Developing an organization capable of strategy implementation and learning. *Human Relations, 49*, 597-619.

Beer, M., & Eisenstat, R. A. (2000). The silent killers of strategy implementation and learning. *Sloan Management Review, 41*, 29-40.

Beer, M., Eisenstat, R. A., & Spector, B. (1990). *The critical path to corporate renewal.* Boston: Harvard Business School Press.

Beers, D. L. (2006). *For the prevention of cruelty: The history and legacy of animal rights activism in the United States.* Athens: Swallow Press/Ohio University Press.

Bennett, W. L. (2003). Communicating global activism: Strengths and vulnerabilities of networked politics. *Information, Communication & Society, 6,* 143-168.

Benson, T. W., & Johnson, B. (1968). The rhetoric of resistance: Confrontation with the warmakers, Washington, D.C., October, 1967. *Today's Speech, 16*(3), 35-42.

Benson, T. W., & Pearce, W. B. (Eds.). (1977). Alternative theoretical bases for the study of human communication: A symposium [Special issue]. *Communication Quarterly, 25*(1).

Bharucha, R. (1998). *In the name of the secular: Contemporary cultural activism in India.* New York: Oxford University Press.

Billingham, P. (Ed.). (2005). *Radical initiatives in interventionist and community drama.* Portland, OR: Intellect.

Boal, A. (1979). *Theatre of the oppressed* (A. Charles & M. O. Leal-McBride, Trans.). New York: Urizen Books.

Boal, A. (1995). *Rainbow of desire: The Boal method of theater and therapy* (A. Jackson, Trans.). New York: Routledge.

Bowen, H. W. (1963a). Does non-violence persuade? *Today's Speech, 11*(1), 10-11.

Bowen, H. W. (1963b). The future of non-violence. *Today's Speech, 11*(3), 3-4.

Bowen, H. W. (1967). A realistic view of non-violent assumptions. *Today's Speech, 15*(3), 9-10.

Boyer, E. L. (1987). *Scholarship reconsidered: Priorities of the professorate.* Princeton, NJ: Carnegie Foundation for the Advancement of Teaching.

Brashers, D. E., Haas, S.M., Klingle, R.S., & Neidig, J.L. (2000). Collective AIDS activism and individuals' perceived self-advocacy in physician-patient communication. *Human Communication Research, 26,* 372-402.

Brashers, D. E., Haas, S. M., & Neidig, J. L. (1999). The patient self-advocacy scale: Measuring patient involvement in health care decision-making interactions. *Health Communication, 11,* 97-121.

Brashers, D. E., Haas, S. M., Neidig, J. L., & Rintamaki, L. S. (2002). Social activism, self-advocacy, and coping with HIV illness. *Journal of Social and Personal Relationships, 19,* 113-133.

Brashers, D. E., & Jackson, S. (1991). "Politically-savvy sick people": Public penetration of the technical sphere. In D. W. Parson (Ed.), *Argument in controversy: Proceedings of the Seventh Speech Communication Association/American Forensics Association Conference on Argumentation* (pp. 284-288). Annandale, VA: Speech Communication Association.

Brouwer, D. (1998). The precarious visibility politics of self-stigmatization: The case of HIV/AIDS tattoos. *Text and Performance Quarterly, 18,* 114-137.

Brouwer, D. (2001). ACT-ing UP in Congressional hearings. In R. Asen & D. C. Brouwer (Eds.), *Counterpublics and the state* (pp. 87-109). Albany: State University of New York Press.

Browning, L. D. (1982). The ethics of intervention: A communication consultant's apology. *Journal of Applied Communication Research, 10,* 101-116.

Browning, L. D., & Hawes, L. C. (1991). Style, process, surface, context: Consulting as postmodern art. *Journal of Applied Communication Research, 19,* 32-54.

Broyles-González, Y. (1994). *El teatro campesino: Theater in the Chicano movement.* Austin: University of Texas Press.

Bugajski, J., & Pollack, M. (1989). *East European fault lines: Dissent, opposition, and social activism.* Boulder, CO: Westview Press.

Bullert, B. J. (2000). Progressive public relations, sweatshops, and the net. *Political Communication, 17*, 403-407.

Burkhalter, S., Gastil, J., & Kelshaw, T. (2002). A conceptual definition and theoretical model of public deliberation in small face-to-face groups. *Communication Theory, 12*, 398-422.

Butler, J. E. (2000). Democracy, diversity, and civic engagement. *Academe, 86*(4), 52-55.

Capo, K. E. (1983). From academic to social-political uses of performance. In D. W. Thompson (Ed.), *Performance of literature in historical perspectives* (pp. 437-457). Lanham, MD: University Press of America.

Carapico, S. (1998). *Civil society in Yemen: The political economy of activism in modern Arabia.* New York: Cambridge University Press.

Carbaugh, D. (1989/1990). The critical voice in ethnography of communication research. *Research on Language and Social Interaction, 23*, 261-282.

Carey, J. W. (1982). The mass media and critical theory: An American view. In M. Burgoon (Ed.), *Communication yearbook* (Vol. 6, pp. 18-33). Beverly Hills, CA: Sage.

Carey, J. W. (1983). The origins of the radical discourse on cultural studies in the United States. *Journal of Communication, 33*(3), 311-313.

Carey, J. W. (1989). *Communication as culture: Essays on media and society.* Boston: Unwin Hyman.

Carlone, D., & Taylor, B. (1998). Organizational communication and cultural studies: A review essay. *Communication Theory, 8*, 337-367.

Carragee, K. M. (1990). Interpretive media study and interpretive social science. *Critical Studies in Mass Communication, 7*, 81-96.

Carragee, K. M. (1991). News and ideology: An analysis of coverage of the West German Green Party by the *New York Times. Journalism Monographs, 128*, 1-30.

Carragee, K. M. (1993). A critical evaluation of the media hegemony thesis. *Western Journal of Communication, 57*, 330-348.

Carragee, K. M. (1996). Critical ethnographies and the concept of resistance. In M. Morgan & S. Leggett (Eds.), *Mainstream(s) and margins: Cultural politics in the 90s* (pp. 126-142). Westport, CT: Greenwood Press.

Carragee, K. M. (2003). Evaluating polysemy: An analysis of *The New York Times'* coverage of the end of the Cold War. *Political Communication, 20*, 287-308.

Carragee, K. M. (2005). Housing crisis: Gaining standing in a community coalition. In D. Croteau, W. Hoynes, & C. Ryan (Eds.), *Rhyming hope and history: Activists, academics, and social movement scholarship* (pp. 79-96). Minneapolis: University of Minnesota Press.

Carragee, K. M., & Roefs, W. (2004). The neglect of power in recent framing research. *Journal of Communication, 54*, 214-233.

Carroll, W. K., & Hackett, R. A. (2006). Democratic media activism through the lens of social movement theory. *Media, Culture & Society, 28*, 83-104.

Carter, K., & Spitzack, C. (Eds.). (1989). *Doing research on women's communication: Perspectives on theory and method.* Norwood, NJ: Ablex.

Caster, P. (2004). Staging prisons: Performance, activism, and social bodies. *TDR: The Drama Review, 48*, 107-116.

Chan, A. (1985). *Children of Mao: Personality development and political activism in the Red Guard generation.* Seattle: University of Washington Press.

Charland, M. (1991). Finding a horizon and telos: The challenge to critical rhetoric. *Quarterly Journal of Speech, 77,* 71-74.

Checkoway, B. (2001). Renewing the civic mission of the American research university. *Journal of Higher Education, 72,* 125-147.

Cheney, G. (1995). Democracy in the workplace: Theory and practice from the perspective of communication. *Journal of Applied Communication Research, 23,* 167-200.

Cheney, G., Wilhelmsson, M., & Zorn, T., Jr. (2002). 10 strategies for engaged scholarship. *Management Communication Quarterly, 16,* 92-100.

Christiansen, A. E., & Hanson, J. J. (1996). Comedy as cure for tragedy: ACT UP and the rhetoric of AIDS. *Quarterly Journal of Speech, 82,* 157-170.

Chvasta, M. (2006). Anger, irony, and protest: Confronting the issues of efficacy, again. *Text and Performance Quarterly, 26,* 5-16.

Cissna, K. N. (1982). Editor's note: What is applied communication research? *Journal of Applied Communication Research, 10,* i-iii.

Cissna, K. N., Eadie, W. F., & Hickson, M., III. (in press). The development of applied communication research. In L. R. Frey & K. N. Cissna (Eds.), *Handbook of applied communication.* Mahwah, NJ: Erlbaum.

Clark, N. (1996). The critical servant: An Isocratean contribution to critical rhetoric. *Quarterly Journal of Speech, 82,* 111-124.

Clark, W. (2000). *Activism in the public sphere: Exploring the discourse of political participation.* Burlington, VT: Ashgate.

Clift, E., & Freimuth, V. (1997). Changing women's lives: A communication perspective on participatory qualitative research techniques for gender equality. *Journal of Gender Studies, 6,* 289-296.

Cloud, D. L. (1994). The materiality of discourse as oxymoron: A challenge to critical rhetoric. *Western Journal of Communication, 58,* 141-163.

Cohen-Cruz, J. (Ed.). (1998). *Radical street performance: An international anthology.* New York: Routledge.

Cohen-Cruz, J. (2006). The problem democracy is supposed to solve: The politics of community-based performance. In D. S. Madison & J. Hamera (Eds.), *The Sage handbook of performance studies* (pp. 427-445). Thousand Oaks, CA: Sage.

Collins, P. H. (2000). *Black feminist thought: Knowledge, consciousness, and the politics of empowerment* (rev. ed.). New York: Routledge.

Condit, C. M. (1988). What makes our scholarship feminist? A radical/liberal view. *Women's Studies in Communication, 11*(1), 6-8.

Condit, C. M. (1993). The critic as empath: Moving away from totalizing theory. *Western Journal of Communication, 57,* 178-190.

Conquergood, D. (1985). Performing as a moral act: Ethical dimensions of the ethnography of performance. *Literature in Performance, 5*(2), 1-13.

Conquergood, D. (1988). Health theatre in a Hmong refugee camp: Performance, communication, and culture. *TDR: The Drama Review, 32,* 174-208.

Conquergood, D. (1991a). "For the nation!": How street gangs problematize patriotism. In R. Troester (Ed.), *Peacemaking through communication* (pp. 8-21). Annandale, VA: Speech Communication Association.

Conquergood, D. (1991b). Rethinking ethnography: Towards a critical cultural politics. *Communication Monographs, 58,* 179-194.

Conquergood, D. (1992a). Life in Big Red: Struggles and accommodations in a Chicago polyethnic tenement. In L. Lamphere (Ed.), *Structuring diversity: Ethnographic perspectives on the new immigration* (pp. 95-144). Chicago: University of Chicago Press.

Conquergood, D. (1992b). Performance theory, Hmong shamans, and cultural politics. In J. G. Reinelt & J. R. Roach (Eds.), *Critical theory and performance* (pp. 41-64). Ann Arbor: University of Michigan Press.

Conquergood, D. (1994). Homeboys and hoods: Gang communication and cultural space. In L. R. Frey (Ed.), *Group communication in context: Studies of natural groups* (pp. 23-55). Hillsdale, NJ: Erlbaum.

Conquergood, D. (1995). Between rigor and relevance: Rethinking applied communication. In K. N. Cissna (Ed.), *Applied communication for the 21st century* (pp. 79-96). Mahwah, NJ: Erlbaum.

Conquergood, D. (1998). Beyond the text: Toward a performative cultural politics. In S. Dailey (Ed.), *The future of performance studies: Visions and revisions* (pp. 25-36). Annandale, VA: National Communication Association.

Conquergood, D. (2002a). Lethal theatre: Performance, punishment, and the death penalty. *Theatre Journal, 54,* 339-367.

Conquergood, D. (2002b). Performance studies: Interventions and radical research. *TDR: The Drama Review, 46,* 145-156.

Conquergood, D. (Producer), & Siegel, T. (Producer & Director). (1985). *Between two worlds: The Hmong shaman in America* [Videotape]. (Available from Filmmakers Library, 124 E. 40th Street, New York, NY 10016)

Conquergood, D. (Producer), & Siegel, T. (Producer & Director). (1990). *The heart broken in half* [Videotape]. (Available from Filmmakers Library, 124 East 40th Street, New York, NY 10016)

Coopman, T. M. (2000). High speed access: Micro radio, action, and activism on the internet. *American Communication Journal, 3*(3). Retrieved May 15, 2006, from http://www.acjournal.org/holdings/vol3/Iss3/rogue4/highspeed.html

Costello, P. J. M. (2003). *Action research.* New York: Continuum.

Crabtree, R. D. (1998). Mutual empowerment in cross-cultural participatory development and service learning: Lessons in communication and social justice from projects in El Salvador and Nicaragua. *Journal of Applied Communication Research, 26,* 182-209.

Craig, R. T. (1989). Communication as a practical discipline. In B. Dervin, L. Grossberg, B. J. O'Keefe, & E. Wartella (Eds.), *Rethinking communication: Vol. 1. Paradigm issues* (pp. 97-122). Newbury Park, CA: Sage.

Craig, R. T. (1995). Applied communication research in a practical discipline. In K. N. Cissna (Ed.), *Applied communication in the 21st century* (pp. 147-155). Mahwah, NJ: Erlbaum.

Craig, R. T., & Tracy, K. (1995). Grounded practical theory: The case of intellectual discussion. *Communication Theory, 5,* 248-272.

Cronin, M., & Hall, P. (1990). A survey of employment opportunities for graduates with a master's in corporate and professional communication: A case study. *Journal of the Association for Communication Administration, 73,* 23-28.

Cronkhite, G. L. (1969). Out of the ivory tower: A proposal for useful research in communication and decision. In R. J. Kibler & L. L. Barker (Eds.), *Conceptual frontiers in speech-communication: Report of the New Orleans Conference on Research and Instructional Development* (pp. 113-135). New York: Speech Association of America.

Cronkhite, G., & Liska, J. (Eds.). (1977). Symposium: What criteria should be used to judge the admissibility of evidence to support theoretical propositions in communication research? [Special issue]. *Western Journal of Speech Communication, 41*(1).

Cushman, D. P. (1989/1990). The role of critique in the ethnographic study of human communication practices. *Research on Language and Social Interaction, 23*, 243-250.

Dallimore, E. J., & Souza, T. J. (2002). Consulting course design: Theoretical framework and pedagogical strategies. *Business Communication Quarterly, 65*(4), 86-113.

Davis, B. D., & Krapels, R. H. (1999). Applied communication consulting. *Business Communication Quarterly, 62*(3), 96-100.

Davis, W. H. (1915). Debating as related to non-academic life. *Quarterly Journal of Public Speaking, 1*, 105-113.

Dawson, J. I. (1996). *Eco-nationalism: Anti-nuclear activism and national identity in Russia, Lithuania, and Ukraine.* Durham, NC: Duke University Press.

Death Penalty Information Center. (2006). *Innocence: List of those freed from death row.* Retrieved May 15, 2006, from http://www.deathpenaltyinfo.org/article.php?scid=6&did=412

Debs, E. V. (1918). Debs's Canton speech. In E. V. Debs, *The Debs white book* (pp. 3-36). Girard, KS: Appeal to Reason.

Deetz, S. (1982). Critical-interpretive research in organizational communication. *Western Journal of Speech Communication, 46*, 131-149.

Deetz, S. (1988). Cultural studies: Studying meaning and action in organizations. In J. A. Anderson (Ed.), *Communication yearbook* (Vol. 11, pp. 335-345). Thousand Oaks, CA: Sage.

Deetz, S. A. (1992). *Democracy in an age of corporate colonization: Developments in communication and the politics of everyday life.* Albany: State University of New York Press.

Deetz, S., & Mumby, D. (1990). Power, discourse, and the workplace: Reclaiming the critical tradition in communication studies in organizations. In J. A. Anderson (Ed.), *Communication yearbook* (Vol. 13, pp. 18-47). Thousand Oaks, CA: Sage.

de Jong, W., Shaw, M., & Stammers, N. (2005). *Global activism, global media.* Ann Arbor, MI: Pluto Press.

DeLeon, D. (Ed.). (1994). *Leaders from the 1960s: A biographic sourcebook of American activism.* Westport, CT: Greenwood Press.

Delia, J. G. (1987). Communication research: A history. In C. R. Berger & S. H. Chaffee (Eds.), *Handbook of communication science* (pp. 20-98). Newbury Park, CA: Sage.

DeLuca, K. M. (1999). *Image politics: The new rhetoric of environmental activism.* New York: Guilford Press.

DeLuca, K. M., & Peeples, J. (2002). From public sphere to public screen: Democracy, activism, and the "violence" of Seattle. *Critical Studies in Media Communication*, *19*, 125-151.

Denzin, N. (2003). *Performance ethnography: Critical pedagogy and the politics of culture*. Thousand Oaks, CA: Sage.

Dewey, J. (1910). *How we think*. Boston: D. C. Heath.

de Witte, H. (Ed.). (2005). *Job insecurity, union involvement, and union activism*. Burlington, VT: Ashgate.

Diani, M. (2000). Social movement networks virtual and real. *Information, Communication & Society*, *3*, 386-401.

Dichter, D. (2004). U.S. media activism and the search for constituency. *Media Development*, *51*, 8-13.

Dijkstra, B. (2003). *American expressionism: Art and social change, 1920-1950*. New York: H. N. Abrams.

Dines, G., & Humez, J. M. (Eds.). (2002). *Gender, race, and class in media: A text-reader* (2nd ed.). Thousand Oaks, CA: Sage.

Dolan, J. (2001a). *Geographies of learning: Theatre and practice, activism and performance*. Middletown, CT: Wesleyan University Press.

Dolan, J. (2001b). Rehearsing democracy: Advocacy, public intellectuals, and civic engagement in theatre and performance studies. *Theatre Topics*, *11*, 1-17.

Dow, B. J. (1994). AIDS, perspective by incongruity, and gay identity in Larry Kramer's "1,112 and Counting." *Communication Studies*, *45*, 225-240.

Dow, B. J. (1996). *Prime-time feminism: Television, media culture, and the women's movement since 1970*. Philadelphia: University of Pennsylvania Press.

Downs, J., & Manion, J. (Eds.). (2004). *Taking back the academy!: History of activism, history as activism*. New York: Routledge.

Durham, M. G., & Kellner, D. M. (2005). *Media and cultural studies: Keyworks* (rev. ed.). Malden, MA: Blackwell.

Eadie, W. F. (1982, November). The case for applied communication research. *Spectra*, pp. 1-2.

Eadie, W. F. (1994). On having an agenda. *Journal of Applied Communication Research*, *22*, 81-85.

Eisenhofer, J. W., & Barry, M. J. (2006). *Shareholder activism handbook*. New York: Aspen.

Elam, H. J. (Ed.). (2003). Theatre and activism [Special issue]. *Theatre Journal*, *55*(4).

Elliott, H. S. (1927). *The why and how of group discussion*. New York: Association Press.

Ellis, D. G. (1982, March). The shame of speech communication. *Spectra*, pp. 1-2.

Ellis, D. G. (1991). The oneness of opposites: Applied communication and theory. *Journal of Applied Communication Research*, *19*, 116-122.

Eno, H. L. (1920). *Activism*. Princeton: NJ: Princeton University Press.

Entman, R. M. (1989). *Democracy without citizens: Media and the decay of American politics*. New York: Oxford University Press.

Entman, R. M., & Rojecki, A. (1993). Freezing out the public: Elite and media framing of the US anti-nuclear movement. *Political Communication*, *10*, 155-173.

Fabj, V., & Sobnowsky, M. J. (1993). Responses from the street: ACT UP and community organizing against AIDS. In S. C. Ratzan (Ed.), *AIDS: Effective health communication for the 90s* (pp. 91-109). Washington, DC: Taylor & Francis.

Fabj, V., & Sobnowsky, M. J. (1995). AIDS activism and the rejuvenation of the public sphere. *Argumentation and Advocacy, 31,* 163-184.

Falconer, T. (2001). *Watchdogs and gadflies: Activism from marginal to mainstream.* Toronto, Canada: Penguin Books.

Farrell, T. B., & Aune, J. A. (1979). Critical theory and communication: A selective literature review. *Quarterly Journal of Speech, 65,* 93-107.

Felshin, N. (1995). *But is it art?: The spirit of art as activism.* Seattle, WA: Bay Press.

Fernandez, T. L. (1968). Jonathan Baldwin Turner at Illinois College: Era of protest. *Today's Speech, 16*(3), 9-14.

Ferree, M. M., & Tripp, A. M. (Eds.). (2006). *Global feminism: Transnational women's activism, organizing, and human rights.* New York: New York University Press.

Fine, M. (2006). Bearing witness: Methods for researching oppression and resistance—A textbook for critical research. *Social Justice Research, 19,* 83-108.

Fine, M. G. (1990). Epistemological and methodological commitments of a feminist perspective. *Women & Language, 13*(2), 35-36.

Fish, S. (2004, May 21). Why we built the ivory tower. *The New York Times,* p. A23.

Fisher, R. E. (1997). *The concept of judicial activism: Its nature and function in United States constitutional law.* Sherman Oaks, CA: Banner Books International.

Fleming, D. (1998). The space of argumentation: Urban design, civic discourse, and the dream of the good city. *Argumentation, 12,* 147-166.

Foley, D., & Valenzula, A. (2005). Critical ethnography: The politics of collaboration. In N. K. Denzin & Y. S. Lincoln (Eds.), *The Sage handbook of qualitative methods* (3rd ed., pp. 217-234). Thousand Oaks, CA: Sage.

Foucault, M. (1979). *Discipline and punish: The birth of the prison* (A. Sheridan, Trans.). New York: Vintage Books.

Freeman, D. E. (1986). A student communication consulting firm: An experiential education option. *Journal of the Association for Communication Administration, 48,* 72-73.

Freire, P. (1970). *Pedagogy of the oppressed* (M. B. Ramos, Trans.). New York: Herder and Herder.

Freire, P. (1994). *Pedagogy of hope: Reliving* pedagogy of the oppressed (R. R. Barr, Trans.). New York: Continuum.

Freire, P. (1997). *Pedagogy of the heart* (D. Macedo & A. Oliveira, Trans.). New York: Continuum.

Freire, P. (1998). *Pedagogy of freedom: Ethics, democracy, and civic courage* (P. Clarke, Trans). New York: Rowman & Littlefield.

Frey, L. R. (Ed.). (1995). *Innovations in group facilitation: Applications in natural settings.* Cresskill, NJ: Hampton Press.

Frey, L. R. (1996). Remembering and "re-membering": A history of theory and research on communication and group decision making. In R. Y. Hirokawa & M. S. Poole (Eds.), *Communication and group decision making* (2nd ed., pp. 19-51). Thousand Oaks, CA: Sage.

Frey, L. R. (Ed.). (1998a). Communication and social justice research [Special issue]. *Journal of Applied Communication Research, 26*(2).

Frey, L. R. (1998b). Communication and social justice research: Truth, justice, and the applied communication way. *Journal of Applied Communication Research, 26,* 155-164.

Frey, L. R. (2000). To be applied or not to be applied, that isn't even the question; but wherefore art thou, applied communication researcher? Reclaiming applied communication research and redefining the role of the researcher. *Journal of Applied Communication Research, 28,* 178-182.

Frey, L. R. (2006a). Across the great divides: From nonpartisan criticism to partisan criticism to applied communication activism for promoting social change and social justice. In O. Swartz (Ed.), *Social justice and communication scholarship* (pp. 35-51). Mahwah, NJ: Erlbaum.

Frey, L. R. (Ed.). (2006b). *Facilitating group communication in context: Innovations and applications with natural groups* (2 vols.). Cresskill, NJ: Hampton Press.

Frey, L. R., Botan, C. H., & Kreps, G. L. (2000). *Investigating communication: An introduction to research methods* (2nd ed.). Boston: Allyn and Bacon.

Frey, L. R., & Cissna, K. N. (Eds.). (in press). *Handbook of applied communication.* Mahwah, NJ: Erlbaum.

Frey, L. R., Pearce, W. B., Pollock, M. A., Artz, L., & Murphy, B. A. O. (1996). Looking for justice in all the wrong places: On a communication approach to social justice. *Communication Studies, 47,* 110-127.

Friedenberg, R. V. (1997). *Communication consultants in political campaigns: Ballot box warriors.* Westport, CT: Praeger.

Friedman, D. (1985). Workers theatre of the 1930s. In B. McConachie & D. Friedman (Eds.), *Theatre for working-class audiences: 1830-1980* (pp. 111-120). Westport, CT: Greenwood Press.

Fuoss, K. (1997). *Striking performances/performing strikes.* Jackson: University of Mississippi Press.

Gamson, W. A. (1992). *Talking politics.* New York: Cambridge University Press.

Gamson, W. A., Croteau, D., Hoynes, W., & Sasson, T. (1992). Media images and the social construction of reality. *Annual Review of Sociology, 18,* 373-393.

Gamson, W. A., & Wolfsfeld, G. (1993). Media and movements as interacting systems: *Annals of the American Academy of Political and Social Science, 528,* 114-125.

Garrett, K. R. (2006). Protest in an information society: A review of literature on social movements and new ICTs. *Information, Communication & Society, 9,* 202-224.

Gastil, J. (2004). Adult civic education through the National Issues Forums: Developing democratic habits and dispositions through public deliberation. *Adult Education Quarterly, 54,* 308-328.

Gastil, J. (2006). Communication as deliberation. In G. J. Shepherd, J. St. John, & T. Striphas (Eds.), *Communication as . . . : Perspectives on theory* (pp. 164-173). Thousand Oaks, CA: Sage.

Gastil, J., & Dillard, J. (1999). Increasing political sophistication through public deliberation. *Political Communication, 16,* 3-23.

Gastil, J., & Levine, P. (Eds.). (2005). *The deliberative democracy handbook: Strategies for effective civic engagement in the twenty-first century.* San Francisco: Jossey-Bass.

Gatenby, B., & Humphries, M. (1996). Feminist commitments in organizational communication: Participatory action research as feminist praxis. *Australian Journal of Communication, 23*(2), 73-88.

Geist-Martin, P., Ray, E. B., & Sharf, B. F. (2003). *Communicating health: Personal, cultural, and political complexities.* Belmont, CA: Thomson/Wadsworth.

Gergen, K. J. (2000). *Invitation to social construction.* Thousand Oaks, CA: Sage.

Gibson, D. (2003). Use of the staged event in successful community activism. *Public Relations Quarterly, 48*(1), 35-40.

Gibson, T. A. (2000). Beyond cultural populism: Notes toward the critical ethnography of media audiences. *Journal of Communication Inquiry, 24,* 253-274.

Gieselman, R. D., & Philpott, J. (1969). Business communication consulting: A survey of faculty practices. *Journal of Business Communication, 7*(1), 15-22.

Gillett, J. (2003). The challenges of institutionalization for AIDS media activism. *Media, Culture & Society, 25,* 607-624.

Ginwright, S., Noguera, P., & Cammarota, J. (Eds.). (2006). *Beyond resistance! Youth activism and community change: New democratic possibilities for practice and policy for America's youth.* New York: Routledge.

Gitlin, T. (1980). *The whole world is watching: Mass media in the making and unmaking of the New Left.* Berkeley: University of California Press.

Glassberg, D. (1990). *American historical pageantry: The uses of tradition in the early twentieth century.* Chapel Hill: University of North Carolina Press.

Goldberg, A. (1983). Resolved: That paid consulting is contrary to the best interests of academia: The affirmative. *Journal of the Association for Communication Administration, 44,* 14-16.

Gómez-Peña, G. (2005). *Ethno-techno: Writing on performance, activism, and pedagogy* (E. Peña, Ed.). New York: Routledge.

Goodall, H. L., Jr. (1989). On becoming an organizational detective: The role of context sensitivity and intuitive logics in communication consulting. *Southern Communication Journal, 55,* 42-54.

Grano, D. A. (2002). Spiritual-material identification in the deep ecology movement. *Southern Communication Journal, 68,* 27-39.

Greenberg, J., & Knight, G. (2004). Framing sweatshops: Nike, global production, and the American news media. *Communication & Critical/Cultural Studies, 1,* 151-175.

Greenwood, D. J., & Levin, M. (2000). Introduction to action research: Social research for social change. In N. K. Denzin & Y. S. Lincoln (Eds.), *Handbook of qualitative research* (2nd ed., pp. 85-106). Thousand Oaks, CA: Sage.

Gregg, R. B. (1971). The ego-function of the rhetoric of protest. *Philosophy and Rhetoric, 4,* 71-91.

Grossberg, L. (1993a). Can cultural studies find true happiness in communication? *Journal of Communication, 43,* 89-97.

Grossberg, L. (1993b). Cultural studies and/in new worlds. *Critical Studies in Mass Communication, 10,* 1-22.

Grossberg, L. (1997). *Bringing it all back home: Essays on cultural studies.* Durham, NC: Duke University Press.

Grossberg, L., Nelson, C., & Treichler, P. A. (Eds.). (1992). *Cultural studies.* New York: Routledge.

Grossberg, L., Wartella, E. A., Whitney, D. C., & Wise, J. M. (2005). *Mediamaking: Mass media in popular culture.* Thousand Oaks, CA: Sage.

Grund, L., Cherwitz, R., & Darwin, T. (2001, December 3). Learning to be a citizen-scholar. *Chronicle of Higher Education.* Retrieved July 6, 2006, from http://chronicle.com/jobs/news/2001/12/2001120302c/careers.html

Guither, H. D. (1998). *Animal rights: History and scope of a radical social movement.* Carbondale: Southern Illinois University Press.

Habermas, J. (1984). *The theory of communicative action: Vol. 1. Reason and the rationalization of society* (T. McCarthy, Trans.). Boston: Beacon Press.

Habermas, J. (1996). *Between facts and norms: Contributions to a discourse theory of law and democracy* (W. Rehg, Trans). Cambridge, MA: MIT Press.

Haedicke, S. C., & Nellhaus, T. (Eds.). (2001). *Performing democracy: Interactional perspectives on urban community-based performance.* Ann Arbor: University of Michigan Press.

Haiman, F. S. (1967). The rhetoric of the streets: Some legal and ethical considerations. *Quarterly Journal of Speech, 53,* 99-114.

Hall, S. (1977). Culture, media and the "ideological effect." In J. Curran, M. Gurevitch, & J. Woollacot (Eds.), *Mass communication and society* (pp. 315-348). London: Edward Arnold/Open University Press.

Hall, S. (Ed.). (1997). *Representation: Cultural representations and signifying practices.* Thousand Oaks, CA: Sage/Open University Press.

Hallin, D. (1987). Hegemony: The American news media from Vietnam to El Salvador, a study of ideological change and its limits. In D. L. Paletz (Ed.), *Political communication research: Approaches, studies, assessments* (pp. 3-25). Norwood, NJ: Ablex.

Hardt, H. (1986). Critical theory in historical perspective. *Journal of Communication, 36*(3), 144-154.

Hardt, H. (1992). *Critical communication studies: Communication, history and theory in America.* New York: Routledge.

Hardt, H. (1993). Authenticity, communication, and critical theory. *Critical Studies in Mass Communication, 10,* 49-69.

Hariman, R. (1991). Critical rhetoric and postmodern theory. *Quarterly Journal of Speech, 77,* 67-70.

Harold, C. (2004). Pranking rhetoric: "Culture jamming" as media activism. *Critical Studies in Media Communication, 21,* 189-211.

Harrison, T. M. (1982). Toward an ethical framework for communication consulting. *Journal of Applied Communication Research, 10,* 87-100.

Hartnett, S. (1998). Lincoln and Douglas meet the abolitionist David Walker as prisoners debate slavery: Empowering education, applied communication, and social justice. *Journal of Applied Communication Research, 26,* 232-253.

Hasian, M., Jr. (2001). Vernacular legal discourse: Revisiting the public acceptance of the "right to privacy" in the 1960s. *Political Communication, 18,* 89-105.

Hauser, G. A. (1998). Vernacular dialogue and the rhetoricality of public opinion. *Communication Monographs, 65,* 83-107.

Hauser, G. A. (2002). *Vernacular voices: The rhetorics of publics and public spheres.* Columbia: University of South Carolina Press.

Hauser, G. A., & Benoit-Barne, C. (2002). Reflections on rhetoric, deliberative democracy, civil society, and trust. *Rhetoric & Public Affairs, 5,* 261-275.

Hauser, G. A., & Grim, A. (Eds.). (2004). *Rhetorical democracy: Discursive practices of civic engagement.* Mahwah, NJ: Erlbaum.

Hawkesworth, M. E. (2006a). *Feminist inquiry: From political conviction to methodological innovation.* New Brunswick, NJ: Rutgers University Press.

Hawkesworth, M. E. (2006b). *Globalization and feminist activism.* Lanham, MD: Rowman & Littlefield.

Held, D. (1982). Critical theory and political transformation. *Media, Culture & Society, 4*, 153-160.

Herman, E. S., & Chomsky, N. (1988). *Manufacturing consent: The political economy of the mass media.* New York: Pantheon Books.

Hertog, J. K., & McLeod, D. M. (1995). Anarchists wreak havoc in downtown Minneapolis: A multi-level study of media coverage of radical protest. *Journalism Monographs, 151*, 1-48.

Hesse-Biber, S. N. (Ed.). (2006). *Handbook of feminist research: Theory and praxis.* Thousand Oaks, CA: Sage.

Hicks, D. (1998). Public debate and the ideal of public reason. *Southern Journal of Forensics, 2*, 350-362.

Hicks, D. (2002). The promise(s) of deliberative democracy. *Rhetoric & Public Affairs, 5*, 224-229.

Hicks, D., & Greene, R. (2000). Debating both sides: Argument pedagogy and the production of the deliberative citizen. In M. Hollihan (Ed.), *Argument at century's end: Reflecting on the past and envisioning the future* (pp. 300-308). Annandale, VA: National Communication Association.

Hicks, D., & Langsdorf, L. (1998). Proceduralist theories of public deliberation: Implications for the production of citizens. In J. Klumpp (Ed.), *Argument in a time of change: Definitions, frameworks, and critiques* (pp. 150-156). Annandale, VA: National Communication Association.

Hickson, M., III. (1973). Applied communications research: A beginning point for social relevance. *Journal of Applied Communications Research, 1*, 1-5.

Hildebrandt, H. W. (1978). Business communication consulting and research in multinational companies. *Journal of Business Communication, 15*(3), 19-26.

Hill, F. (1983). A turn against ideology: Reply to Professor Wander. *Central States Speech Journal, 34*, 121-126.

Hitchcock, D. (2002). The practice of argumentative discussion. *Argumentation, 16*, 287-299.

Holsworth, R. D. (1989). *Let your life speak: A study of politics, religion, and antinuclear weapons activism.* Madison: University of Wisconsin Press.

Horkheimer, M., & Adorno, T. W. (1972). *Dialectics of enlightenment* (J. Cumming, Trans.). New York: Herder and Herder.

Hoynes, W. (2005). Media research and media activism. In D. Croteau, W. Hoynes, & C. Ryan (Eds.), *Rhyming hope and history: Activists, academics, and social movement scholarship* (pp. 97-114). Minneapolis: University of Minnesota Press.

Hung, C-j. F. (2003). Relationship building, activism, and conflict resolution. *Asian Journal of Communication, 13*, 21-49.

Hyde, B., & Bineham, J. L. (2000). From debate to dialogue: Toward a pedagogy of nonpolarized public discourse. *Southern Communication Journal, 65*, 208-223.

Inomata, T., & Cohen, L. S. (Eds.). (2006). *Archaeology of performance: Theaters of power, community, and politics.* Lanham, MD: Altamira Press.

Iraq Coalition Casualty Count. (2006, October 3). Retrieved October 4, 2006, from http://www.icasualties.org/oif/

Ishikawa, Y. (2002). Calls for deliberative democracy in Japan. *Rhetoric & Public Affairs, 5*, 331-345.

Ivie, R. L. (1998). Democratic deliberation in a rhetorical republic. *Quarterly Journal of Speech, 84,* 491-505.

Jarboe, S. (1989). Teaching communication consulting and training (or, reminisces of a trainer). *Southern Communication Journal, 55,* 22-41.

Jarboe, S. (1992). They do it for the money (?): A response to G. M. Phillips. *Journal of Applied Communication Research, 20,* 225-233.

Jennings, J. (Ed.). (1997). *Race and politics: New challenges and responses for Black activism.* New York: Verso.

Jensen, K. B. (1990). Television futures: A social action methodology for studying interpretive communities. *Critical Studies in Mass Communication, 7,* 129-146.

Johnson, E. P. (2006). Black performance studies. In D. S. Madison & J. Hamera (Eds.), *The Sage handbook of performance studies* (pp. 446-463). Thousand Oaks, CA: Sage.

Johnson, T., Nagel, J., & Champagne, D. (Eds.). (1997). *American Indian activism: Alcatraz to the Longest Walk.* Urbana: University of Illinois Press.

Johnson, T. R. (1996). *The occupation of Alcatraz Island: Indian self-determination and the rise of Indian activism.* Urbana: University of Illinois Press.

Johnson-Cartee, K. S., & Copeland, G. A. (1997). *Inside political campaigns: Theory and practice.* Westport, CT: Praeger.

Jones, J. L. (2002a). Performance ethnography: The role of embodiment in cultural authenticity. *Theatre Topics, 12,* 1-15.

Jones, J. L. (2002b). Teaching in the borderlands. In N. Stucky & C. Wimmer (Eds.), *Teaching performance studies* (pp. 175-190). Carbondale: Southern Illinois University Press.

Jones, T. S., & Bodtker, A. (1998). A dialectical analysis of a social justice process: International collaboration in South Africa. *Journal of Applied Communication Research, 26,* 357-373.

Jørgensen, C. (1998). Public debate—An act of hostility? *Argumentation, 12,* 431-443.

Kahn, R., & Kellner, D. (2004). New media and internet activism: From the "battle of Seattle" to blogging. *New Media & Society, 6,* 87-95.

Kaplan, F. F. (Ed.). (2006). *Art therapy and social action.* Philadelphia: J. Kingsley.

Keck, M. E., & Sikkink, K. (1999). *Activists beyond borders: Advocacy networks in international politics.* Ithaca, NY: Cornell University Press.

Kellner, D. (1990). *Television and the crisis of democracy.* Boulder, CO: Westview Press.

Kellner, D. (1995). *Media culture: Cultural studies, identity, and politics between the modern and the postmodern.* New York: Routledge.

Kemmis, S., & McTaggart, R. (2005). Participatory action research: Communication action and the public sphere. In N. K. Denzin & Y. S. Lincoln (Eds.), *The Sage handbook of qualitative research* (3rd ed., pp. 559-603). Thousand Oaks, CA: Sage.

Kennedy, D. (1997). *Academic duty.* Cambridge, MA: Harvard University Press.

Kerr, H. P. (1959). The rhetoric of political protest. *Quarterly Journal of Speech, 45,* 146-152.

Kershaw, B. (1992). *The politics of performance: Radical theatre as cultural intervention.* New York: Routledge.

Kibler, R. J., & Barker, L. L. (Eds.). (1969). *Conceptual frontiers in speech-communication: Report of the New Orleans Conference on Research and Instructional Development.* New York: Speech Association of America.

Kielbowicz, R. B., & Scherer, C. (1986). The role of the press in the dynamics of social movements. In K. Lang & G. E. Lang (Eds.), *Research in social movements, conflicts and change* (Vol. 9, pp. 71-96). Greenwich, CT: JAI Press.

Kim, J., Wyatt, R. O., & Katz, E. (1999). News, talk, opinion, participation: The part played by conversation in deliberative democracy. *Political Communication, 16,* 361-385.

Klope, D. C. (1994). Creationism and the tactic of debate: A performance study of guerrilla rhetoric. *Journal of Communication & Religion, 17,* 39-51.

Knight, G., & Greenberg, J. (2002). Promotionalism and subpolitics: Nike and its labor critics. *Management Communication Quarterly, 15,* 541-570.

Korza, P., & Bacon, B. S. (Eds.). (2005). *Art, dialogue, action, activism: Case studies from animating democracy.* Washington, DC: Americans for the Arts.

Kosokoff, S., & Carlmichael, C. W. (1970). The rhetoric of protest: Song, speech, and attitude change. *Southern Speech Journal, 35,* 295-302.

Kowal, D. M. (2000). One cause, two paths: Militant vs. adjustive strategies in British American women's suffrage movements. *Communication Quarterly, 48,* 240-255.

Kreps, G. L. (1989). A therapeutic model of organizational communication consultation: Application of interpretive field methods. *Southern Communication Journal, 55,* 1-21.

Kreps, G. L., Frey, L. R., & O'Hair, D. (1991). Applied communication research: Scholarship that can make a difference. *Journal of Applied Communication Research, 19,* 71-87.

Kurpius, D. D., & Mendelson, A. (2002). A case study of deliberative democracy on television: Civic dialogue on C-SPAN call-in shows. *Journalism & Mass Communication Quarterly, 79,* 587-601.

Kuypers, J. A. (2000). Must we all be political activists? *American Communication Journal, 4*(1). Retrieved June 24, 2006, from http://acjournal.org/holdings/vol4/iss1/special/kuypers.htm

Lampert, K. (2005). *Traditions of compassion: From religious duty to social activism.* New York: Palgrave Macmillan.

Lange, J. (1984). Seeking client resistance: Rhetorical strategy in communication consulting. *Journal of Applied Communication Research, 12,* 50-62.

Lawton, W. (1968). Thoreau and the rhetoric of dissent. *Today's Speech, 16*(2), 23-25.

Lemish, D. (2002). Gender at the forefront: Feminist perspectives on action theoretical approaches in communication research. *Communications: The European Journal of Communication Research, 27,* 63-78.

Lengel, L. B. (1998). Researching the "other," transforming ourselves: Methodological considerations of feminist ethnography. *Journal of Communication Inquiry, 22,* 229-250.

Levinas, E. (1969). *Totality and infinity* (A. Lingis, Trans.). Pittsburgh, PA: Duquesne University Press. (Original work published 1961)

Levine, P., Fung, A., & Gastil, J. (2005). Future directions for public deliberation. *Journal of Public Deliberation, 1*(1), Article 3. Retrieved June 28, 2006, from http://services.bepress.com/cgi/viewcontent.cgi?article=1003&context=jpd

Lewis, J. (1999). Reproducing political hegemony in the United States. *Critical Studies in Mass Communication, 16,* 251-267.

Lewis, J. (2001). *Constructing public opinion: How political elites do what they like and why we seem to go along with it.* New York: Columbia University Press.

Leyland, W. (Ed.). (2002). *Out in the Castro: Desire, promise, activism.* San Francisco: Leyland.

Lomas, C. W. (1960). The agitator in American politics. *Western Speech, 24,* 76-83.

Lomas, C. W. (1963). Agitator in a cassock. *Western Speech, 27,* 14-26.

Lubin, D. M. (1994). *Picturing a nation: Art and social change in nineteenth-century America.* New Haven, CT: Yale University Press.

Madison, D. S. (2005a). *Critical ethnography: Method, ethics, and performance.* Thousand Oaks, CA: Sage.

Madison, D. S. (2005b). Critical ethnography as street performance: Reflections of home, race, murder, and justice. In N. K. Denzin & Y. S. Lincoln (Eds.), *The Sage handbook of qualitative research* (3rd ed., pp. 537-546). Thousand Oaks, CA: Sage.

Madison, D. S. (2006). Staging fieldwork/performing human rights. In D. S. Madison & J. Hamera (Eds.), *The Sage handbook of performance studies* (pp. 397-418). Thousand Oaks, CA: Sage.

Makau, J. M. (1996). Notes on communication education and social justice. *Communication Studies, 47,* 135-141.

March, J. G. (1991). Organizational consultants and organizational research. *Journal of Applied Communication Research, 19,* 20-31.

Markowitz, L. (2000). *Worker activism after successful union organizing.* Armonk: NY: M. E. Sharpe.

Martin, H. H. (1966). The rhetoric of academic protest. *Central States Speech Journal, 17,* 244-250.

Mattson, K. (2002). Do Americans really want deliberative democracy? *Rhetoric & Public Affairs, 5,* 327-329.

Mauch, C., Stolzfus, N., & Weiner, D. R. (Eds.). (2006). *Shades of green: Environmental activism around the globe.* Lanham, MD: Rowman & Littlefield.

McAdam, D. (1996). The framing function of movement tactics: Strategic dramaturgy in the American civil rights movement. In D. McAdam, J. D. McCarthy, & M. N. Zald (Eds.), *Comparative perspectives on social movements: Political opportunities, mobilizing structures, and cultural framings* (pp. 338-355). New York: Cambridge University Press.

McBurney, J. H., & Hance, K. G. (1939). *The principles and methods of discussion.* New York: Harper & Brothers.

McCall, M. M. (2000). Performance ethnography: A brief history and some advice. In N. K. Denzin & Y. S. Lincoln (Eds.), *Handbook of qualitative research* (2nd ed., pp. 421-433). Thousand Oaks, CA: Sage.

McCaughey, M., & Ayers, M. D. (Eds.). (2003). *Cyberactivism: Online activism in theory and practice.* New York: Routledge.

McChesney, R. W. (1999). *Rich media, poor democracy: Communication politics in dubious times.* Urbana: University of Illinois Press.

McChesney, R. W. (2004a). Media policy goes to main street: The uprising of 2003. *Communication Review, 7,* 223-258.

McChesney, R. W. (2004b). *The problem of the media: U.S. communication politics in the twenty-first century*. New York: Monthly Review Press.

McEdwards, M. G. (1968). Agitative rhetoric: Its nature and effect. *Western Speech*, *32*, 36-43.

McGee, J. J. (2003). A pilgrim's progress: Metaphor in the rhetoric of Mary Fisher, AIDS activist. *Women's Studies in Communication*, *26*, 191-213.

McGuire, M., & Slembeck, E. (1987). An emerging critical rhetoric: Hellmut Geissner's *Sprechwissenschaft*. *Quarterly Journal of Speech*, *73*, 349-358.

McHale, J. P. (2004). *Communicating for change: Strategies of social and political advocates*. Lanham, MD: Rowman & Littlefield.

McHale, J. P. (Producer/Director), Wylie, R. (Producer/Editor), & Huck, D. (Producer/Assistant Editor). (2002). *Unreasonable doubt: The Joe Amrine case* [Videotape]. (Available from Hampton Press)

McKerrow, R. E. (1989). Critical rhetoric: Theory and praxis. *Communication Monographs*, *56*, 91-111.

McKerrow, R. E. (1991). Critical rhetoric in a postmodern world. *Quarterly Journal of Speech*, *77*, 75-78.

McKerrow, R. E. (1993). Critical rhetoric and the possibility of the subject. In I. Angus & L. Langsdorf (Eds.), *The critical turn: Rhetoric and philosophy in postmodern discourse* (pp. 51-67). Carbondale: Southern Illinois University Press.

McNiff, J., & Whitehead, J. (2002). *Action research: Principles and practice* (2nd ed.). New York: RoutledgeFalmer.

McNiff, J., & Whitehead, J. (2006). *Action research: Living theory*. Thousand Oaks, CA: Sage.

Meehan, E. R, & Riordan, E. (Eds.). (2001). *Sex and money: Feminism and political economy in the media*. Minneapolis: University of Minnesota Press.

Meikle, G. (2002). *Future active: Media activism and the internet*. New York: Routledge.

Melcher, C. (1995). Non-expert expertise: Chronicling the success of AIDS and breast cancer activists. In S. A. Jackson (Ed.), *Argumentation and values: Proceedings of the Ninth Speech Communication Association/American Forensic Association Conference on Argumentation* (pp. 356-361). Annandale, VA: Speech Communication Association.

Merriam-Webster Online. (2006). *Activism*. Retrieved May 15, 2006, from http://www.m-w.com/dictionary/activism

Meyers, R. A., & Brashers, D. E. (2002). Rethinking traditional approaches to argument in groups. In L. R. Frey (Ed.), *New directions in group communication* (pp. 141-158). Thousand Oaks, CA: Sage.

Mienczakowski, J. (1995). The theatre of ethnography: The reconstruction of ethnography into theatre with emancipatory potential. *Qualitative Inquiry*, *1*, 360-375.

Miller, G. R. (1995). "I think my schizophrenia is better today," said the communication researcher unanimously: Some thoughts on the dysfunctional dichotomy between pure and applied communication research. In K. N. Cissna (Ed.), *Applied communication in the 21st century* (pp. 47-55). Mahwah, NJ: Erlbaum.

Miller, G. R., & Sunnafrank, M. J. (1984). Theoretical dimensions of applied communication research. *Quarterly Journal of Speech*, *70*, 255-263.

Monks, R. A. G. (1999). *The Emperor's nightingale: Restoring the integrity of the corporation in the age of shareholder activism.* Reading, MA: Perseus Books.

Montgomery, D., Wiseman, D. W., & DeCaro, P. (2001). Toward a code of ethics for organizational communication professionals: A working proposal. *American Communication Journal, 5*(1). Retrieved July 3, 2006, from http://acjournal.org/holdings/vol5/iss1/special/montgomery.htm

Morley, D. (1980). *The nationwide audience.* London: British Film Institute.

Morley, D. (1992). *Television, audiences, and cultural studies.* New York: Routledge.

Mosco, V. (1996). *The political economy of communication: Rethinking and renewal.* Thousand Oaks, CA: Sage.

Muir, C. (1996). Using consulting projects to teach critical-thinking skills in business communication. *Business Communication Quarterly, 59*(4), 77-87.

Mumby, D. K. (1993). Critical organizational communication studies: The next 10 years. *Communication Monographs, 60*, 18-25.

Murphy, T. A. (2004). Deliberative civic education and civil society: A consideration of ideals and actualities in democracy and communication education. *Communication Education, 53*, 74-91.

Neal, L. (1968). The Black arts movement. *TDR: The Drama Review, 12*(4), 29-39.

Nielsen, J. M. (Ed.). (1990). *Feminist research methods: Exemplary readings in the social sciences.* Boulder, CO: Westview Press.

Noakes, J. A., & Wilkins, K. G. (2002). Shifting frames of the Palestinian movement in US news. *Media, Culture & Society, 5*, 649-671.

Novek, E. (1999). Service is a feminist issue: Transforming communication pedagogy. *Women's Studies in Communication, 22*, 230-240.

Novek, E. (2005). "The devil's bargain": Censorship, identity and the promise of empowerment in a prison newspaper. *Journalism: Theory, Practice & Criticism, 6*, 5-23.

O'Hair, D., Kreps, G. L., & Frey, L. R. (1990). Conceptual issues. In D. O'Hair & G. L. Kreps (Eds.), *Applied communication theory and research* (pp. 3-22). Hillsdale, NJ: Erlbaum.

Oleson, V. (2005). Early millennial feminist qualitative research: Challenges and contours. In N. K. Denzin & Y. S. Lincoln (Eds.), *The Sage handbook of qualitative methods* (3rd ed., pp. 235-278). Thousand Oaks, CA: Sage.

Oliver, P. E., & Myers, D. J. (1999). How events enter the public sphere: Conflict, location, and sponsorship in local newspaper coverage of public events. *American Journal of Sociology, 105*, 38-87.

Olomo, O. O. O. (2006). Performance and ethnography, performing ethnography, performance ethnography. In D. S. Madison & J. Hamera (Eds.), *The Sage handbook of performance studies* (pp. 339-345). Thousand Oaks, CA: Sage.

Olson, K. M., & Olson, C. D. (2003). Problems of exclusionary research criteria: The case against the "usable knowledge" litmus test for social justice communication research. *Communication Studies, 54*, 438-450.

Online Etymology Dictionary. (2006). *Theory.* Retrieved May 15, 2006, from http://www.etymonline.com/index.php?term=theory

Ono, K. A., & Sloop, J. M. (1992). Commitment to "telos"—A sustained critical rhetoric. *Communication Monographs, 59*, 48-60.

Palczewski, H. (2001). Cyber-movements, new social movements, and counter-publics. In R. Asen & D. C. Brouwer (Eds.), *Counterpublics and the state* (pp. 161-186). Albany: State University of New York Press.

Palmeri, T. (2006). Media activism in a "conservative" city: Modeling citizenship. In O. Swartz (Ed.), *Social justice and communication scholarship* (pp. 149-173). Mahwah, NJ: Erlbaum.

Park-Fuller, L. (2003). Audiencing the audience: Playback Theatre, performative writing, and social activism. *Text and Performance Quarterly, 23,* 288-310.

Pearce, K. A., & Pearce, W. B. (2001). The Public Dialogue Consortium's school-wide dialogue process: A communication approach to develop citizenship skills and enhance school climate. *Communication Theory, 11,* 105-123.

Pearce, K. A., Spano, S., & Pearce, W. B. (in press). The multiple faces of the Public Dialogue Consortium: Scholars, practitioners, and dreamers of better social worlds. In L. R. Frey & K. N. Cissna (Eds.), *Handbook of applied communication.* Mahwah, NJ: Erlbaum.

Pearce, W. B. (1998). On putting social justice in the discipline of communication and putting enriched concepts of communication in social justice research and practice. *Journal of Applied Communication Research, 26,* 272-278.

Pearce, W. B., & Pearce, K. A. (2000a). Combining passions and abilities: Toward dialogic virtuosity. *Southern Communication Journal, 65,* 161-175.

Pearce, W. B., & Pearce, K. A. (2000b). Extending the theory of the coordinated management of meaning (CMM) through a community dialogue process. *Communication Theory, 10,* 405-423.

Peeples, J. A. (2003). Trashing South-Central: Place and identity in a community-level environmental justice dispute. *Southern Communication Journal, 69,* 82-95.

Pestello, F. G., Saxton, S. L., Miller, D. E., & Donnelly, P. G. (1996). Community and the practice of sociology. *Teaching Sociology, 24,* 148-156.

Peterson, K. (2006, August 3). *Wash., New York say no to gay marriage.* Retrieved August 22, 2006, from http://www.stateline.org/live/ViewPage.action?site NodeId=136&languageId=1&contentId=20695

Pezzullo, P. C. (2001). Performing critical interruptions: Stories, rhetorical invention, and the environmental justice movement. *Western Journal of Communication, 65,* 1-25.

Pezzullo, P. C. (2003). Resisting "National Breast Cancer Awareness Month": The rhetoric of counterpublics and their cultural performances. *Quarterly Journal of Speech, 89,* 345-365.

Phillips, G. M. (1992). They do it for the money. *Journal of Applied Communication Research, 20,* 219-224.

Pickerill, J. (2003). *Cyberprotest: Environmental activism online.* New York: Manchester University Press.

Pilotta, J. J., McCaughan, J. A., Jasko, S., Murphy, J., Jones, T., Wilson, L. et al. (2001). *Communication and social action research.* Cresskill, NJ: Hampton Press.

Pingree, R. J. (2006). Decision structure and the problem of scale in deliberation. *Communication Theory, 16,* 198-222.

Pini, B., Brown, K., & Previte, J. (2004). Politics and identity in cyberspace: A case study of Australian women in agriculture online. *Information, Communication & Society, 7,* 167-184.

Plax, T. G. (1991). Understanding applied communication inquiry: Researcher as organizational consultant. *Journal of Applied Communication Research, 19*, 55-70.

Poe, S. D. (2002). Technical communication consulting as a business. *Technical Communication, 49*, 171-180.

Pollock, M. A., Artz, L., Frey, L. R., Pearce, W. B., & Murphy, B. A. O. (1996). Navigating between Scylla and Charybdis: Continuing the dialogue on communication and social justice. *Communication Studies, 47*, 142-151.

Quigley, D., Sanchez, V., Handy, D., Goble, R., & George, P. (2000). Participatory research strategies in nuclear risk management for native communities. *Journal of Health Communication: International Perspectives, 5*, 305-331.

Rakow, L. F. (2005). Why did the scholar cross the road? Community action research and the citizen-scholar. In S. H. Priest (Ed.), *Communication impact: Designing research that matters* (pp. 5-17). Lanham, MD: Rowman & Littlefield.

Real, M. (1984). Debate on critical theory and the study of communications: A commentary on ferment in the field. *Journal of Communication, 34*(4), 72-80.

Reason, P., & Bradbury, H. (Eds.). (2001). *Handbook of action research: Participative inquiry and practice.* Thousand Oaks, CA: Sage.

Reber, B. H., & Berger, B. K. (2005). Framing analysis of activist rhetoric: How the Sierra Club succeeds or fails at creating salient messages. *Public Relations Review, 31*, 185-195.

Redding, C. (1979). Graduate education and the communication consultant: Playing God for a fee. *Communication Education, 28*, 346-352.

Reed, T. V. (2005). *The art of protest: Culture and activism from the civil rights movement to the streets of Seattle.* Minneapolis: University of Minnesota Press.

Reinharz, S. (with Davidman, L.). (1992). *Feminist methods in social research.* New York: Oxford University Press.

Rhoads, R. A. (1998). *Freedom's web: Student activism in an age of cultural diversity.* Baltimore: John Hopkins University Press.

Ristock, J. L., & Pennell, J. (1996). *Community research as empowerment: Feminist links, postmodern interruptions.* New York: Oxford University Press.

Rogers, E. M. (1994). *A history of communication study: A biographical approach.* New York: Free Press.

Rojecki, A. (1999). *Silencing the opposition: Antinuclear movements and the media in the Cold War.* Urbana: University of Illinois Press.

Rojecki, A. (2002). Modernism, state sovereignty and dissent: Media and the new post-Cold War movements. *Critical Studies in Media Communication, 19*, 152-171.

Rosenfield, L. W. (1983). Ideological miasma. *Central States Speech Journal, 34*, 119-121.

Rude, L. G. (1969). The rhetoric of farmer labor agitators. *Central States Speech Journal, 20*, 280-285.

Rushing, J. H., & Frentz, T. S. (1991). Integrating ideology and achetype in rhetorical criticism. *Quarterly Journal of Speech, 77*, 385-406.

Ryan, C. (1991). *Prime time activism: Media strategies for grassroots organizing.* Boston: South End Press.

Ryan, C. (2005). Successful collaboration: Movement building in the media arena. In D. Croteau, W. Hoynes, & C. Ryan (Eds.), *Rhyming hope and history: Activists,* academics, and social movement scholarship (pp. 115-136). Minneapolis: University of Minnesota Press.

Ryan, C., Carragee, K. M., & Meinhofer, W. (2001). Theory into practice: Framing, the news media, and collective action. *Journal of Broadcasting & Electronic Media, 45*, 175-182.

Ryan, C., Carragee, K. M., & Schwerner, C. (1998). Media, movements, and the quest for social justice. *Journal of Applied Communication Research, 26*, 165-181.

Ryfe, D. M. (2002). The practice of deliberative democracy: A study of 16 deliberative organizations. *Political Communication, 19*, 359-377.

Ryfe, D. M. (2005). Does deliberative democracy work? *Annual Review of Political Science, 8*, 49-71.

Said, E. (1989). Representing the colonized: Anthropology's interlocutors. *Critical Inquiry, 15*, 205-225.

Salter, L. (2004). Structure and forms of use: A contribution to understanding the "effects" of the internet on deliberative democracy. *Information, Communication & Society, 7*, 185-206.

Sanchez, J., & Stuckey, M. E. (2000). The rhetoric of American Indian activism in the 1960s and 1970s. *Communication Quarterly, 48*, 120-136.

Sandmann, L. R., & Lewis, A. G. (1991). Land grant universities on trial. *Adult Learning, 3*, 23.

Sanford, V., & Angel-Ajani, A. (Eds.). (2006). *Engaged observer: Anthropology, advocacy, and activism.* New Brunswick, NJ: Rutgers University Press.

Santiago, C. D. (1972). *A century of activism.* Manila, The Philippines: Rex.

Schiller, H. I. (1989). *Culture, Inc.: The corporate takeover of public expression.* New York: Oxford University Press.

Schiller, H. I. (1996). *Information inequality: The deepening social crisis in America.* New York: Routledge.

Schoening, G. T., & Anderson, J. A. (1995). Social action media studies: Foundational arguments and common premises. *Communication Theory, 5*, 93-116.

Schragge, E. (2003). *Activism and social change: Lessons for community and local organizing.* Orchard Park, NY: Broadview Press.

Schramm, W. (1997). *The beginnings of communication study in America: A personal memoir* (S. H. Chaffee & E. M. Rogers, Eds.). Thousand Oaks, CA: Sage.

Scott, R. L., & Smith, D. K. (1969). The rhetoric of confrontation. *Quarterly Journal of Speech, 55*, 1-8.

Seaton, C. E. (1996). *Altruism and activism: Character disposition and ideology as factors in a blockade of an abortion clinic: An exploratory study* (2nd ed.). Lanham, MD: University Press of America.

Seibold, D. R. (1995). *Theoria* and *praxis*: Means and ends in applied communication research. In K. N. Cissna (Ed.), *Applied communication in the 21st century* (pp. 23-38). Mahwah, NJ: Erlbaum.

Seibold, D. R. (2000). Applied communication scholarship: Less a matter of boundaries than of emphases. *Journal of Applied Communication Research, 28*, 183-187.

Sender, K. (2001). Gay readers, consumers, and a dominant gay habitus: 25 years of the *Advocate* magazine. *Journal of Communication, 51*, 73-99.

Sheffield, A. D. (1926). *Creative discussion: A statement of method for leaders and members of discussion groups and conferences* (3rd ed.). New York: American Press.

Shepherd, C. (1998). *A study of the relationship between style I art and socio-political change in early mediaeval Europe.* Oxford, England: British Archaeological Reports.

Shi, Y. (2005). Identity construction of the Chinese diaspora, ethnic media use, community formation, and the possibility of social activism. *Continuum: Journal of Media & Cultural Studies, 19,* 55-72.

Shoemaker, P. J. (1984). Media treatment of deviant political groups. *Journalism Quarterly, 61,* 66-75, 82.

Shotter, J. (1997). On a different ground: From contests between monologues to dialogic contest. *Argumentation, 11,* 95-112.

Sirianni, C., & Friedland, L. (1997, January/February). Civic innovation and American democracy. *Change,* pp. 14-23.

Smith, D. H. (1967). Social protest . . . and the oratory of human rights. *Today's Speech, 15*(3), 2-8.

Smith, J., McCarthy, J. D., McPhail, C., & Augustyn, B. (2001). From protest to agenda building: Description bias in media coverage of protest events in Washington, D.C. *Social Forces, 79,* 1397-1423.

Smith, R. A., & Siplon, P. D. (2006). *Drugs into bodies: Global AIDS treatment activism.* Westport, CT: Praeger.

Sobnowsky, M. J., & Hauser, E. (1998). Initiating or avoiding activism: Red ribbons, pink triangles, and public argument about AIDS. In W. E. Elwood (Ed.), *Power in the blood: A handbook on AIDS, politics, and communication* (pp. 25-38). Mahwah, NJ: Erlbaum.

Sowards, S. K., & Renegar, V. (2004). The rhetorical functions of consciousness-raising in third wave feminism. *Communication Studies, 55,* 535-552.

Spano, S. (2001). *Public dialogue and participatory democracy: The Cupertino community project.* Cresskill, NJ: Hampton Press.

Spano, S. (2006). Theory and practice in public dialogue: A case study in facilitating community transformation. In L. R. Frey (Ed.), *Facilitating group communication in context: Innovations and applications with natural groups: Vol. 1. Facilitating group creation, conflict, and conversation* (pp. 271-298). Cresskill, NJ: Hampton Press.

Sprague, J. (2005). *Feminist methodologies for critical researchers: Bridging differences.* Walnut Creek, CA: AltaMira Press.

Staggenborg, S. (1991). *The pro-choice movement: Organization and activism in the abortion conflict.* New York: Oxford University Press.

Stengrim, L. (2005). Negotiating postmodern democracy, political activism, and knowledge production: Indymedia's grassroots and e-savvy answer to media oligopoly. *Communication & Critical/Cultural Studies, 2,* 281-304.

Stevenson, M. R., & Cogan, J. C. (Eds.). (2003). *Everyday activism: A handbook for lesbian, gay, and bisexual people and their allies.* New York: Routledge.

Stewart, C. K. (1991, November). *Research in organizational communication.* Paper presented at the meeting of the Speech Communication Association, Atlanta, GA.

Stewart, J. (1983). Reconsidering communication consulting. *Journal of Applied Communication Research, 11,* 153-167.

Stockdill, B. C. (2003). *Activism against AIDS: At the intersection of sexuality, race, gender, and class.* Boulder, CO: Lynne Rienner.

Strine, M. S. (1991). Critical theory and "organic" intellectuals: Reframing the work of cultural critique. *Communication Monographs, 58*, 195-201.

Strine, M. (1992). Art, activism, and the performance (con)text: A response. *Text and Performance Quarterly, 12*, 391-395.

Stringer, E. T. (1999). *Action research* (2nd ed.). Thousand Oaks, CA: Sage.

Stucky, N. (2006). Fieldwork in the performance studies classroom: Learning objectives and the activist curriculum. In D. S. Madison & J. Hamera (Eds.), *The Sage handbook of performance studies* (pp. 261-277). Thousand Oaks, CA: Sage.

Sunwolf. (2006). Empathic attunement facilitation: Stimulating immediate task engagement in zero-history training groups of helping professionals. In L. R. Frey (Ed.), *Facilitating group communication in context: Innovations and applications with natural groups: Vol. 1. Facilitating group creation, conflict, and conversation* (pp. 63-92). Cresskill, NJ: Hampton Press.

Sussman, L. (1982). OD as muddling: Implications for communication consultants. *Communication Quarterly, 30*, 85-91.

Swan, S. (2002). Rhetoric, service, and social justice. *Written Communication, 19*, 76-108.

Swartz, O. (1997). *Conducting socially responsible research: Critical theory, neopragmatism, and rhetorical inquiry.* Thousand Oaks, CA: Sage.

Swartz, O. (2004). Partisan, empathic and invitational criticism: The challenge of materiality. *Ethical Space: The International Journal of Communication Ethics, 1*, 28-33.

Swartz, O. (2005). *In defense of partisan criticism.* New York: Peter Lang.

Swartz, O. (Ed.). (2006). *Social justice and communication scholarship.* Mahwah, NJ: Erlbaum.

Taylor, P. (2003). *Applied theatre: Creating transformative encounters in the community.* Portsmouth, NH: Heinemann.

Tenopir, C., & King, D. W. (2000). Towards electronic journals: Realities for scientists, librarians, and publishers. *Psycoloquy, 11*(84). Retrieved May 15, 2006, from http://psycprints.ecs.soton.ac.uk/archive/00000084/#html

Theodore, A. (2002). "A right to speak on the subject": The U.S. women's antiremoval petition campaign, 1829-1831. *Rhetoric & Public Affairs, 5*, 601-624.

Thomas, J. (1993). *Doing critical ethnography.* Newbury Park, CA: Sage.

Thousands march for immigrant rights: Schools, businesses feel impact as students, workers walk out. (2006, May 1). Retrieved May 12, 2006, from http://www.cnn.com/2006/US/05/01/immigrant.day/index.html

Toc, H. (1971). "I shot an arrow in the air . . .": The performing arts as weapons of social change. *Journal of Communication, 21*, 115-135.

Toch, H. H., Deutsch, S. E., & Wilkins, D. M. (1960). The wrath of the bigot: An analysis of protest mail. *Journalism Quarterly, 27*, 173-185.

Tuchman, G. (1978). *Making news: A study in the construction of reality.* New York: Free Press.

Turner, V., & Turner, E. (1982). Performing ethnography. *TDR: The Drama Review, 26*, 33-50.

Turner, V., & Turner, E. (1988). Performance ethnography. In V. Turner, *The anthropology of performance* (pp. 139-155). New York: Performing Arts Journal.

Ugwu, C. (Ed.). (1995). *Let's get it on: The politics of Black performance.* Seattle, WA: Bay Press.

Van de Donk, W., Loader, B. D., Nixon, P. G., & Rucht, D. (Eds.). (2004). *Cyberprotest: New media, citizens, and social movements.* New York: Routledge.

van Erven, E. (1992). *The playful revolution: Theatre and liberation in Asia.* Bloomington: Indiana University Press.

Varallo, S. M., Ray, E. B., & Ellis, B. H. (1998). Speaking of incest: The research interview as social justice. *Journal of Applied Communication Research, 26,* 254-271.

Wander, P. (1983). The ideological turn in modern criticism. *Central States Speech Journal, 34,* 1-18.

Wander, P. (1984). The third persona: An ideological turn in rhetorical theory. *Central States Speech Journal, 35,* 197-216.

Wander, P., & Jenkins, S. (1972). Rhetoric, society, and the critical response. *Quarterly Journal of Speech, 58,* 441-450.

Warren, K. B. (1998). *Indigenous movements and their critics: Pan-Maya activism in Guatemala.* Princeton, NJ: Princeton University Press.

Weiss, A. (2002). *Principles of spiritual activism.* Hoboken, NJ: KTAV.

Weissberg, R. (2005). *The limits of civic activism: Cautionary tales on the use of politics.* New Brunswick, NJ: Transaction.

Welsh, S. (2002). Deliberative democracy and the rhetorical production of political culture. *Rhetoric & Public Affairs, 5,* 679-708.

West, M., & Gastil, J. (2004). Deliberation at the margins: Participant accounts of face-to-face public deliberation at the 1999-2000 world trade protests in Seattle and Prague. *Qualitative Research Reports in Communication, 5,* 1-7.

Whedbee, K. E. (2003). The tyranny of Athens: Representations of rhetorical democracy in eighteenth-century Britain. *Rhetoric Society Quarterly, 33*(4), 65-85.

Whedbee, K. E. (2004). Reclaiming rhetorical democracy: George Grote's defense of Cleon and the Athenian demagogues. *Rhetoric Society Quarterly, 34*(4), 71-95.

Whillock, R. K. (1989). Political empiricism: The role of a communication scholar as a consultant for one mayoral election. *Southern Communication Journal, 55,* 55-71.

Wigginton, E. (Ed.). (1991). *Refuse to stand silently by: An oral history of grass roots social activism in America, 1921-64.* New York: Doubleday.

Williams, D. C., Ishiyama, J. T., Young, M. J., & Launer, M. K. (1997). The role of public argument in emerging democracies: A case study of the 12 December 1993 elections in the Russian Federation. *Argumentation, 11,* 179-195.

Williams, R. (1975). *Television: Technology and cultural form.* New York: Schocken Books.

Wolfe, C. (1997). *Judicial activism: Bulwark of freedom or precarious society?* (rev. ed.). Lanham, MD: Rowman & Littlefield.

Wood, J. T. (1995). Theorizing practice, practicing theory. In K. N. Cissna (Ed.), *Applied communication in the 21st century* (pp. 181-192). Mahwah, NJ: Erlbaum.

Wood, J. T. (1996). Social justice research: Alive and well in the field of communication. *Communication Studies, 47,* 128-134.

Yoder, J. (1969). The protest of the American clergy in opposition to the war in Vietnam. *Today's Speech, 17*(3), 51-59.

Young, I. M. (2000). *Inclusion and democracy.* New York: Oxford University Press.

Zald, M. (1996). Culture, ideology, and strategic framing. In D. McAdam, J. D. McCarthy, & M. N. Zald (Eds.), *Comparative perspectives on social movements: Political opportunities, mobilizing structures, and cultural framings* (pp. 261-274). New York: Cambridge University Press.

Zoller, H. M. (2005). Health activism: Communication theory and action for social change. *Communication Theory, 15,* 341-364.

PART I

Managing the Media

1

AT THE CHECKPOINT

Journalistic Practices, Researcher Reflexivity, and Dialectical Dilemmas in a Women's Prison*

Eleanor Novek
Rebecca Sanford

Monmouth University

Although communication researchers can play an active role in assisting marginalized groups and communities in the quest for social justice, there are some contexts in which the good intentions of researchers, no matter how altruistically motivated, theoretically informed, or methodologically sensitive, run up against blunt pragmatic and ethical challenges. For example, engagement with a subjugated population may require the appeasement of those who oppress the group, and conditions that researchers define as

*We wish to thank the American Association of University Women for awarding us the Community Action Grant that made it possible for us to purchase computer equipment, books, and other research resources for the women involved in the journalism classes described in this chapter.

oppressive may also contain structures that subjugated groups can use for resistance. Thus, the work of activist research may generate paradoxes that researchers cannot ignore.

In 2001, we encountered these and other contradictions when we began teaching journalism classes at a state prison for women in the northeastern United States. As communication professors and researchers, we initiated an inmate newspaper project in the tradition of social justice research: "the engagement with and advocacy for those in our society who are economically, socially, politically and/or culturally underresourced (Frey, Pearce, Pollock, Artz, & Murphy, 1996, p. 110). As we worked with the women inmates to establish a prison newspaper, we hoped to study several aspects of this form of communication closely: (a) the ways these women understood their prison worlds and expressed their understanding in journalistic writing; (b) the manner in which the inmates were able to use, and hopefully benefit from, the intrinsic values of journalistic practice; and (c) the tactics used by prison journalists to overcome the contextual constraints they faced. We also were interested in observing relational development among the women in the journalism project because the influence of incarceration on relationships suggests ways of understanding that are outside the scope of conventional research.

A house of corrections is a fitting setting for activist research. Foucault (1979, p. 232) called the prison "a detestable solution" that has generated disquiet and debate in societies that employ it, is useless at stopping criminality, and, in fact, is responsible for institutionalizing and reproducing violence. Depending on the political climate at the time, societies have variously viewed prisons as engines for the punishment of lawbreakers or as vehicles for the rehabilitation or "correction" of social miscreants. In recent decades, U.S. public policy has favored tougher sentencing laws, more jails, harsher punishment, and more executions, leading to a period of astonishing growth in the nation's prison-industrial-complex. Rates of incarceration have tripled in the last 2 decades, and the United States now imprisons more of its citizens per capita than any nation in the world (The Sentencing Project, 2001).

In mid-2003, an estimated 2.1 million men and women were serving sentences in jails or prisons, and another 4.8 million were on probation or parole (Glaze & Palla, 2004), meaning that an estimated 480 prison inmates per 100,000 U.S. residents were incarcerated in state or federal prisons (Harrison & Karberg, 2004). Rates of incarceration were disproportionately high for Black, non-Hispanic U.S. Americans. In June 2003, 4,834 African American men out of every 100,000 were incarcerated, as compared to 1,778 Hispanic men out of every 100,000 and 681 non-Hispanic White men out of every 100,000 (Harrison & Karberg, 2004). Nearly 10% of all African American men in the United States in their 20s and 30s were in prison in 2002 (Maguire & Pastore, 2003).

The female population of the U.S. corrections system doubled in the last 2 decades. In mid-2003, the number of women incarcerated in state or federal prisons reached 100,102, an all-time high, and at year's end, there were an estimated 61 women sentenced per 100,000 women in the United States (Harrison & Karberg, 2004). Most of the women in prison are over the age of 30, have at least a high school diploma or equivalency certificate, and are women of color (Pollock, 2002). Most are single mothers of young children and have grown up in single-parent households (Pollock, 2002). More than 40% report a history of physical or sexual abuse (Girshick, 1999). Women inmates are more likely than men to be incarcerated for a drug offense, or to have committed crimes under the influence of drugs or alcohol; have a shorter criminal record; and are less likely to be incarcerated for violent crimes and more likely, if serving time for a violent offense, to have victimized a relative (Pollock, 2002). Fifty-two percent of incarcerated women are African American, although they make up only 14% of the nation's population (Human Rights Watch, 1996). Moreover, more than a quarter of all women in custody are mentally ill (Human Rights Watch, 2003).

With a staggering 3.2% of the nation's adult population, or 1 in every 32 adult residents in prison or jail or on probation or parole in 2003, there is an urgent need for research and activist engagement in prisons. Activist communication researchers approach prisons and the people incarcerated there from diverse perspectives. Some activist scholars view the corrections system mainly as a problematic social construct that degrades society at large and, consequently, focus their research on broad societal concerns, including human rights and the death penalty (Conquergood, 2002); the rise of the correctional-industrial-complex and the historic connections between capitalism, incarceration, and slavery (Hartnett, 2000); or the oppositional codes of discourse that perpetuate violence in prisons (Huspek & Comerford, 1996). A number of other researchers approach prisons as "schools" and work at the individual level to teach better survival skills to prisoners (e.g., Corcoran, 1985; Duguid, 1988). Others, particularly feminists, view penal institutions as oppositional sites where activists can witness and share the stories of exiled people whose voices are not heard in public discourse (e.g., Anderson, 1996; Shaver, 1993; Valentine, 1998).

Our roles as prison teachers, researchers, and activists are often a contradiction of many terms. As researchers, we have gathered data on the ways women inmates understand the prison experience, benefits they may derive from journalistic practice within that context, and ways their relationships are shaped by the prison setting. However, as we worked with imprisoned women to try to make their lives better, in ways significant or small, we also experienced the tensions inherent in the engaged performance of prison research.

We found ourselves asking questions without clear answers: In the reg-imented structure of the corrections system, how could we encourage inmates who had been silenced to claim their voices and express themselves, but to do so in ways that would not bring harsh repercussions from custo-dial authorities? Given that we maintained our access to the prison by demonstrating obedience to administrative rules, how can we, at the same time, advocate critical thinking about those rules to our inmate students? How do we advocate for the rights of incarcerated women and demonstrate our concern for them as human beings but also approach them as a research population to observe and analyze?

In this chapter, we discuss some of the multilayered paradoxes we encountered in our prison journalism research and explore their implica-tions for activist communication scholars. First, we describe the context of this work and the research methods we used. Because the prison setting imposes an ingenious array of constraints on all who enter its gates, out-siders need to understand the interplay of influences that affect communica-tion and social interaction in this environment. We also consider the prison as a social universe with respect to how the institution functions in society and imposes mechanisms of control and evaluation on prisoners. We take particular note of the prison's profound impact on incarcerated women and the suffering they experience. We then explore the roles of writing and rep-resentation in our research, using feminist theory to help focus on our strug-gles to fairly and compassionately represent the incarcerated women with whom we worked and make meaning of the ways they represented them-selves in writing. We closely consider prison journalism and its potential as an empowerment strategy for incarcerated women, interpreting the verbal skill development, sense of group connection, and crossing of social bound-aries inherent in journalistic practice as enabling communicative action. In this light, we also examine the contradictions inherent in the growth of rela-tionships between women in prison. Finally, we share some of the lessons we have learned from this research about communication activism.

CONTEXT AND METHODS

Prison newspapers have a long and important history in the United States, where they have served both a political function as a voice for inmate rights and a practical purpose as a vocational training opportunity (Morris, 2002). In 2001, Sanford, a graduate student and university instructor, had already been working at the Clara Barton Correctional Facility for Women (a pseu-donym) for 3 years, teaching community college courses on interpersonal communication and business writing. Novek, a former public affairs reporter turned university journalism professor, joined her in 2001, after developing an interest in prison journalism. We designed a proposal to establish a journalism class at that prison and create a newspaper written and published by and for inmates. After reviewing our proposal, the prison superintendent gave us permission to set up the program, but warned us not to let the newspaper become an organizing tool for inmate disobedience. In addition, any writings slated for inclusion in the newspaper would be screened by the superintendent prior to publication, and any materials deemed unacceptable would be censored.

We began to visit the prison every other week, dividing our time between the prison's minimum- and maximum-security areas to teach a journalism class in each wing. Our classes ranged in size from a low of 6 to a high of 18 women at a time. Any inmate who wished to join the class was welcome; any woman wishing to drop out could do so at any time without penalty. Some class participants never actually wrote an article; some contributors of articles never attended a class. These class characteristics, combined with the regular arrival of new prisoners, the day-to-day conflicts of incarceration, and the release of women who have completed their sentences, meant that the number and skills of participating journalists fluctuated significantly over time. Still, in the first 36 months, the members of the prison journalism class produced 23 issues of a 24- to 47-page newspaper.

Class lessons included the technical skills of journalism and wide-ranging group discussions based on news of the day and topics of interest to our students. Our teaching units covered news judgment, generating story ideas, understanding the ramifications of newsworthy issues, and group decision making regarding the publication. We also taught the women how to organize an article in news style (e.g., inverted pyramid and concise writing); conduct interviews; argue and write opinion columns; edit their own and others' work; improve their use of grammar, spelling, and punctuation; design the newspaper pages; and use word-processing and layout software. The department of corrections paid for the printing of the newspaper and allowed the women to share office space with another program.

However, we discovered early on that our expectations for the outcomes of the lessons would have to be adjusted to fit the context of the prison, where even simple journalistic practices, such as gathering news, are fraught with difficulty. The prison has an ingenious array of regulations that limit inmates' ability to communicate, and these constrain every one of journalism's typical information-gathering tools.

For example, incoming mail and publications are opened and inspected, and outgoing mail is read if officials suspect that it contains "disapproved content" (which may include complaints to elected officials or requests for information or assistance from certain outside organizations). Telephone calls are limited to 15 minutes, may only be made to a short list of pre-screened recipients, and may be monitored. Inmates have no access to the internet. Women living in different residence halls within the prison may not freely associate except at work or in class, and women living in different security wings may send each other letters but cannot speak on the telephone or face to face. Access to daily newspapers, magazines, books, and television is rationed, and specific issues in those media may be censored. Library hours are brief, and library collections are minuscule, consisting mostly of tattered romance novels, true-crime thrillers, out-of-date encyclopedias, pop-psychology tomes, and fashion magazines. Facing all of these constraints and more, inmate journalists are denied access to many of the information channels taken for granted by traditional journalists and are, therefore, often unable to produce articles that take the conventional form of news stories.

Still, these inmates have persisted, and the newspaper has grown into a monthly publication with a strong reputation at the prison, appreciated by inmates and staff members alike. Over the course of 3.5 years, we have taught more than 100 inmates in journalism classes and published 30 issues of the prison newspaper. In the process, our sense of commitment to these women continued to increase. Reinharz (1992) described the nurturing impulses and reciprocation that occur in some feminist fieldwork as a "closeness/distance dilemma" (p. 67). In an inquiry, she noted, researchers may form relationships with participants that influence the researchers' levels of involvement, sharing of information and tangible items, and motivations for action. When the time comes for the traditional, distanced reporting of their observations, researchers may be unable to pull back to a state of "objectivity." We grew to like, admire, and respect many of our participants as the program developed, and this often-mutual affinity caused us to experience, remember, and care—and report—differently than we might have otherwise.

Although we do not see this relational connection as a dilemma for activists per se, the context of a prison makes it problematic for researchers, as we discuss later. However, as researchers, we agree with Conquergood (2002, p. 146) that the dominant way of knowing in the academy, "that of empirical observation and critical analysis from a distanced perspective," is not appropriate when activist researchers deal with disadvantaged groups. Conquergood argued that a better model of knowing involves a personally engaged, embodied approach, a conversational copresence of speaking and listening that is "grounded in active, intimate, hands-on participation and personal connection: 'knowing how,' and 'knowing who.' This is a view from ground level, in the thick of things" (p. 146).

In gathering and presenting the data we acquired in this project, we used methodological triangulation—including participant observation, interviewing, and textual analysis—in an attempt to present this "knowing how" and "knowing who." Clearly, participant observation was integral to the teaching role we held, and, as a research method, it provided opportunities for ongoing interpersonal interaction with the incarcerated women and enabled ethnographically thick description of the setting and social interactions we engaged in and witnessed. Interviewing allowed us to understand inmates' experiences from their perspective and represent those experiences in their words. Textual analysis of the women's writings offered evidence of the themes and issues of importance to the inmates, as well as of their styles of self-expression.

These methods were grounded in the broad category of social justice research, wherein the research is undertaken to improve conditions for subjugated or underresourced groups (Frey et al., 1996). These methods also were informed by a collaborative dialogic approach to participation by those being studied—that is, the belief that all human beings have the ability to create knowledge, not only those deemed to be "experts" or "professionals" (Servaes, 1996; Whyte, 1989). Dialogic research, thus, involves collaboration between committed researchers and the members of a community who, together, engage in analyzing a social environment for the purpose of creating some needed action or change.

At times, the women in our journalism classes at the Clara Barton prison were engaged participants in this research. Several long-time class participants have reviewed drafts of our published writings and conference presentations; although their remarks were never critical, we responded to their subtle prompts about our observations when constructing the view of the prison we represented to outsiders. In one case, before we made a conference presentation, we asked the women to represent themselves in writing, and we read their remarks verbatim at the conference. The writers were delighted when we reported later how the audience had responded to their words. The women also have surveyed their fellow inmates about the meaning and value of the newspaper project to them (whether as participant-authors or as readers), compiling a special edition that focused on the newspaper's origins and emergence as an important part of inmate culture at the Clara Barton prison.

Conquergood (1995) also argued that communication researchers must be deeply committed to the politics of emancipation, claiming that "as engaged intellectuals we understand that we are entangled within world systems of oppression and exploitation. . . . Our choice is to stand alongside or against domination, but not outside, above, or beyond it" (p. 85). In the prison, however, our choices sometimes were less clear. Although our work was grounded in compassion for and copresence with the prisoners and we were and are committed to their distinct worth as human beings, we are simultaneously undecided about the role of prisons in society, sensitive to the types of crimes our class members have committed, and aware of the damage they have done to themselves and others.

We have used the theoretical frameworks explicated next to make sense of the context of prison, generally, and this women's prison, specifically, as we examine not only the circumstances in which we operated but also our parts in reproducing and maintaining a troubling social system. We critique the prison as a social construct but also assess our roles as we functioned within it. As researchers and scholars, we had the opportunity to collaborate with these incarcerated women in their current setting and learn more about them. However, as noted by Fonow and Cook (1991), we remain aware that, at the end of the day, we got to go home, but for these women, the prison *was and is* home. As a result of this awareness, we spent countless hours discussing the wisdom and purpose of virtually everything we did in this setting. Thus, we do not take lightly the responsibility that comes with our research, realizing that there may be no best way to put such knowledge forth.

PRISON AS A SOCIAL UNIVERSE

Krippendorff (1989) argued that power

> does not reside in objective conditions outside social relationships but in the reality constructions invented, talked about, held on to and complied with by all those involved and on both sides of the inequality. The reality we know is not a given but continuously constructed and reconstructed in discourse with others. (pp. 186-187)

Standing outside the electronic cyclone fences strung with concertina wire at the entrance to the maximum-security wing of the Clara Barton prison, one can ponder Krippendorff's premise about the social construction of reality; however, at institutions like this one across the United States, the physical reality of prison feels very much like a given, the only reality that our lawmakers have imagined it possible to construct.

Foucault's (1979) seminal work on society, power, and imprisonment noted the structural parallels between prisons and other institutions of social control, such as armies, schools, and factories, that seek to manage and monitor human behavior. However, he argued that the prison is a more comprehensive and far-reaching structure because, unlike more specialized social institutions, the prison assumes total responsibility for incarcerated people, containing and sustaining their bodies, dictating and restricting every aspect of their conduct and labor, and influencing their mental, moral, and spiritual attitudes, in some cases for their entire lives. The prison, said Foucault, "combines in a single figure discourses and architectures, coercive regulations and scientific propositions, real social effects and invincible utopias, programmes for correcting delinquents and mechanisms that reinforce delinquency" (p. 271).

Although the courts establish the length of an inmate's sentence, Foucault (1979) said that it is the people responsible for administering detention—such as the warden, guards, chaplain, psychologist, and parole evaluator—who establish the actual severity of the penalty by the way they carry it out. These custodians are granted impressive autonomy to impose society's "formidable right to punish" (Foucault, p. 90) on transgressors and maintain obedience throughout the prison population. Thus, it is the day-to-day judgment of the custodial staff, not the courtroom verdict or the theory of law, that most influences every aspect of an inmate's treatment once she or he is imprisoned. In classifying each inmate's character and evaluating all of her or his daily actions and behaviors, prison authorities further adjust and customize the penalties of incarceration for each individual.

Huspek and Comerford (1996) contended that the ways of knowing used by prison personnel to categorize and classify inmates are a self-defeating set of discursive practices. When inmates enter the penitentiary system, prison authorities expect them to serve out the conditions of their sentences submissively. However, as Huspeck and Comerford noted, inmates discursively defined as "model prisoners" by the prison establishment are set up for victimization by other inmates. Only inmates who adopt the oppositional behaviors that identify them as "problem inmates" can stave off abuse from and earn the respect of their peers. When they do this, however, they fall ever further in the esteem of prison authorities and earn harsher treatment by the penal system, including longer prison sentences.

Custodial definitions and evaluations can certainly affect an inmate's life profoundly. Cathy (all names used are pseudonyms), one of the first editors of the prison newspaper, was well regarded in the prison's minimum-security wing for her warm personality and excellent clerical skills. Although she had a long prison sentence, she had earned the trust of administrators over time and enjoyed a number of small freedoms and privileges, such as a private cell and participation in a number of educational programs. We recruited Cathy and trained her to be the editor, which meant that she would be paid as a paraprofessional for her work and have limited other responsibilities. She began to manage the newspaper filing system and serve as a central contact person for the articles and artwork submitted by other prisoners via internal prison mail. With her in place, the newspaper reached its monthly publication goal and established regular deadlines and routines.

One morning we arrived for our usual staff meeting and found that our editor was gone. After an escape attempt in a distant men's prison, state officials had started looking hard at all minimum-security potential flight risks, and any inmate with a certain number of years left on his or her sentence was

transferred to a more secure location. Cathy fit the criterion and, consequently, had been relocated abruptly to a treatment wing of the prison, a
location we could not access without escorts and special permission. She will
not be able to take part in the newspaper again for many years. In a single
afternoon, Cathy was reclassified as a security risk; she lost her privileges
and we lost our newspaper editor.

In what may be an even crueler example of the capricious nature of custodial treatment, Jocelyn was ready to be released on parole after serving
about a year at Clara Barton. Her family and children were waiting for her,
thrilled that she was finally coming home. The day before her release, she
visited the administration building where she signed all her exit paperwork,
had her photograph taken (in the event of parole violation or future offense),
and met with her social worker, who wished her well. The office phone rang
and Jocelyn left. On her way out of the building, the social worker called her
back in to tell her that the parole had been revoked—for reasons that would
never be revealed. Her joy turned to shock and disbelief. As an inmate, she
could not simply pick up the telephone at will to find out what had happened or seek legal help or family support. Feeling desperate and helpless,
Jocelyn would watch another 5 long months drag by before she was paroled.

Thus, researchers who enter the prison universe encounter a disjointed
reality constructed of explicit but often capricious regulations, mechanisms,
classifications, and evaluations. Whatever our philosophical and theoretical
views of prisons as social institutions, we also must recognize the personal
anguish experienced by human beings who are incarcerated. We may
acknowledge and support the need for social institutions and mechanisms
that punish people who harm others or we may join the movement crusad-
ing for the abolition of prisons and the substitution of community-based
restitution programs. We may condone the prison as a necessary evil or condemn it as ineffective, inhumane, and barbarous (or fall somewhere between
these two extremes). Regardless of these perspectives, however, we must feel
compassion for those whom the state has decreed must suffer, for in a
prison, even to the casual observer, the suffering of the incarcerated is extensive and acute.

PRISON'S SPECIAL IMPACT ON WOMEN

As the statistics reported previously reveal, the increasing numbers of incarcerated women and the effects of prison on them and their families have
become a pressing social concern. Some of the most painful anguish of
women in prison results from their isolation from their family. Ritchie
(2002) estimated that 75% of women in prison are mothers and two-thirds
have children under the age of 18. Belknap (2000) noted that incarcerated

women are far more likely than incarcerated men to have custody of their children before imprisonment and be their emotional and financial providers; therefore, "one of the greatest differences in stresses for women and men serving time is that the separation from children is generally a much greater hardship for women than for men" (p. 176). Often, the forced separation of inmate mothers and children was sudden and unexpected. The impact of that separation on the women is captured in a truism that Ross (1996) attributed to the observations of prison workers: When male inmates arrive in prison, they demand to see their lawyers, whereas women immediately want to know how their children are. When prisons are located geographically far from women inmates' families, Johnson (2003) observed, family bonds are even more difficult to maintain over time and the "women may become despondent, and children may lose their connection to their primary parent" (p. 281).

A second cause of trauma faced by incarcerated women is damage from past abuse and the ongoing threat of more abuse in prison. Although more than 40% of incarcerated women report a history of physical or sexual abuse (Girshick, 1999), few of these women get access to programs or counseling for sexual victimization (Belknap, 2000). A significant number of women inmates also encounter such mistreatment in prison, where most of the guards are men (although female correction officers also commit sexual abuse). Sexual misconduct can range from being patted down or strip-searched by a male officer to overt sexual encounters and sexual assault. In 1996, Human Rights Watch interviewed inmates, correction officers, and staff at women's prisons in California, Georgia, Illinois, Michigan, New York, and the District of Columbia and found widespread evidence of custodial sexual misconduct and assault.

Another cause of great suffering for women inmates is their desperate need for healthcare. As epidemics of HIV, AIDS, hepatitis C, and tuberculosis sweep the nation's prisons, the state of inmate healthcare declines. Belknap (2000) maintained that the lack of skilled or available medical care for any condition is one of the major problems in women's prisons, and inmates' requests for medical care often are mocked and dismissed by prison authorities. Male inmates are four times more likely than female prisoners to see a physician instead of a nurse and more likely to actually receive treatment for illnesses (Belknap, 2000). Women inmates also need gynecological services, obstetrical care, and treatment for specific cancers (Johnson, 2003), but their access to these health services is severely limited and the care they get, if and when they do receive it, often is substandard.

The policies of individual prisons can magnify the problem. For example, if inmates at the Clara Barton prison need tests or major procedures performed at a remote hospital, they cannot be informed in advance of the dates or times of the scheduled procedures, lest they plot an escape while they are out of the prison. If they demand care for an ailment with which the prison doctor is unfamiliar, they may be labeled as "complainers" and treated with derision by the prison custodial staff. In an unguarded moment, a staff member with many years of prison experience admitted to one of us that the medical care provided to the women was "terrible. It's worse than the men get. I've never seen anything as bad in the men's prisons." Moreover, when women were diagnosed with a serious illness, such as cancer or AIDS, the state did not release them early to their families or other conditions where they might have some relief. "They just send them back here to die," the same staff member said.

One day, Roberta, one of our students in her 20s, disappeared. We learned that she had a stroke and had been moved to the prison hospital, in the maximum-security wing. One of us had a single opportunity to visit her. The hospital looks more like a crowded clinic than a critical care facility. To get in, patients and doctors must pass through locked outer doors and a sally port entrance with security screening. As visitors pass from one locked holding area to another, they can see patient rooms constructed in a circle around the nurses' station and hallways crowded with people and equipment carts. The halls smell of stale food from dinners long ago and faint traces of cigarette smoke—not the clean, antiseptic aromas experienced in a traditional hospital. It hardly seemed like the place for a stroke victim, or anyone with a serious health problem, to receive care.

After several months, Roberta returned to the class, a shadow of her former self. She could hardly walk unassisted, had trouble focusing, often slurred her words, and complained of pain in her head. She went repeatedly to see the prison physicians, but complained that her tests were delayed, she had few consultations with a brain specialist, medications were prescribed but their effects not adequately monitored or explained to her, and follow-up care seemed nonexistent. Her access to sound medical treatment was always getting bogged down in paperwork or security procedures. Privately, some prison staff observed that Roberta needed someone from outside the prison to get involved and "make noise" to get her treatment underway, but prison employees are not supposed to be personally involved with inmates, and if they were to advise Roberta about securing better medical care, they would risk losing their jobs.

One of us was deeply moved by Roberta's plight and, acting as a friend, not as a researcher, she intervened and made inquiries with people in legal and medical fields outside the prison in an attempt to get Roberta better care. By acting on this impulse, she could have jeopardized her access to the prison in the future. Indeed, other volunteers in similar situations had been banned from a nearby prison for involving themselves in an inmate's problems. By defying prison regulations to aid one member of our class, she risked losing her access to the class itself and all of the other women in it.

Fortunately, Roberta did eventually get the examinations and tests she needed, and the intervention went unnoticed by prison authorities, but not before this became an issue that we had to negotiate as researchers.

THORNY THICKETS OF REPRESENTATION

Our knowledge of the suffering that many inmates endure runs counter to popular perceptions of prisons, which often are exaggerated by media representations of prisons as stimulating, macho, excitingly violent places. We felt a special responsibility to treat the women of Clara Barton prison fairly in our representations of them, so as not to compound the injustices they already face, nor extend the lurid and widespread pop-cultural images of prison life. Our orientation as feminist scholars led us to focus on two aspects of representation: (a) ways in which we represented the women with whom we worked, and (b) ways in which these women represented themselves through their own writings. Accordingly, we tended to collect data with the underlying assumption that they would help us to understand and explain the prison world and the women in it more fully. However, some contradictions surfaced.

In conducting ethnographic research, Skeggs (1995) noted, observers may come to believe that they have "access to a particular form of knowledge which others may not know about; that it is authentic and privileged" (p. 199). Although researchers' experiences form part of their data, the inclusion of those experiences in the interpretive process must be linked to the recognition that those data are not complete. In this case, our understanding of prison life was highly dependent on what the women in our classes chose to share with us. The students may not have intentionally misled us, but if they felt they could not safely divulge certain information in a given situation (perhaps because there were other inmates or officers within earshot), our ability to understand the meaning of that situation was limited.

This issue is especially salient, Reinharz (1992) pointed out, "when there are differences of social class, race, ethnicity, or sexual preference" (p. 65). The population of the Clara Barton prison contains a majority of women of color and many women who come from poverty (prison staffers say they do not have specific data available regarding these characteristics, although detailed demographic and personal information is collected from each inmate when she is admitted). Given our roles as White, heterosexual college professors and our standing as "outsiders" to the prison itself, the information we gathered and the meanings we made of it were highly situated. The ways we represented the women of Clara Barton prison, thus, were shaped and delimited by our observations and bodily experiences; shared truths from our participants, as expressed through a web of institutional constraints; and our responses to the dilemmas of closeness and distance we felt with and because of these women.

People unfamiliar with correctional institutions often regard those who work at prisons through a fantasy lens of their own and are unaware of the many shades of meaning in any representation of prison experience. Some, imagining the chaotic prisons they have seen in movies and television shows, asked us, "Aren't you scared to death in that place? Do the inmates ever try to *do* anything to you when you are there?" Others found the enterprise ennobling, like missionary work, saying, "You're doing so much for those women." Their view of such work seemed to elevate the researcher to a high moral ground and anoint her or him as a model of self-sacrifice who is a deserving recipient of gratitude. For empirical and ethical clarity, the activist researcher must resist these constructions, something that is not always easy to do.

It is tempting to inflate our sense of self-worth as we venture in and out of the prison gates. Inmates become part of that construction, especially when they tell us how we are the only ones who care about them or how different and caring we are compared to the prison staff. One of us is particularly susceptible to flattery and had a decidedly interpersonal focus in her interactions that produced collegial relationships with participants that were self-reinforcing experiences. Thus, the dissemination of our research results felt like a betrayal of colleagues to her. In the same way that many people feel uncomfortable presenting their family members' private histories to a room full of scholars, she found sharing her observations in academic or other public settings decidedly awkward.

Her reaction was not lessened by the behavior engaged in by some other researchers who study incarceration. On several occasions, we have participated in academic conference panels featuring other prison scholars and activists. Here, far from the harsh surroundings of the prison, in comfortable meeting rooms equipped with the latest communication technologies, many of our fellow researchers do seem motivated to uphold the human rights of inmates. Others, however, put themselves forward as noble adventurers braving danger, or as missionaries giving of themselves to uplift the downtrodden. Some audiences for these presentations express an interest in social justice, but others seem bent on titillation, looking for accounts of their peers reporting back from the belly of the beast. As activists, how can we avoid the charity model of teaching and conducting research in prison and the demonization of inmates or the romanticism of activism that may accompany it?

We found that the answer to this question was to focus on our responsibility to the women with whom we work. One inmate told us that she wanted herself and her peers to be represented by others as just "women who made a mistake. We truly would like to have people look at us like human beings and not monsters." As we conducted this research, we struggled to understand our observations and help these women tell their stories without stigmatizing or endangering them. In our studies, we concealed the specific identities of the institution and the women with whom we worked, lest their words or stories be recognizable to prison authorities or others. (We assumed that the worlds of inmates and the publics we inhabited were not mutually exclusive but may well intersect in ways not unanticipated.) As we seek a balance between protecting the inmates we worked with from exploitation and raising public awareness about their plight, we hope to generate research reports that are less exploitive than some we have seen presented on convention panels or published in anthologies on prisons.

We also are concerned about what happens when the women represent themselves in writing. Gaucher (2002) observed that prison writing springs from the relationship between the prisoner and the prison; writing and other forms of artistic expression, therefore, "become resistance, a means of survival and a testament to surviving the dislocations of prison life" (p. 12). According to Scheffler (2002), all women prisoners' texts are political, "each speaking uniquely for silenced women behind bars and prison walls" (p. xxi). Written work by female prisoners, however, as Scheffler noted, is scarce compared to written work created by male prisoners. This is no doubt due to the pressures of poverty among incarcerated women, which demand a focus on basic survival, not self-expression; the subsistence struggles facing these women on release from prison; the shortage of educational programs offered in prisons (especially in women's prisons); and the lack of privacy and quiet to express themselves in the written form.

Writing for an inmate newspaper provides a means for participants to express their voice and nurtures the agency that accompanies such expression; in prison, these are in short supply. However, we are mindful of Lorde's (1984) observation that the "transformation of silence into language and action is an act of self-revelation, and that always seems fraught with danger" (p. 42). When a writer's words are published, a dialogue with the larger society is made possible. At that point, the choices these women have made—such as whether to disclose personal or sensitive information or to engage critical themes and topics—become even more important.

We watched as, increasingly, these women prisoners challenged themselves to take on sensitive issues. Many issues of the newspaper contained articles about the harshness of U.S. correctional policies, including mandatory minimum sentencing; the loss of parental rights, voting privileges, and educational opportunities for inmates; incompetent medical care; and inhumane treatment inside the prison walls. Others wrote about violence in the home, battering of partners and children, sexual abuse, and neglect.

Numerous essays implored the people who were in similar situations as these women to put drug and alcohol addiction behind them, or to take charge of their life and conquer the passivity that prison breeds in inmates.

This transformation from silence to language and, possibly, subsequent action carries a number of tensions within it. Some of the women writing for the newspaper were revisiting painful personal experiences to bring them to the public's attention. Nancy wrote relentlessly about domestic violence, her battered face bearing the evidence of her scars. Martina, a breast cancer survivor, wrote about her frustration in trying to get treatment for breast cancer while being incarcerated. Sheryl wrote about the impossibility of controlling her diabetes on a prison diet of noodles and white rice and sporadic, ill-timed shots of insulin. Marlene wrote of her religious conversion behind bars. Such self-expression may add to some women's sense of vulnerability.

The highly personal experiences expressed in these newspaper articles led many authors to be resistant to critique and obsessive about their work. This was complicated in a setting where editing and censorship may occur on many levels; changes in copy were made by the women organizing the newspaper, us in our capacity as teachers, and by administrators who suppressed the more critical articles submitted for publication. At some times, even the smallest editing changes were seen by the women as violations and led to fierce quarrels among class members. In other instances, however, the process was indeed silencing. Donna, for instance, had published many sorrowful poems that described her experience of sexual abuse, but when she turned an account into a first-person narrative article, it was censored by the warden, and she quit the newspaper soon after. Pearl wrote that, in composing articles for the newspape:

> We cannot express exactly how we feel. We have to write so that administration sees fit and because of that, I stunt myself as well as others who may be able to benefit from what I or anyone else may have to say.

However, as the newspaper took its place as a recognized element in the social fabric of the prison, the writers became increasingly aware of the power of their pens. They were approached by readers with compliments, suggestions, or criticisms. They also realized that the prison administrators and staff read their work, and they became eager for even more exposure. In sum, the women prison authors became aware that they had a voice and can be heard, the first time many had had such an empowering experience. However, when publication of their work was delayed due to space limits or receipt after a deadline, they felt victimized, and when others criticized their writing or challenged its assumptions, bitter resentment percolated. Claiming one's voice, thus, becomes a double-edged sword in prison: Once the women have a taste of purpose and power, they feel even more deprived without them.

JOURNALISM AS A PATH TO EMPOWERMENT

Scholars generally analyze the news media in terms of their influence on society or appeal to audiences, but a few have focused on the ways that news routines have social effects on journalists themselves. Novek (1995) used Habermas's (1984) concept of "communicative action" to explain how the routines of journalism have an intrinsic capacity to empower practitioners in their social lives. Habermas described *communicative action* as a dynamic that takes place when people arrive at shared interpretations of situations and events and act cooperatively as a result of those understandings. Communicative action, thus, is seen as a powerful social energy that benefits those who engage in it.

When urban high school students produced a community newspaper, Novek (1995) found, a form of communicative action took place. The practices of gathering and selecting the news helped the youth to explore important issues as a group and expand their sense of group connection outward into their community. Through dialogue with each other and interaction with community members, "participants agreed upon common values and predicaments shared by themselves and their communities. . . . Some began to feel competent using communication strategies to move from one social group to another, or to reach out to previously unknown groups" (Novek, p. 86). The shared understandings of the young journalists and their outreach into many public environments led them to feel part of an empowering "community of interest" and play more engaged roles in their social worlds (Novek, p. 73; see also Christian, this volume).

This is what we hoped to see taking place at the prison as a result of the newspaper effort there. We knew that the concept of "empowerment" was problematic in the prison context, where the prison's structures and regulations discourage women from taking any initiative whatsoever and sharply limit their opportunities to communicate with the world outside. We hoped, however, that in addition to the development of individual skills, we would see evidence of the women achieving a sense of group connection and reaching out beyond the boundaries of their previous experiences, and, in some instances, we did. In a reflective essay, Carol wrote that being a member of the newspaper staff had affected her life profoundly because it allowed her to share her experiences with an audience. As she explained, her nightmares, secrets, and

> things I never wanted to remember are now being heard and shared with others. I feel that if there is a woman, mother, sister, or aunt that can be helped by my writing poems [or] thoughts, I am pleased with that. Just knowing I helped or could help another, then my job is done.

Because the women writers were proud of their efforts, they sometimes sent copies of the Clara Barton prison newspaper to friends or family members incarcerated in other prisons. On one occasion, a prisoner organization at a men's prison saw the publication and reached out to the Clara Barton women. The men were publishing an occasional magazine devoted to deterring young people from crime, and they asked the women to submit articles for their magazine. Although the women in the classes were pleased to be recognized, they were even more excited about the fact that a group of imprisoned men had been allowed to form a nonprofit organization to engage in outreach to the outside world. As Martina said, "I just don't understand how that can be done inside a prison but if they can do it, then maybe we can do it here."

Members of the classes began talking about developing a proposal for starting their own organization and wrote to the men for start-up advice and copies of their magazine. A supervised conference call was set up between the two groups. The Clara Barton prison population contributed dozens of essays for the men's magazine. The ripples of this communicative action soon spread as more of the women inmates developed ideas for additional forms of community outreach. One woman planned to connect inmates to the homebound elderly through a pen-pal program, another woman envisioned partnering prisoners with a missionary organization to raise public awareness about the needs of prisoners and their families, and a third woman planned to establish an advocacy organization to help imprisoned women get better medical care. Such efforts take prison authorities many months to review and approve, and the organizers may be released before they reach fruition, but they plant seeds of hope in the women who stay behind, improving the chances of such projects succeeding.

We saw numerous other examples of these women prisoners desiring to take coordinated action for the betterment of their fellow inmates, stimulated, in part, by their participation in the class and with the newspaper. For instance, Jessica decided to survey the inmate population to study the possible link between childhood sexual abuse and adult drug addiction. She received authorization from prison administrators to develop a survey questionnaire and worked with her peers to design it (although later, she felt betrayed when the administration appointed a college intern to take over the survey). Frustrated that her formal requests for various types of service and assistance were never acknowledged by prison authorities, Tracy created a log-in sheet to help other inmates keep track of such requests. Martina staged a breast cancer awareness event, inviting healthcare professionals to the prison to teach the women how to examine themselves for early signs of cancer. Women from the minimum-security wing lobbied for a volleyball tournament with the women from the maximum-security wing, although such events had been banned for a long time.

The journalism class may not have been fully responsible for inspiring all of these goals, but we believe that it equipped participants with confidence in their communication skills, a shared sensibility, and an energetic sense of possibility, at least sometimes. As class member Carla noted, the newspaper was a small but important outlet that allowed many inmates to express themselves and connect to other women. "It carries a lot of important information to inmates and there is always room for a better-informed inmate," she wrote. "The paper has positively affected my self-esteem and improved my headspace all around. I feel like I am accomplishing something, being a part of something, and also learning a trade."

Habermas (1984) envisioned an ideal form of communicative action taking place in a social world where there was no disparity of power, speakers were free from domination by other speakers, and decisions to act were rational choices. However, when people are subjugated, Conquergood (2002) contended, they "do not have the privilege of explicitness, the luxury of transparency, the presumptive norm of clear and direct communication, [and] free and open debate on a level playing field that the privileged classes take for granted" (p. 146). Critical of Habermas's approach as too idealistic, Flood (1990, p. 174) warned of "the possibility of coercive forces working against the potential for emancipation" and argued that there are specific conditions under which communicative action might be impeded or impossible to achieve.

Prisons offer examples of these conditions. Certainly, prison routines are structured to prevent independently coordinated social action because prison authorities worry that inmates will organize to resist their authority. Thus, the inmates at Clara Barton prison get little practice in learning to work cooperatively with others and rarely act as cooperative team members unless compelled to do so (e.g., the road gangs that pick up trash on the highways). Although they share many similar problems with the rest of the inmate population, some of the women prisoners feel separated from the others by a deep lack of trust and a maddening sense of competition over even the most trivial-seeming of resources. They show little desire to bond into a "community of interest" and may take part in group communication, when required to do so, without developing any sense of connection or loyalty to others.

An example of this problem was expressed in the actions of an inmate called Sheryl. After many months of active participation in the newspaper project, Sheryl learned that she would soon be released from prison. Although never very congenial, she now began to actively start arguments with other women in class. She sat at a separate table from the others during class and complained incessantly when her writings, often very lengthy, were shortened for the newspaper.

A quarrel erupted over one of the last articles Sheryl submitted before leaving. A number of essays she wrote for the newspaper had been critical of the prison, and an administrator had censored her most recent article and reprimanded her for her attitude. Just before leaving, she submitted another essay that was just like the censored one, insisting that it be published as written. Some of the other newspaper participants were very worried, wondering if Sheryl's actions might goad administrators into shutting down the paper. "You know how [the warden] can flip like a light switch," one of the women protested. Selfishly, Sheryl answered, "Well, I hope when that switch is flipped, I'll be gone." At that moment, the months of shared effort and experiences with the other class members seemed to count for nothing to her.

Although this situation and similar experiences we have had do not cancel out the intrinsic value of journalistic practices for the inmates, they certainly lowered our expectations of communicative action. These occurrences demonstrated that not all of the women felt a sense of connection or shared values with their classmates as a result of the journalism project, and not all of the women proved interested in or capable of cooperative effort. However, we continue to believe that interaction and connection with others in the daily relationships of a working group—in this case, on a newspaper—can have a profound impact on the lives of women at the prison.

RELATIONSHIPS BEHIND PRISON WALLS

As they worked in close contact on the newspaper over time, we expected that the women would develop relationships with one another, and we wanted to observe these relationships closely. Current research on the development of friendships and romantic relationships has been conducted with participants who are free (e.g., Duck, 1973; Knapp & Vangelisti, 1996; Rawlins, 1992), not on those located in heavily isolated and guarded contexts that influence the type and trajectory of their relationship formation. Given the constraints of prisons and the ways in which relationships may differ in these circumstances from ordinary ones, the behaviors, practices, and ways of understanding affiliation within the prison context are worthy of attention. The newspaper classes allowed us to observe these interactions discreetly.

It did not really surprise us that some women in the newspaper project found it difficult to work cooperatively with others. At the same time that new prisoners are incarcerated with hundreds or thousands of other strangers (depending on the type of correctional facility in which they are housed, security level of their sentence, and estimated flight risk), they also are starkly isolated from contact with friends and family members on the "outside." Therefore, the relationships they develop with fellow inmates may not follow the typical trajectories of "friendship" or "colleague" that are familiar in much of the research on interpersonal and group relationships.

Although something the inmates call "friendship" does develop in prison, such connections are shaped by the context of incarceration and the lack of alternative relational choices. Inmates' relatively low educational levels, their unaddressed learning or emotional disabilities, and the racial disparities within correctional institutions also may influence the ways inmates develop and maintain relationships in prison. Time, especially the extended period of a lengthy prison sentence, alters relationships with loved ones back home and also is likely to have an impact on the ways in which an inmate forms connections with fellow prisoners.

Connections with fellow inmates can be emotionally costly. On one occasion, as a member of the class prepared to move to a halfway house, Tricia, a long-time newspaper participant, wished her well, her eyes brimming with tears. Sanford, one of the authors, spoke to Tricia, commenting that it must be difficult to watch friends leave. Tricia said that the relationships she made in prison were doomed to end, regardless of their quality or importance. She knew that parolees may not associate with inmates, nor may they visit the particular prison where they once served time. Opportunities for relational maintenance are reduced to cards and letters, a communication medium that easily falls by the wayside in the excitement and stress of a newly freed inmate's life. Tricia wiped away her tears as she watched her colleague gather her things, and said to Sanford:

> I used to be able to hold it together. I can't no more. You lose people over and over again—and sometimes they even come back, so you lose them twice—but after a while, it just wears on you. You can't have friends here, [in] this place.

She then added, "You shouldn't have friends here, either. It never gets easier to say goodbye."

One of the key areas in communication research on interpersonal relationships is the understanding of how self-disclosure works to create and maintain relationships. In the literature on relationships among people who are not incarcerated, self-disclosure frequently is cited as a catalyst that moves people closer, whereas the lack of self-disclosure is seen to end relationships (see, e.g., Altman & Taylor, 1973; Derlega, Metts, Petronio, & Margulis, 1993; Knapp, 1983). This perspective assumes that participants are free to share or not share certain information at their discretion. However, self-disclosure as the lynchpin of relationship formation and maintenance may not be entirely applicable in the prison context. *Self-disclosure* involves sharing information about the self with others that would not otherwise be known, but in prison, such sharing may not be the best way to demonstrate trust between friends. Existing in a web of classification and evaluation, inmates often cannot prevent other members of the prison community from learning many intimate details about their lives.

For example, when women first are admitted to Clara Barton prison, they are housed in a special maximum-security wing for anywhere from a few weeks to several months to be sorted out and classified according to their offense and length of sentence. A decrepit gymnasium is used for this purpose, crammed with as many as 100 metal bunk beds. A row of shower stalls lines the far wall, with flimsy plastic curtains. Toilets are built into a low, concrete-block honeycomb instead of being full stalls, so that women's heads and shoulders are visible as they sit down to relieve themselves. Here, the women spend 24 hours a day, except for meals in the mess hall, surrounded by strangers, and with their weaknesses and humiliations on public display. In this atmosphere, although they are not supposed to, guards and prison administrators may discuss the particulars of a woman's criminal history within easy earshot of others. To overcome this lack of privacy, inmates may avoid self-disclosure when building rapport with each other.

However, the women in our classes often chose to share personal information with us and with each other. These women often discussed healthcare issues in prison and felt comfortable enough to disclose their personal experiences or illnesses. When making a point during one class discussion, Marjorie, an inmate of the maximum-security wing, began by telling us that she was terminally ill and had spent time in the prison hospital on many occasions. Lynette, who was released to a halfway house but returned to prison on a parole violation, said she wanted to write about the healthcare available in halfway houses for HIV-positive women, an interest that stemmed from her own diagnosis.

These disclosures were contextually appropriate, but also could have been risky for the women. On more than one occasion, inmates with HIV or hepatitis C have spoken of being shunned or mistreated when word of their condition spread. One woman wrote, "I have overheard numerous conversations of women in prison stating that they were afraid to use the toilet behind someone with the virus, [or] they didn't want to shower after someone infected." Another inmate wrote of women intentionally spreading false rumors that someone was HIV infected to isolate that person from the other women. However, despite these possible consequences, the women in our classes still felt it was important to share their experiences.

In another departure from traditional relational analysis, we recognize that prison "friends" may serve a different function for these women than the friends people would choose to be part of their life back home. Incarcerated women often use familial terms (e.g., "mother," "brother," and "aunt") to describe close relational partners and members of significant social networks in prison. These relationships and types of "family" networks are primarily context driven and occur within the isolation of a women's prison in ways in which they could not exist in the mainstream world. For instance, Samantha, one of our students, referred to another inmate as her "Mami" because the older woman had taken her under her wing, and she expressed feelings of closeness and gratitude resembling those in some mother-daughter relationships. Although she was anticipating her release soon, Samantha did not want to lose her connection with this woman; as she explained, "When I look at Mami, I want to take her in my bag with me. I want to leave and forget this whole thing, but I don't want to forget her."

Another relational theory of interest within the prison context is that of relational dialectics. *Dialectical tensions*, paired opposites of motivation and behavior that exist simultaneously and create interpersonal dilemmas, are present in every relationship. Baxter and Montgomery (1996) explained that "contrary themes illustrate the multifaceted process of social life" and that social life itself "is a dynamic knot of contradictions, a *ceaseless interplay* between contrary or opposing tendencies" (p. 3). In our work at Clara Barton prison, we encountered tensions that affected our orientation to activist research, our specific actions, and the inmates in our classes.

These tensions influenced the relationships the women had among themselves, as well as between themselves and the researchers. For example, women at Clara Barton were constantly managing how involved to be with one another—forming relationships and care-taking—and how much independence they needed to maintain to have a sense of self and not be excessively wrapped up in the day-to-day hubbub of the facility. There is no clear answer that works for all people, and women tended to vacillate between involvement and independence. This vacillation held when we looked at relationships formed and maintained between our students and us. For example, Jenna, a participant from the maximum-security wing, attended classes for months, full of ideas for stories and improvements to the newspaper. Then, suddenly, she withdrew from participation and shunned invitations to join the meetings. Months later, she returned as though no time had passed and resumed her role as outspoken contributor. Her colleagues took it all in stride; many of them had done the same thing at some point.

LESSONS LEARNED ABOUT COMMUNICATION ACTIVISM

In some ways, facilitating a journalism class and newspaper project in a women's prison is similar to teaching or conducting research in many other settings. However, in many other ways, the experience is different and has taught us new ways of understanding and acting that we believe are applicable to other activist contexts as well. For example, researchers often stress the idea that their research participants are meritorious and possess voices that need to be heard in society, but when the engaged population is a stigmatized or demonized one, as prisoners are, it is even more important that activist researchers be committed to this belief. The women in our classes saw themselves as regular people who had made mistakes and were paying society's price for those mistakes. They were not the "women in cages" or sociopathic monsters often portrayed in movies and on television, but people who potentially can contribute to the society that shuns them. Celebration of their humanity was and is the single-most pressing message we carried back from inside the prison walls.

One of the more challenging tensions that has surfaced in the context of our research on incarceration is that of "access-activism." Much is at risk when prison authorities allow research to be conducted within their confines. Information that travels outside the institution may create security hazards; expose inmates, custodial staff, or administrators to manipulation in various ways; or make known human-rights violations behind bars. Therefore, the entrée vital to conducting research and follow-up in a prison is simply not granted to most scholars. When it is, access must be maintained through the favor of those in power in the institution. In doing activist work at Clara Barton prison, we always were aware that our admission might be cut off in a moment's notice if we fell from grace in the eyes of prison administrators. This bore itself out in our work; in the morning we might facilitate a classroom discussion that was highly critical of the prison administration and, in the afternoon, advise an inmate journalist to tone down the level of criticism of the administration in her newspaper article. Were we conceding defeat or just being practical? Eventually, we did lose our access; a security crackdown on inmate computer use affected the journalism program, and volunteers like us made way for state employees who could monitor more attentively computer access.

Working in the prison, we learned that activists need to be flexible, persistent, and patient. The process of getting things done in a prison is agonizingly slow and arbitrary. We came to anticipate that something unexpected would happen on every visit; our best-laid plans were thwarted time and again. However, with enduring determination, we sometimes were able to construct alternate realities at the prison. For instance, story and project ideas that initially were ruled out by the warden eventually were accepted; inmate activities formerly seen as insurgent, such as organizing for a group project, were tentatively approved; and the circulation of the inmate newspaper has led to some changes at the prison, some of which were minor (e.g., an annual volleyball tournament between the minimum- and maximum-security wings, as recommended by writers in the newspaper) and some of which were more significant (e.g., the newspaper staff's daily access to a small office with computers, unheard of when we began). Thus, we felt reason to be encouraged by these accomplishments.

However, we also learned that we cannot save the world and that, sometimes, the women prisoners we taught and worked with did not want to save themselves. Although we were motivated by an activist desire to obtain social justice for the women spending years of their life behind bars, our best intentions meant nothing when these women felt no sense of agency or direction to do the same, or when depression or mental illness silenced them. If never shared, prison writings may express their authors' private thoughts, but cannot offer comfort or hope to others. The best strategies for action and empowerment will not blossom without committed effort on the women's part and the conviction that their efforts can be successful.

Even with dedication and drive, the women in our classes faced daunting odds when they were released. If imprisoned women are to break the cycle of poverty, crime, and recidivism, they require marketable skills and confidence, attributes they are not likely to develop during a typical term of incarceration. Learning to create an inmate newspaper may sharpen women's writing and computer skills and give them a taste for communication on a broader level than they have previously experienced, but when they leave the prison, they will not automatically become professional journalists. Most of the women will not have access to computers, a printing press, or the space and time to think and write. Their need for economic self-sufficiency will be acute, even as their employment opportunities are permanently delimited by the felony convictions on their records. The benefits derived from a prison journalism class, therefore, may be meaningful, but may not be substantive enough to translate into a foundation for survival in the world.

Through our embodied experiences inside Clara Barton prison's barbed wire and iron gates, we also came to understand that the idea of prison is an enormously entrenched meaning system that our society enthusiastically embraces despite its terrible flaws. Prisoners, guards, lawmakers, and citizens all construct the carceral world through imperfect views. No single individual or research team, no matter how committed, can reverse the damage we do as a society so wholly invested in incarceration. If we are going to make prisons more humane or find more productive ways to deal with people who break laws, we need to build a coordinated advocacy network that reaches many levels of society at once. A number of organizations devoted to such goals already exist—such as the American Friends Service Committee and the Fortune Society, which provide legal and informational resources to incarcerated people and support programs for inmates returning to society—and activist scholars must make connections with these groups and strengthen the human rights movement they represent.

Finally, although we advocate broad engagement, we also recognize the value of micro-level or local action. We have seen how individual acts of consideration, kindness, and compassion can lift an inmate's spirits and lighten her burden. We have watched women develop inner courage and strength and begin to reshape themselves as human beings. We have come to see that our efforts at the prison, although touched by misgivings and contradictions, constitute a significant copresence with women whose struggles we witness and support.

CONCLUSION

Ultimately, we have learned that the drama of survival in prison is a struggle for the humanity of us all. Prison researchers spend time with people who have been shunned by society, cast out, and then hidden from public consciousness by a web of disciplinary regulations and punitive practices. As researchers, we may want to help, but we operate in a hostile environment where help is hard to define and a price may be extracted for answers to the questions we wish to ask. The setting is challenging to enter, understand, and document. As outsiders, researchers may be granted access to prisons, but we are never fully integrated into their environments. Inmates, corrections officers, and administrators all arrive at separate interpretations of the prison experience, using distinct and unique discourses unfamiliar to researchers. Meanings must be negotiated and explained again and again, yet we can never be sure that our understandings are congruent with either the general inmate knowledge of the prison or the general custodial understanding of the institution.

It is a paradox that the strategic and instrumental importance of communication is so apparent in an environment that seeks to structure and stifle its every expression. We believe, however, that communication scholars may learn a great deal by studying the world of corrections and can make an important contribution to social justice by calling public attention to the experiences of inmates. As our communication activism continues, we hope to help inmates gain access to education and, thereby, to self-determination, and continue to make public the voices of incarcerated people to help them illuminate and challenge the conditions under which they work and live.

REFERENCES

Altman, I., & Taylor, D. A. (1973). *Social penetration: The development of interpersonal relationships.* New York: Holt, Rinehart and Winston.

Anderson, S. (1996). Ethnography as advocacy: Allowing the voices of female prisoners to speak. In P. M. Spacks (Ed.), *Advocacy in the classroom: Problems and possibilities* (pp. 408-421). New York: St. Martin's Press.

Baxter, L. A., & Montgomery, B. M. (1996). *Relating: Dialogues and dialectics.* New York: Guilford Press.

Belknap, J. (2000). *The invisible woman: Gender, crime, and justice* (2nd ed.). Belmont, CA: Wadsworth.

Conquergood, D. (1995). Between rigor and relevance: Rethinking applied communication. In K. N. Cissna (Ed.), *Applied communication in the 21st century* (pp. 79-96). Mahwah, NJ: Erlbaum.

Conquergood, D. (2002). Lethal theatre: Performance, punishment, and the death penalty. *Theatre Journal, 54*, 339-367.

Corcoran, F. (1985). Pedagogy in prison: Teaching in maximum security institutions. *Communication Education, 34*, 49-58.

Derlega, V. J., Metts, S., Petronio, S., & Margulis, S. T. (1993). *Self-disclosure.* Newbury Park, CA: Sage.

Duck, S. W. (1973). *Personal relationships and personal constructs: A study of friendship formation.* New York. Wiley.

Duguid, S. (1988). "To inform their discretion"—Prison education and empowerment. *Journal of Correctional Education, 39*, 174-181.

Flood, R. L. (1990). *Liberating systems theory.* New York: Plenum Press.

Fonow, M. M., & Cook, J. A. (1991). Back to the future: A look at the second wave of feminist epistemology and methodology. In M. M. Fonow & J. A. Cook (Eds.), *Beyond methodology: Feminist scholarship as lived research* (pp. 1-5). Bloomington: Indiana University Press.

Foucault, M. (1979). *Discipline and punish: The birth of the prison* (A. Sheridan, Trans.). New York: Vintage Books.

Frey, L. R., Pearce, W. B., Pollock, M., Artz, L, & Murphy, B. A. O. (1996). Looking for justice in all the wrong places: On a communication approach to social justice. *Communication Studies, 47*, 110-127.

Gaucher, B. (2002). The *Journal of Prisoners on Prisons*: An ethnography of the prison industrial complex in the 1990s. In B. Gaucher (Ed.), *Writing as resistance: The* Journal of Prisoners on Prisons *anthology 1988-2002* (pp. 5-30). Toronto: Canadian Scholars' Press.

Girshick, L. B. (1999). *No safe haven: Stories of women in prison.* Boston: Northeastern University Press.

Glaze, L., & Palla, S. (July 2004). Probation and parole in the United States, 2003. *Bureau of Justice Statistics Bulletin.* Retrieved September 10, 2004, from http://www.csdp.org/research/ppus03.pdf

Habermas, J. (1984). *The theory of communicative action: Vol. 1. Reason and the rationalization of society* (T. McCarthy, Trans.). Boston: Beacon Press.

Harrison, P., & Karberg, J. (May 2004). Prison and jail inmates at midyear 2003. *Bureau of Justice Statistics Bulletin.* Retrieved September 10, 2004, from http://www.ojp.usdoj.gov/bjs/pub/pdf/pjim03.pdf

Hartnett, S. (2000). Prisons, profit, crime, and social control. A hermeneutic of the production of violence. In A. Light & M. Nagel (Eds.), *Race, class, and community identity* (pp. 199-221). Amherst, NY: Humanity Books.

Human Rights Watch (1996). *All too familiar: Sexual abuse of women in U.S. state prisons.* Retrieved June 6, 2002, from http://www.hrw.org/summaries/s.us96d.html

Human Rights Watch (2003). *Ill-equipped: U.S. prisons and offenders with mental illness.* Retrieved September 10, 2004, from http://www.hrw.org/reports/2003 /usa1003/index.htm

Huspek, M., & Comerford, L. (1996). How science is subverted: Penology and prison inmates' resistance. *Communication Theory, 6,* 335-360.

Johnson, P. C. (2003). *Inner lives: Voices of African American women in prison.* New York: New York University Press.

Knapp, M. L. (1983). *Interpersonal communication and human relationships.* Boston: Allyn and Bacon.

Knapp, M. L., & Vangelisti, A. L. (1996). Relationship stages: A communication perspective. In K. M. Galvin & P. J. Cooper (Eds.), *Making connections: Readings in relational communication* (pp. 134-141). Los Angeles: Roxbury.

Krippendorff, K. (1989). The power of communication and the communication of power: Toward an emancipatory theory of communication. *Communication, 12,* 175-196.

Lorde, A. (1984). *Sister outsider: Essays and speeches.* Trumansburg, NY: Crossing Press.

Maguire, K., & Pastore, A. L. (Eds.). (2003). *Sourcebook of criminal justice statistics 2002.* Retrieved February 16, 2004, from http://www.albany.edu/sourcebook/ index.html

Morris, J. M. (2002). *Jailhouse journalism: The fourth estate behind bars.* New Brunswick, NJ: Transaction.

Novek, E. (1995). Buried treasure: The community newspaper as an empowerment strategy for African American high school students. *Howard Journal of Communications, 6,* 69-88.

Pollock, J. M. (2002). *Women, prison, and crime* (2nd ed.). Belmont, CA: Wadsworth Thomson Learning.

Rawlins, W. K. (1992). *Friendship matters: Communication, dialectics, and the life course.* New York: Aldine de Gruyter.

Reinharz, S. (with Davidman, L.). (1992). *Feminist methods in social research.* New York: Oxford University Press.

Ritchie, B. (2002). The social impact of mass incarceration on women. In M. Mauer & M. Chesney-Lind (Eds.), *Invisible punishment: The collateral consequences of mass imprisonment* (pp. 136-149). New York: New Press.

Ross, S. (1996). The writings of women prisoners: Voices from the margins. In M. Morgan & S. Leggett (Eds.), *Mainstream(s) and margins: Cultural politics in the 90s* (pp. 85-102). Westport, CT: Greenwood Press.

Scheffler, J. A. (Ed.). (2002). *Wall tappings: An international anthology of women's prison writings, 2000 to the present.* New York: Feminist Press at the City University of New York.

Servaes, J. (1996). Introduction: Participatory communication and research in development settings. In J. Servaes, T. L. Jacobson, & S. A. White (Eds.), *Participatory communication for social change* (pp. 13-25). Thousand Oaks, CA: Sage.

Shaver, L. D. (1993). The relationship between language, culture and recidivism among women offenders. In B. R. Fletcher, L. D. Shaver, & D. G. Moon (Eds.), *Women prisoners: A forgotten population* (pp. 119-134). Westport, CT: Praeger.

Skeggs, B. (1995). Theorising, ethics, and representation in a feminist ethnography. In B. Skeggs (Ed.), *Feminist cultural theory: Process and production* (pp. 190-206). New York: Manchester University Press.

The Sentencing Project. (2001). *Prisoners re-entering the community.* Retrieved June 6, 2002, from http://www.sentencingproject.org/pdfs/1036.pdf

Valentine, K.B. (1998). "If the guards only knew": Communication education for women in prison. *Women's Studies in Communication, 21,* 238-243.

Whyte, W. F. (1989). Advancing scientific knowledge through participatory action research. *Sociological Forum, 4,* 367-385.

2

A MARRIAGE OF LIKE MINDS AND COLLECTIVE ACTION

Civic Journalism in a Service-Learning Framework

Sue Ellen Christian

Western Michigan University

Sometimes we go overboard trying to find something that is relevant when a lot of times it's right under our nose. It's something that's really touchy and overlooked, and for that reason alone, it's important. Things happen because of it—like fights. People die because of it and people are afraid because of it—meaning interracial problems. It's important to confront things that scare us and make us uncomfortable so we can learn to deal with them better.

—A student journalist on writing about segregation for a special edition of her high school newspaper as part of the Student Newspaper Diversity Project

Journalism has long been an agent of social change. From advocacy journalism to muckraking to new journalism, there is a tradition in journalism of promoting engagement and action in society. A notable era in the history of journalism's public role was that of the muckrakers of the early 1900s. Led by Lincoln Steffans, whose series on municipal corruption was published in the influential *McClure*'s magazine, muckraking journalists had an agenda of investigation, advocacy, and reform (Eksterowicz & Roberts, 2000; Kutler, 2003). Muckraking exposés on corruption helped to prompt Progressive-era reforms. As Eksterowicz (2000) wrote in his essay on the history and development of public journalism, "The muckraker operated within and commented upon (and outright aided) the social, economic, and political changes affecting the general culture" (p. 6). Had it not been for the revelations of the muckrakers on the beef trust or life insurance companies, for example, historians believe that the Progressive movement would not have received the public support needed for successful reform. This journalistic tradition of seeking change and reform is the very heritage that investigative journalists of today call on when seeking, for instance, to expose fraud and illuminate governmental or other systems gone awry. It should be noted, as well, that journalism can be and has been an effective inhibitor of social change. Extensive research shows that the power structures of media relations departments, established sources' access to media, the media's agenda-setting role, and journalistic laziness also can play a role in maintaining the status quo (e.g., Fico & Freedman, 2001; Kensicki, 2004; Kim, Scheufele, & Shanahan, 2002).

One of the most recent manifestations of journalism's advocacy role is the movement called "civic," or "public", "journalism" that was labeled and defined nearly 9 decades after Steffans's groundbreaking series. *Civic journalism* has been defined as many things, including an effort to make citizens and journalists more engaged and informed about public life and local culture (Rosen, 2000). Glasser and Craft (1996) noted that public journalism "denotes a simple but controversial premise: The purpose of the press is to promote and improve, and not merely report on or complain about, the quality of public or civic life" (p. 153). Merritt (1997) contended that public journalism is still "experimental"; it cannot be boiled down into a simple, 1-paragraph, practical definition. Instead of focusing on "what is" public journalism, Merritt emphasized the "why" of public journalism, noting that, like it or not, journalism has an important impact on public life and, therefore, has an obligation to engage citizens in public life. Civic journalism, although not without its vocal critics, has gained and maintained a foothold in many newsrooms nationwide. Much of civic journalism is rooted in the concept of "community," with journalists viewing their newspapers as integral "citizens" of the local community — with a vested interest in that community and not just as neutral bystanders. It is at this community crossroads, this public square of advocacy and social change, that civic journalism and service learning meet.

Journalism is a natural vehicle for a service-learning project—a project with the elements of education, civic responsibility, experience, and reflection—elements that typically define *service learning* (The National Community Service and Trust Act of 1993, cited in Corbett & Kendall, 1999; National Society for Experiential Education, 1998, cited in Katula & Threnhauser, 1999). The service-learning foundation of learning through experience, or learning by doing, already is inherent in the publication process. Teaching journalism, unlike teaching philosophy or any other discipline rooted in theory, is (save for topics such as ethics, history, and media law) predominately vocational—practical, hands-on—in orientation. Students learn by finding story topics, researching those topics, and organizing and writing the information they gather into cogent, cohesive stories. The broad framework of service learning allows room for a project that aims to teach students how to "commit" civic journalism. However, the pairing of service learning and civic journalism goes beyond the simple learning-by-doing mantra; the two movements share some of the same DNA—they are rooted in community, civic life, activism, democracy, and participation as tools for social change.

Another similarity between the movements is that although both are rooted in long-standing traditions, both are fairly young in their development as stand-alone entities, with civic journalism being the junior of the pair. Both also hold tremendous promise; they are rooted in a hopeful, powerful premise of democracy in action, of humans' ability to change and be changed. Both, however, also risk becoming a tool for passivity as opposed to change in that they can serve a status quo that sometimes inhibits change.

It is from these two movements that the Student Newspaper Diversity Project was born. The project is a community effort that I spearhead that involves the student staff of a public high school newspaper in southwest Michigan and select journalism and communication students from Western Michigan University. The 15-week project results in a once-a-year special edition of a high school newspaper that focuses on a diversity issue relevant to the local community. The creation of the Student Newspaper Diversity Project has attempted to solve three disparate needs: (a) the educational need to get a local high school newspaper staff to concentrate on serious topics that resonate outside the school walls; (b) the experiential need to find additional sites (e.g., aside from the campus paper, which is wholly student run and bars faculty involvement) to provide undergraduate journalism and graduate communication students with opportunities to serve as editors of a newspaper; and (c) the outreach need to provide a link between local high school journalism programs and our university journalism program. To be honest, the project also attempted to solve a fourth, more personal, problem: As a former, full-time journalist, I wanted to spend at least a few hours a week in a newsroom, no matter the nature and size. Satisfying those needs meant that the Student Newspaper Diversity Project naturally became a service-learning project—one characterized by partnership-building in a community, student engagement, and civic education.

As participants in the project focused on a theme of meaning to the school and its community, it was evident that our publishing mission needed to involve many aspects of civic, or public, journalism. The newspaper project, thus, is rooted in the movements of civic journalism and service learning, both of which seek to encourage democracy in a community through awareness and activism. In this chapter, I examine the Student Newspaper Diversity Project and the lessons learned from it. I frame discussions of the project from the perspectives of service learning and civic journalism, which are, as just discussed, in many ways compatriots with similar goals. I first describe the Student Newspaper Diversity Project and address the pedagogical, theoretical, ethical, and practical issues that arose in doing the project from both a civic journalism and service-learning perspective. I conclude the chapter with reflection and evaluation of the project, including the impact of the project on the students involved and lessons learned about communication activism.

THE STUDENT NEWSPAPER DIVERSITY PROJECT

The National Communication Association's (NCA) Communicating Common Ground initiative, begun in 2000, provided the focus of the special diversity editions of the newspaper. Communicating Common Ground is about highlighting, celebrating, and fostering diversity, and that goal became the theme of our project's special edition as well. As part of the Communicating Common Ground initiative, our project joins more than 50 other partnerships that link K-12 classrooms with universities to combat hate and hate crimes through communication instruction that seeks to foster respect for and appreciation of diversity. The initiative is a national effort promoted by the NCA, Southern Poverty Law Center, Campus Compact, and the American Association for Higher Education.

Our project, begun in 2002, seeks to promote understanding and awareness among people who are unlike each other for any number of reasons— such as age, gender, race, ethnicity, sexual orientation, and religion—by devoting an entire student-produced newspaper to a diversity theme. The project has evolved since its inception, but for its first 3 years, the project followed a model pairing a high school newspaper staff of 13-18 students with graduate and undergraduate communication students who serve as mentors and editors to the high school staff. The university students participate as part of undergraduate and graduate research assistantships for which they receive a university stipend. There have been African American, Indian, Asian, Latino, and White university students participating in the project over those 3 years, and all have had some background in journalism. The involvement of university students has been limited to 1-2 per year due to difficulties in scheduling, a limited number of university assistantships, and the impracticality of involving too many editors, student or faculty, in one publication.

The student newspaper is a for-credit high school class taught by a faculty advisor who is an English teacher; she and I work as partners to oversee the process, including editing each story. The special edition—entitled simply "Common Ground" by the student staffers—is just one of six editions of the newspaper produced during the academic year by the high school staff, but it is the only one devoted to a single theme and such serious content. The newspaper is disseminated free of charge to the high school students, school board members, other area high school teachers, key city leaders, and English teachers in the community for use in classroom discussions. In our first 2 years, advertisement sales and project grants from the Southern Poverty Law Center enabled us to print extra copies of the newspaper (1,500 instead of the usual 1,000). In 2004, thanks to additional grants from the local Kalamazoo Community Foundation, the special edition was included as an insert in the community newspaper and delivered to approximately 50,000 subscribers and posted online.

I purposely selected an urban public high school in southwest Michigan of about 1,300 students for this diversity project. The school is approximately 50% White, 45% African American, and 5% Hispanic. More than 40% of the students are considered economically disadvantaged; in the school district, about 9% of students have limited English proficiency and nearly 12% of households are run by a single parent, compared to 10% countywide (Standard & Poor's, 2003).[1]

Within this setting, our Common Ground project seeks to fulfill both an internal and an external purpose. The internal purpose is to educate high school students on the newspaper staff about the basics of writing, researching, and reporting using a compelling diversity issue inspired by their school community. These activities hone students' abilities to gather and analyze information, develop critical-thinking skills, and present information clearly and authoritatively. The project also has sparked awareness, understanding, and struggle within students as they report on sensitive issues in their midst. The external purpose is to promote community readers' awareness about a local diversity issue, educate readers about that issue, and connect high school students with their community.

The project is the one time in the year that the high school newspaper staff dedicates its resources to producing a special edition focusing on a single theme that extends beyond the school walls. Far more typical are the other five editions the students publish in any given year that are happily cluttered with more intramural news. That content tends toward a potpourri of news articles, features, and columns on topics such as what kind of soda pop to put in the hallway vending machines or whether identification badges for students really are necessary. For decades, the newspaper has been overseen by a faculty advisor and English teacher, but it is largely run by students taking the course for credit. It has a reputation of attracting some of the best writers in the school.

The students involved in the project identify the overall theme of the special edition by selecting topics from grassroots community concerns. In the first year of the project, we chose to examine the nature of Islam and discrimination against Muslim Americans in our mid-sized midwest U.S. community. In the second year, we examined desegregation and integration in the local public school district—a theme prompted by racial division at the high school at which the student newspaper is based. Our third-year project focused on the multiple issues that contemporary teenagers encounter and looked specifically at teens within the newspaper's high school—their safety, academic performance, social life, and diversity.

The demographic character of the newspaper staff differs each year but, typically, 13-18 students are on staff and the majority of those students are White and upper class. In our first year, two students were aiming to be the first from their families to attend college. In our second year, 3 of the 16 students were African American and two were biracial. In our third year, of the 13 staffers, one was of Indian heritage and one was African American.

The project team begins meeting several weeks prior to the start of the reporting phase of the special edition to discuss a theme (with each edition, I have found it most successful to involve myself and my university students earlier and earlier in the process, as much as 4 weeks ahead of the actual work on the special edition). A few days are devoted to brainstorming and exploring possible diversity themes, and after consensus is reached, students begin pitching individual stories that fit that theme. With the guidance of the newspaper advisor, me, and our university editing team, students research and report their stories. Each story is read several times for content, accuracy, and copyediting by me, the advisor, university research assistants, and classroom peers. Frequent one-on-one sessions are held with the student journalists to discuss story focus, the issues of bias and fairness in reporting and writing, story organization, and word choice. Student journalists are in charge of creating their own graphics and taking photographs to accompany stories, and they are each assigned a page or two of the edition to copyedit.

Before printing, the paper is reviewed by administrators at the high school for content and accuracy. This is no small moment, for in 1988, in

Hazelwood School District v. Kuhlmeier et al., the U.S. Supreme Court ruled that limits could be set on the free press rights of high school students. Kopenhaver and Click (2002) found that due to that decision, most high school publications self-censor their work prior to administrative review to avoid controversy, confrontation, and possible censure of the faculty member involved in the newspaper. Although the Supreme Court ruling did not specify who is responsible for problematic content in high school newspapers, as Kopenhaver and Click's work showed, in real-world experience, advisors most often are held responsible for such problems, with discipline ranging from a visit to the principal's office to removal from advising duties to firing (Student Press Law Center, 2001, 2002, 2003). After the edition returns from the printer, the newspaper staff members, with a pride akin to parents passing around photos of their newborn child, devote one class period to hand-delivering copies of their creation to each class in the high school.

Throughout the project, we hold several staff meetings that always prove to be important for sharing concerns, obstacles, and successes; teaching journalism skills; and honing the focus of the special edition. Taken together, the meetings create an important sense of unity and an atmosphere of free discourse and democracy. We have used these meetings to discuss controversial issues, such as how to report and write a story about fighting at the school. We also swap information on related story topics, brainstorm sources, and share personal prejudices or biases that changed over the course of working on the edition. Although it is hardly overt—we discuss the definition and purpose of civic journalism only in a cursory way, for example—the entire process, as explained in the next section, is interwoven with the principles and practices of both service learning and civic journalism.

THEORY, RESEARCH, AND PRACTICE IN SERVICE LEARNING AND CIVIC JOURNALISM

In this section, I examine the history and goals of civic journalism, critiques of whether the movement advocates for change in an effective way that maintains objectivity or devolves into pandering to the status quo and readers' changing interests, and also look at the Student Newspaper Diversity Project through the prism of civic journalism. I then examine the history and goals of service learning, researchers' calls for such learning to be less objective and involve more critique of structural inequalities, and briefly apply service learning to my project.

History and Goals of Civic Journalism

When filtering service learning through the prism of a student newspaper course in which reporting and writing for publication are the foundations of the course, the result has clear connections to civic journalism. The Pew Center for Civic Journalism (2003) described civic journalism as a philosophy and a set of values. Central to the movement is the credo that journalism has an obligation to public life—one that goes beyond providing information and facts in a news story to actually affecting public life and empowering a community. Rosen (2000), in a debate on what constitutes public journalism, claimed that the movement seeks to link "active and interested citizens to one another, with the news organization as a kind of 'switching device,' in the hope that a more engaged, interactive, and informable public might result" (p. 680).

In 1990, the call for journalists to become more activist and connected to local communities came forth from various parties, including James K. Batten, then chief executive of Knight-Ridder; Burl Osbourne, editor of the *Dallas Morning News* and incoming president of the American Society of Newspaper Editors; and David Broder, political reporter for the *Washington Post* (Rosen, 2002). The theme was that "it was time to do something about the withdrawal and disengagement of citizens, and the press would have to be the do-er" (Rosen, 2002, p. 118). David "Buzz" Merritt, former editor and senior vice president of the daily newspaper the *Wichita Eagle*, described the next step in the evolution of public journalism this way:

> For what became known as public journalism, the pivotal moment came in 1991 at a discussion organized by The Kettering Foundation and Syracuse University. It was there that some journalists who had been thinking about the decline in public life—particularly political life— encountered academics, most notably Jay Rosen of New York University, who had been looking at the problem from their different perspective. (cited in Merritt, 2002, ¶ 13)

Civic journalism departs from traditional journalism, in part, because it is overt in stating unself-consciously that it wants to help people to be better citizens by participating more in local public life and fostering dialogue about important social issues. Traditional journalism is far less direct—and idealistic—about its purposes, which tend toward conveying information as neutrally as possible and allowing readers, or the public, to decide whether to act on that information. Civic journalism, however, takes this process to the next step by conducting community forums, focus groups, citizen polls, and other feedback techniques to promote citizen involvement and action.

The critiques of civic journalism come from two primary directions—one professional and one political. One set of criticisms stems from the perspective that civic journalism is nearly a foil to traditional journalism and, thus, the criticism centers on the alleged lack of objectivity and detachment in civic journalism—hallmarks of traditional journalism. The other set of criticisms generally aims at the stated purpose of civic journalism to engage communities and instigate reform even though it neglects structural inequities and problems that hinder structural reform for political reasons—because attacking the very foundations of a community does not track well with community engagement. I first look at the primary critique of civic journalism—the critique that cuts to the heart of what journalism is and should be.

Civic Journalism: Advocacy or Pandering?

Some scholars have divided traditional journalism and civic journalism into a choice by journalists to either report on the workings of society as disengaged observers who, by their disengagement and use of routine sources (e.g., sources of power), perpetuate the status quo, or, conversely, to consciously elect to engage in not only the presentation of information but also an exploration of solutions, including raising alternative solutions (Altschull, 1996; Friedland & Nichols, 2002). Altschull (1996) joined other critics of traditional journalism by stating that "objectivity is a mechanism for ensuring the status quo" (p. 169). In contrast, civic journalism encourages journalists to be subjectively involved and adopt an agenda-setting role.

In an analysis of public journalism, *The Los Angeles Times* media writer David Shaw (1999) articulated the difference between taking readers' views into consideration in determining newspaper content and "editing a newspaper based largely on focus group research" (p. 73). Newspapers published chiefly in response to public forums and polls ultimately pass over issues essential to democratic society; studies have shown that people do not really know what they want to read in the paper until they see it, Shaw noted. Anderson, Dardenne, and Killenberg (1996, p. 162) countered Shaw's concerns by proposing that journalism can serve as an "inclusive civic university" and expand whom it listens to without sacrificing its present strengths. They envisioned a form of journalism that encourages dialogue, in which the news is not owned and controlled by journalists alone but where the creation of news and opinion occurs through a relationship between journalists and the people of the community.

Such a perspective on civic journalism has been critiqued, however, with the chief concern being that such a relationship sets up a newspaper to pander to the public. Mike Hoyt (1995), a senior editor at *Columbia Journalism Review*, wrote that "a newsroom that would seek to market itself as the

community's pal is the kind that could reflexively refrain from doing anything that might offend that community" (p. 29). Voakes (1999) registered
the critique that civic journalists are catering to citizen views instead of serving as facilitators in determining what the public needs to know. Charity
(1996), writing as a proponent of public journalism in the *National Civic
Review*, noted that "to the truly earnest critics, though, we're pandering to
the crowd, and in the process throwing away the press's ostensibly dearest
possession, detachment" (p. 12). Charity answered that criticism by arguing
that ordinary men and women never have indicated that the press dictates
their beliefs and opinions and that polls show that the public distrusts the
disengaged, "objective" press.

The essence of civic journalism is to ameliorate the self-imposed boundaries of traditional journalism in favor of a more active, engaged reporting
and writing perspective. Novek (1999) noted that "unlike traditional forms
of journalism, publicly oriented newsmaking explicitly encourages young
people to participate in community life" (p. 145). Civic journalism encourages journalists to take up an issue as a cause in print, but critics of civic journalism have voiced concerns over the loss of the watchdog role of the press
as embodied in the First Amendment. The question they pose is how journalists can be watchdogs over the very entities with which public journalism
tells them to partner as part of a community approach to news.

In a published account (Merritt & McMasters, 1996) of a debate with
Merritt, Paul McMasters, past president of the Society of Professional
Journalists, raised the concern that public journalism eschews any detach-
ment on the part of journalists, arguing:

> In our passion for connecting with other citizens, in our role as journal-
> ists, we blur the distinction. The citizen has a role and the journalist has
> a role. That's the reason those 45 words of the First Amendment carved
> out a special niche for journalists of all the professions. (p. 176)

Merritt asserted that public journalism does include objectivity:

> I say public journalism includes objectivity insofar as journalistic objec-
> tivity can exist, but as journalists we do need to care about whether pub-
> lic life goes well. That does not mean our dictating how it ought to go
> or how we ought to get there. But the fundamental of public life is that
> it's public, and people are engaged in it, and so journalists ought to do
> their job in ways that reengage people in public life, so they can make
> decisions about what's going on. (p. 177)

Merritt advocated that journalists stop functioning as observers who
sniff out conflict and polarize issues, avoiding gray areas and areas of agree-

ment (Merritt & McMasters, 1996). In contrast, Shaw (1999), in his review of Rosen's (1999) book *What are Journalists for?*, asserted that some civic journalism initiatives involve staff members taking participatory and leadership positions in forums and activities sponsored by their newspapers. With such involvement, asked Shaw, "How do they report on problems—logistical, ethical, or legal—that involve their colleagues and employers?" (p. 75). Similarly, Davis (2000, p. 689) agreed with the need for some healthy detachment by journalists, noting that "many veteran, reasonable and wary practitioners" are not just in favor of building good fences but good walls that separate journalists from pressures such as profit, advertising, and popularity contests with the public.

In many ways, the choice facing journalists is parallel to the choice for those engaged in service learning, as articulated by Artz (2001) and other scholars. Journalism can continue to criticize individual actors in the reporting of stories in neat, two-party opposing viewpoints, or it can challenge the social order by seeking out sources who lack power (such as interviewing homeless people in addition to interviewing policymakers). Similar to service learning, which can become enamored with the *process* as opposed to examining the *framework* within which the process takes place, civic journalism has been faulted for conveniently opting out of an examination of structural inequities in society. This soft-lens approach can result in a romanticized portrait of community. Civic journalism, the argument goes, is too busy connecting neighbors and building community partnerships to question whether the very foundation on which the community stands is flawed. To critics of civic journalism, the movement poses a conflict of purposes; it is as if journalists are members of the very community commissions and governing boards they are covering; consequently, how could those same journalists even question the existence and operations of those bodies?

Civic Journalism, Service Learning, and the Student Newspaper Diversity Project

The Student Newspaper Diversity Project is rooted in the strong tradition of newspapers as agents of social change. The credo of civic journalism is that journalists should act as involved, engaged citizens *of* their communities rather than dispassionate and uninvolved reporters *on* those communities. In that vein, the newspaper project selects a theme that is designed to hold a mirror up to the community with the intention of raising citizen awareness and understanding; it is, of course, hoped that increased understanding will spark change.

The Student Newspaper Diversity Project is intimately connected to an idea—promoting diversity within the community in which it is situated—

and promulgating that idea for the betterment of the community through goals as varied as reduced hate speech and discrimination to simple regard of others unlike oneself in a community. In that sense, the project is more akin to civic journalism than traditional journalism. The project team desires the Common Ground edition to have an impact and, in fact, my research projects have sought to measure that impact empirically, a measurement I have found difficult to make due to the complexity of isolating a single edition of a school newspaper on readers' attitudes and stereotypes. Little research has been done on the impact of specific newspaper articles and editions because the effects of such interventions are so difficult to separate from other factors that affect peoples' attitudes and beliefs, including other media, family, and friends.

As part of the evaluation of the 2002 edition, I conducted a survey of students with my colleague, Dr. Maria Lapinski, to assess the impact of the newspaper on students' knowledge and attitudes about Muslims and Islam. We surveyed 132 students drawn from a convenience sample from the high school at which the Common Ground edition is produced and from the other public high school in the school district. Students were surveyed about their attitudes toward Muslims and knowledge of Islam. The students at the high school at which the newspaper is produced completed the survey questionnaire before and after reading the Common Ground edition that focused on Muslims and Islam; the students at the other high school in the district completed the survey questionnaire at the beginning and end of the same time period but did not read the Common Ground edition.

What emerged from this survey research (see Christian & Lapinski, 2003) was further confirmation of the so-called "contact hypothesis," which asserts that contact with an "unlike other"—someone different than oneself—will positively affect an individual's attitude toward that person or group (Allport, 1954; Pettigrew, 1998). The high level of student knowledge regarding Islam and the corresponding high percentage of students attributing positive stereotypes to Muslims because of significant exposure to that group of people is a concept embedded in the contact hypothesis and supported by later research (e.g., Nesdale & Todd, 2000). Consistent with contact theory, a strong association emerged in the survey results between readers who knew someone from the diversity group in question—in this case, Muslims—and positive attitudes and stereotypes about that group.

That said, the Student Newspaper Diversity Project hardly embodies the full spectrum of civic journalism as a innovative movement, as our ideas for stories typically do not come from focus groups, we do not hold town meetings or conduct citizen polls, and we do not devote space in our edition for substantial, unfettered citizen comment. I subscribe to the approach that students must learn some of the "rules" of traditional journalism before they can break them as civic journalists. Simply put, the impetus and energy for our project comes from civic journalism, but the basic skills and techniques emphasized in the project are not unique to civic journalism; they are the bedrock journalistic principles of accuracy, fairness, thorough reporting, credible sourcing, and clear writing. We aim to equip young people with communication skills that will not only help them to contribute to their vocation—be that journalism or not—but also con-tribute to public life.

Our goal, thus, is not so different from newspapers surveyed in a Pew Center for Civic Journalism study by Friedland and Nichols (2002), which found that more than half of newspapers engaged in civic journalism-designed projects to primarily inform the public and raise awareness of pub-lic issues. These goals are shared by civic journalism and traditional journal-ism alike. Novek (2002, p. 174), for instance, put the "theoretical framework of civic journalism into practice" by collaborating with a high school English teacher to team-teach a civic journalism class (there were no univer-sity students involved) and publishing a community-focused newspaper for high school students in a large inner-city U.S. high school (see also Novek & Sanford, this volume). Novek (1999) asserted that civic journalism encourages young people to participate in their communities and wrote that "in the field of education, civic journalism may also be used as a learning strategy that combines teaching communication skills with community serv-ice" (p. 145). This project continues that tradition.

Civic journalism seeks to melt the perceived divide between "us" and "them"—that is, between journalists and the public. Novek (1999) noted that in her civic journalism service-learning projects, students contribute to the common good by gathering information about local concerns, making them public, and seeking their solutions. Indeed, many of the students pro-ducing the Common Ground edition are the "them" whom we seek to cover. For example, one student on the newspaper staff spent the night in jail after her mother called the police on her for getting in a fight with her sib-ling. Some of the high school student staff members will be the first in their families to attend college; others are translators for their parents in an English-speaking society. If this project were located at the suburban high school 5 miles away, or at the parochial high school down the street, there might be more of a sense of dividing lines, a sense of the "us" and "them"— that we are outsiders looking in on the community.

Since the U.S. Supreme Court decision limiting the free press rights of student publications, there has been great debate over whether that decision causes newspaper faculty advisors to self-censor to avoid controversial top-ics that would elicit administrative censorship and discipline, which, as noted earlier, often centers on the newspaper's faculty advisor. In a national survey of high school principals and newspaper advisors, three-fourths said that their school newspapers engaged in self-censorship (Kopenhaver & Click, 2002), and 87% indicated that school principals should have the right to prevent publication of articles that they think would be harmful, even if such articles might not be found to be obscene or disruptive (which are some of the guidelines specified by the *Hazelwood* decision) by a court of law. Nearly 80% of those survey respondents also said they thought that most parents prefer the school newspaper to print "good" news rather than controversial news.

In the third year of our project, the project team wrestled mightily with the portrayal of issues facing the students at the high school at which the newspaper is based. The conflict involved the following debate: Too much negative information in an article might mean that administrators would not allow its publication, but a one-sided, wholly positive account conflicted with the project's educational goals of teaching balance and truth-telling in news. We were publishing at a time of budget cuts in school funding, White flight from the public schools, and a general distrust of student journalists as rabble-rousers. These factors prompted an excessively difficult prior review of that year's special edition, not to mention the fact that the edition would be delivered to 50,000 community readers of the local paper.

In light of obstacles to conducting comprehensive critical analyses of relevant social issues, Artz (2001) advised that "limited" service-learning projects should be undertaken, an assertion I find both realistic and preferable in a single-semester experience. Consequently, we tackle one, 16-20-page edition in 10 weeks. In addition to the aforementioned goals of teaching basic reporting and writing skills, other goals include linking youth to their community in a constructive and concrete way and raising the profile of students' unique points of view in the greater community. We, thus, want to engage students in the public life of their high school and their larger community by involving them in pertinent, compelling social issues.

Interestingly, research indicates that projects such as the Student Newspaper Diversity Project certainly do not guarantee that students will practice civic journalism should they enter the profession of journalism. A survey of college students and professional journalists by McDevitt, Gassaway, and Perez (2002) showed that as students move into the professional newsroom, their support of civic journalism gives way, to some extent, to placing a higher value on journalistic autonomy; that is, on the journalist in the traditional role, as independent from community forces and advocacy roles. Such autonomy can preclude the purposeful community engagement that civic journalism advocates. The researchers suggested that college instruction should encourage a broader conception of journalistic interdependence, one that includes breaking from traditional practices that may limit the role of the press in community life. This project, we hope, helps to diminish the fallout that can occur with the transition from classroom to professional newsroom. Participating students may not practice civic journalism per se, but they may carry with them the value of engagement in important issues facing the communities in which they work and live.

The U.S. philosopher John Dewey is, in many ways, the link between service learning and civic journalism, and frequently is cited in discussions of both movements (see, e.g., Anderson et al., 1997; Giles & Eyler, 1994; Lisman, 1998; Novek, 1999; Rosen, 1995, 2000). Anderson et al. (1997) noted that Dewey was the instigator of the idea that "community exists through discussion among its citizens, not just among their representatives" (p. 106). These authors extended Dewey's position by describing a "conversational commons" that journalists enable by creating a newspaper that is a site of public dialogue shared by all citizens—that is, the readers of the paper. Anderson et al. linked the many similar goals and traits of education and journalism, explaining that "they share a mission: broadly stated, to facilitate the learning of an informed community of decision-makers. Education is journalistic and journalism is educational" (p. 105; see also Barber, 1992). Civic responsibility, citizenship, civic engagement, knowledge, and learning; the same words that pepper the definition and description of service learning also are central to descriptions of civic journalism.

Definitions of service learning (and civic journalism, for that matter) abound, but many encompass what Stanton, Giles, and Cruz (1999) called the joining of "two complex concepts: community action, the 'service,' and efforts to learn from that action and connect what is learned to existing knowledge, the 'learning'" (p. 2). They added that service-learning advocates distinguish their form of activism from volunteerism by "evoking the concept of reciprocity between server and served" (p. 3). The served, ideally, is receiving something of value through the service-learning project, and the server is gaining knowledge and experience. In particular, Katula and Threnhauser (1999) stated that one of the benefits of service learning is that it heightens students' civic engagement. Waterman (1997) noted that the outcomes sought through service learning include enhancing students' learning of material that is part of their traditional in-school curriculum, promoting personal development, fostering the development of civic responsibility and other values of citizenship, and accruing benefits to the community. Panici and Lasky (2002) stated that service learning is a way that the academy can acknowledge its commitment to or renew its civic responsibility to its local community.

Several critics of service learning view it as too objective, similar to the criticism often leveled at traditional journalism. Novek (1995) wrote that her public journalism service-learning project, in which students actively participated in producing a product (a newspaper), differed from many forms of service learning, in which students may be "placed" to work in service organizations. Novek's distinction alluded to the danger that such placed students typically work for free with perhaps little ownership of the organization's mission and even less educational instruction in their time there. Increased involvement may help to address the problems faced in a service-learning setting for such placed students, but also at issue is the student's position of detachment—an unemotional, distanced position that hinders deeper learning. Such students are not creatively engaged in a hands-on process meant to encourage in-depth learning, as the founders of service learning envisioned. In a similar critique, faculty members who oversee service-learning projects sometimes are seen as separate, detached observers, isolating themselves from the experience that their students undergo (Bachen, 1999). They remain bystanders and overseers of the action rather than engaged learners themselves. Inherent in this critique of service learning is the recommendation that faculty should involve themselves more fully in the projects, as experiential partners rather than as classroom monitors.

Some scholars, including Katula and Threnhauser (1999), have noted that experiential education, in which they include service learning, in addition to other forms of hands-on education, creates a symbiotic relationship between the university and the corporate world, "providing cheap labor for it and subordinating the educational needs of students to the needs of business and industry" (p. 252). As Katula and Threnhauser asked:

> The university may pride itself on being a part of the community because of its service-learning requirement, but if the student is required to pay tuition to work at a homeless shelter and then returns to a campus where little or no formal reflection on that experience is had, who then has reaped any value? (p. 252)

Others continue to question the role that charity plays in the activity, noting that, in many cases, the service often involves educated, affluent students helping, at arm's length, undereducated, poor people. In particular, service-learning advocates as critics have voiced concern about service learning as bordering on sheer charity and lacking a critical component that does nothing to educate students about root causes of the inequality that prompted the service learning in the first place (see, e.g., Artz, 2001; Frey, Pearce, Pollock, Artz, & Murphy, 1996; Herzberg, 1994).

In a refreshingly honest appraisal of his experiences with a literacy-tutoring project that included two semesters of composition, a sociology course, and students serving as tutors in a community, Herzberg (1994) concluded that service learning and community service do not automatically raise questions about social structures, ideologies, and social justice. He voiced concern that students were not learning about the nature of the problems that compelled the very existence of the social service organizations (such as a homeless shelter or soup kitchen) at which the students worked in their service-learning projects.

In an essay on their service-learning writing project at Michigan State University, Cooper and Julier (1997) asserted that effective citizenship requires an "immanent critique" of proposed solutions to social problems, in addition to immersing students through direct experience in those problems. By critically analyzing possible solutions to social ills, students learn that democratic processes are "complicated, demanding, frustrating, tentative, and often as messy as they are important" (Cooper & Julier, p. 92). Artz (2001) further noted that "service-learning can become either an institutionalized version of charity, inadvertently defending the status quo, or service-learning can consciously put certain intellectual enterprises at the service of the search for social justice and liberation" (p. 242). A service-learning agenda that challenges structural conditions and involves societal-level critique will greatly favor the latter result, Artz asserted.

Perhaps, as noted in the commentary by Artz (2001), too few service-learning projects challenge structural conditions. For a service-learning project at a local homeless shelter, for example, critically examining the reasons behind why the homeless shelter is needed in the first place leads to larger, complicated political questions. Most teachers and students are not prepared to go beyond the actual service-learning component (out of sheer time constraints, if nothing else), let alone branch into political critique. A failure to wrangle with embedded, institutional inequities is a concern voiced by both critics of service learning and civic journalism; the complaint against both movements, thus, is strikingly similar.

The service-learning framework of the Student Newspaper Diversity Project is designed to enhance students' learning of the academic material, promote their self-esteem, foster their responsibility both professionally as journalists and civically as citizens, and thrust the focus of the project outward toward serving the community. The project also attempts to avoid service-learning's charity trap to a certain extent. Instead of seeking out those who are oppressed by social injustice and "helping" them, as is the goal of many service-learning projects, the student journalists working on a diversity theme are, in fact, dependent on those who are oppressed to help them as journalists by providing their life stories, information, knowledge, and experience. The role of the student journalist is to engage in communication with these individuals to better understand issues, challenge irrationalities, and illuminate the truth about whatever issue they are covering.

REFLECTIONS ON COMMUNICATION ACTIVISM AND AN EVALUATION OF THE STUDENT NEWSPAPER DIVERSITY PROJECT

The Student Newspaper Diversity Project fundamentally is about impact. Each edition has been marked by the tremendous anticipation of student reporters eager to see some influence of their work on the community. Research conducted in conjunction with the Common Ground editions sought to measure the impact of these editions on readers' attitudes and stereotypes. Looking inward instead of outward, the project affected the student reporters and editors largely through the personal knowledge they gained about their stereotyping of others and skill-based knowledge in reporting such complex stories. The students also have had to come to terms with the effects of censorship (both by administrators and the project team itself) on final editions. A final measure of impact—the staying power of the project—indicates that it appears to be in good hands, as there is evidence of student ownership of the concept of publishing a newspaper devoted to a topic of diversity meaningful to the local community, with or without grant money or university involvement. This evaluation and reflection section discusses the impact of the newspaper edition on readers, as well as on the students involved. I then continue with a discussion of two of the central elements affecting success of the project—developing student ownership and censorship by the school district administrators—and conclude with a look at future plans for the project.

Seeking and Measuring Impact of the Newspaper on Readers

By concentrating on a diversity theme, the newspaper's special edition effectively highlights the needs, issues, and experiences of marginalized groups in the community. Moreover, articles oftentimes illuminate the need for political, social, and educational reform in the community. For example, as mentioned previously, articles in our 2001 edition focused on Muslims of Middle Eastern descent and included news stories about discrimination faced by a local Muslim American businessperson, as well as an explanation of Muslim religious beliefs and a description of a reporter's visit to the local mosque. Articles in our 2002 edition focused on desegregation and integration in the public schools in the community and included stories on the dearth of minority teachers in a high school with a student population that is nearly half African American, the practice of "tracking" minority students into more remedial classes, and the pros and cons of affirmative action. If readers so choose, articles can provide the momentum for discourse on inherent inequalities in a system, be they political, social, or educational. Letters to the editor of the high school newspaper, as well as discussions in classes throughout the high school, indicate that at least some level of discourse is occurring.

One student journalist commented that she expected change to result from the special edition. In a research interview I conducted with her on the day the 2002 edition hit the hallways, the student said:

> I hope when the paper comes out and all the readers get a feel for the paper, I hope the things we do open their eyes and they see things differently, like we have. The whole issue is about building understanding and acceptance. There are a lot of things that people wanted to talk about and once you talk about it, you learn to tolerate it and accept it.

Another student said:

> I know that obviously I'm not going to solve the world's problems with my article. I have this dream somehow, it'll make it to *The New York Times* and spontaneously all of America will turn around, but I have a pretty good feeling that that's not going to happen. I got out of it a ton. It was really great to actually put all this work into one issue that was for the most part dedicated to [the theme].

Newspaper stories can create ripple effects. A look at the Pulitzer Prize winners in journalism in any given year will reveal that more than a few newspapers brought about change due to their reportage. For example, the Pulitzer winners for public service in 2004 were *The New York Times* staff writers David Barstow and Lowell Bergman, who chronicled deaths and injuries among U.S. workers due to safety violations by employers. Their series led to an investigation by the U.S. Occupational Safety and Health Administration and federal charges against foundry manufacturer managers. To be fair, it is important to mention that newspapers do not always make the impact their editors may crave. A 1996 public journalism initiative by the Pew Center for Civic Journalism and *The Bergen Record*, a mid-sized daily newspaper in northern New Jersey, included 9 weeks and 54 full pages of coverage on the 1996 New Jersey Senate race, but a thorough analysis of the project showed little impact on readers' knowledge of the issues in this campaign, especially when up against a deluge of television commercials by candidates (Blomquist & Zukin, 1997).

For the Student Newspaper Diversity Project, there have been some discernable effects of our work. In the fall of 2002, the edition's impact was evident in several ways: letters to the editor, classroom discussions, additional community grant funding, and a special 4-part series in the local community newspaper. The community newspaper, which has a circulation of more than 70,000, took up the same topic of desegregation as our project theme just a few weeks after our special edition was published. The Common Ground special edition won an award from the state scholastic press organization and was highlighted in several media outlets.

That said, specific, direct action in response to our project has been difficult to measure and seems to be negligible. Specifically, there have been no discernable school reforms due to this project. For example, there has not been a special effort to hire more minority faculty members due to the segregation in the public schools theme of one of our special editions. The student journalists became aware as they reported their stories that institutional reform was a long and slow process; interestingly, many sources indicated as much in their interviews with students. The students learned through their school district sources what to expect in terms of any immediate change in the problems about which they wrote.

As part of the evaluation of the 2002 edition, as previously explained, Lapinski and I conducted a survey of students to assess the impact of the newspaper on students' knowledge and attitudes about Muslims and Islam (Christian & Lapinski, 2003). Although the results supported the contact hypothesis, the results did not show statistically significant changes in attitudes or knowledge due to reading the Common Ground edition.

In the third year of the project, in early 2004, when the Common Ground edition was distributed throughout the county in which the high school is based, I sought to gather community members' reactions through feedback forms designed to elicit readers' assessment of the newspaper's impact on their attitudes about that year's special edition theme—the diversity of issues facing teens in one public high school (seen by some as an unsafe, unproductive learning environment) in the local community, from safety to social issues. The data are preliminary, but many readers responded that they learned something new about a school and a student body in their community, and they generally felt more positive about that school after reading the edition. One reader, who said the edition prompted her to talk to other residents about issues raised by the articles, wrote, "We need to get more of this good talk out in the community and neighboring communities for all to hear!"

How the Project Affected Participating Students

The Student Newspaper Diversity Project affected the high school and university students involved in two important ways—one attitudinal and the other academic—as revealed in individual interviews and focus groups conducted with students throughout the project. First, students remarked often that they felt their prejudices or perspectives on diversity issues were being challenged and altered in some cases, due to their work on the project. Second, students believed that they learned important lessons about practicing the craft of journalism. In both instances, the input and influence of peers was essential. For the university students involved in the project, they reported that they were particularly invigorated by the opportunity to serve as mentors and role models to the high school students. My university students enjoyed the equal status they were given as editors overseeing individual reporters and articles, and they learned in this way about the power of the press and their own public and social responsibility as part of the editing team of a published newspaper. In evaluations, the university students said that trying to help a high school student journalist move from a story's conception to its publication was most educational, as it taught the university students important lessons concerning bias, balance, accuracy, and story organization. One university student, who is now working at a large urban daily newspaper, said that the project helped her to understand and value the editing process in ways that classroom learning had not.

As for the high school journalists, their reflections emphasized the influence of their peers in learning to appreciate other points of view, particularly from a classmate in a racial, ethnic, or socioeconomic group unlike their own (Christian & Prater, 2003). One biracial student journalist said:

> Even after looking at everyone's articles, you can see what impact it can make on readers. I read [name of student author]'s article on White guilt. I never really thought about it in that aspect. Different people will see other sides of issues because of this.

Second, student reflections separated the activist component of the project from the educational component of learning journalistic skills. In a 2002 post-publication interview, one high school student commented on the act of reporting on a sensitive subject, such as the lack of racial integration in the community, saying:

> I think it's important, you know, to discuss that sort of stuff because it's out there and if you put it out in the paper, people will read it and [begin] fixing stuff, finding the problems and then trying to solve them.

That student wrote an article about educational tracking of minority students; in reporting the story, he interviewed the assistant superintendent and teachers at all levels of the K-12 curriculum. He learned important lessons about interviewing and the need for reporting accuracy. For instance, he said, "It's really touchy . . . and I've gotta make sure it's right. I know that. It was really difficult to get interviews." Other students commented on how the edition forced them to interview someone other than a class-mate or favorite teacher, and they asserted that getting out into the commu-nity helped them to realize what the job of a professional journalist was like.

Developing Student Ownership of the Project

In the project's first year, in an effort to model the type of theme we were aiming for in terms of breadth, depth, and reader impact, I brought the theme idea to the high school staff rather than letting the staff come up with its own theme concept, a decision that proved to be a mistake. With the focus, as previously mentioned, on the discrimination of people of Middle Eastern descent, particularly Muslims, post-September 11, 2001, students wondered whether the focus was on all Muslims or just Muslims from the Middle East (as opposed to African American Muslims, for example), and whether the focus was on people from the Middle East, in general, includ-ing Hindus or other religious affiliations. These questions stemmed largely from the fact that the theme was assigned; it did not evolve from their under-standing of their community. Not helping matters was the confusion between the faculty advisor and me over which one of us ultimately was "in charge": She looked to me, as the creator and facilitator of the project, to lead; I thought that as she ultimately was responsible for the newspaper's content, she should have the final say over difficult editing decisions.

In the following 2 years, several important changes occurred. The uni-versity team entered the students' lives even earlier in the semester, several weeks before the project began and as the staff was still working on one of the regular editions, meaning that the university team became part of the daily newsroom operation rather than being visitors. We also visited the high school newspaper class more often, began discussions early in the semester about possible ideas for a theme, and brainstormed the ideas in sev-eral sessions to build consensus. Students then pitched their story ideas and chose their reporting partners on the staff. The result was a far more cohe-sive group that welcomed the university team's presence as opposed to see-ing us as outsiders. In addition, the faculty advisor and I sought to improve our communication and actively lead as partners. One-on-one interviews conducted with students post-publication pointedly asked them about the ownership of the project and the leadership roles of their faculty advisor and me. There was a unanimous feeling that the project was theirs (to the point that several said they would continue it even if the university students and I were not involved) and that the advisor and I shared control and authority in the classroom with regard to the newspaper and its content. These simple changes in communication, thus, made for a far more enriching and positive experience for all involved.

Regardless of what the future holds in terms of grant funding, the university-high school partnership, or administrative censorship, the Common Ground edition as produced by the high school newspaper staff likely will continue for years to come. The special theme edition has captured the imagination of the newspaper faculty advisor and the student staff; they particularly like the one-time challenge of going into the community to find stories and meet sources. Students in the high school understand that the newspaper does this innovative edition just once a year, and they want to be on the staff during the semester the edition is produced. Interest and excitement about the project also has been aided by media coverage; the project has been profiled twice in the school district's newsletter, twice in university newsletters, and three times in the local community paper.

How Censorship Affected Content

Our project is evidence that not all forms of communication activism are created equally, as there are legal, educational, and, at times, social limits to the forms that communication activism can take. In our case, the limits involve censorship; due to the 1998 *Hazelwood* decision, the topics that can be raised, and the manner in which they are addressed, are subject to administrative review. School officials can cut sections of stories and entire articles if they deem it necessary for a variety of reasons, ranging from accuracy and relevance to offensive language or controversial topics. Although administrators must provide reasons for their edits, the criteria for prior review are quite broad and include sweeping statements, such as, "A school need not tolerate student speech that is inconsistent with its basic educational mission" (*Hazelwood v. Kuhlmeier*, 1988). The notion of First Amendment rights and the concept of academic freedom that prevail in higher education, thus, cannot be exercised as liberally as is customary when a project is based at a secondary education institution, as is this project.

Administrative censorship affected the newspaper's content most severely in 2004, when the Common Ground edition focused on the diversity of students and issues at the school at which the student newspaper is based. Some administrative cuts seemed warranted, such as the deletion of an anecdote in an article about student fights that named a minor student who had been suspended for fighting. Other cuts are best described as a "Brave New World" approach to language, such as the demand that the word "fight" be replaced with the word "confrontation." In all, two full-length articles and an editor's note were cut from the edition, in part, because they were deemed controversial, and numerous edits were required before the edition was published and distributed to readers of the local community paper; this new, expanded audience likely was the cause for such heavy administrative editing.

One of the spiked articles detailed the number of fights at the school each year and included a substantive discussion with school administrators in charge of student discipline about innovations in punishing students involved in fights, such as an in-school suspension that sought to instruct students on how to channel their aggression more positively. This article was cut because it was deemed controversial and, ostensibly, inaccurate. Administrators said that the number of fights reported at the school, a figure the school district itself supplied to the national school evaluation web site on which we found the information, was incorrect. (Administrators refused to directly supply to student reporters the specific information on the number of fights at the school.) Another article sought to examine the use of drugs among teenagers and largely relied on national statistics from the federal government. Although some quotes included from students referred in general to the use of alcohol and drugs among peers, no names of students appeared. These student quotes, however, were largely of concern to administrators who felt they could reflect poorly on the students quoted and the school as a whole, and, to be generous, it could be argued they merely were secondhand observations (for credibility, we chose not to include in the article any anonymous interviews with actual substance abusers), although peer observations certainly are appropriate in such an article. Finally, the editor's note detailed the administration's extensive prior review and stated the staff's objection to such vigorous editing on what the staff members believed were exaggerated grounds. The front-page editor's note was the staff's attempt to explain to readers why this special edition was not as complete or as accurate as it could have been. It was the staff's attempt to defend itself against possible reader criticism that the articles or edition were incomplete or soft-peddled the truth; not surprisingly, the note was cut by the administration.

The administrative censorship, which stretched for weeks and primarily involved the school's dean of students and, apparently, also the school district's attorney, taught students many unfortunate, although realistic, lessons, including the politics of their educational bureaucracy. Another result of the censorship is that the project may not continue as it has been structured; for 2005, the faculty advisor and I scaled down the scope of the high school project. Specifically, we did not seek to publish the special edition community-wide, and we did not involve university students and myself in the entire edition start-to-finish. Instead, students in my upper level undergraduate specialized reporting and writing course worked with the high school students at two key points in the publishing process: story conception and brainstorming sources, and final story editing. This approach was successful, as it fostered better communication with school administrators that resulted in a more edifying and clear-cut prior-review process, which we also experienced with the 2006 high school edition. In addition, the university undergraduate class in 2005 began publishing its own course newspaper as part of the Student Newspaper Diversity Project; it is free from administrative prior review and shares the same diversity theme as the high school edition, but is wholly unique in its content and is distributed to the greater community in print and, in 2006, online.

In addition to administrative review, and in large part because of it, the project team has engaged in self-censorship. One notable example was the decision in 2003 by the faculty advisor and me to redact paragraphs from a story about ethnic labels. The student author included two paragraphs on the use of the word "nigger" as a slang term. After several meetings as a staff and with the student author, the faculty advisor and I chose to take out the paragraphs against the wishes of the author, who felt that such editing substantially weakened his story. The advisor and I based our editing decision on several factors, including the fact that the story's focus was on socially acceptable labels for African Americans over time, such as "colored" or "Negro," not on slang terms; journalistically, then, the paragraphs did not fit in the article. In addition, we were concerned about the potential unrest the inclusion of the "n"-word might prompt within the school and, thereby, detract from the rest of the newspaper and other students' very worthwhile articles.

Some staff members supported our decision, whereas others did not. As part of the project evaluation, we asked the student author to write down his reflections on the article and how it was handled. He wrote:

> The censorship argument was absolutely the dumbest. If the administration is going to censor the article in prior review, let them [sic] do it. Let's not pre-censor it so they don't have to do their job. I think the overriding reason the section was cut was that the advisor felt uncomfortable printing it, because some of the responsibility would lie with her. That is absolutely a valid argument. I still would have fought it, but it would make more sense. About half the staff [members] approached me at one time or another and said they agreed with my reasons for keeping it in, and a couple said something about how gutsy it was to include the section. I felt good about hearing their support and I felt that backed up my opinions of the readership at our school.

The student was correct in his assessment that the advisor was uncomfortable printing those paragraphs and, in fact, from the high school administration's point of view, all the responsibility for that decision would lie with her. Many members of the student newspaper staff did, indeed, champion the paragraphs, mostly in the spirit that they were part of the author's original work and the article should, thus, stand just as is. To me, this point of view stems from inexperience and naivete regarding the purpose and value of editing. I appreciate the student author's argument that we should not pre-censor ourselves; however, the faculty advisor and I believed that those two paragraphs would so concern administrators as to potentially make the entire prior review of the edition that much more loaded with aggressive edits and overzealous deletions that substantially could affect the work of still more student reporters.

Future Plans

There is a saying that "democracy is messy" and so, too, are engaged learning and civic journalism. Significant criticisms of both service learning and civic journalism have been raised here. I do not plan to abandon the Student Newspaper Diversity Project, however, for three reasons. First, in focus groups, one-on-one interviews, and anonymous written evaluations, students reported that they enjoyed learning in the engaged, interactive way that service learning so naturally promotes. Students also reported that they learned both academic and social concepts through this partnership. In terms of academic concepts, they learned the importance of using informed and diverse sources, story organization, and accuracy. In terms of nonacademic learning, in project evaluations, both high school and university students reported that they understood how complex and political a bureaucracy can be, how powerful the press is when reporting information that is known only by a select few, how enriching the role of a mentor can be (for university students), and how their attitudes and biases changed as a result of working on the diversity newspaper editions.

Second, I find it pedagogically invigorating to teach key concepts of journalism through service learning and in the setting in which students ultimately will work: a newsroom in the real world with actual sources and compelling issues, and not a classroom laboratory. Through this project, students learn that issues are not as black and white as a sample workbook press release would have them believe. The purpose of this project is not to teach students to become political and social reformers, or even to become civic journalists. However, students do learn that the press inextricably is linked to social and political reforms—both the rendering and inhibition of such reforms—and journalism students need exposure to that societal role to fully understand the profession and learn concepts and lessons that textbooks cannot teach them. Lastly, engaged learning, as well as the practice of journalism, expose the community to students, and vice versa, and through that exposure, dialogues can occur and understanding and even respect can result. It is of value for a community to see the results of the public education of local students and to have a tangible project to look at, discuss, and react to (and, in this case, even clutch in their hand over morning coffee). It is of value for students to have a vehicle to demonstrate their skills to their friends and neighbors and have a voice in their community; through the Student Newspaper Diversity Project, students use their skills to communicate the issues they think are worth talking about.

As noted earlier, the Student Newspaper Diversity Project likely will evolve in the coming years in terms of scale, scope, and partnerships, seeking new relationships with other K-12 classrooms and even community groups. Although the partners may change, the result of the project will remain constant: the publication of a single edition of a newspaper devoted to a diversity theme relevant to the local community. Project goals include becoming economically self-sufficient, increasing university and community ownership, and involving more undergraduate university students in the project. I have independently pursued grants to fund the project, initially to free up the high school newspaper staff from selling ads to support the paper so that students could focus on the reporting and writing of the special edition, and later to expand the number of copies printed. I have received three external grants for the project, one from the Southern Poverty Law Center and two from the Kalamazoo Community Foundation. If the community newspaper becomes a partner in the project by donating printing fees, we could become truly self-sustaining. The power of our editorial content will likely be the single-most important factor in continuing to build the support of school, university, and community members for our project.

The university has been supportive of the endeavor and, in 2003, awarded grants to support two undergraduate journalism students to serve as research assistants and creative collaborators on the project. Only graduate communication students were involved in the project's first 2 years, and I am continually exploring additional ways in which more of my undergraduate journalism students can get involved in the project. One option is to create an undergraduate civic journalism course, similar to those outlined in articles such as McDevitt's (2000), which would contribute to the diversity project. This model could be adapted to an existing mid-level writing and reporting skills course at my university. Under this model, our community partner would include both a high school newspaper staff and a neighborhood association in the community. High school and university journalism students would work together on articles. In this adapted course, students would be required to write profiles of neighborhood residents that emphasize issues of diversity, discrimination, or prejudice in the residents' lives. Students also would research the demographic, economic, and social issues within the neighborhood, endeavors that could lead to pulling property records at the city clerk's office or studying changes in crime rates—valuable tasks to learn for future reporters.

CONCLUSION

As the Student Newspaper Diversity Project changes and evolves, the focus will remain the same: a marriage of service learning and civic journalism aimed at promoting journalistic skills, student awareness of civic issues, public dialogue, and, ultimately, appreciation of one another, especially others unlike ourselves. Civic journalism and service learning are fields rich with potential, but both are evolving. Consider the following passage about public journalism from Eksterowicz and Roberts (2000):

> The future of the public journalism movement remains in doubt. No one expects the movement to give birth to a new generation of "muckrakers" intent upon instigating a new populist or progressive movement. Yet an opportunity does exist for the movement to focus its energy on helping to persuade the American people that civic involvement in not a dirty phrase. (p. 187)

Similarly, service learning is still undergoing scrutiny and evaluation as researchers seek to assess student learning and outcomes (e.g., Corbett & Kendall, 1999). Rosen, a leading proponent of civic journalism, has used Dewey's (1927) treatise, *The Public and Its Problems*, as a philosophical starting point for his critical examinations of journalism as it is practiced today (cited in Eksterowicz & Roberts, 2000). Dewey advocated connections between people and their communities, and his philosophy is at the root of the service-learning movement as well (see, e.g., Katula & Threnhauser, 1999). Dewey asserted that students must actively participate in democracy to help shape it. In the same way, Dewey saw the newspaper as an "educator of the public par excellence," and as a means for citizens to get informed and connected to shape their democracy (Friedland, 2000, p. 123).

The pursuit of an engaged citizenry that participates in creating a healthy democracy is a tenet of both civic journalism and service learning. These two movements undoubtedly will continue to evolve, being rooted as they are in democracy through participation and citizen activism. This form of democracy calls for communication activism of the toughest but truest sort—communication in our own communities.

NOTE

1. The specific web site address for these statistics is not given because it would reveal the identity of the school at which the newspaper is based, which is not

permissible as per the agreement with the human subjects institutional review board that approved this research.

REFERENCES

Allport, G. W. (1954). *The nature of prejudice.* Reading, MA: Addison-Wesley.

Altschull, J. H. (1996). A crisis of conscience: Is community journalism the answer? *Journal of Mass Media Ethics, 11,* 166-172.

Anderson, R., Dardenne, R., & Killenberg, G. M. (1996). The American newspaper as the public conversational commons. *Journal of Mass Media Ethics, 11,* 159-165.

Anderson, R., Dardenne, R., & Killenberg, G. M. (1997). The American newspaper as the public conversational commons. In J. Black (Ed.), *Mixed news: The public/civic/communitarian journalism debate* (pp. 96-117). Mahwah, NJ: Erlbaum.

Artz, L. (2001). Critical ethnography for communication studies: Dialogue and social justice in service-learning. *Southern Communication Journal, 66,* 239-250.

Bachen, C. M. (1999). Integrating communication theory and practice in community settings: Approaches, opportunities, and ongoing challenges. In D. Droge & B. O. Murphy (Eds.), *Voices of strong democracy: Concepts and models for service-learning in communication studies* (pp. 13-24). Washington, DC: American Association for Higher Education.

Barber, B. R. (1992). *An aristocracy of everyone: The politics of education and the future of America.* New York: Ballantine Books.

Blomquist, D., & Zukin, C. (1997). *Does public journalism work? The campaign central experience: Summary and key findings.* Retrieved April 29, 2004, from http://www.pewcenter.org/doingcj/research/r_does.html

Charity, A. (1996). Public journalism for people. *National Civic Review, 85,* 7-13.

Christian, S. E., & Lapinski, M. (2003). Support for the contact hypothesis: High school students' attitudes toward Muslims post 9-11. *Journal of Intercultural Communication Research, 32,* 247-263.

Christian, S. E., & Prater, A. (2003). Publishing the n-word in a student newspaper: A dialogue on the racial, ethical, and educational issues. *Journal of Intergroup Relations, 3,* 20-38.

Cooper, D., & Julier, L. (1997). Democratic conversations: Civic literacy and service-learning in the American grains. In L. Adler-Kassner, R. Crooks, & A. Watters (Eds.), *Writing the community: Concepts and models for service-learning in composition* (pp. 79-94). Washington, DC: American Association for Higher Education.

Corbett, J. B., & Kendall, A. R. (1999). Evaluating service learning in the communication discipline. *Journalism & Mass Communication Educator, 53*(4), 66-76.

Davis, S. (2000). Public journalism: The case against. *Journalism Studies, 1,* 686-689.

Dewey, J. (1927). *The public and its problems.* New York: Holt, Rinehart & Winston.

Eksterowicz, A. J. (2000). The history and development of public journalism. In A. J. Eksterowicz & R. N. Roberts (Eds.), *Public journalism and political knowledge* (pp. 185-187). Lanham, MD: Rowman & Littlefield.

Eksterowicz, A. J., & Roberts, R. N. (2000). Epilogue: Public journalism and the future. In A. J. Eksterowicz & R. N. Roberts (Eds.), *Public journalism and political knowledge* (pp. 185-187). Lanham, MD: Rowman & Littlefield.

Fico, F., & Freedman, E. (2001). Setting the news story agenda: Candidates and commentators in news coverage of a governor's race. *Journalism & Mass Communication Quarterly, 78,* 437-449.

Frey, L. R., Pearce, W. B., Pollock, M. A., Artz, L., & Murphy, B. A. O. (1996). Looking for justice in all the wrong places: On a communication approach to social justice. *Communication Studies, 47,* 110-127.

Friedland, L. A. (2000). Public journalism and community change. In A. J. Eksterowicz & R. N. Roberts (Eds.), *Public journalism and political knowledge* (pp. 121-142). Lanham, MD: Rowman & Littlefield.

Friedland, L. A., & Nichols, S. (2002, September). *Measuring civic journalism's progress: A report across a decade of activity.* Washington, DC: Pew Center for Civic Journalism. Retrieved September 2, 2003, from http://www.pewcenter. org/doingcj/research/r_measuringcj.html

Giles, D. E., Jr., & Eyler, J. (1994). The theoretical roots of service-learning in John Dewey: Toward a theory of service-learning. *Michigan Journal of Community Service-Learning, 1,* 77-85.

Glasser, T., & Craft, S. (1996). Public journalism and the prospects for press accountability. *Journal of Mass Media Ethics, 11,* 152-158.

Hazelwood School District v. Kuhlmeier et al., 484 U.S. 260, 108 S. Ct. 562, 98 L. Ed. 2d 592 (1988).

Herzberg, B. (1994). Community service and critical teaching. *College Composition and Communication, 45,* 307-319.

Hoyt, M. (1995). Are you now, or will you ever be, a civic journalist? *Columbia Journalism Review, 34,* 27-33.

Katula, R. A., & Threnhauser, E. (1999). Experiential education in the undergraduate curriculum. *Communication Education, 48,* 238-255.

Kensicki, L. J. (2004). No cure for what ails us: The media-constructed disconnect between societal problems and possible solutions. *Journalism & Mass Communication Quarterly, 81,* 53-73.

Kim, S. H., Scheufele, D. A., & Shanahan, J. (2002). Think about it this way: Attribute agenda-setting function of the press and the public's evaluation of a local issue. *Journalism & Mass Communication Quarterly, 79,* 7-25.

Kopenhaver, L. L., & Click, J. W. (2002). Students learn about free press through censored school newspapers. *Communication: Journalism Education Today, 35,* 24-33.

Kutler, S. I. (Ed.). (2003). *Dictionary of American history: Vol. 5. La Follette to nationalism* (3rd ed.). New York: Charles Scribner's Sons.

Lisman, C. D. (1998). *Toward a civil society: Civic literacy and service learning.* Westport, CT: Bergin & Garvey.

McDevitt, M. (2000). Teaching civic journalism: Integrating theory and practice. *Journalism & Mass Communication Educator, 55*(2), 40-49.

McDevitt, M., Gassaway, B. M., & Perez, F. G. (2002). The making and unmaking of civic journalists: Influences of professional socialization. *Journalism & Mass Communication Quarterly, 79,* 87-100.

Merritt, D. (1997). Public journalism, independence, and civic capital . . . Three ideas in complete harmony. In J. Black (Ed.), *Mixed news: The public/civic/communitarian journalism debate* (pp. 180-184). Mahwah, NJ: Erlbaum.

Merritt, D. (2002, July 8). *Public journalism: Where it has been; where it is headed.* Retrieved April 29, 2004, from http://www.imdp.org/artman/publish/article_14.shtml

Merritt, D., & McMasters, P. (1996). Merritt and McMasters debate public journalism. *Journal of Mass Media Ethics, 11,* 173-183.

Nesdale, D., & Todd, P. (2000). Effect of contact on intercultural acceptance: A field study. *International Journal of Intercultural Relations, 24,* 341-360.

Novek, E. M. (1995). Buried treasure: The community newspaper as an empowerment strategy for African American high school students. *Howard Journal of Communications, 6,* 69-88.

Novek, E. M. (1999). Read all about it! Using civic journalism as a service-learning strategy. In D. Droge & B. O. Murphy (Eds.), *Voices of strong democracy: Concepts and models for service-learning in communication studies* (pp. 145-154). Washington, DC: American Association for Higher Education.

Novek, E. M. (2002). Good news! Using civic journalism to teach community participation. In T. A. McDonald, M. P. Orbe, & T. Ford-Ahmed (Eds.), *Building diverse communities: Applications of communication research* (pp. 171-185). Cresskill, NJ: Hampton Press.

Panici, D., & Lasky, K. (2002). Service learning's foothold in communication scholarship. *Journalism & Mass Communication Educator, 57,* 113-125.

Pettigrew, T. F. (1998). Intergroup contact theory. *Annual Review of Psychology, 49,* 65-85.

Pew Center for Civic Journalism. (2002, November 4). *Community impact, journalism shifts cited in new civic journalism study.* Retrieved September 2, 2003, from http://www.pewcenter.org/doingcj/spotlight/index.php

Rosen, J. (1995). Public journalism: A case for public scholarship. *Change, 27,* 34-39.

Rosen, J. (1999). *What are journalists for?* New Haven, CT: Yale University Press.

Rosen, J. (2000). Questions and answers about public journalism. *Journalism Studies, 1,* 679-683.

Rosen, J. (2002) Community connectedness: Passwords for public journalism. In R. P. Clark & C. C. Campbell (Eds.), *The values and craft of American journalism: Essays from the Poynter Institute* (pp. 116-122). Gainesville: University Press of Florida.

Shaw, D. (1999). The press as player. *Columbia Journalism Review, 38,* 73-75.

Standard & Poor's. (2003). *School evaluation services.* Retrieved May 1, 2004, from http://www.ses.standardandpoors.com/

Stanton, T. K., Giles, D. E., Jr., & Cruz, N. I. (1999). *Service-learning: A movement's pioneers reflect on its origins, practice, and future.* San Francisco: Jossey-Bass.

Student Press Law Center. (2001). Administrators reprimand adviser for column. *SPLC Report, 22*(2), 40. Retrieved March 10, 2005, from http://www.splc.org/report_detail.asp?id=688&edition=18

Student Press Law Center. (2002). *Student media advisers and the law.* Retrieved March 10, 2005, from http://splc.org/legalresearch.asp?id=51

Student Press Law Center. (2003). Schools target advisers as scapegoats. *SPLC Report, 25*(1), 37. Retrieved March 10, 2005, from http://www.splc.org/report _detail.asp?id=1053&edition=27

Voakes, P. (1999). Civic duties: Newspaper journalists' views on public journalism. *Journalism & Mass Communication Quarterly, 76,* 756-774.

Waterman, A. S. (1997). An overview of service-learning and the role of research and evaluation in service-learning programs. In A. S. Waterman (Ed.), *Service-learning: Applications from the research* (pp. 1-24). Mahwah, NJ: Erlbaum.

3

COMMUNICATION ADVOCACY

Learning and Change in the Media Literacy and Violence Prevention Project

Leda Cooks

Erica Scharrer

University of Massachusetts, Amherst

Activist research, by its very nature, promotes the idea of research as intervention, as an interruption in the way things are that produces some type of change for social betterment. This understanding can be traced back to ontological assumptions about the state of humans' *being* that lies in their *doing*—their movement from one (psychological) state or (social) position to another. The epistemology of change that frames our knowing what, how, and whether movement has occurred, thus, is conceptualized in terms of expectations met and goals achieved. When we work for social change, the discourse becomes infused with moral character; the terms "should," "ought to," and "better," for instance, imply a state of being other than that which presently exists. The language of change is future oriented in defining problems, assessing needs, and offering and implementing solutions. Yet, it could reasonably be argued that actual activism and change occur somewhere *in between* intention and outcome, grounded in experiences made meaningful in the present rather than in the future. We adopt the latter perspective and look at the ontology and epistemology of communication activism through a social constructionist perspective on learning and change.

Whereas much of the research on social action focuses on change or outcomes and the participants involved, little attention is paid to the epistemological assumptions underlying the theory, research, pedagogy, and evaluation of change. Shotter and Gergen (1994) noted that traditionally, epistemology has ignored the situational, developmental, and relational features of communication, presuming, instead, that "isolated, unsituated ideal individuals gain orderly knowledge of passive objects, objects that react to their probings and manipulations but that do not answer back, that is, that do not communicate with them" (p. 5). In the conceptualization, operationalization, and evaluation of social action, the presumption of change, its manifestation in practice, and the criteria on which change is evaluated often rely on traditional assumptions about human passivity with regard to meaning making; that is, that meaning is constructed *outside* the communicative process and rests in some objectifiable reality. In media campaigns focused on drug abuse, for instance, ends (changed behavior) rely often on assumptions about the viewing audience and the influence of media messages. Such campaigns often include both attitudinal and behavioral dependent measures, which pertain to use of the information by the viewing audience. These campaigns envision and strive for a singular end at which time and point a desired effect has been achieved. The effect occurs in these studies independent of the communication process through which meaning is made; communication, thus, often is viewed as a tool that produces the end goal.

In contrast to an approach that views communication as a tool for acquiring information, central in much of social constructionist thought is John Dewey's (1922) work in pragmatism, in which he asserted that ideas about the self, culture, education, and other matters are formed through communication. Dewey described social action not in terms of ends, which imply a start and stop to meaning, but in terms of "ends in view." Cronen (1995) explained that "ends in view are not prior to communication; rather they are constructed and reconstructed in communication" (p. 221). This means that our notions of what changes occur through interventions, as well as how to assess those changes, should be seen not as outcomes that start and stop with any particular project but as processes through which change is understood in the ongoing context of its interpretation.

Building on the idea that learning occurs somewhere *in between* class-room and community settings, in this chapter, we introduce the concept of *learning-as-change*. Learning-as-change indicates and makes conscious the assumption that learning and change are grounded in the same social processes; in other words, when we learn, we are assumed to have changed somehow and in some way that can be recognized or indicated through socially and culturally understood symbols and structures. Thus, learning cannot and does not occur outside this symbolic frame. Although this explicit equation of learning with change is by no means new, its implications for developing and practicing a reflexive approach to the process of learning in communication activism is one important goal of this chapter.

We provide a basis for the understanding and analysis of learning-as-change by describing and assessing a communication activism project, The Media Literacy and Violence Prevention Program (hereafter, the MLVPP). The MLVPP is an ongoing university/community service-learning project that involves multiple courses and constituencies in teaching and learning about mediated and interpersonal violence and conflict resolution strategies.[1] The project provides a richly complex setting for looking at the multiple ways in which meanings of learning and change are constructed in use, as well as the ways our ideas about change frame our assessments of the effectiveness of community service learning for students and local communities. Of particular concern are the ways we frame and interpret learning about media literacy, media violence, and interpersonal conflict as affecting advocacy and transformation among university students and community constituencies (sixth graders, their teachers, and their families).

In earlier work on the topic of learning in community service learning (detailed elsewhere in Cooks, Scharrer, & Paredes, 2004), we built a theoretical structure for examining learning in activist and community service-learning programs.[2] Our approach to learning brought together concepts from social constructionist, critical pedagogy, and community service-learning scholarship to articulate a perspective that stressed critical engagement, participatory and relational processes, and citizenship. In this chapter, we demonstrate the ways an assessment of change using individual outcomes can be complemented by an interactionist perspective on the ways change is constructed in and through discourse. Thus, we offer a conceptual approach to the interpretation of communication activism that locates individual learning and transformation within a social context, and we provide an assessment of a specific project (the MLVPP) using this approach. In the following section, we discuss the theoretical contributions of media literacy scholarship and practice to our communication activist program. We then describe the project, its goals, and its assessment using qualitative data to evaluate change as we have constructed it. We conclude the chapter by revisiting our conceptualization of change and its implications for communication activism research.

MEDIA LITERACY:
THEORY, RESEARCH, AND PRACTICE

With young people in the United States spending about 3.5 hours watching television per day (Comstock & Scharrer, 1999) and over 6 hours per day with all forms of media (Roberts & Foehr, 2004), fostering "media literacy" appears to be a crucial pursuit (Zettl, 1998). Advocates have argued for the adoption of media literacy as a subject to be taught in kindergarten through 12th-grade classrooms, as well as a topic to be explored in after-school programs and by community organizations (Kubey, 1998). At present, all of the 50 U.S. states have added media literacy to their curriculum frameworks (Kubey & Baker, 1999).

There has, however, been considerable dissension among scholars and practitioners regarding how to conceive and carry out media literacy curricula (Kubey, 1998). There is vast variability in the orientations, assumptions, philosophical foundations, and perspectives of those who engage in media literacy instruction and, consequently, much accompanying variability in how and where such instruction is performed. Encompassed under the term "media literacy" is instruction that occurs in both schools and the community; carried out by classroom teachers, library media specialists, or visiting guests; and that is its own subject or is integrated into English, communication, language arts, or other areas of the curriculum.

After much disagreement and debate, and despite the many differences that scholars and practitioners bring to the table, a common definition of media literacy has emerged. Those gathering at the Aspen Institute Communications and Society Program's National Leadership Conference on Media Literacy to discuss the principles and practices of *media literacy* agreed to define it as "the ability to access, analyze, evaluate, and communicate messages in a wide variety of forms" (Hobbs, 1998, p. 16; see also Aufderheide, 1997). Media literacy, then, includes the study of all types of media, their characteristics, and their relationships to both audiences and other social forces, as well as the development of skills pertaining to media use (e.g., constructing a web site, operating a video camera, and writing a newspaper story).

Most media literacy theorists and practitioners also agree on a small number of guiding principles that include the notions that (a) media simultaneously construct and reflect reality, (b) there are values embedded in media messages, (c) audience members often respond differently to media,

(d) media have commercial implications, and (e) each medium has unique codes, conventions, and aesthetics (Aufderheide, 1997). Thus, most scholars argue that media literacy should entail the analysis of media texts (such as individual depictions and content patterns), media audiences (including how they respond to media), and the context in which those texts are produced (such as by analyzing the political and economic power of media institutions) (Aufderheide, 1997; Potter, 1999). A unifying theme is that media literacy students should view media texts as resulting from a series of decisions made and social and institutional processes affecting those decisions (Hobbs, 1998). Furthermore, a central element of media literacy education (as it has developed in the United States) is fostering a complex understanding of the relationships among media texts, audiences, and contexts so that the commercial structure of the media system—the production of texts designed to appeal to an audience of a particular size or type—is made transparent.

Encouraging these perspectives on the media often is referred to as promoting "critical thinking" about the media as a central goal in media literacy. Similarly, the objective of *critical autonomy* often is discussed in media literacy scholarship, defined as students developing their own, independent ability to critique the media in any setting or situation (Buckingham, 1998). For visual media, specifically, *critical viewing* is a goal (Singer & Singer, 1998), which Elizabeth Thoman (1999), Director of the Center for Media Literacy, defined as "learning to analyze and question what is on the screen, how it is constructed and what may have been left out" (p. 133). Silverblatt (1995) also identified awareness of the influx of messages received from the media and their effects on audiences as key goals of media literacy education.

There is a great deal of debate as to the nature and effectiveness of media literacy and media literacy programs that is beyond the scope of this chapter. However, it is important to note that the media literacy and violence prevention curriculum that we describe here attempts to bridge the gap between two camps in media literacy scholarship: an intervention-oriented, media effects-based approach and a cultural studies-based perspective (Scharrer, in press).[3] The MLVPP curriculum attended to many of the positions advocated by those in the cultural studies-based camp by inviting the sixth graders' opinions and experiences with the topics and avoiding being "preachy" or didactic, although much of the material discussed in the curriculum was about the potential for media violence to be associated with negative consequences for audience members. In addition to this goal, however, we wanted to introduce an idea of media literacy that went beyond the abstract critique of the media to discuss its use or usefulness in the everyday lives of students. Specifically, our interest was in bringing together the examination of and critical thinking about the media with the interpersonal dynamics of conflict experiences in the lives of children and to foster some dialogue about the connections, if any, between mediated and interpersonal violence. In the section that follows, we describe the design and implementation of the project.

THE MEDIA LITERACY
AND VIOLENCE PREVENTION PROJECT

The MLVPP is an ongoing undergraduate interclass (TV Violence, Conflict and Mediation, and Public Speaking) project/partnership between the Department of Communication at the University of Massachusetts, Amherst and three area public school 6th-grade classes. Undergraduate students who elect to take the community service-learning (CSL) credit (offered in conjunction with their course) design and implement a media literacy and conflict resolution program for area sixth graders. Before the program begins each year, the responsible faculty members meet with some of the teachers and principals to get their input on the program's design. This design then is applied to all 6th-grade classroom settings so that the program is administered consistently. The CSL project takes place in two phases: first, in weekly meetings at the beginning of the semester to design and discuss curricula and curricular materials for the sixth graders, and then in the program implementation, which occurs in the area schools.

In the program described here, 20 participating undergraduate students, who varied only modestly in terms of race and ethnicity and slightly more in terms of class,[4] spent 6 hours in five local 6th-grade classrooms. Ninety sixth graders participated in the program.[5] The undergraduate students implemented, in teams of four members, the curriculum that they had spent the earlier part of the semester designing, using some of the materials created by former undergraduates engaged in the project as a starting point. The materials created by this project year's undergraduate students included a reading packet written in easy-to-understand language that explained concepts and models in the study of media violence and with respect to interpersonal conflict; interactive, role-playing exercises for the sixth graders to engage in; discussion questions to be posed; media content to analyze; and a creative media-production exercise.[6] The undergraduate students met hourly once a week in a CSL colloquium, as well as more informally outside of school in groups, to plan and design the materials used to interact with the sixth graders about the topic, practice in-school presentations and assign roles, and reflect with one another on their teaching experiences. They formed groups of four—with each group comprised of at least one person from each course—and each group was assigned to work consistently with one 6th-grade classroom.

As the in-school program took place, the undergraduate participants continued to meet weekly to reflect on how the program was going, problem solve difficult situations involving sensitive interactions with the sixth graders (e.g., reports of witnessing real violence), and plan for subsequent sessions. We, the faculty members/authors, taught the CSL colloquium and, along with two participating graduate students, observed the sessions that were conducted with the sixth graders. All the meetings (with CSL undergraduates and facilitators) and the in-school sessions were videotaped, and the videotapes were viewed in the following week's meeting to facilitate a discussion of interactions with the sixth graders, as well as to document specific evidence of the program's successes and challenges.

A pretest questionnaire using both quantitative and qualitative measures was administered on the first day of the in-school sessions (before beginning the program) to measure the 6th-graders' pre-existing knowledge and critical thinking about the topics the program covered. After the initial data collection, the actual program began. The conflict education element of the program was introduced first and began with a conversation around the sixth graders' experiences of conflict and their thoughts about why conflicts occur. The undergraduate students also introduced and explained some models that can be applied in the resolution of conflict. For instance, the reading packet contained a description of the lens model (Wilmot & Hocker, 2001), which suggests that people in conflict should consider the issue from one another's perspective. A favorite of the sixth graders was a model that we called the "LTA model," which stood for *listen* to the other party when in conflict; then *think* about various points of view, options, and consequences; and then *act*. To segue to the media literacy segment of the program, the sixth graders were asked to think of ways that conflicts are resolved or mediated on television, in video games, and in the movies.

The media literacy element of the in-school presentations then focused on ways in which violence was shown in the media and whether the depicted violence would likely encourage or discourage negative effects on audiences (e.g., learning aggression, experiencing fear or a view of the world as mean and dangerous, or becoming desensitized to violence). Four of the five factors that Smith et al. (1998) identified in their national television violence study as those that constitute particularly high-risk depictions for older children and adolescents (ages 7-18) were discussed in the program: (a) violence perpetrated by appealing media characters, (b) violence that is rewarded, (c) violence that is justified, and (d) violence that occurs without consequences. Each factor was defined in the reading packet, discussed with the sixth graders, and identified in the media clips used. The factors were discussed as they are shown in media portrayals, and then the sixth graders indicated whether those media depictions were realistic compared to their real-life conflicts.

The media clips the undergraduate students selected for use and analysis in the in-school sessions were 30-second to 2-minute snippets from popular television programs, movies, and music videos that at least partially targeted a young audience. Scenes from the movies *Shrek*, *Spy Kids*, and *The Lion King* are examples of clips that were analyzed by the sixth graders in discussions led by the undergraduate students. To analyze the video clips, the sixth graders were asked to consider whether any or all of the four high-risk portrayal factors were present and how conflict was addressed or resolved in the clip. Positive as well as negative features of the clip were discussed, and the sixth graders volunteered other critical observations about what they saw. The final portion of the program was devoted to the sixth graders' video-production projects, in which they scripted a story based on a conflict from their own experience. The sixth graders then were taught to use a video camera and filmed their productions, with the final session devoted to viewing the productions.

The remainder of this chapter focuses on our aims for the project, as well as the ways we went about assessing its effectiveness with regard to the concepts of media literacy, conflict resolution, and communication activism. In the first section, we look at the goals of the project with respect to promoting critical thinking and describe an assessment of those goals. The second section looks at the epistemological assumptions embedded in our discussion of learning-as-change and then, using the concepts of discursive force (Hymes, 1972) and positioning (Davies & Harré, 1990), analyzes the videotaped interactions of the project and the journals of the undergraduate student participants.

The Goals of the Project

Defining and measuring critical knowledge and attitudes about the media is no easy task. Much has been written about the elusiveness of the concept of critical thinking and the difficulty in measuring whether and to what degree it has occurred (see, e.g., Ruminski & Hanks, 1995; Wright, 2002). One component of critical thinking that the present project attempted to tap into is the development of critical attitudes about the media, a central part of critical thinking (Loo & Thorpe, 1999; Wright, 2002). Indeed, Watson and Glaser (1994), the creators of a critical-thinking appraisal scale, include attitudes pertaining to the recognition of problems and the consideration of evidence as one of three components used to define critical thinking (along with knowledge and skills). Critical attitudes are important because they are called on in the process of "applying, analyzing, and evaluating information" (Ruminski & Hanks, 1995, p. 5). In the curricular design of the MLVPP, the 6th-grade students apply information they have learned about media violence and conflict resolution and consider their own attitudes on these subjects to make independent judgments of particular media practices and depictions, as well as particular ways to address conflict in their lives.

Ediger (2001) also argued, however, that critical thinking is most effective when background material is first provided to students to enable them to engage in an informed and effective critique. Such an approach—the presentation of information by instructors followed by open-ended critical discussion by students—was utilized in the media literacy and interpersonal conflict curriculum described here, for the reasons outlined earlier and also because it may help to avoid some of the pedagogical pitfalls that can occur in media literacy.[7] This project, thus, combined the presentation of information gleaned from media and conflict theory and research (e.g., factors in media portrayals of violence, possible effects of viewing mediated violence, and models associated with effective conflict mediation) with in-class discussion in which the 6th-grade students' views and experiences with the topics examined were invited.

Assessment: Pre-Program and Post-Program Questionnaire Responses

A number of items on the questionnaire administered to the sixth graders before the program had begun and then after the program had ended 5-6 weeks later asked for their responses to open-ended questions pertaining to the topics covered in the program. For example, one question asked the sixth graders what they thought of when asked to define the term "conflict." Responses were somewhat similar before and after the program, with the vast majority of sixth graders using terms such as "disagreement," "misunderstanding," "argument," "fighting and yelling," and "issues or problems between two people" to define conflict. However, after the program, a greater number of sixth graders mentioned that conflicts could be verbal or nonverbal, which was a point raised during the program. Examples of their statements included "I think of people having an argument, not always physical" and "I think of fighting, verbal or physical, when I hear the word conflict." Responses after the program also differed from those before in that the sixth graders tended to broach the issue of resolution when explaining their conflicts, which was a central focus of the instruction regarding this topic. Examples from their responses included "Conflict to me means a problem that can usually be solved in a nonviolent way" and "I think of mediation and conflict resolution."

Another open-ended question posed to the sixth graders asked how many different ways they could think of to resolve a conflict. Before the program began, the responses were fairly simple, straightforward, and relatively undeveloped, such as "You can resolve a conflict with a 'solution'," "You can resolve a conflict by calming down," and "Walk away and ignore the problem." After the MLVPP, the sixth graders elaborated more in their responses regarding conflict mediation, and many drew on the models that they had learned in class. Examples from their responses included "LTA. Lens Model. Looking at both sides of the story. Apologizing"; "Come up with an idea you both like . . . apologize and finally take the blame if it was your fault"; and "To resolve a conflict, you could talk to them, write a note, think like you are in their shoes."

An additional, open-ended question focused primarily on the media violence analysis part of the MLVPP, asking the sixth graders to consider how television violence differs from violence occurring in the real world. Before the program began, responses to this question emphasized somewhat superficial, obvious differences, such as television is simply not real and because actors are involved, there is no actual harm. Examples of their statements included "On TV, it is fake"; "TV is not real, and actors play in place of a real response"; and "Real-life violence can really hurt." After the MLVPP ended, responses tended to, again, be more elaborate in nature, were arguably more sophisticated (less obvious), and used the language introduced in the program to respond to the question. Examples from their responses included "Violence on TV usually doesn't show the 'aftermath' of the victim"; "On TV it is not real but in real life, people get hurt and get into trouble and even get the death penalty or could screw up their life forever"; "TV violence goes away the minute the director stops shooting, but real-life violence results in many consequences"; and "In TV, no one gets seriously hurt and is hardly ever punished." Thus, the topics of consequences and rewards—introduced, defined, and discussed in the curriculum—had a central place in the 6th-grade students' post-program responses.

Overall, although the sixth graders still focused on television violence being unreal (a rather rudimentary observation when taken literally), they provided greater detail and justification for *how* it is unreal, *why* it is unreal (e.g., the role of the director), and the *potential ramifications* of its lack of realism. Thus, we see evidence in their post-program quotes that some of the principles of critical thinking appear to have been effectively (if occasionally only modestly) employed. In particular, the sixth graders pointed to ways in which television content was an artificial construction by contrasting it with real-life interactions. In doing so, they successfully made connections between mass and interpersonal communication and, thereby, met a central goal of the program. They discussed the principles and values embedded in mediated representations of violence and conflict by focusing on both what was included in such depictions and what was left out (e.g., realistic consequences). They expressed that television content was not "a given" but, rather, resulted in a series of processes and decisions made by individuals, as is evident in the quote given previously that considered the role of the director. They also speculated about the responses of audiences to the content they viewed. Finally, although not as frequent as other observations, some of their responses used the language of the codes and conventions of television production, such as by mentioning plots, directors, and camera shots.

Assessment: Analysis of a Media Clip

As another means of assessing the program, we asked the sixth graders to view a media clip and "write down anything that is important or interesting to note about the clip." The sixth graders analyzed the clip before the program began and then analyzed the same clip (in response to the same, open-ended prompt) after the program ended. The clip was from the television cartoon *Jonny Quest*, featuring a scene in which Jonny and the rest of his crime-fighting team travel to India to try to determine why one of the team members, Pasha, is haunted by a memory of his stepfather trying to kill him with a knife. The Quest team members break into a store and are confronted by a group of Indian men who attack them. All characters in the scene use physical violence, such as punching, kicking, and pulling others down with a rope, and the team is captured as the 3-minute clip ends. The clip was chosen for its depictions of conflict and the stereotypes it assumed (of gender and of South Asian Indians), as well as because we believed that because the target audience for the cartoon is younger than age 12, the sixth graders would not already be exceedingly familiar with the episode or the scene and, therefore, would be responding to it for the first time.

In their pre-program (MLVPP) written responses to this media clip, most of the sixth graders noted the presence of violence and also provided a description of the scenes in the clip. Examples included "Bad guy rip phone off wall. Man gets knocked out. Big fight"; "Violence shows people getting beaten up. Knife"; and "Threatening, breaking, and entering; lots of violence; knife. I thought for a cartoon it had a lot of violence in it."

The 6th-graders' post-program responses often went beyond description or notation of the violence to provide analysis of the conflict. Some of them used the media literacy language introduced in the program, such as: (a) consequences ("People did something bad and there wasn't a consequence"; "Fake. Didn't show the poor people getting hurt in fighting scene"; and "There would be blood . . . broken bones or stuff like that"); (b) rewards and punishments ("It was too violent but the guy is obviously gonna get away"; "I think it was very fake and extremely violent . . . but the police would be all over it in real life"; and "It's kind of rewarded violence because he gets rewarded for what he did"); (c) justified violence ("It's violent and it's justified because the people kidnapped his father" and "Justified. Shows beating up people is 'fun'"); and (d) likeable characters ("The good guys always win"; "The good guy never dies or loses a fight"; and "It was pretty violent. It probably would affect kids that watch it and look up to Johnny Quest"). These analyses of the ways in which violence was presented in the video clip demonstrate two of the central principles of media literacy: media as a form of social construction and values embedded in media content. They also demonstrate that the program seems to have provided the sixth graders with tools—specific concepts, words, and phrases—to engage in critical analysis of media (as well as in critical analysis of conflict and mediation, as was demonstrated in the questionnaire responses).

As seen in the last quote just presented, some of the 6th-graders' responses demonstrated a concern for the potential effects on audiences of this portrayal of violence, thus illustrating the learning of another media literacy principle regarding audience responses. Examples of such learning included the students' statements of "It doesn't show real life. But this is bad for little kids because they think this can really happen"; "It's a children's show so it could affect little kids"; "I think that somebody could get affected by that clip"; and "This is a kid's show! It is so violent! Kids could pick up a lot from this. This is also a fake show, but little kids who watch won't know." It is interesting to note that the sixth graders were not concerned about the potential effects of viewing such violence on themselves but, rather, the effects on younger kids. This appears to be evidence of the "third-person effect," in which a person believes him- or herself to be invulnerable to negative media influence but that such influence can occur for others (see Scharrer, 2002b). We discuss the children's concern for the media's power over others as part of their learning process later in the chapter.

A few of the 6th-graders' post-program responses mentioned the decision-making role of those involved in the creation of media, another central component of media literacy. Examples of such statements included "I think about how unrealistic it is is something important to notice because when it suits the plot, the characters are overly powerful or underpowerful" and "The violence wasn't realistic and the media exaggerated too much."

The 6th-graders' responses also demonstrated an integration of the material presented in the instruction regarding interpersonal conflict resolution and the material pertaining to the analysis of mediated conflict and violence. Examples of those responses included "In the clip there was a lot of fighting. It could have been resolved in a different way. Not by almost killing him"; "There was a lot of violence. The conflicts could have been resolved peacefully"; "There was a person trying to kill someone. That shouldn't be the way to solve something like that"; "I don't think violence helped the situation at all"; "One of the men used violence to solve his problem and that wasn't right. They should have talked it out"; and "Try to find a peaceful resolution or run away." These quotes show that the sixth graders were able to extend the analysis of the media to the analysis of interpersonal conflict, and vice versa, which was an important and unique goal of our program.

A few of the 6th-grade students, however, pointed out positive elements of the clip, saying, for instance, "I think it was important that the whole team [the *Jonny Quest* protagonists] tried to help other people" and "The violence is cool." Still others thought that because the violence was justified in the story's plot, the characters "had a right to defend themselves" (e.g., "I think it would sort of be OK for the good people to fight back"). Responses to the clip, thus, did vary, with some of the sixth graders resisting a negative interpretation of the clip. We believe that these responses illustrate that our efforts to convey that there were multiple valid ways to think about this material, rather than only adopting the terms and models we discussed, were successful. The sixth graders' resistance provides an important check on our framing of the clip and insight into the social process of punctuating learning rather than evidence of the failure or success of learning per se.[8]

REPOSITIONING LEARNING AS CHANGE

In the previous section, we described the 6th-grade students' learning that resulted from the program based on the changes in their responses to the open-ended pre- and post-questions we asked.[9] In the section that follows, we reflect on our own and our undergraduate students' epistemological assumptions in constructing, implementing, and assessing the MLVPP with respect to the goal of social change. This section examines the ways the undergraduate students negotiated (i.e., struggled over) their roles in their stories about teaching, learning, and social change in the community and their own lives. In particular, we look at the undergraduate students' reflections on their experience throughout the program, as well as their interactions with the various constituencies involved in the project (i.e., teachers, other undergraduate students, graduate students, and sixth graders). We utilize videotaped recordings of undergraduate students interacting with faculty in the colloquium associated with the project, as well as recordings of undergraduate students interacting with sixth graders in the classroom. In addition, we discuss the reflections of the undergraduate students in journals they kept during the project. This in-depth analysis of both interaction and reflection complement each other, as we examine the undergraduate students' actions and interpretations of teaching and learning in the project.

An important part of our assessment of learning-as-change (through the MLVPP) from a social constructionist perspective has to do with the positions one takes up with regard to the larger narrative of social action and activism. We use "position" here in the fashion of Davies and Harré (1990), as a metaphor for discussing ways individuals are constituted and reconstituted through social interactions and discursive practices. As participants in one another's story lines, interactants, through discourse, either explicitly or implicitly make subject positions available that may (or may not) be taken up (i.e., adopted, acted into) by another person. Davies and Harré described this positioning in discursively produced story lines as similar to the ways that readers of stories are positioned in alignment with or opposition to various characters, thus opening up the possibility for multiple, even contradictory readings.

In the analysis that follows, we are interested in the positions adopted by the undergraduate students in relation to the larger narrative of social change produced through discussion (via the project) of learning about media literacy and conflict education as tools for social change. We are particularly concerned with the subject positions they adopt, as well as those they leave behind. Specifically, we wonder if they avow a teacher/subject position with all the privileges that accrue, or whether they place others (e.g., teachers, community members, the ignorant, or the powerful) in that subject position, and render themselves invisible—neither self nor other. Davies and Harré (1990) noted that even though a speaker may position another in a story line, that other may (a) understand the cultural positions at work in the discourse differently than the speaker; (b) pursue his or her own story line, unaware of the story line that was implied by the first speaker; or (c) be aware of the speaker's implicit story line but choose, instead, to resist it. How interlocutors understand the story lines in which they are embedded, then, is a critical element in establishing whether positions are taken up or not. The usefulness of the theoretical concept of positioning "is that it serves to direct our attention to a process by which certain trains of consequences, intended or unintended, are set in motion" (Davies & Harré, p. 51).

Positioning the Other in Narratives of Social Change

In the journals completed by the undergraduate students (the media literacy instructors) and the videotaped recordings of the CSL colloquia and 6th-grade classroom sessions,[10] the "other" in need of change was explicitly stated in the goals and expectations at the beginning of the semester. One undergraduate student's goals, illustrative of those expressed in the majority of the journals, were as follows: "I would like to learn how media violence affects young people. Do they act more violently after watching something violent? Are they scared by what they see? Have they become desensitized?" Another undergraduate student stated a commonly articulated goal:

> I would like to see how a few sessions with these young people can maybe alter their way of perceiving media violence, or even media and violence separately. If I can help to get even just one child thinking more critically, I will feel as though I have made a difference.

"Making a difference" seemed to be a central concern of many undergraduates participating in the program, which certainly implies a concern for social activism and change. Nonetheless, making a difference still seemed to emphasize the subject position within the change narrative; after all, the sixth graders had to comply with their position within the narrative to confirm the subject's (undergraduate students') need to "make a difference."

Although she did not alter the subject/object position within the larger narrative, one undergraduate's journal entry placed the sixth graders in the position of determining the necessity or effectiveness of action for media literacy:

> I would like to learn what action young people think we should take toward violence in the media. Should we teach people about media literacy like we are doing? Should we advocate for less violence in the media? If yes, how?

Contrasted with the journal entries, however, are the actual interactions that took place during the in-class sessions with the sixth graders. Interestingly, although the sixth graders seemed to accept the conflict frameworks we presented as possibilities for dealing with their own conflicts, they did not readily adopt their positions as learners, in general, or targets of conflict resolution education or (especially) media literacy, in particular. When, as mentioned previously, in a few instances, the undergraduate students presented information that demonstrated the negative effects of viewing violent behavior on television or especially in video games, the sixth graders often would respond that they were not affected by such violence or that they enjoyed viewing violence on television. They often stated that their younger brothers and sisters were more likely to be affected by violent content on television than were they.[11]

Thus, the object of change in the larger narrative produced through the program often was deferred to an "other." The signification of the sixth graders by the undergraduate students as the objects of change was deferred by their own interpretations of the media literacy material. The sixth graders seemed to reflect this same view, believing (at least implicitly) that by the time they reached third or fourth grade, they were sophisticated consumers of the media and, consequently, were not affected by violent content on television and in the video games they played. In this regard, the sixth graders positioned themselves as potential subjects of social action and activism through educating their younger brothers, sisters, and others they knew who were more vulnerable than themselves. This point has important implications for our approach to learning-as-change and we return to in the next section of this chapter.

Other identity positions adopted by the undergraduate student teachers, as well as by the sixth graders, reflected their dominant place in a majority White, male, middle-class society. In discussions about race and gendered representations in the media, some of the sixth graders expressed their belief that Blacks and poor people were primarily responsible for the violence perpetuated inside and outside the 6th-graders' community. One sixth grader appeared to sum up the concerns of many when he said that he would never go to Springfield, MA because he saw on the news that that was where all the Black people lived and Black people were violent. In this manner, the social geography of Blackness (and poverty, as mentioned in other conversations) was perpetuated through television news programs, as well as through the Whiteness of the sixth graders' own communities. In this manner, those seen as being in need of social change again were deferred—this time to those people who were, at least from the sixth graders' perspective, raced, classed, and gendered—rendering invisible the privilege of a White position as the agent of change.[12]

Implicated, perhaps, in the previous point, the focus on the object (the *who* of change processes) raises an important concern for communication activists, regardless of whether they are engaged in professional (e.g., research, teaching, and service) or personal activism. The undergraduate students' emphasis on the teacherly role separates and distances the (undergraduate and 6th-grade) students from themselves as the potential objects of the change process. Before the project began, the undergraduates did not position themselves as learners in the education-as-social-change narrative, and many expressed surprise from the first time they met the sixth graders and throughout the program at how deeply they were affected by their interactions with the youth and how much they learned from them. By taking on the dominant (i.e., subject) position in the narrative, the undergraduate student teachers assumed and bypassed the moral question of *who* exactly is implicated as needy, problematic, and requiring a solution in change processes. Although, from a social constructionist perspective, the undergraduate students could never construct their own subjectivities apart from the position of the sixth graders, their positioning in the context of the social action narrative allowed them considerable agency over the terms and conditions of change.

In this manner, the self as change-*able* became an important theme for activism on the part of the undergraduate students participating in the project. Reviewing the response papers and journals written as part of the project, we could see that those who were most surprised by their own changes during the course of the semester seemed the most committed at the end to continuing to work on advocacy projects. In the movement back and forth from viewing the self as teacher and as learner, these undergraduates seemed to sense the possibilities for growth with/in the community rather than through a sense of giving to the community. Indeed, this sense of possibility for collaborative work seemed to foster a stronger sense of purpose for the undergraduate students beyond this project.[13]

Another promising theme (overlapping substantially with the changeable self) that emerged throughout the taped interactions and reflection responses is that of the self as response-*able*. This idea was expressed in several ways; most notably, through the responsibility described by the undergraduates to properly represent and convey the content of the program, the increased capacity of those undergraduates to develop a repertoire of responses to sixth graders' questions about that content, and the ability to be flexible in their responses to the contexts in which the program occurred. For instance, in one elementary school where bullying incidents had recently become a problem, the conflict materials were particularly relevant to the concerns of those sixth graders (and to their teachers and guidance counselors who also sat in on the program). In responding to the bullying incidents described by the sixth graders, the undergraduate teachers decided to devote more in-class time to exploring the interpersonal dynamics of these episodes and possible conflict resolution strategies that could be used. This strategy also meant balancing and connecting the conflict dynamics and frameworks to the media literacy material in ways that might otherwise not have occurred to the undergraduate group. One of the undergraduates expressed this idea of response-ability in her comment:

> I felt like we learned together, which was so key in making this experience so impacting. Part of learning is knowing how to think critically, which seems so self-evident, but yet is something that we overlook because we think it is that simple. I was thrilled we started out with this concept and followed into the topic of conflict, which then led perfectly into media violence. But it was the way we all worked together to maintain the process. . . . The way everything "flowed" on all levels was very rewarding.

As we re-viewed the videotaped interactions and analyzed the journals and response papers written by our undergraduate students, we saw reflected in the discourse a general orientation to the teaching (subject) and learning (object) of social change. The positions adopted by both the undergraduates and the sixth graders can be seen as encompassing all three of the previous points discussed by Davies and Harré (1990). First, the undergraduate students positioned themselves and others in a narrative of social activism that involved educating *others* about media literacy and conflict resolution. Second, the sixth graders took up or resisted this narrative through using and acting on the vocabulary offered to them (as in their stated use of the "LTA" model when conflicts occurred) or deflecting the object position in the narrative (which, importantly, still engaged the social processes of learning and change). Third, through teaching sixth graders critical-thinking skills with regard to the media and critical-engagement skills for resolving their own and others' conflicts, our project hoped to effect social change on a variety of levels and for several constituencies. The assessment as to whether the program was successful in meeting its goals, however, is much more complicated, as we have demonstrated in this chapter.

Although they were not the primary focus of the program, we feel it is important to mention the 6th-grade teachers and the principals who also were (to varying degrees) part of the creation and ongoing process of this partnership. Our original contacts for the program in each school were the principals, and their enthusiastic responses to and degree of involvement in the program, we believe, contributed to its positive evaluation on the part of other teachers not involved with the program, parents of these sixth graders, and the local parent-teacher organization.[14] We have no direct indication, however, of the impact of principals' support on the program or, for that matter, on the other constituents potentially affected by the project. As part of our assessment process, we interviewed the 6th-grade teachers before and after the program, and their responses were uniformly positive and enthusiastic. However, the 6th-grade teachers varied widely in their levels of engagement with the project. Some teachers participated in the program by prompting their 6th-grade students to explore particular conflicts or recent events that had occurred in popular culture/media that had been topics of discussion in the classroom. Other teachers, however, chose not to participate at all, either by physically leaving the classroom when the project was taking place or (perhaps) psychologically leaving through grading papers or engaging in other work that took their attention elsewhere. In our follow-up interviews with the teachers, however, all of them considered the program to be extremely effective and useful. When pressed as to how the program was useful, some teachers discussed the critical-thinking skills their students learned from the program and how they (the teachers) made connections to other topics (e.g., in social studies or history) on which the sixth graders were asked to consider and reflect. All of the teachers mentioned bullying and discussed ways that the conflict curricula linked to other programs that tried to address social problems in the schools (e.g., drug abuse resistance education [DARE]). The teachers also were very supportive of the media literacy content in the program, and, although they varied in terms of how and how much the media were addressed in their curricula, the teachers readily concurred that more programmatic attention needed to be paid in the classroom to media systems and effects.

Finally, we should note that the evolution of the project into a partnership has created a sense of community among us (the facilitators) and the teachers and administrators with whom we work. There is a sense of expectation and responsibility as our project has become part of the curricula at these schools. As we become part of the functioning of this larger system, the consequences of the program can be measured in terms of the siblings of former participants we now see in classes, the undergraduate students who move on to work as teachers or community activists, and the parents who become advocates for more media literacy programs in the schools.

LEARNING-AS-CHANGE AND ITS IMPLICATIONS

At this point, we return to our concept of learning-as-change and raise several implications for activist media and conflict practitioners, teachers, and scholars interested in developing and implementing a social constructionist view of learning and change processes. First, Dewey's (1922) notion of "ends-in-view" implies a view of learning as punctuated moments in an ongoing process of meaning-making. For communication activists, this raises the possibility of moving beyond an understanding of learning as the acquisition of skill sets to thinking about how people co-create situations of *usefulness* for particular ideas and ways of being/doing. Thus, in the MLVPP, concepts of media literacy, conflict resolution, and social change were developed and made meaningful through their resourcefulness for interpretation *with/in* social situations. In other words, these concepts only find their use in practice, in action.

Second, building on the previous point, an approach to learning-as-change views learners' *resistance* as a necessary part of determining the usefulness of (in this case, media literacy and conflict resolution) concepts in specific social scenes. In this view, resistance becomes another way of struggling over position with regard to narratives in general (e.g., of conflict or with regard to media violence), or the meaning of a particular narrative itself. For communication activists, this means looking reflexively at our narratives and the ways we orient toward particular subject positions, as well as the ways that resistance on the part of others may be resistance to an object position that we have created in the narrative.

Third, we hope that we have shown ways in which both individual and social assessments of learning and change can complement one another and provide a check on assumptions about learning as movement, as chronological, or as acontextual. Through our use of a multimethodological approach to the design and assessment of the MLVPP, we have been able to complicate our view of the effectiveness or success of our program and work toward both celebrating our successes and making changes in the program we might otherwise not have envisioned (e.g., through assessing individual claims of change contextually). We hope that our approach to learning-as-change will prompt others involved in communication activism to explore the ways they frame change processes in their projects and how those frames construct and reflect back on their conceptualization, operationalization, and assessment of social change. Moreover, we hope that as a result of such assessment, our fellow activists will make changes in their own projects that reflect *social* and not just *individual* consequences.

CONCLUSION

As part of our pedagogical goals for the Media Literacy and Violence Prevention Program, we asked our undergraduate students to come up with goals and expectations that they had for their participation in the program. In raising the specter of a future orientation, we assumed the ontological-epistemological connections outlined early in this chapter. Through asking these students to describe their goals and expectations, we assumed the moral value of activism with regard to media literacy and conflict resolution and presumed the nature of the problem and who should be the agents of change toward its management or transformation. These assumptions marked the subjects and objects/targets of our change efforts, as well as starting and ending points for evaluation of the program's success.

Although these assumptions seem almost unavoidable in the context of providing evidence of change about intervention programs for funding institutions and research purposes, the actual processes of change are much more complex and need further analysis. Change presumes movement from some static point to some other point in time and space. Rather than being seen as the punctuation of meaning assigned to instances of communicative behavior, we tend to see action and activism as starting from somewhere—some social problem or issue that already has been defined, with matters of definition emanating from those in positions of power.

In the Media Literacy and Violence Prevention Program, change was implicated both through the learning process of the participating undergraduate students and sixth graders and the assessment of learning via pre- and post-questionnaires, response papers, journals, and videotaped recordings of the process. We have used these measures (and many others[15]) through the 6 years of this project to evaluate the success of, and make changes in, our efforts to engage students in our local communities (both undergraduates and sixth graders) in learning and to advance critical thinking about course content, as well as its application to social and community systems. Although we believe that these measures are useful, they do not challenge conventional or traditional modes of conceptualizing teaching and learning. Our goal in the project, as well as in this chapter, has been to complicate the analysis of learning and social activism through individual assessment measures by moving toward an analysis of learning as it was constructed both through interaction and reflection on the interaction that took place during the project. We were interested in the ways movement in and through the media literacy and conflict curricula were negotiated; that is, in what terms and experiences students took up, gave further expression, or left behind. As communication activism grows as an intellectual endeavor and practical commitment in academia and beyond, we need to continue to place the *act* of communication at the center of meaning-making.

NOTES

1. *Conflict resolution* is a phrase often contested due to its assumptions that conflicts can and should be resolved. Although we do not believe that all conflicts are or should be resolved, we adopted this term for the project because it was the most popular and widely understood term, among children, regarding conflict processes. Other terms, such as *conflict education* or *conflict management*, might be more appropriate for use with adults.
2. Although that project explicitly linked community service learning with social activism, it is important to note that many community service-learning projects do not address issues of social change but, rather, help existing social programs (e.g., students helping out in soup kitchens).
3. Much of the theory and research regarding media literacy falls fairly neatly into one of these two camps (Kubey, 1998). Those in the intervention-oriented, media effects-based camp begin with a view of the relationship between media exposure and effects on audiences—their thoughts, attitudes, and behaviors—and conceive of media literacy as an attempt to mitigate or mediate that relationship. From this perspective, attempts are made to shape audience members' responses to media to intervene between media exposure and media effects that are largely seen as negative in nature. Examples include teaching young children that commercials are attempts to persuade them so that they will not be misled, teaching teenagers to critique advertising messages about alcohol so that they do not develop favorable views of drinking, or teaching teenage girls to evaluate the ideal of thinness exhibited by media characters to discourage their own dissatisfaction with their bodies. Some scholars have found that such media literacy discussions can, indeed, mitigate media influence (see, e.g., Austin & Johnson, 1997; Brown, 2001; Cantor, 2000; Scharrer, in press). Interventionists typically focus media literacy instruction on young participants because they believe that children and teenagers are more susceptible to media influence than are adults

due to the limited number of real-world experiences they have at their disposal to counter media messages (Comstock & Scharrer, 1999), and because their sense of identity is in flux, which may make them vulnerable to persuasion.

The cultural studies perspective views media literacy instruction that attempts to "inoculate" against the negative effects of media exposure as ineffective and misguided, largely for two intertwined reasons (see Buckingham, 1998; Hart, 1997; Tyner, 1998). First, such endeavors devalue and deemphasize the experiences of pleasure many youth derive from their relationships with the media. This is problematic pedagogically because it can shut down discussion of what young people actually experience in their lives and, thereby, contribute to a disconnection between lived experiences and the type of knowledge or learning that is valued in schools (Sholle & Denski, 1994). Furthermore, it can result in young people's resistance to media literacy that they perceive is telling them what to do or think. This resistance could either be expressed directly or indirectly by simply telling media literacy instructors what they want to hear, but not actually buying a word of it. Second, interventions can be construed as elitist in that media educators are purporting to know what is best for youth and making potentially dogmatic judgments of "high" and "low" culture. Indeed, the notion that appreciation and enjoyment of the popular not be viewed as "base" or negative and that audiences not be seen as needing protection from what they enjoy is a central concept in cultural studies. Rather than framing media literacy as intervention, then, those operating from this perspective tend to focus on pursuits such as understanding the conventions of media-making, media production, and self-expression; global critique of media institutions and the overarching political-economic system; and discussion of various readings of media texts.

4. Based on self-descriptions reported in their journals and in class discussion, 15 students identified as White, two as African American, and three as Asian or South Asian. Ten of these students reported themselves to be first-generation college students, although their class status was never explicitly requested.

5. The 90 sixth graders were from five different classrooms in three towns in the northeast United States. The towns were chosen because of their proximity to the university, and the classrooms were chosen due to the desire of the teachers and principals to participate. Therefore, the participants constitute a nonrandom convenience sample. U.S. Census Bureau figures from 1990 indicate that the median yearly household income in the three towns was $34,591. The population of the three towns was 1.6% Black or African American, 2.9% Asian or Asian American, 2.1% Latino/Latina, and 93.4% White or Caucasian. The average age of the sixth graders was 12. Just over half (51.1%) of the students were male (48.9% female). The sixth graders were not asked to report their race or ethnicity, nor were the income levels of their households studied. Therefore, the census data for the area are the closest approximation of these characteristics.

6. The sixth graders wrote scripts based on conflicts experienced and constructed alternative nonviolent endings based on the conflict resolution and media violence discussions. They acted out these scripts and videotaped their performances and, thereby, learned video-production skills, which also are an important part of media literacy. Examples of the conflict scenes that they scripted, acted

out, and videotaped include an argument centered around a group of friends who could not agree what television program to watch and a dispute over an object that multiple parties wanted to use at the same time.

7. Teachers of media literacy have been critiqued by those from the cultural studies-based camp for teaching what and how media are bad for children without acknowledging the pleasures and experiences that media audiences bring to viewing. Informed advocates of media literacy, therefore, discuss the need for teaching that acknowledges the enjoyment people get from the media but still promotes skills that allow people to be critical of media messages and practices.

8. The idea of a punctuation of learning comes from Dewey (1922) and Bateson (1979), among others, who believe that learning, much like communication, is a continuous process. We (educators, researchers, and people in general) too often frame learning as an event, with starting and stopping points around which we can organize concepts-to-be-learned.

9. In other publications based on this project (Scharrer, 2002a, 2004; Scharrer, Cooks, & Paredes, 2002), we detailed a quantitative assessment of student learning in the MLVPP.

10. We videotaped the entire process of the project from beginning to end, from planning to implementation and follow-up. We analyzed the tapes with our undergraduate students during the weekly meetings and again for this analysis. In doing so, we were able to examine differences between ways the undergraduates represented their interactions with the children and how they unfolded via visual documentation. In this manner, we learned that change occurred somewhere *in between* our complexly located interactions and the ways that we represented them to ourselves and others.

11. An interesting aside is that we found the same phenomenon among the undergraduate students facilitating the MLVPP, who suggested that they were not affected by the violence they saw but were concerned about younger people's vulnerability to media effects. This, again, provides observational evidence of the third-person effect—the notion that individuals believe "others" to be more susceptible to media effects than themselves—that has been found in past research (see, e.g., Scharrer, 2002b).

12. It is beyond the scope of this chapter to address the place of White identity in this particular project, although it played a strong role in the identification of subject and object positions with regard to the potential activism narratives produced by both the undergraduates and the sixth graders.

13 Although the large majority of the undergraduate students who participated in this project have been seniors and follow-up with them beyond a couple of months has been difficult, the few juniors who participated that we later contacted remained interested in working as advocates after they graduated. Several have asked to be a part of the project again, and one is involved in a current, albeit different, version of the program. We are trying now to track more closely the undergraduates and sixth graders in the years subsequent to the project.

14. The principals introduced and discussed the program with other school staff in our presence at one school and at another in an all-faculty workshop we led on media literacy. We heard from other teachers who wished to be involved in the program (based on reports from those participating) and parents who called us

directly to discuss the program or who came to the Parent Teacher Organization (PTO) meetings we attended.

15. We also have conducted statistical analyses of the impact of the program on the sixth graders/community members (using control groups) and have begun to track participants after the completion of the program to discuss its usefulness in their lives. These supplemental sources of data support the basic findings presented in this chapter.

REFERENCES

Aufderheide, P. (1997). Media literacy: From a report of the National Leadership Conference on Media Literacy. In R. Kubey (Ed.), *Media literacy in the information age: Current perspectives* (pp. 79-86). New Brunswick, NJ: Transaction.

Austin, E., & Johnson, K. (1997). Effects of general and alcohol-specific media literacy training on children's decision making about alcohol. *Journal of Health Communication, 2,* 17-42.

Bateson, G. (1979). *Mind and nature: A necessary unity.* Toronto: Bantam Books.

Brown, J. A. (2001). Media literacy and critical television viewing in education. In D. G. Singer & J. L. Singer (Eds.), *Handbook of children and the media* (pp. 681-697). Thousand Oaks, CA: Sage.

Buckingham, D. (1998). Media education in the UK: Moving beyond protectionism. *Journal of Communication, 48*(1), 33-43.

Cantor, J. (2000). Media violence. *Journal of Adolescent Health, 27*(2S), 30-40.

Comstock, G., & Scharrer, E. (1999). *Television: What's on, who's watching, and what it means.* San Diego, CA: Academic Press.

Cooks, L., Scharrer, E., & Paredes, M. (2004). Rethinking learning in service learning: Toward a communication model of learning in community and classroom. *Michigan Journal of Community Service Learning, 10*(2), 44-56.

Cronen, V. (1995). Practical theory and the tasks ahead for social approaches to communication. In W. Leeds-Hurwitz (Ed.), *Social approaches to communication* (pp. 217-242). New York: Guilford Press.

Davies, B., & Harré, R. (1990). Positioning: The discursive production of selves. *Journal for the Theory of Social Behaviour, 20,* 43-63.

Dewey, J. (1922). *Human nature and conduct; an introduction to social psychology.* New York: Henry Holt.

Ediger, M. (2001). Assessing methods of teaching in the school setting. *Education, 122,* 123-128.

Hart, A. (1997). Textual pleasures and moral dilemmas: Teaching media literacy in England. In R. Kubey (Ed.), *Media literacy in the information age: Current perspectives* (pp. 199-211). New Brunswick, NJ: Transaction.

Hobbs, R. (1998). The seven great debates in the media literacy movement. *Journal of Communication, 48*(1), 16-32.

Hymes, D. (1972). Models of the interaction of language and social life. In J. J. Gumperz & D. Hymes (Eds.), *Directions in sociolinguistics: The ethnography of communication* (pp. 35-71). New York: Holt, Rinehart and Winston.

Kubey, R. (1998). Obstacles to the development of media education in the U.S. *Journal of Communication, 48*(1), 58-69.

Kubey, R., & Baker, F. (1999). *State by state standards for media literacy* [Table]. Retrieved April 14, 2004, from www.med.sc.edu:1081/statelit.htm

Loo, R., & Thorpe, K. (1999). Psychometric investigation of scores on the Watson-Glaser critical thinking appraisal new forms. *Educational and Psychological Measurement, 59,* 995-1003.

Potter, W. J. (1999). *On media violence.* Thousand Oaks, CA: Sage.

Roberts, D. F., & Foehr, U. G. (with Rideout, V. J., & Brodie, M.). (2003). *Kids and media in America: Patterns of use at the millennium.* New York: Cambridge University Press.

Ruminiski, H. J., & Hanks, W. E. (1995). Critical thinking lacks definition and uniform evaluation criteria. *Journalism & Mass Communication Educator, 50*(3), 4-12.

Scharrer, E. (2002a, May). *Sixth graders take on television: Media literacy and critical attitudes about television violence.* Paper presented at the meeting of the International Communication Association, Washington, DC.

Scharrer, E. (2002b). Third-person perception and television violence: The role of out-group stereotyping in perceptions of susceptibility to effects. *Communication Research, 29,* 681-704.

Scharrer, E. (2004, August). *"I noticed more violence": The effects of a media literacy program on knowledge and attitudes about media violence.* Paper presented at the meeting of the Association for Education in Journalism and Mass Communication, Toronto, Canada.

Scharrer, E. (in press). Closer than you think: Bridging the gap between media effects and cultural studies in media education theory and practice. In A. Nowak, S. Abel, & K. Ross (Eds.), *Media education as pedagogy: Essays on identity and critical thinking.* Cresskill, NJ: Hampton Press.

Scharrer, E., Cooks, L., & Paredes, M.C. (2002, October). *Measuring learning in community service learning: A research project.* Paper presented at the Service Learning Research Conference, Nashville, TN.

Sholle, D., & Denski, S. (1994). *Media education and the (re)production of culture.* Westport, CT: Bergin & Garvey.

Shotter, J., & Gergen, K. (1994). Social construction: Knowledge, self, others, and continuing the conversation. In S. A. Deetz (Ed.), *Communication yearbook* (Vol. 17, pp. 1-54). Thousand Oaks, CA: Sage.

Silverblatt, A. (1995). *Media literacy: Keys to interpreting media messages.* Westport, CT: Praeger.

Singer, D. G., & Singer, J. L. (1998). Developing critical viewing skills and media literacy in children. *Annals of the American Academy of Political and Social Science, 557,* 164-180.

Smith, S. L., Wilson, B. J., Kunkel, D., Linz, D., Potter, W. J., Colvin, C. M. et al. (1998). *National television violence study* (Vol. 3). Thousand Oaks, CA: Sage.

Thoman, E. (1999). Media literacy education can address the problem of media violence. In W. Dudley (Ed.), *Media violence: Opposing viewpoints* (pp. 131-136). San Diego, CA: Greenhaven Press.

Tyner, K. (1998). *Literacy in a digital world: Teaching and learning in the age of information.* Mahwah, NJ: Erlbaum.

United States Census Bureau. (1990). *1990 Census population, demographic, and housing information.* Retrieved September 21, 2004, from http://quickfacts.census.gov/qfd/states/25000lk.html

Watson, G., & Glaser, E. M. (1994). *Watson-Glaser critical thinking appraisal manual.* San Antonio, TX: Psychological Corporation.

Wilmot, W., & Hocker, J. L. (2001). *Interpersonal conflict* (6th ed.). Boston: McGraw-Hill.

Wright, I. (2002). Challenging students with the tools of critical thinking. *Social Studies, 93,* 257-261.

Zettl, H. (1998). Contextual media aesthetics as the basis for media literacy. *Journal of Communication, 48*(1), 81-95.

4

ACADEMIA MEETS LGBT ACTIVISM

The Challenges Incurred in Utilizing Multimethodological Research

Van M. Cagle

The Gay & Lesbian Alliance Against Defamation (GLAAD) exists to promote fair, accurate, and inclusive representation of lesbian, gay, bisexual, and transgender (LGBT) people and events in news and entertainment media. Whereas prominent LGBT organizations, such as the Human Rights Campaign (HRC) and the National Gay and Lesbian Task Force (NGLTF), advance civil rights for LGBT people through lobbying elected officials and public education campaigns, GLAAD focuses all of its efforts on lobbying the media in an attempt to guarantee balanced coverage of LGBT issues. For example, during the past 5 years, as antigay hate crimes increasingly have been spotlighted in the media, due to the murder of Matthew Shepard in

1996, GLAAD has conducted workshops with journalists who cover hate crimes to insure that respectful treatment is given to victims. More recently, in 2003, GLAAD challenged broadcast media to give equal time to gay spokespersons when discussing the historic *Lawrence and Garner v. Texas* (2003) case.[1] Likewise, in 2003, GLAAD conducted successful meetings with over 200 national and regional newspaper editors who had refused to print same-sex commitment ceremony announcements, but who changed their policies after those meetings. During the past few years, on the entertainment front, GLAAD has been especially proactive in serving as a source of information for television and film scriptwriters who are developing LGBT characters and storylines.

Although seemingly ironic, GLAAD actually maintains that it is not a "political organization" per se because it has never formally endorsed any political candidates, party issues, or legislative bills. This somewhat plebian view of "politics" is a bit more sophisticated than one might imagine, however, in that the organization often finds that the media are more willing to look to GLAAD as a resource and respect its opinions if a position of "relative neutrality" is maintained in regard to political issues with strong partisan overtones. For example, in 2003, GLAAD succeeded in pressuring MSNBC to remove ultraconservative talk-show host Michael Savage from the air, not because GLAAD was perceived as having a left-wing agenda that stood in stark contrast to Savage's extreme right-wing politics but because GLAAD staff members focused specifically on factual inaccuracies in Savage's claims about gay men and lesbians.

This type of organizational tactic harkens back to GLAAD's early days. Formed in New York in 1985, GLAAD began as a small media-watchdog group that succeeded in correcting newspaper stories that were presenting erroneous and sensational information about people with AIDS. As GLAAD's work evolved during the 1990s, it developed into a national organization with a full-time staff that took on the job of monitoring national and regional U.S. news media on a daily basis to identify content that defames LGBT people, as well as those stories that ignore the importance of LGBT perspectives. During the past 14 years, GLAAD also has engaged in entertainment media outreach by advising directors, writers, and producers about methods for presenting nonstereotypic LGBT characters and themes. More recently, GLAAD's Regional Media Program has grown to serve local communities and media outlets across the country through monitor-and-mobilize campaigns, training sessions for media personnel, and on-the-ground community and media support.

In 1999, GLAAD implemented an organizational strategy to conduct academic research that analyzed the social and cultural significance of LGBT representations in media through the institution of a Research & Analysis Program. During Spring 2000, GLAAD conducted a nationwide search for an academic staff person to head the program. Because I hold a doctorate in communication from the University of Illinois at Urbana, with emphases in cultural studies, media studies, and media research methods, and because I also had experience as an assistant professor of media at Tulane University and as a researcher in developmental studies at the University of Illinois at Urbana, I applied for and was offered the position as GLAAD's first director of research and analysis.

On arriving at GLAAD in August 2000, I formally launched the Center for the Study of Media & Society (CSMS), a research think tank whose charge is to promote intersections between the worlds of media scholarship and GLAAD's media activism. Since the inception of the CSMS, my primary goal has been to commission, and subsequently supervise, research that offers GLAAD "hands-on" findings that can be used internally and in discussions with media professionals. At the same time, because I believe that the CSMS should strive to advance LGBT media studies beyond GLAAD, commissioned research projects are organized to serve a variety of academic audiences, including university- and college-based scholars, graduate and undergraduate students, and independent researchers. Because GLAAD-sponsored research serves academia, as well as activism, all commissioned papers, research initiatives, and internal reports, thus, are designed to be conceptually sophisticated, yet practical and concrete.

This chapter is an account of my experiences as director of research and analysis at the CSMS from my arrival on August 14, 2000 through the date of my departure on April 30, 2004. Because GLAAD's work, as described in this chapter, remains contemporaneous, and because CSMS research is still available at http://www.glaad.org/programs, I made the decision to employ present tense in the chapter, when appropriate, and when describing GLAAD's interaction with scholarly researchers.[2]

In this chapter, I present the most common problems that I encountered when attempting to commission "practical research" that fosters connections between academia and media activism. In so doing, I explain some of the principal start-up techniques that I employed during my first year at GLAAD, when the organization was in the process of adjusting to the CSMS as a new department and program. In the process, I discuss challenges I have experienced within an organization that is not overly familiar with the particularities of academic research, especially its reliance on theoretical terminology and specialized languages, as well as the more-measured pace at which such research generally moves in comparison to media activism. In the second half of the chapter, I identify four general tensions that one might experience when aspiring to build connections between the world of scholarship and the world of LGBT activism. Although my focus is on a particular type of media activism, my intention is to educate as wide a readership as possible so that the lessons that I have learned may be applied to a variety of contexts in which academicians and activists work together in an attempt to bring about social change.

THE ISSUE OF PRACTICALITY: WHAT KIND OF WORLD DOES GLAAD LIVE IN?

Although a majority of GLAAD's activists have undergraduate college degrees, most are trained in so-called "practical" fields, such as journalism, business, graphic design, media production, computer science, and public relations. Moreover, because of the nature of their work, GLAAD activists describe themselves as "media technicians" and not "academicians." For these reasons, those who wish to engage in activist-driven media research must do so through developing a respect for and understanding of the background knowledge, as well as the day-to-day practices, that permeate the world of media activism.

On a daily basis, GLAAD's news activists engage in what they commonly refer to as "sexual orientation training 101." In many cases, they interact with newspaper and television journalists who are either unfamiliar with or not convinced of the reasons why certain terms or descriptions and particular types of written and visual portrayals may be perceived as offensive to LGBT individuals and groups. Consequently, news activists must employ a number of journalistic skills when educating media professionals about issues relating to defamation; awareness is raised through messages from activists that are instructive, convincing, and compelling, yet succinct. Journalists value brevity, which means that activists must be able to quickly pinpoint the problems or issues at hand and offer concise, credible information.

Along related lines, on-air discussions with news broadcasters are framed by rapidity, as well as by the types of spokespersons who are frequently utilized. Programs such as *The O'Reilly Factor* and *Crossfire* (which feature GLAAD activists roughly 5-10 times per year, depending on the issues at hand) rarely allow for more than 3-6 minutes of total speaking time per interviewee. When appearing on these and other talk-show programs, GLAAD activists are not only explaining concepts such as "defamation" of LGBT people and groups (e.g., social/cultural "stigmas" and stereotypes) and offering proactive methods for including LGBT perspectives in news stories and entertainment media, they almost always are attempting to counter the opinions of extreme right-wing organizations. Indeed, in an effort to achieve "balance," news programmers regularly pair LGBT activists with spokespersons from fringe-right groups, with the result that activists are forced into the position of having to present some rather simplistic and obvious claims, ones that may seem redundant to some queer audience members. For example, in debates about same-sex civil unions, opponents often frame the issue around essentialist terms, such as "gay lifestyle," which avoid the particular topic at hand by assuming that gayness can, indeed, be reduced to one and only one, "lifestyle." (To consider the absurdity of such a claim, consider the polar opposite: "straight lifestyle.") In such cases, activists must spend time rehearsing what have become tired arguments that there is no "gay lifestyle"; gay people are diverse, coming from all social classes, races, and economic backgrounds, and, hence, there is no identificatory "way of being" that effectively "summarizes" one's sexual orientation.

Although news activists are limited by time and format restrictions, GLAAD's entertainment media activists also face particular constraints when conducting their work. When entertainment media activists engage in outreach efforts, they are assisting with programming that is designed to reach what the media industry refers to as the "mushy mainstream." Even a cursory glance at the content of blockbuster films, prime-time television, and daytime dramas reveals that a majority of writers and producers are not risk-takers. Understanding the limitations posed by conventional media, but also realizing their innovative potential, GLAAD's entertainment activists advise writers and producers about appropriate language and "fair representation" and also serve as a resource for the development of queer characters and storylines. Here, again, because of the hurried pace of production schedules, conciseness on the part of activists is a key strategy in conducting meetings with media professionals. In presentations to media executives, PowerPoint outlines and media-style sound bites play a central role in creating effective messages that accomplish GLAAD's goals.

Because GLAAD's media activists must organize their work in accordance with journalistic logics and practices, the type of academic research that the organization seeks is that which offers quantitative data and/or qualitative findings that will be easily (and quickly) translatable during discussions with media professionals. At the same time, all CSMS projects must serve a programmatic academic mission by illuminating contemporary issues in queer media studies; indeed, the research center is not designed to be a functional number-crunching arm that simply churns out data. Although LGBT researchers who work with LGBT organizations might prefer that activism and academia coexist in a complementary relationship, there is a certain reality that also must be addressed in that academic editors and journal review boards do not always value the types of policy-oriented components that GLAAD requires of its commissioned researchers, and the types of intellectual analyses that support the CSMS's academic goals are not always aligned with the exact needs of GLAAD. In addressing these concerns, in my role as director of research and analysis, I develop guidelines for commissioned researchers that attempt to balance their scholarly needs, such as conducting publishable studies, with the activism needs of GLAAD.

ACADEMIA MEETS ACTIVISM: DEVELOPMENT AND CHALLENGES

Early Organization of the CSMS

The introduction of the CSMS to GLAAD in August 2000 posed new internal challenges for an organization that largely was unaccustomed to utilizing academic research and insights. The foundational method for building alliances between LGBT activism and academia was to form a National Research Advisory Board (NRAB), which consists of 24 LGBT researchers who are among the most-respected scholars in their fields. Larry Gross and Catherine Stimpson serve as the co-chairs, and the board consists of Kevin Barnhurst, Fred Fejes, Joshua Gamson, Lisa Henderson, Meg Moritz, Charles Nero, Ken Sherrill, Arlene Stein, and Suzanna Walters, to name a few.

Because a majority of the NRAB members have long had strong ties to gay and lesbian activism, and because most are seasoned scholars with experience in conducting and publishing research, during the formative stages of the program, I relied on the NRAB to assist with a number of start-up tasks, such as writing effective contracts, developing copyright policies, and locating researchers for projects. Such procedures, although seemingly mundane, actually required a great deal of problem solving. For example, in taking into account the contemporaneous nature of GLAAD's work with media practitioners, we had to develop a turnaround policy for research that is more stringent than that of most academic research centers. We also had to create contractual agreements that would allow researchers full copyright ownership of their work, but also permit GLAAD, the funding source, to cite sections of those reports at the organization's discretion. Correspondingly, we had to address the concerns of those scholars who feared that by allowing the CSMS to post their reports on the organization's web site, future scholarly publication efforts might be hindered. Policy development in all areas, therefore, necessitated that we collectively address a number of important dilemmas, many of which had no clear-cut precedents or answers.

As the research program has developed, the NRAB has continued to serve many important functions. Members read proposals and provide evaluative comments, act as a support network by providing me with useful advice, and assist in promoting the Center's work. Although most academic think tanks have advisory boards, GLAAD's NRAB is not a board "in name only." Members are enthusiastic and dedicated. Because the contributions of original members have played a crucial role in the institutionalization of the CSMS, all prospective members are required to pledge a 2-year commitment that honors a series of expectations regarding *active* service.

Although advisory board members remain important to the Center's work, they are not directly involved in GLAAD's internal operations. At an internal level, projects are developed through the reciprocal efforts of me, as director, and GLAAD's Communications Team, which consists of 16 media activists. During several scheduled meetings per year, team members submit requests for projects that they believe will assist in supporting and solidifying their day-to-day work. In turn, I attempt to weigh their requests against the realities of research costs and calculate the probability of commissioning the specific types of projects they are soliciting. Although the Communications Team and I typically agree on topic areas to pursue, complications arise if proposed topics are underresearched in the field of media studies or if I view requests as impractical, academically unsound, or not feasible due to budgetary constraints. (Although the budget for research initiatives and commissioned papers increased over time, the total budget, excluding salaries, decreased. The total operating budget, excluding salaries, was typically modest, with $150,000 allotted for the CSMS in 2001 and approximately $75,000 in 2003.)

For example, in complex research-related discussions, especially during times when activists are collectively concentrating their efforts on current issues about which they have much emotional investment, such as media coverage of hate crimes or "antigay" commentary in broadcast news, research-related meetings may take on a contentious tone. To offer one illustration, during my first year at GLAAD, when a great deal of energy was being directed toward raising public awareness of rap singer Emenim's "homophobic" messages on *The Marshall Mathers LP*, I frequently received requests from Communications Team members to commission studies that would determine that antigay actions among adolescents are directly linked to antigay song lyrics. Although such requests might be slighted by a majority of academic media researchers in that the "hypodermic needle" model of media (see McQuail, 1994) has long been considered obsolete (cf. Grossberg, Wartella, & Whitney, 1998), those activists who called for this project claimed that such a study would provide them with much-needed support for arguments they were making about Emenim's lyrics. During the process of offering explanations regarding the improbability of commissioning this particular type of research, ensuing discussions revealed that heightened emotional investment in an issue can result in disharmonious meetings at which activists inadvertently are situated in opposition to the world of scholarly research, even though the Communications Team and I have common goals. In particular, my explanations regarding the unlikelihood of being able to segregate those adolescents who have committed antigay acts, as well as my discussions regarding the dangers of oversimplifying causal relationships between media violence and people's violent behavior, were taken to mean that I did not support the organization's stand on Emenim's "homophobic lyrics." Indeed, during one of the most-heated debates, I was asked to become "more of an activist and less of a scholar." After attempting to reach common ground on a number of occasions and not succeeding, I decided that large group meetings, at which I was obviously outnumbered, did not offer the best context for beginning negotiations about research with the Communications Team.

In giving consideration to a number of possible options, I developed a method that has succeeded in procuring more convivial discussions of hot-button topics. Specifically, 2 weeks prior to all meetings, I send a form to members of the Communications Team that requests a list of projects that will directly support their work during the upcoming 8 months. Team members also identify the research methods they prefer for each project, and they offer explanations regarding the ways in which topics might promote organizational goals. Once the form is submitted, I have the opportunity to address submissions on an individual basis—in person, by telephone, or through e-mail. By the time that large group meetings occur, we typically have reached common ground and are able to have thought-provoking discussions that lend themselves to the refinement of project requests. The process also has advanced the overall goals of the research division at GLAAD by educating activists about media research methods and the ways in which media scholarship can drive proactive agendas within the organization. In addition, the personal approach to working with individual members of the Communications Team has raised awareness of my role in the organization and furthered my understanding of the activists' work as well.

Styles of Communication

Although the use of forms has resulted in more effective interactions with media activists, during my first year at GLAAD and continuing to the present, I have had to repeatedly address an issue regarding variance in styles of communication; in particular, the tendency of activists to demand that intellectual ideas be described in concrete, accessible language. To clarify, at the time that I took the directorship position, I frequently wrote (and spoke) in a manner that was customary to teaching and writing in the area of cultural studies, as I was informed that I was hired to be an "expert" who should strive to exude professorial expertise in accordance with my academic background. One rather frustrating outcome was that after I had been at GLAAD for several months, colleagues recommended to me that during meetings and in written reports I needed to simplify the academic language I used and, in particular, make theoretical concepts less idiomatic. To be more specific, the request came after what I now see as a quite humorous interaction in which, during the course of a 5-minute conference call, it was requested that I explain "Gramsci's concept of hegemony" (Gramsci, 1992) and the key points of "Foucauldian genealogy" (Foucault, 1984). Although I was referencing a submitted proposal and certainly did not employ the "language of cultural studies" in everyday conversations, I later came to realize that I often took on an "academic tone" in my formal writing and speech. I also began to see that because the activist world moves at a more frantic day-to-day pace than the world of research and academia (in general), a certain amount of clarity is expected; accordingly, an "easy style" is equated with "effectiveness" (Warner, 2002, p. 141).[3]

As I have already suggested, journalistic vernacular is the mainstay of media activism largely due to the rapid nature of the work being conducted and because of the need to influence the media using language that they understand. Conversely, because I was so acclimated to academic life, I placed strong value on theoretical terminology, intricate details, and the claim-evidence method of argumentation. Given that the requests to subdue academic style were extended to cover all contexts in which I communicated with activists, I was, consequently, required to rethink language use throughout all of my daily activities. Even the manner in which I composed e-mails had to be revised, as I was accustomed to academic listservs and university discussion groups, where scholars are rarely chastised for "length" or "complexity" per se. In attempting to adjust to a largely unfamiliar style, the process became quite tedious as, for example, it was mandated that in describing research projects, I avoid even the slightest hint of scholarly language and include only one to two sound bites, no matter the type of information I was sharing. Along related lines, I also was asked to revise all CSMS web pages in accordance with traditional journalistic standards. For example, in one case, I was asked to delete the term *heteronormativity* from the description of a research project, due to a concern that it might be perceived in a "negative manner" among readers who are unfamiliar with academic language. When I stated that the primary audience for the CSMS's web page is a scholarly one, and that the term has more positive connotations than a term such as *homophobia*, the request was still issued, as it was assumed that my word choice might result in misunderstanding among readers who are unacquainted with cultural studies and queer theory.

Although I was willing to make these changes and certainly was understanding of the diverse needs of a broad array of internal and external audiences, I noticed a particular discrepancy between the ways in which cultural studies scholars and media activists view language. To reach a popular audience, LGBT media activists strive to produce what they distinguish as "neutral writing," a style that attempts to use an "apolitical" tone to reach a wide readership, whereas most scholars whose work derives from contemporary cultural studies view all language as political and, therefore, they attempt to challenge readers. Even when writing for "mass publics," the language of cultural studies attempts to contest the structures of journalistic normalcy because those structures are seen as suggestive of the misguided notion that "good writing" is only achieved through imagining the numerical extensiveness of a reading audience. The language of cultural studies *requires* rigorous definitions; it is intentionally contentious and there are no positions that are "unbiased."

Because I strongly subscribe to this point of view, I initially took issue with the requirements that were being imposed on my writing and speech and questioned the need for academic insights to always be reduced to a few snappy sound bites. I argued, as Warner (2002, p. 141) did, that it is a mistake to always equate "accessible prose" with "good writing," especially if the author is presenting complex ideas; as such, I interpreted criticisms about my style as an attack against my academic profession and grounding. At the same time, although I continue to maintain this position to varying degrees, depending on the issue at hand, I also have come to realize that unless communication abides by certain normative rules within activist-oriented contexts, documents go unread and discussions go "unheard"; for these reasons, I adapted to the standards that characterize media activism. Hence, the lesson to be learned for scholars is that anti-intellectualism among activists is not always linked to resentment of academia, although, as I discuss later, competition between academics and activists is common in certain contexts. As becomes more apparent in other sections of this chapter, in situations in which scholars and activists interact, it is necessary for scholars to produce writing and speech that can be understood by a wide variety of publics including, most importantly, activists, who are, in a sense, "lay readers." In this regard, when communicating with media activists, intellectuals must employ methods that make ideas fungible, translatable, repeatable, summarizable, and restatable (Warner, 2002).

The Process of Research Management: Locating Appropriate Scholars

Once the Communications Team and I decide on potential projects, I proceed by reviewing the research that has been conducted in the topic areas that we wish to investigate. As this process occurs, I attempt to determine if the topics under consideration have received any analysis by any scholar, and if one or more studies are located, I then compose a literature review that allows team members to determine if their research requests need modification or refinement. I also rely on published studies to serve as a "referral mechanism"—a particularly intriguing essay may lead me to a prospective applicant, or I may seek the author's assistance in locating a researcher who might be appropriate for a project.

Although this process of surveying research may seem obvious, the biggest challenge faced along these lines is that, in many cases, the type of "hands-on" LGBT media research that GLAAD desires has few direct precedents and, hence, I must look to broad areas of study to find relevant information. For example, in March 2002, GLAAD requested a project to assess LGBT representations in Spanish-language print and television news media in the United States. At the end of several weeks of intensive research, I concluded that no prior studies had been conducted in this area, and subsequently engaged in a 2-month process of searching for an appropriate scholar by contacting a wide range of Spanish-language specialists, until I located a researcher whose expertise fit GLAAD's needs. Although there is no necessary correlation between a successful CSMS project and high-caliber research that already has addressed a specific activist-oriented issue or problem, my point is that, in many cases, the types of policy-directed studies that GLAAD requests are not always readily commissionable due to underrepresentation in the field of media studies and LGBT studies.

For all of these reasons, if prominent scholars cannot be located, I must issue national calls for research in newsletters and on academic e-mail listservs. This typically results in receiving 50-200 proposals, some of which are not always related to the project guidelines but, rather, are attempts to persuade the CSMS that funding is deserved nonetheless. For example, after posting a call in a number of national newsletters for a project on youth web sites, I received 52 applications, yet only one was specific to the area that GLAAD wished to fund. I then researched the applicant's published reports, discovered that his research was particularly impressive, and, after several conversations, we agreed on an outstanding project that analyzed commercial and noncommercial, youth-oriented, queer web sites and how today's queer youth wish to be represented on the web (Alexander, 2003).

Negotiations and Contracts

Once a researcher for a particular project is located, it is standard for her or him and GLAAD to engage in 2-3 months of dialogue and negotiations before agreeing on the parameters of a commissioned study. In many cases, during the time that GLAAD is seriously evaluating an application, the organization typically requests "more than" a scholar has proposed to accomplish, or the Communications Team members may request specific technical revisions to a proposal. As this process transpires, I act as a liaison in an attempt to arrive at contractual terms that are agreeable to all parties. Because scholars are receiving sizable funding for projects, at least in GLAAD's eyes (in 2003, $8,000-$10,000 for research initiatives, $1,500-$3,000 for commissioned papers), commissioned researchers usually are willing to include components that GLAAD requests; at the same time, few of them wish these components to go unused in their publications. Indeed, many scholars engage in negotiations with GLAAD to develop projects that are not solely designed to give "hands-on" data to activists. In other words, GLAAD typically requests quantitative data with only 1-2-sentence explanations per statistic, if that much. Prominent media studies journals, however, typically do not publish essays that contain unadorned content analyses, statistics that are not grounded in theoretical elaboration, or five key sound bites that can be pitched to the media. Keeping these issues in mind, I attempt, whenever possible, to alleviate scholars' concerns by working with applicants to create research designs that will successfully intermesh both academic and activist goals.

To offer one example, when conducting preliminary research for a potential study on representation of sexual orientation in popular video games, I determined that a majority of analyses in this area had examined gender, class, and race (e.g., Kinder, 1991; Provenzo, 1991; Sherry, 2001), but they had not analyzed queer sexuality. In addition, the most rigorous study, conducted by Children Now (2001), employed basic quantitative analysis to show variations in racial and gender representations among video games. Because GLAAD had requested a project that would analyze queer sexuality in the most-popular video game of all time, *The Sims*, the organization needed results that would allow for comparisons with findings on gender, class, and race from other studies, and because no study had yet looked at sexuality in video games, I spent 2 months assisting a selected applicant in completing the details of a project proposal. Although the scholar was trained to produce the quantitative components that GLAAD had requested, her major strengths were in cultural studies, queer theory, and qualitative research methods. She was, however, amenable to employing basic quantitative methods, and I assisted her in creating a project that would produce the statistical data that GLAAD had requested and also arranged a contract that would allow this scholar to write a compelling theory-oriented paper as well (Consalvo, 2003).

In a manner similar to that just described, I also offered assistance to a scholar (Harrington, 2001) who was proposing to study the first lesbian character of centrality in daytime soap operas (Bianca on *All My Children*). I arranged for a fan poll that assessed attitudes about the inclusion of the lesbian character to be posted on SoapCentral.com, the most widely hit web site for soap fans. Because GLAAD has many industry connections, I also was able to assist this researcher in gaining access to interviews with a number of media insiders, including Eden Reigal (the actress who plays Bianca), soap writers, and soap publicists. The outcome of these types of projects was threefold: (a) each provided GLAAD with the type of data it needed to proceed more effectively with its work with media professionals, (b) the complexity of the analysis allowed for submission of the work to scholarly journals or books, and (c) the projects allowed me to hone my skills in developing studies that employ multiple research methods.

Producing Studies and Achieving Projected Results

All GLAAD-sponsored research requires two main end products: (a) a paper that is sent to me for approval and, after final editing, is placed on GLAAD's web site; and (b) a topline summary that provides GLAAD's activists with the key points from the paper. The online paper is intended to serve academic audiences, and because the CSMS aspires to reach as many scholarly readers as possible, including graduate and undergraduate students, authors must attempt ("in good faith") to compose documents that are understandable to readers outside their field(s). This means that terms that are specific to a particular field or research area must be clarified, and any theories employed must receive more "basic" explanations than those that might be found in scholarly articles and books intended to reach specialized readers. To achieve the type of interdisciplinary symmetry preferred by the CSMS, final composition requires that authors maintain the intellectual integrity of the paper but also compose it so that it may be used as a teaching tool in graduate and undergraduate courses in media, cultural studies, gender studies, and LGBT studies.

On completion of the paper, I assist the researcher in composing a topline summary, which presents the main points of the study and proposes ways in which GLAAD might use the findings. Because I am an employee of GLAAD, scholars depend on me to sift through their study and assist them in translating research results into policy recommendations for GLAAD. Composing the topline summary usually is the most difficult part of the writing process, as GLAAD requires that summaries be devoid of academic language, no longer than five pages, and must consist solely of bullet-point phrases. To abide by this corporate method, which is common to topline market-research summaries, the findings from a study must be framed quite differently than they are in the online report. For example, one report (Roque Ramírez, 2003) included over 73 pages of statistics and analysis, the majority of which would be of significance to GLAAD, but the information had to be condensed in such a way so as to highlight only the main statistical findings. In another case, an author (Sender, 2002) developed a lengthy, complex argument based on 40 in-depth interviews with marketing professionals, and she and I struggled to extract the intricacy of the argument in accordance with the required composition style.

What also makes the process of writing topline summaries exceedingly stressful, both for scholars and for me, is that the summary usually is the only report that is read by GLAAD's Communications Team. Unfortunately, this means that the pressure to produce a high-quality topline summary is heightened because a study's perceived "value" typically is based only on the information presented in this report. Simply put, 8-12 months of research and writing are "reduced" to a few short pages. The submission of a topline summary, thus, is laden with a certain amount of anxiety, especially because the interpretation of this final product is sometimes difficult to control once it has been sent via e-mail to all parties at the bicoastal offices of GLAAD.

To offer an example, in composing a summary of a study on college freshmen's attitudes regarding gay characters and themes in youth media, the researcher (Streitmatter, 2003) and I used the term "18-year-olds" in three key places, as opposed to the more specific term "18-year-old respondents." In other words, the author had surveyed 200 18-year-old college students, but had not conducted a random sample that allowed for inferences about a whole population of 18-year-olds. Even though the use of "18-year-olds" was a slight oversight and most definitely should have been corrected prior to the submission of the final report, by the time the summary had been read, a number of readers expressed concern that the entire study was flawed, and even the revision of the topline report did little to alleviate this concern. As I previously explained, activism moves at a fast pace, and after quickly submitting a revised version of the report, the GLAAD Media Awards were occupying the full attention of the Communications Team; thus, those who had previously critiqued the report were, in turn, occupied with more high-profile public events. Therefore, to my knowledge, the revised report never was actually read.

In another case, a multifaceted, 120-page study (Harrington, 2001) of the "Bianca" character on *All My Children* contained five components, none of which were easily explained in a topline report. After drafting the required 5-page explanation, the author and I, instead, opted for a 15-page bullet-point summary that listed the major findings and recommendations. Believing that this document would be very well received, given the findings, as well as GLAAD's advisement efforts for the soap opera, I questioned the lack of feedback on this document. In turn, I was informed that the report represented an "academic study," and that team members were "uncertain" as to how the findings were applicable to GLAAD's work. When I explained that the topline report contained poll data that were especially pertinent to GLAAD's work in entertainment media, that it supported the organization's work with ABC, that it was written in corporate style, and that it could be effectively pitched to the entertainment press, I was informed by many members of the Communications Team that the study could, indeed, be used to support claims regarding LGBT visibility in the media. However, the Entertainment Media Manager, who was in charge of external promotion of entertainment research, maintained that the report was "not worthy of attention" because the poll information was framed by a "scholarly textual analysis," which he viewed as "inappropriate" for purposes of publicity.

Understandably, both Harrington (2001) and I were pleased with GLAAD's overall assessment, yet disappointed with the evaluation offered by the Entertainment Media Manager. In turn, Harrington worked with a Miami University of Ohio news editor to compose a press release that was successfully placed in over 15 top-tier U.S. newspapers. As a result of Harrington's promotion, I also was profiled by *The Advocate*, the leading U.S. LGBT news magazine, as one of the nation's "leaders" in LGBT media research ("LGBT Innovators," 2001). Needless to say, the fact that I took matters into my own hands did not result in my work being "more accepted" at GLAAD, nor did anyone congratulate me or Harrington; instead, we were viewed as scholars who had "overstepped our boundaries" and not listened carefully to the advice of the Entertainment Media Manager. Thus, I point to this type of discordant relationship to stress the tensions that occurred between LGBT media research and GLAAD's internal staff. Many staff members were simply unwilling to promote quite excellent studies, and claims that CSMS research could not obtain press coverage were, in this case and in others, proven to be false (an issue I address in great detail in the latter section of the chapter).

In a majority of cases, however, topline reports served their internal purpose, notwithstanding the issues I have outlined. One clear-cut example occurred in October 2003, when a researcher (Grace, 2003) and I composed a topline report that was based on his study of national and regional media coverage of the bias-motivated crimes that were committed against Matthew Shepard and Billy Jack Gaither. The findings in his study were very precise: A majority of national media utilized stereotypes about the West and the South in attributing blame for the crimes, whereas regional media employed a more complex approach by avoiding regional stereotypes and including diverse perspectives of local citizens, LGBT people, students, and others. The study also demonstrated that if the victim of an antigay hate crime did not fit certain cultural preconceptions about homosexuality, press treatment reflected bias. In the media's view, Matthew Shepard's story was one of a hate-crime victim who was easily consumable, in that he was a young, attractive, out-of-the-closet college student. In contrast, Billy Jack Gaither's story was quite different, and much less consumable, because he was older, working class, overweight, in the closet, and a country music fan.

In composing the topline report that was based on this study, the author and I provided summary statistics that showed how coverage of the two cases differed, with special focus on the fact that regional media provided more fair and balanced coverage of both cases. The statistics, for example, pointed to the fact that Matthew Shepard's murder resulted in over 10,000 stories worldwide, whereas Gaither's murder resulted in only eight national news stories. More importantly, the statistics provided content analysis of the types of descriptions journalists used when writing about the two cases. This information was seen as especially important to those news activists who had advised journalists with respect to these two hate crimes because this was the first study to compare national and regional coverage of antigay hate crimes. In this case, team members not only carefully read the topline report but the study as well, and they referenced both reports when discussing antigay hate crimes with national and regional journalists.

Promotion of CSMS Studies

When GLAAD's Executive Director, the Communications Team, and I have approved the topline report and the paper, external promotion of CSMS research occurs. Three times per year, I announce studies through capsule reports in the Center's newsletter, which is mailed to 1,500 scholars and 500 university department chairpersons in the United States. With the release of each particular study, I make an announcement on various public listservs, provide a link to the online version of the document, and request that potential readers provide me with information regarding the ways in which the study is used in the classroom, community-organizing efforts, and other contexts. Over the course of a calendar year, I typically receive at least 250 letters from various individuals and groups telling me that they have used the studies CSMS produces. Students who are conducting research in LGBT media studies frequently write to thank the CSMS for providing studies in underresearched topic areas and that our work offers them much-needed information and insights. High school, college, and university instructors consistently state that GLAAD-sponsored studies have served as effective teaching tools. I also receive letters from individuals who lead coming-out seminars and gay Alcoholics Anonymous groups that share the ways in which certain studies have been used to spark discussions about issues of concern to specific populations of gay men and lesbians. In addition, I receive letters from a broad range of nonacademic readers who say that our studies have broadened their perspectives on LGBT issues.

To further advance the mission of the CSMS, I also promote three or four of the Center's projects per year through panels that I organize for yearly presentations at the conferences of the National Communication Association, International Communication Association, and U.S. Cultural Studies Association. I also encourage other LGBT organizations to make use of our research, and, in many cases, this type of bridge-building leads to alliances. For example, when a project on media coverage of the September

2002 campaign to repeal the Miami Dade Human Rights Ordinance[4] (Fejes, 2003) was completed, it not only was used by the GLAAD news team in advisement on media campaigns but also by the National Gay and Lesbian Task Force, which was studying tactics that might encourage politicians to support ballot initiatives that address LGBT civil rights. After we completed a study (Streitmatter, 2003) of young people's attitudes regarding LGBT characters and themes in popular youth television programs, I sent the study to the Gay, Lesbian, and Straight Educational Network (GLSEN), which, in turn, utilized the findings to develop focus group research that currently is being used to engage in a public awareness campaign.

Along related lines, as the CSMS developed a respectable body of work, other research centers have increasingly requested my assistance in developing appropriate methodologies for their studies. For example, I advised the Institute for Gay and Lesbian Strategic Studies (IGLSS) on research that analyzed media coverage of the Roman Catholic Church scandal, and I also advised the First Amendment Center on a project that focused on the religious right's attack on children's programming that was perceived as containing a "gay agenda." I also collaborated with the National Gay and Lesbian Task Force on an internal project that surveyed public attitudes toward "coming out." Given the multiple ways in which CSMS-sponsored research is used both as a tool for educators and students and to build connections with other research centers, it is clear that CSMS studies must have demonstrated that they have the ability to advance social change for LGBT people and groups.

FRAMING THE CHALLENGES:
THE MOST COMMON STRUGGLES FACED
IN RESEARCHER-ACTIVIST COLLABORATIONS

Although I have explained some of the challenges that reoccur as the process of scholarly-activist research management transpires, to make my experiences more generalizable, I identify here four of the most significant tensions that one might experience in contexts in which academia meets LGBT activism. The purpose of this section is to further clarify and put into perspective the role that "practical" research plays not only in the contemporary landscape of LGBT politics but also in relation to current trends in queer media studies. I conclude the section with a brief explanation of three GLAAD-sponsored studies to demonstrate ways in which the privileging of multimethodological research has managed to solve many of the dilemmas that are addressed throughout this chapter.

The Expertise of Activists Versus the Expertise of Scholars

GLAAD's activists see their work as occurring in the "trenches" of the LGBT movement, and they frequently presuppose a disconnect between their work and that of academia. Because LGBT media activists often have previous work histories in corporate media environments, media activism, in general, often maintains a competitive edge, which translates into a fear of possible outcomes, should academic insights supercede the knowledge base of activism. Among GLAAD's media activists, this tension is especially strong because activists not only work behind the scenes but they also are the "face" of the organization and they appear in the media. Media producers and broadcasters consider them to be "spokespersons for the LGBT movement" and, in many cases, rightfully so, they view themselves as "LGBT leaders." Because they have high media profiles and conduct work "in the field," they frequently have concern regarding the potential ways in which commissioned studies might be spotlighted in public spheres, leading to questions such as: What might happen should commissioned scholars produce studies that are widely recognized by media professionals? What might happen should commissioned researchers be sought by the media as primary sources? Will commissioned researchers come to represent new "media spokespersons" who compete with activists' expertise? Put simply, will scholars overtake "our" turf? These are the types of perceived outcomes that contribute to a general mistrust of academics among some media activists. It is a mistrust that is somewhat ironic in that those activists who issue calls for research projects often are the very ones who are hesitant to use and promote completed studies in their own work because of these concerns.

Among those activists who do use research, another type of tension persists: There is a strong preference for quantitative data per se (e.g., statistical tables, bar graphs, and pie charts) as opposed to quantitative studies that are accompanied by theoretical explanations and critical-oriented studies that are driven by cultural studies theories and queer theory. In many cases, activists maintain a "common-sense" understanding of academic theorizing (in general) as something that is irrelevant to "reality," as in the expression, "Well, that's a nice idea, *in theory*." Among LGBT media activists, in particular, it is axiomatic that "academic theorizing," especially that which derives from cultural studies and queer theory, is largely irrelevant, perhaps because they are rarely, if ever, asked to contemplate complex ontological and epistemological problems in their everyday work. Given these tensions, activists will readily accept a nationwide public opinion poll that claims to measure attitudes about LGBT issues, but these same activists remain largely unconvinced as to the ways in which theories of identity and representation might offer insights into the cable television show *Queer as Folk*. Simply put, LGBT media activists view themselves to be at the forefront of *practical* struggle and, to them, scholarly research, unless it consists of quantitative *data* (with no theoretical grounding), is extraneous, self-serving, and overly seductive.

That said, a common activist comment about academic research is, "Skip the theory; give us the *hard facts*"; in this case, as implied earlier, "hard facts" are considered to be *unadorned* quantitative data, usually in the form of simple cross-tabulations that contain the results of survey research, or summary charts that list the results of content analysis (again, with no interpretation of the results included). This kind of claim is related, at least in part, to the fact that the news media frequently present the public with uncomplicated snapshot polls that are easily consumable and seem to offer ready-made answers for news consumers. Along these same lines, when GLAAD made a decision in 2003 to fund research projects conducted by large-scale polling and market research firms, the assumption was that 3-4 sound bites would be delivered, rather than an in-depth topline report, accompanied by a book of data that would require at least some "translation" on the part of the organization. Here again, the assumption was that "research will produce 'uncomplicated' results," and that "400 pages of banner data will 'analyze themselves.'"

Although LGBT media activists tend to value only quantitative data (sans the theory) and denounce critical-oriented research, some prominent queer theorists have fueled the aforementioned tension in that they have condemned LGBT activism altogether because they see it as exclusionary and reductive (cf, Seidman, 1997; Warner, 1999). They view LGBT activism as subscribing to nationalist or ethnic models of identity that reject and marginalize many acts and identities of LGBT individuals. Indeed, Warner (1999) and Seidman (1997) both claimed that in an unyielding attempt to gain acceptance by mainstream heterosexual culture, contemporary LGBT activism ignores the diverse voices that make up LGBT communities. In accordance with this position, activism is perceived as acquiescing to those normative systems of power that it claims to resist. As some queer studies scholars also maintain,[5] mainstream LGBT research takes as its starting point the unification of sexual identity (i.e., the assumption that all gay people are fundamentally "similar," due to sexual orientation), and because of this, mainstream LGBT research does not account for the ways in which gender and sexuality operate as "cultural fictions"—that is, as performative effects of reiterative acts (Jagose, 1996, p. 84). In other words, as both Seidman and Warner (1999) contended, "identity" is comprised of "fragments," not "unified wholes," and, in fact, the "public 'gay lifestyle'" that so often is "denounced" by LGBT activists should, instead, be acknowledged in a more proactive, positive manner because it does represent one of the most potent and popular ways in which gay men, in particular, have "histor-ically" connected through club cultures, bars, and other public venues. A number of queer theorists have, consequently, pointed to the "hypocrisies" of the organized LGBT movement, which, according to their view, has con-sistently denounced the multiplicity of gay identities, the wide range of vari-ance in sexual desires among LGBT people, and, in particular, shunned those who do not fit within heterosexually prescribed, preordained roles of nor-malcy (Warner, 1999).

At the other end of the spectrum, scholars who do choose to engage in LGBT activist-driven research often are profoundly aware of their positions of privilege, and this can result in other types of tensions. For example, in conducting research and composing their reports for GLAAD, scholars sometimes become overly self-conscious about balancing a style that is accessible to "real-world" activists and one that is more consistent with the style of scholars in their field. Similarly, commissioned researchers some-times become concerned about whether their research findings will coincide with GLAAD's organizational stands on LGBT issues.

In addressing these issues, I try to bridge gaps between academia and activism. I stress to scholars that their research is being conducted to assist in making GLAAD's arguments more compelling and complex. I also remind scholars that GLAAD is funding them to produce benchmark studies, and that if the "applicability factor" turns out not to be high, the studies are not necessarily discredited out of hand, as I, in my role of director, recognize that CSMS studies often provide important outreach to the academic communi-ty. In turn, I remind activists that many LGBT scholars also are activists who have actively worked for LGBT civil rights throughout their careers. Hence, gay scholarship and activism have much more in common than activists cus-tomarily presume. I also reinforce the fact that the scholars with whom I have worked typically shun the media spotlight, for they often view main-stream media attention that focuses on them, and not on the research itself, as co-optation, and they have no desire to appear in the media as spokesper-sons for GLAAD. Hence, in essence, I educate scholars about better skills for communicating with activists, and I alleviate activists' concerns regarding the perceived "threat" of scholarship. At the same time, the tensions that I have described are deep-seated and there is no easy solution, with similar issues tending to reoccur with each commissioned study.

The Pace of Academic Research Versus Media Activism

The academic world, in general, is organized around ongoing contemplation of research questions, and scholarly research usually is based on long-term

goals. It is common practice to give research questions thorough consideration through reading and rereading relevant theoretical works in the field;
designing, testing, and redesigning research methods; revising manuscripts
several times prior to submission to a journal or book; and other activities.
However, the world of media activism is ordered around practices for *react-
ing* to the immediacy of current events. Each day, GLAAD's activists must
consume national and regional broadcast and print media, speak with journalists, appear on live broadcasts, write press releases that reach a wide readership, attend fundraisers, and conduct media training seminars. In many
cases, turnaround for a project, such as a press release or even a talk, from the
time of conception to the time of delivery, is 2-3 hours. Along related lines,
GLAAD's activists often scan 3-4 newspapers prior to leaving their home
each morning, and watch a considerable number of national and local news-
casts, because if a newsworthy LGBT event has occurred, one or all of them
will likely be interviewed that day by a major national or local news media
outlet. The very nature of media activism, therefore, necessitates a more
spur-of-the-moment approach than that which characterizes academia.
Because their work is oftentimes necessarily reactive as opposed to proactive
and contemplative, media activists, therefore, have to adjust to the unique-
ness of the CSMS research program, one that does not deliver immediate
answers, and where answers cannot be offered until projects are completed.

One outcome of this tension is that scholars consistently are frustrated
in that they feel pressure to accommodate an activist world that requests
"results" from ongoing projects, as if such results will serve as definitive
research findings. Likewise, because media activists place such a strong value
on "quick hits" and sound bites, researchers often complain that the complexity of their final reports typically is ignored. In particular, those scholars who are trained to value theoretical and methodological sophistication
find it problematic to work with an organization that requires that they con-
dense findings in a manner that is more reflective of market research and
newspaper writing than writing for the social sciences.[6] In many cases, there
is a sense of being caught between two activist-driven logics: the "scholarly"
mission to write within the academy about complex issues regarding power,
sexuality, and gender, and the "activist" mission to educate GLAAD
through lay language that is not always held in high esteem in the academy.

Differences in Interpretation: The Case of "Representation"

In determining the fairness and "accuracy" of media representations,
GLAAD activists often see meaning as the function of *a* gay, *a* lesbian, *a*
bisexual, or *a* transgender identity, or, in the case of defamation, as a func-

tion of the ways in which an author's *presumed* intent is *perceived* as being relative to particular (unsubstantiated, yet "theorized") "concrete" actions.[7] For example, the GLAAD Entertainment Media Director often claimed in discussions with me that if a term such as *faggot* is uttered in a popular medium, the author, as well as the text, are homophobic, and, by default, it is assumed that the author and the text are necessarily reinforcing or producing attitudes that directly coincide with homophobic *behavior*. Because a primary goal of GLAAD's media activism is to combat such defamation, this reasoning has, at times, resulted in requests by the Communications Team to commission research projects that demonstrate ways in which "antigay representations" act in a causative manner to produce antigay attitudes or actions among viewers/receivers.

Because cause-effect analyzes of media are difficult, if not impossible, to produce, especially when attempting to suggest links between complex social behaviors and single media-related explanations, such as the effects of listening to particular popular songs; and because it would be extremely difficult to isolate an audience that has watched or listened to "homophobic content" and acted on it and is willing to discuss its homophobic actions; and because it is unlikely that a researcher could segregate particular antigay actions as direct outgrowths of particular media texts, this type of behaviorist research cannot be conducted and funded. Although some media-effects researchers have suggested causal patterns, especially in studies that attempt to link exposure to media violence to aggressive behaviors (see, e.g., Green, 1994; Huesmann, Moise-Titus, Podolski, & Enron, 2003), recent trends in both uses and gratifications research and "new audience research" suggest a pluralist view of audiences as active and, consequently, media-related attitudes and behaviors are seen as being relative to personality characteristics and social and cultural situations (cf. Grossberg et al., 1998). Even though LGBT media activists at GLAAD consistently argued that "it was my job to find media-effects researchers" who would conduct linear cause-effect research for the organization, I explained that "linear models of aggression" died in the 1930s, and that although correlational studies may show relationships between media violence and aggressive behavior, none of these studies assume that media violence is the only variable related to particular forms of aggression or even particular attitudes about aggression (see, e.g., Schutte, Malouff, Post-Gorden, & Rodasta, 1988).

Despite these arguments and their substantive validation, there is obviously a strong tension between activists who request studies that show direct cause-effect patterns between media representations of violence and people's aggressive behavior(s) and those media scholars whose research employs conjunctural analysis to account for diverse interpretations of media and the interrelated conditions of historical and situational specificity. In particular, the academic-activist tension is exacerbated because conjunctural analysis always suggests *a range* of responses to media as a result of examining intertextual relations, including political economy, production, audiences, texts, and the conjoined conflictual components of any interpretative process. As Grossberg (2003) suggested, those scholars who employ conjunctural analysis never say, "*This* is what is going on," but *rather*, "*This* is going on, *and* this, *and* this, *and* this, *and* this, and so on." Given that these are the dominant tenants of conjunctural analysis, researchers who utilize this theoretical/methodological framework would not be surprised to find a *variety* of responses to Eminem's "antigay lyrics," for instance, and would even expect that some self-identified gay young people are not only fans of his music but that they also may hear liberating messages in the songs that activists deem as "homophobic."[8]

Along somewhat related lines, a tension also arises due to the dominant trend in queer-oriented media studies to analyze mainstream audience reception of queer characters and themes in entertainment media (Palmer-Meta & Hay, 2002; Streitmatter, 2003). Ironically, although media activists frequently speak publicly about the increasing acceptance of LGBT characters and themes in popular culture, these same activists typically are unimpressed by research that substantiates such claims because their common assumption is that the recent proliferation of media representations of queer people, especially in entertainment media (such as reality television and situation comedies), as well as the rise in the number of queer characters and themes in pay-for-view cable programs and mainstream films, demonstrates that a majority of viewers do, in fact, accept queer characters and storylines. In other words, an increase in visibility often is equated, quite simply (and sometimes, simplistically), with "progress."[9] For this reason, activists request data that suggest that defamation has lived consequences. In those cases in which researchers discuss the *contradictions* posed by representations that media activists have defined as either progressive or defamatory, or when researchers discuss a range of ways in which audiences may interpret media, convincing rationales are required because such research challenges firmly held convictions of LGBT activists who perceive that the media operate in a causal manner to produce specific behaviors and attitudes.

Queer Theory Versus Identity Politics

The purpose of addressing identity politics in relation to queer theory is not to construct an argument that favors one over the other but, instead, to recognize that because queer theory has made a substantial impact on gay and lesbian studies over the past 13 years, it is important to briefly discuss ways it can affect the work of an academic research center that is located within an organization that subscribes to a fairly rigid model of identity politics. At the onset of this description, it is worth noting that although the CSMS has commissioned research that employs queer theories, I generally receive either no responses or unenthusiastic responses when contacting queer theorists in communication and sociology to determine if they would be interested in conducting research for GLAAD or to invite them to join the NRAB. Because tensions exist between LGBT activists and queer theorists—mainly because LGBT activists typically subscribe to a fixed model of identity politics that assumes the necessity of a gay/straight binary, whereas queer theorists contest the usefulness of that binary—I address here some of the central arguments that queer theorists have made or might make when analyzing models of LGBT identity politics. I then explain particular ways in which queer theoretical scholarship can work to advance the goals of LGBT activism, with a focus on LGBT media research centers.

The traditional model of identity politics assumes that LGBT people are in many ways "different" from heterosexuals because they are a minority group that has experienced oppression by the majority group. Along related lines, the model takes as a starting point the assumption that lesbian and gay identities are "real" and "stable" (Kopelson, 2002, p. 180); accordingly, there are particular common bonds among minority members, and, hence, they are seen as a community of individuals that is cohesive (as exemplified by the common use of the term "gay community" among LGBT activists, and LGBT media activists, in particular). To advance social and cultural progress, LGBT media activists who subscribe to this model see LGBT visibility as a primary goal.

Because LGBT media activists focus on mainstream media's representations of LGBT people and events, they often are criticized by queer theorists for attempting to legitimate homosexuality through assimilation into heterosexual culture. Queer theorists argue that traditional gay identity politics name a unified gay identity that does not recognize the diverse range of queer *sexual* identities but, instead, argue for certification by a heterosexual world—based on the logic that a gay sexual orientation is a *fundamental identity formation* that is or has the potential of becoming *as normative* as one that is heterosexual. Along these lines, as some queer theorists (cf. Highleyman, 1995; Jagose, 1996; Kopelson, 2002; Savoy, 1994) maintain, the rigidity of this view leads to the reinforcement of boundaries between homosexual/heterosexual categories, especially because gay activists often exclude those who are seen as "not gay enough" and those who are seen as "not straight enough." In addition, queer theorists contend that although LGBT activism claims to speak for all (or most) LGBT people and groups, activists actually view some identities as "authentic" (the "good, upstanding 'straight-acting' gays") and others as "inauthentic" (those LGBT people who are likely to be rejected by mainstream culture, based on looks or demeanor, such as "masculine-acting" lesbians or "effeminate-acting" gay men) (cf. Warner, 1999). Similarly, as Warner (1999) argued, the LGBT movement actively works to desexualize gayness—to stress through public declarations that being gay has little to do with sex but everything to do with being a respectable citizen. In a similar manner, some queer theorists maintain that the "normative" model that LGBT activists usually aspire to is actually a "heterosexual, White male model" that serves as a cultural yardstick, one that, in accordance with this view, should only hold relevance for the *performance* of diverse queer identities, not as a *barometer* for the production of "acceptable" queer identities (see Warner, 1999). According to this argument, instead of trying to make sexual and gender minorities more "straight," non-normative sexual cultures should aim to make the mainstream "more queer" (Highleyman, 1995; Warner, 1999). For example, Warner (1999) suggested that "against assimilation, one could insist that dominant culture assimilate to queer culture, not the other way around. Straight culture has already learned much from queers and it shouldn't stop now" (p. 74). Along related lines, Warner (1999) also contended that among those in the gay and lesbian movement:

> Sex and sexuality are seen as "irrelevant" in an attempt to fight stigma. . . . As soon as a [gay and lesbian] movement was organized, embarrassment became a permanent condition of its politics. . . . Drawing the curtain over the sexual culture without which it could not exist, it speaks whatever language of respectability it thinks will translate. (pp. 46-49)

In a manner that addresses this very issue, Joan Garry (2003), GLAAD's Executive Director, maintained:

> I get uncomfortable talking about sex. As a good Irish-Catholic girl, public discussions of that most private of associations bring out the prude in me. When my school-age kids bring it up, we don't talk about the mechanics, but about love, family, respect, safety, honesty and responsibility. Otherwise, sex is a private matter between my partner and me.
>
> So I'm always taken aback when people confuse sexual orientation with what someone does in the bedroom—as if they could divine what my partner and I do behind closed doors simply by knowing we are partners. And as a gay civil-rights leader, I spend a lot of time fighting those who maliciously try to convince people that being gay is not a key ingredient of who someone is, but simply what someone does in bed. . . . Being gay or straight is just that—a state of being. It's not a sex act. Sexual orientation is as fundamental as a person's sex, age, skin color or fingerprints. Gay people—and on some level, most straight people—know this to be true. (¶ 1-3)

Given that my purpose is not to explicate the various—as well as the more complex—arguments of queer theory, especially in light of the fact that it takes many forms and is difficult to capture succinctly (Schlager, 1998), I turn from this brief summation to the suggestion that much media-oriented academic research that employs queer theories and themes is, indeed, activism in that it serves a "practical mission" in the academy by challenging the ideological and political nature of the media. However, even as queer theory has this type of practical mission, through teaching students about models of identity that they may never have considered, its academic research often is not translatable to the world of policymaking. Queer theory actually resists incorporation into LGBT policymaking because queer theorists typically do not hold respect for the kind of identity politics that is so entrenched in gay activism. Nonetheless, although activists and queer theorists may disagree in certain areas, they obviously share certain broad commitments in terms of developing counter-hegemonic strategies for addressing oppressive heterosexual norms. One major difference, however, is that LGBT media activists typically do not have opportunities to deploy complex theories of power and knowledge in their everyday work; they are cultural technicians, not theoreticians.

As previously explained, GLAAD's news activists live in a world where they are required to react quite quickly, not to questions that allow for intricate and detailed discussions that are easily framed by queer theories of cultural representation and identity but to journalists who typically see sexuality as a foundational component of identity, the subcultural expression of a homosexual minority, or as a "choice." Hence, although queer theory has argued that identity politics inevitably exclude potential subjects in the name of representation (see Jagose, 1996), and it has described LGBT activist-oriented positions on diversity as simplistic and failing to make space for "difference within difference" (Kopelson, 2002, p. 24), it is important to realize that to proceed at all, gay activists must often seek, or in some cases *appear to seek*, complicity with the very identificatory regimes that they—in *theory*—may wish to counter.

For these reasons, for GLAAD's media activists to function organically and work to affect change for people who *self-identify* as gay, lesbian, bisexual, or transgender, the organization stresses an identity project that is based in practice on what Hall (1993) referred to as the "fictional necessity" (p. 135) of the arbitrary closure of meaning around identity, a provisional "cut" in language (p. 136), which makes the naming of identity, as well as acting in the name of identity, possible. As Hall saw it, identity and the production of identity are reflected in the stories that people produce about themselves. Such stories do not reflect essential truths about "identity" (despite self-perceptions) but, instead, are narratives that are "situational" or "positional" (Hall, pp. 136-137). When diverse individuals come together in the name of identity, according to Hall, it is possible for mobilization to occur around one or more organizing features, despite the hybridity of identity.

Although Hall (1993) did not argue that perceptions of "identity as stable" produce binary logics, among LGBT media activists, it is fair to say that dualistic reasoning often is an obligatory practice. To fight homophobia in the media, LGBT media activists must frequently take the stand that there is an "LGBT world" and a "straight world"; there are progressive and nonprogressive representations, even as "positive" and "negative" are terms that media activists no longer commonly use. One outcome is that given the concerns of activists, versions of queer theory and other poststructuralist and deconstructionist approaches that offer critiques with no concrete alternatives often are seen as stumbling blocks to effective, strategic activism. However, as demonstrated by some CSMS projects (e.g., Cagle, 2001; Consalvo, 2003; Roque Ramírez, 2003), queer theory offers important insights into the complex ways in which media commonly construct queer sexuality through the lens of heteronormative conventions (for details, see the previously listed studies). Because queer theory provides unconventional ways to conceptualize identity; because it increasingly is becoming popularized among young people in LGBT studies programs; and because queer youth groups often now include references in their monikers that have some basis in queer theory, such as LGBTQQ (lesbian, gay, bisexual, transgender, *queer*, and *questioning*), GLAAD most likely will begin to give more credence to theoretical perspectives that derive from queer theory. In other words, because queer theoretical concepts increasingly have become a part of the lexicon of queer youth, and because GLAAD intends to appeal to a college-age (18-22-year-old) demographic, it will be necessary for the organization to rethink the implications of the gay/straight binary that has long served as the model for describing sexual orientation and give stronger consideration to queer theoretical critiques and reconceptualizations of identity politics.

At the present time, most GLAAD activists see queer theory as offering an interesting philosophical puzzle, yet they remain largely unconvinced about ways in which it can be incorporated into their work. As I have already suggested, due to the particular day-to-day activities in which media activists engage, they typically prefer quantitative studies that, in their view, offer "hard facts" in the form of data that are gleaned from content analyses and survey research. For activists, "facts" regarding "how much" and "how often" offer compelling selling points, and quantitative scholarship moves media policymakers (Lempert, 2001). Many activists, thus, believe that strategic policy analysis as informed by quantitative research should become more integral to LGBT advocacy, especially as the nation's top-20 conservative think tanks spent $1 billion dollars during the 1990s alone to produce and disseminate polling studies that support legislation that counters the grassroots efforts of LGBT and other activist movements (National Committee for Responsive Philanthropy, 1999).

Although GLAAD is not involved in U.S. congressional lobbying efforts, a "think-tank model" has played a primary role in defining the type of research that the organization finds most useful when lobbying media professionals. When GLAAD activists meet with media executives, it makes sense that they would want to have statistical data that suggest that mainstream audiences gain a better understanding of LGBT diversity through observing "balanced" representations in media. Similarly, when the news team engages in on-air debates, it would be extraordinarily helpful to be able to use representative survey data to counterattack the often-skewed survey research conducted by organizations such as the Family Research Council (see Pietrzyk, 1994). In addition, when attempting to argue that queer young people need more affirmative representations in media, it would be beneficial to show, through reliable and valid nationwide survey studies, that programs such as the *Real World, Dawson's Creek*, and *Buffy the Vampire Slayer*, which contain young lesbian and/or gay characters, have encouraged adolescents to become either "more" or "less" comfortable with their sexuality. At the same time, as previously discussed, these types of studies are not only costly but often difficult to execute effectively. Thus, combining the desire for particular kinds of quantitative data with the problematics of conducting research that is cost effective and valid produces a series of dilemmas that come to the forefront. How, then, does a media research center, amidst significant budget constraints, address the needs of LGBT media activists?

ADDRESSING THE NEEDS/PROBLEM SOLVING

In light of the challenges posed by funding, and in an ongoing attempt to solve the problems that I have outlined in this chapter, the CSMS employs a number of administrative methods that attempt to achieve compromises. One method has been to commission scholars who are able to obtain matching university or organizational grant funds for projects and, thereby, facilitate research that offers the type of comprehensive data that GLAAD prefers, as the CSMS has not, as of 2004, had the resources to fund large-scale surveys of public attitudes about LGBT depictions in media. Another method that has been utilized is to fund a broad spectrum of commissioned papers and initiatives per year, so that for every project that is specifically directed toward a quantitative, data-driven need of GLAAD's, there is another that offers a more theory-driven, critical-cultural approach. To offer an example, in 2000, in an effort to launch the CSMS as a multidisciplinary research center, GLAAD funded a research initiative that was comprised of five studies of the television show *Will & Grace* (Cagle, 2001), which was one of the first popular prime-time comedies to feature two openly gay male characters. One commissioned scholar conducted focus group research on gay and lesbian viewers, another conducted a quantitative survey of midwestern U.S. college viewers, another conducted textual analysis of gay identity markers on the program, another employed queer theories and feminist perspectives to look at the rigidity of gender stereotypes on the program, and the fifth conducted a content analysis of the voices of the gay male characters on the program (Cagle, 2001). In funding this initiative, GLAAD, thus, saw the need for balance and commissioned studies that, as a set, incorporated diverse methodological approaches.

To offer another illustration, in 2001, as previously explained, Harrington conducted a study of the lesbian storyline on *All My Children*, and, in doing so, she combined a history of homosexuality in daytime serials, data from structured interviews with industry insiders, analysis of letters to the editor of soap fanzines, an examination of the ways in which the storyline was treated in the entertainment press, quantitative survey results obtained through responses generated from advertisements placed in several soap opera publications, and data from an online poll that was arranged by the CSMS and SoapCentral.com. Although there was disagreement over media promotion of the project, the project was, nonetheless, of particular importance to GLAAD because the organization had served in an outreach capacity during the foundational stages of storyline development in 2000, when two polls conducted by SoapCentral.com in October 2000 and November 2000 showed negative reactions to or ambivalence toward the forthcoming storyline. Harrington's multimethodological report not only provided data that were useful to GLAAD by showing that during the course of 8 months, ambivalent viewers increasingly supported the storyline and its address of social issues relating to lesbian teens, but it also offered a benchmark study for LGBT media scholarship because it was the first study to comprehensively assess depictions of homosexual themes and characters on daytime television dramas.

Between September 1, 2003 and February 28, 2004, in conducting a GLAAD-sponsored study, Roque Ramírez (2003) tracked and analyzed news coverage of LGBT people, groups, and events in the two dominant Spanish media in Los Angeles: *La Opinión*, the longest-running Spanish-language newspaper in the United States; and Univisión's Channel 34, the most-widely watched television channel in the U.S. Latino community. In the first portion of the study, Roque Ramírez utilized cultural studies, interpretive anthropology, and queer theory to analyze the contextual dimensions of LGBT representations in those Latino immigrant communities that place strong value on family, religion, and gender conformity. The main portion of the project then consisted of several interrelated components. To offer a brief summation, Roque Ramírez conducted a content analysis of Channel 34 news and determined that a majority of reports on LGBT issues occurred on the 11:30 p.m. broadcast, leading to the conclusion that the earlier 6 p.m. broadcast had deemed LGBT coverage to be "adult" in nature and not fitting for the early evening news. In looking at specific segments, Roque Ramírez found that "homophobic jokes" were prevalent, even though the news, in general, offered fair and balanced coverage of LGBT issues. In analyzing the third component of the study, the newspaper *La Opinión*, he discovered that of the total number of articles (280) referring to LGBT people, issues, or events, the greatest number (202) involved indirect coverage that occurred when LGBT people and events were mentioned as part of a larger story, not as the focus of the story per se. Although indirect coverage was consistently unbiased in nature, *La Opinión* consistently omitted LGBT perspectives in indirect, as well as direct, news stories. Even though this description highlights only a few of his findings, the point is that Roque Ramírez developed a project that not only offered GLAAD data that it used in negotiations with Spanish-language media professionals but the project also presented a deeply contextual cultural analysis of the ways in which Spanish-language news serve particular Latino communities.

Aside from their innovative subject matter, what distinguished each of these GLAAD-sponsored scholars was a commitment to engaging in a balancing act; for instance, some had to use a sizable portion of their grant funding to obtain assistance in gathering quantitative data that would be useful to GLAAD, whereas others chose to gain knowledge of methods in which they were not otherwise trained. In all cases, the outcome was research that could be put to use in practical ways.

A FINAL NOTE ON PRACTICALITY AND LESSONS LEARNED ABOUT COMMUNICATION ACTIVISM

The issue of the practicality of research has been central to this chapter. This issue is one that the scholars commissioned by GLAAD struggled with during the course of their study and LGBT media activists dealt with during the conception stage and at the completion stage of each study. The conception stage has been thoroughly covered in the chapter, but what has not been discussed is the fact that, for some key GLAAD activists, the issue of practicality does not always revolve solely around the question of "How might we apply research findings to our work?" Instead a more-pressing question for the Director of Communications and the Director of External

Communications is, "What are the *sound bites* from the study (or studies) that we can effectively pitch to the media in such a way that will gain *mainstream* media coverage of the study/studies?" Although commissioned scholars and I work diligently to craft sound bites that are based on the research findings, it probably is apparent to most readers that not every academic research project contains media sound bites. Academic research is notoriously difficult to market to mainstream media, and scholars rarely, if ever, equate the value of their studies with mainstream media publicity. Although all GLAAD-sponsored studies are, of course, commissioned to provide data and insights that Communications Team members can use in their day-to-day work with the media, if the Communications Director and the External Communications Director at GLAAD determine that studies cannot be effectively marketed to mainstream media, research projects often are deemed "unsuccessful."

This conclusion is perhaps based on a standard of performance that is applied to the entire Communications Team, but when the same standard is applied to the academic research division, it is not always appropriate. To explain, Communications Team members are expected to not only monitor and advise the media but they also are expected to author and subsequently place press releases in national and regional mainstream media. Thus, for example, if an antigay hate crime occurs in a northeastern U.S. state, the Northeast Regional Media Manager is expected to author a press release about the crime and place it in one or more regional newspapers in that part of the country. In turn, on a quarterly basis, the number of stories that Communications Team members place typically are counted and tallies often are "promoted" in GLAAD's newsletters for donors/supporters and quarterly reports to GLAAD's Board of Directors. Along related lines, excerpts of full stories that GLAAD places also are regularly included in board reports and newsletters. Thus, one of GLAAD's guiding assumptions is that the organization must not only monitor and advise mainstream media but it also must engage in a consistent and aggressive public relations campaign to get GLAAD's "name" in the media, as media visibility offers a tangible means for demonstrating that the organization is conducting important work. GLAAD is quite successful in this regard; for example, approximately 95% of all copy that GLAAD activists pitched to national and regional mainstream daily newspapers in 2003 was placed.

Although this type of journalistically inspired model is appropriate to the work of media activism per se, it is one that does not always translate well to the world of academic research. At the most fundamental level, the division of labor at GLAAD is strictly delegated in that Communications Team members are the only staff allowed to pitch stories to the media. Consequently, as Director of Research & Analysis, although I write summations of studies that lend themselves to the composition of press releases, I am not permitted to overstep my job duties and conduct independent public relations work with the media. At the same time, in an attempt to bridge the gap between public relations and academia at the internal level, between 2001 and 2004, scholars and I consistently studied GLAAD's press releases, talked to others at LGBT organizations with research departments, and examined scholarly studies that received mainstream press attention. The most consistent finding of my research was that although all research directors faced the same problems that I did, several had been successful in placing press releases about their research studies in mainstream media. In such cases, the studies that received press attention were those that typically contained some type of "startling" or "unusual" information. With this information in hand, I began to draft press-release-style documents on those CSMS studies that also contained startling or interesting findings (cf. Cagle, 2001; Harrington, 2001; Fejes, 2003; Streitmatter, 2003) and sent these documents to the Director of Communications and the Director of External Communications. However, despite the fact that I streamlined the process and focused on the unusual, and despite the fact that the CSMS produced over 25 first-of-their-kind studies by well-known scholars from 2000-2004, 22 of which included startling or unique findings, GLAAD only composed and pitched two press releases that focused on scholarly research. When I questioned why this was the case, I was informed on several occasions that scholarly researchers tend to be "difficult people to work with" in that when they are contacted to provide quotations for press releases, they typically engage in "lengthy academic discussions" about the ways in which their work potentially is going to be promoted. In other cases, I was told that to make research "interesting" to the press, it had to undergo more "spin" than that which I had provided, and researchers were not willing to concede to such spin. At other times, I was informed that press releases that focused on academic research were simply not a priority, given the fact that "gay marriage," *Lawrence and Garner v. Texas* (2003), The GLAAD Media Awards, and other issues and events were of more immediate concern to GLAAD. Needless to say, scholars and I often became quite frustrated as we believed that GLAAD—which consists of national experts in media promotion—could have made a more concerted effort to write and place press releases about LGBT research, given that two key GLAAD staff members often judge academic research based on its ability to "generate media attention."

Perhaps the most important lesson to be learned from these interrelated experiences is that researchers who are commissioned by media activist organizations may want to consider from the start how their work will be evaluated with respect to the knowledge that it contributes, its potential to gain publicity, or its accordance with both requirements. Along related lines, those academicians who are considering research directorship jobs at media activist organizations also may want to obtain a clear understanding about the ways in which studies will be evaluated by all organizational leaders, and exactly what role they, as directors, will play in the promotion of studies. Most important, media activists, LGBT or otherwise, should be aware that media scholars, in particular, often are uneasy about producing quotes that spin their work purely for promotional reasons, and they also wish to have their work accurately represented in the media.

Aside from these lessons, it is important to point out that during the past 4 years, although GLAAD has made great advances in understanding the necessity and utility of academic research, the Communications Team still often relies on one consistent method that was in place prior to the establishment of the CSMS: simple number counting. In other words, the team typically "counts" the number of LGBT characters or themes in enter-tainment in any given year and then compares the numbers to those of pre-vious years. The premise of this process is quite basic: An increase in LGBT visibility is assumed to equal an increase in progress toward reducing homo-phobia (even though this type of "number counting" says nothing about the content or context of programs with LGBT themes and characters). In fact, even as late as 2004, 4 years after the CSMS was established, GLAAD still relied heavily on this type of straightforward number counting as a way of showing "where we (as 'LGBT people') have come and where we are going." Although I have never openly disagreed with such a perspective, what I have done is explain to GLAAD's staff the ways in which CSMS-sponsored research provides *accessible* content-analytic data, *easy-to-com-prehend* survey data, and *uncomplicated* focus group research (and so forth) that can add *credibility* to the number counting and, in turn, perhaps offer a more sophisticated viewpoint. However, although many at GLAAD read the CSMS studies and use them for informative purposes, and although the majority of GLAAD's staff members understand my point of view and agree with it, they still prefer the number-counting method that has been in place for over 10 years because, once again, they claim that the media typi-cally want sound bites, not academic research. This perhaps points to one of the most frustrating lessons that scholars and I have had to learn: No matter how accessible we make the research, whether using simple bar graphs, pie charts, cross-tabs, or tables, GLAAD is an organization that actually prefers "tried-and-true" methods. Thus, no matter the tactics taken by researchers and research directors at LGBT activist organizations, it should not come as a surprise if research is not used to "add credibility" to organizational stands. In other words, the academic/activist dichotomy is one that is diffi-cult to overcome, even when one attempts to do so through some obvious methods and means.

Finally, because several key staff members have come to GLAAD from the world of corporate communications and public relations, a prevalent view is that scholarly research should be proprietary and provide quick turn-around in terms of delivery. The majority of senior-level staff members at GLAAD are accustomed to polling firms and market research, where snap-shot polls are sometimes conducted over a period of a day or a few days and data are delivered within a week. Consequently, because academic research cannot be "controlled" in the same ways that research typically is at market-ing companies and polling firms—where studies oftentimes are conducted to confirm existing opinions or to test (and then retest) a new concept or prod-uct—academic research too often is viewed as a "loose cannon" at GLAAD. To offer a few pertinent examples, over the course of 4 years, various indi-viduals at GLAAD have posed questions such as, "What might happen should a study examining the extreme right 'support' the antigay positions of the extreme right?" "Can't we locate a scholar who can simply produce a study that demonstrates, beyond a reasonable doubt, that Newspaper A is 'more homophobic' than Newspaper B?" "How might the 'XYZ' network perceive GLAAD, should an audience study show that a gay-themed pro-gram on 'XYZ' is seen in an unfavorable light by LGBT respondents?" Because scholarly research cannot and should not be "managed" in the same ways that market research or proprietary studies often are, there is a persist-ent fear at GLAAD that CSMS studies might contradict GLAAD's stand on LGBT issues and, even more significantly, that some studies might destroy important relationships that GLAAD has built with the media.

These concerns are not to be slighted; after all, what organization wants to fund projects that counteract its organizational mission and goals? What the concerns do point to though are lessons that both commissioned schol-ars and GLAAD have learned. Much like market researchers, commissioned researchers are obliged to produce studies that provide GLAAD with actionable findings. In the process of reading these studies, GLAAD has learned that research is, in fact, not a "loose cannon." Even when studies have contradicted some of the positions that GLAAD has taken on certain issues, the majority of staff members at GLAAD realize that this is one of the consequences of research and that GLAAD-sponsored LGBT media scholars have no ill intent; they are "on GLAAD's side," so to speak. On the other hand, several key individuals at GLAAD continue to mull over CSMS reports as if they are classified government documents. In fact, prior to post-ing a study on the web, I often receive a barrage of questions about the author's credentials, methods, and findings (even though these questions are addressed upon commissioning a study). GLAAD-sponsored scholars and I understand the reasoning behind such questions and, consequently, we pro-vide clear and concise answers. The result is that GLAAD has posted on its web site each study that it has commissioned. Perhaps the most important lesson to be learned, then, is that nonprofit activist organizations, such as GLAAD, often wish to commission proprietary types of research projects.

However, diplomatic discussions and effective negotiations between scholars and the organizations can lead to productive relationships both during the process of research and at the time that studies are completed.

CONCLUSION

In this chapter, I described the reasons that GLAAD requested practical research from media scholars. In turn, I demonstrated the difficulties that scholars and I faced in attempting to bridge the gaps that exist between academia and media activism. It is my hope that readers will be able to take the lessons I have learned and apply them to contexts in which activists and academics are attempting to work together, whether these be in university settings, in the field, or at activist organizations such as GLAAD. Above all, an underlying message to scholars is that research that is produced for activist organizations does make a difference by offering hands-on findings that can be used in activists' daily work. Equally important, activist-driven research can serve multiple missions by providing studies that inspire students, community activists, and nonacademic researchers. Given that the majority of research initiatives and papers commissioned at the CSMS also have been accepted as academic books or journal articles, activist-driven research also has the ability to forthrightly motivate the scholarly community and, in turn, lead scholars to the work of sponsoring activist organizations, such as GLAAD.

Finally, this "model," so to speak, whereby academics and activists stimulate each other in varying ways and to varying degrees, although seemingly simple, actually is quite complex. Even though the production of *activist-driven research per se* is the ultimate goal of most U.S. nonprofit research centers, activists need to give much stronger consideration to the importance of actually talking to scholars; indeed, organizations such as GLAAD should utilize scholars in a consulting capacity, as many are quite willing to provide insights and opinions that could maximize GLAAD's work with the media. Similarly, as evidenced by the anecdotes provided in this chapter, activists should develop more respect for those theoretical opinions that diverge from their own, and they should recognize the importance of using and promoting the academic work that activism has sponsored. At the same time, scholars who work with activists must recognize the importance of writing and speaking in vernacular that is journalistic, thereby taking into account the significant contextual differences that guide both the academic and the activist worlds. When each of these issues is understood more fully and addressed in a more congruous manner by academics as well as by activists, the communication activism that guides the academic-activist worlds will become more provocative, dynamic, and, ultimately, more rewarding.

NOTES

1. For over 200 years, the police, states, and the federal judiciary had used so-called "sodomy laws" as a legal reason to arrest and imprison LGBT people. One outcome was that police were permitted to "spy" on LGBT people to obtain information on their private sex lives. On June 26, 2003, the U.S. Supreme Court overruled all state laws regarding sodomy and, thereby, recognized that all men and women, regardless of sexual orientation, have a right to (sexual) privacy.

2. In September 2003, GLAAD made a formal decision to close the CSMS and outsource funding for the program to high-end market research companies and polling firms. In all public and private discussions regarding this decision, GLAAD made it abundantly clear that the decision had nothing to do with the success of the CSMS, my job performance as Director of Research & Analysis, or the quality of projects conducted at the CSMS. Instead, GLAAD claimed that the decision was based on the advice of McKinsey & Company, a consulting firm that had evaluated the organization's work, conducted an assessment of programs, and provided a strategic plan. One of McKinsey & Company's key recommendations was that GLAAD should no longer fund academic research because market research and polling studies would likely gain greater media attention than academic research. Although the outsourcing of research can be viewed as a reasonable decision in many regards, one unfortunate outcome of the GLAAD/McKinsey decision was that the National Research Advisory Board (NRAB) co-chairs and the NRAB members were not consulted during the *process* of determining this quite significant decision. When GLAAD was considering the move to market research, my input also was not sought. The decision, instead, was presented to me after the fact, in mid-December 2003. One month later, during a series of conference calls in January 2004, GLAAD announced the decision to NRAB members, including the two co-chairs. This particular method of "announcing" the decision to the very scholars who had assisted in formulating the CSMS, and who had helped with the center's projects, growth, and success, in turn, has resulted in a significant rift between NRAB members, many renowned LGBT scholars, and GLAAD.

3. Although Warner (2002) did not discuss activism directly, his points regarding public intellectuals and writing for "mass publics" are especially useful for my analysis. He actually suggested that within these contexts, an easy style is not always effective.

4. On September 10, 2002, citizens in Miami-Dade County Florida voted by a margin of 53-47% to retain that county's Human Rights Ordinance, which includes a ban on discrimination based on sexual orientation. The study examined the media climate surrounding the pro-ordinance and anti-ordinance campaigns.

5. This insight came as a result of conversations that I had with those scholars who conduct queer theoretical work. Because these scholars were discussing matters in confidence, it is not appropriate to list them as references.

6. The majority of the research that the CSMS commissions comes from sociology or communication.

7. The italicization of "a" is meant to suggest an "organized" or "unified" identity.

8. Indeed, GLAAD received numerous e-mails from young gay fans stating that Emenim was not homophobic but was portraying "Slim Shady," a character who may have expressed homophobic remarks in the context of a "conceptual album" and stage show. This reasoning is reminiscent of that used by Alice Cooper fans in the 1970s, who often claimed, rightfully so, that Alice was a stage character and that his productions were morality plays.

9. At the same time, GLAAD often has argued that the television landscape portraying LGBT people lacks cultural diversity. For example, entertainment television frequently portrays gay men as White, upper middle- to upper class, refined, well educated, and stylish in terms of dress.

REFERENCES

Alexander, J. (2003). *In their own words: LGBT youth writing the world wide web.* New York: GLAAD Center for the Study of Media & Society. Retrieved October 4, 2004, from http://www.glaad.org/programs/csms/papers.php

Cagle, V. (2001). *Research initiative on* Will & Grace. New York: GLAAD Center for the Study of Media & Society. Retrieved November 30, 2003, from http://www.glaad.org/programs/csms/initiatives.php?PHPSESSID=65257cf06 382c1790cc634b1cf376547

Children Now. (2001, December). *Fair play? Violence, gender and race in video games.* Retrieved January 3, 2002, from http://publications.childrennow.org/publications/media/fairplay-2001.cfm

Consalvo, M. (2003). *It's a queer world after all: Studying* The Sims *and sexuality.* New York: GLAAD Center for the Study of Media & Society. Retrieved November 30, 2003, from http://www.glaad.org/programs/csms/papers.php

Fejes, F. (2003). *The September 2002 campaign to repeal the Miami-Dade Human Rights Ordinance.* New York: GLAAD Center for the Study of Media & Society. Retrieved November 30, 2003, from http://www.glaad.org/programs/csms/papers.php

Foucault, M. (1984). *The Foucault reader* (P. Rabinow, Ed.). New York: Pantheon Books.

Garry, J. (2003, June 16). Sexual orientation: A state of being, not just a sex act. *USA Today,* p. 15A. Retrieved September 12, 2003, from http://www.usatoday.com/usatonline/20030616/5244939s.htm

Grace, A. B. (2003). *Matthew Shepard and Billy Jack Gaither: The politics of victimhood.* New York: GLAAD Center for the Study of Media & Society. Retrieved November 30, 2003, from http://www.glaad.org/programs/csms/papers.php

Gramsci, A. (1992). *Prison notebooks* (Vol. 1., J. A. Buttigieg, Ed.; J. A. Buttigieg & A. Callari, Trans.). New York: Columbia University Press.

Green, R. G. (1994). Television and aggression: Recent developments in research and theory. *Media, Children, and the Family: Social, Scientific, Psychodynamic, and Clinical Perspectives, 151-152,* 21-44.

Grossberg, L. (2003, June). *Cultural studies and U.S. conservatism.* Speech presented to the meeting of the U.S. Cultural Studies Association, Pittsburgh, PA.

Grossberg, L., Wartella E., & Whitney, D. C. (1998). *Mediamaking: Mass media in a popular culture.* Thousand Oaks, CA: Sage.

Hall, S. (1993). Minimal selves. In A. Gray & J. McGuigan (Eds.), *Studying culture: An introductory reader* (pp. 134-138). New York: Edward Arnold.

Harrington, C. L. (2001). *Conditions of represent-ability: Homosexuality on All My Children.* New York: GLAAD Center for the Study of Media & Society. Retrieved November 30, 2003, from http://www.glaad.org/programs/csms/initiatives.php

Highleyman, L. (1995). Identities and ideas: Strategies for bisexuals. In N. Tucker (Ed.), *Bisexual politics: Theories, queries, and visions* (pp. 73-92). New York: Haworth Press. Retrieved July 8, 2003, from http://www.black-rose.com/articles-liz/bipol.html

Huesmann, L. R., Moise-Titus, J., Podolski, C-L., & Eron, L. D. (2003). Longitudinal relations between children's exposure to TV violence and their aggressive and violent behavior in young adulthood: 1977-1992. *Developmental Psychology, 39,* 201-221. Retrieved: December 1, 2003, from http://www.apa.org/journals/dev/press_releases/march_2003/dev392201.html

Jagose, A. (1996). *Queer theory: An introduction.* New York: New York University Press.

Kinder, M. (1991). *Playing with power in movies, television, and video games: From Muppet Babies to Teenage Ninja Mutant Turtles.* Berkeley: University of California Press.

Kopelson, K. (2002). Dis/integrating the gay/queer binary: "Reconstructed identity politics" for a performative pedagogy. *College English, 65,* 17-35

Lawrence and Garner v Texas, 539 U.S. 448 (2003).

Lempert, R. O. (2001). Activist scholarship. *Law & Society Review, 35,* 25-31.

LGBT innovators. (2001, August 14). *The Advocate.* Retrieved October 7, 2004, from http://www.advocate.com/html/issuelinks/843_4links.asp

McQuail, D. (1994). *Mass communication theory: An introduction* (3rd ed.). Thousand Oaks, CA: Sage

National Committee for Responsive Philanthropy. (1999, March). *$1 billion for ideas: Conservative think tanks in the 1990s.* Washington, DC: Author. Retrieved October 31, 2003, from http://www.ncrp.org/cgi-bin/SoftCart.exe/Store/p-012.html?L+scstore+ptfs6338ffade7ad+1084131569

Palmer-Mehta, V., & Hay, K. (2003). *The anti-gay hate crime story line in DC Comic's Green Lantern: An analysis of reader responses.* New York: GLAAD Center for the Study of Media & Society. Retrieved November 30, 2003, from http://www.glaad.org/programs/csms/papers.php

Pietrzyk, M. E. (1994). *Queer science.* Retrieved March 20, 2004, from http://www.indegayforum.org/authors/pietrzyk/pietrzyk53.html

Provenzo, E. F., Jr. (1991). *Video kids: Making sense of Nintendo.* Cambridge, MA: Harvard University Press.

Roque Ramírez, H. N. (2003). *A language of (in)visibility: Latina and Latino LGBT images in Spanish-language television and print media.* New York: GLAAD Center for the Study of Media & Society. Retrieved November 30, 2003, from http://www.glaad.org/programs/csms/initiatives.php

Savoy, E. (1994). You can't go homo again: Queer theory and the foreclosure of gay studies. *English Studies in Canada, 20,* 129-152.

Schlager, N. (Ed.). (1998). *St. James Press gay and lesbian almanac.* Detroit, MI: St. James Press.

Schutte, N. S., Malouff, J. M., Post-Gorden, J. C., & Rodasta, A. L. (1988). Effects of playing videogames on children's aggressive and other behaviors. *Journal of Applied Social Psychology, 18,* 454-460.

Seidman, S. (1997). *Difference troubles: Queering social theory and sexual politics.* New York: Cambridge University Press.

Sender, K. (2002). *"Business, not politics": Gays, lesbians, bisexuals, and transgender people and the consumer sphere.* New York: GLAAD Center for the Study of Media & Society. Retrieved November 30, 2003, from http://www.glaad.org /programs/csms/initiatives.php

Sherry, J. (2001).The effects of violent video games on aggression: A meta-analysis. *Human Communication Research, 27,* 409-431.

Streitmatter, R. (2003). *How youth media can help combat homophobia against American teenagers.* New York: GLAAD Center for the Study of Media & Society. Retrieved November 30, 2003, from http://www.glaad.org/programs /csms/initiatives.php

Warner, M. (1999). *The trouble with normal: Sex, politics, and the ethics of queer life.* New York: Free Press.

Warner, M. (2002). *Publics and counterpublics.* New York: Zone Books.

5

UNREASONABLE DOUBT

Using Video Documentary to Promote Justice

John P. McHale

Illinois State University

Video and film documentary can be a powerful, humanizing form of communication, especially when used in conjunction with other forms of communication activism. In particular, documentary video/film can educate the public about the important and divisive issue of capital punishment. This chapter traces the development and use of a video documentary that I and others made to assist a marginalized citizen in securing justice by helping to prevent the execution of an innocent man. The video production, undertaken in conjunction with an ethnographic investigation of activists' use of media, was catalytic in halting a death penalty execution.

In this chapter, I explicate how this ethnographic investigation of activists' use of media informed the production of this video documentary in the effort to stop the execution of Joe Amrine, a Missouri man living on death row for 17 years for a prison murder he was found guilty of committing, despite there being neither witnesses nor evidence against him. I trace my involvement with Amrine's case—particularly the creation of *Unreasonable Doubt: The Joe Amrine Case* (McHale, Wylie, & Huck, 2002), a video documentary about his case, trial, and torturous limbo in prison—and the public relations battle to attract attention to Amrine's plight. These activities recursively informed the development of a theory of activist communication (McHale, 2004). I examine the literature on the use of video/film documentary as an activist tool; provide background information on my involvement in Joe Amrine's case; explain the preproduction, production, postproduction, promotion, and exhibition of the video documentary; identify the effects of the documentary; and outline some lessons learned from this experience about communication activism. As demonstrated, the video documentary and the media attention it generated were important factors in the battle to save Amrine's life and, hopefully, in the wider battle to stop the death penalty as it currently is used in the U.S. justice system.

THE USE OF VIDEO/FILM DOCUMENTARY AS AN ACTIVIST TOOL

Although little work has been done on activists' use of documentary video/film, much work has been done on the effects of the media in general. The concern that media, including film, could have strong effects on people began with the philosophical and sociological consideration of the unique characteristics of industrialized, mass society (Durkheim, 1933; Tönnies, 1940) and continued through the study of media propaganda (Hovland, Janis, & Kelly, 1953; Lasswell, 1935; Lippmann, 1922). Research on the impact of the media subsequently moved toward an assumption of limited effects (Janis et al., 1959; Katz & Lazarsfeld, 1955; Klapper, 1960; Lazarsfeld & Merton, 1948; Schramm, 1954; Schramm, Lyle, & Parker, 1961), with scholars generally concluding that the media could have some effect when their messages were consistent with those from other socializing groups (e.g., family and peers) and institutions (e.g., education and religion).

This type of media-effects research, conducted in a mainstream, social-scientific tradition in the United States stood in sharp contrast to an alternate approach, largely European in origin, that started with the early work of the Frankfurt School, followed by later research linked to the British cultural studies tradition (e.g., Adorno, 1991; Fiske & Hartley, 1978; Fromm, 1976; Hall, 1982; Marcuse, 1964), which focused on the ideological role of the media. These explorations of media ideology assumed that people experience prolonged media exposure to ideological positions that are consistent with other cultural influences. Perhaps because of this perspective, a move toward viewing the media as having moderate effects (more impact than assumed under a limited effects perspective but less than originally assumed by the strong effects perspective) arose in the United States after the 1960s in theoretical perspectives such as social learning theory (Bandura, 1971), agenda setting (McCombs & Shaw, 1972), spiral of silence (Noelle-Neumann, 1984), and cultivation analysis (Gerbner, 1999). Accompanying research demonstrated that long-term exposure to ubiquitous media frequently produced significant influence on individuals. Little of this research, however, focused on the impact of activists' use of documentary video/film or activists' use of documentary in conjunction with other activist communication.

Some work has been done on the impact of political film. Feldman and Sigelman (1985), for instance, studied the effects of the television film *The Day After*, about midwestern U.S. survivors of a hypothetical nuclear war between the United States and the Soviet Union, and found that viewers reported learning more about the possible implications of nuclear war but did not change their opinions about what policies would best avoid such a conflict. Lenart and McGraw (1989), however, did find that U.S. citizens who viewed *Amerika*, a made-for-television film about a fictional invasion of the United States by Soviet military forces and their Central American allies, showed an increase in conservative views about relations between the United States and the Soviet Union. These two studies were sensitive to the context in which viewers saw these films (e.g., taking into account whether people watched them alone or with other people and the location where they watched the films), but they did not focus on video/film documentary or its use by activists.

There also is a rich tradition of scholarship on the use of media by activists (e.g., Goodman, 2003; Ryan, 1991; Ryan, Carragee, & Meinhofer, 2001; Ryan, Carragee, & Schwerner, 1998), although there exists little on the use of documentary video/film for that purpose. The lack of such research is unfortunate, for there is a history of using video/film documentary as a medium for social protest and reform. For instance, John Grierson used film documentary in Britain in the 1920s and 1930s to raise public consciousness about social problems, and his work was influential in creating a number of subsequent documentaries on social conditions in Great Britain and the impact of imperialism abroad (Barnouw, 1993). The documentary film work of Pare Lorentz in the United States during the 1930s, including *The Plow that Broke the Plains* (1936) and *The River* (1937), promoted social change by highlighting problems of rural poverty. On the other side of the political spectrum, the Nazis used documentary film—most notably, the work of Leni Riefenstahl (e.g., *Triumph of the Will*)—to promote their agenda in Europe. In more recent years, filmmakers such as Errol Morris (*Thin Blue Line* and *Fog of War*) and Michael Moore (*Roger and Me, Bowling for Columbine*, and *Fahrenheit 9/11*) have promoted progressive agendas through film.

Although there has been little study of the political or social impact of video/film documentaries, there have been considerable critical analyses of such work, such as Bohn's (1977) study of the films from the U.S. World War II documentary series *Why We Fight*. Much of this work has been text-based, engaging in close readings/analyses of the content and form of film documentaries (see, e.g., Nichols, 1981, 1991, 1994), but frequently not examining issues related to the influence of these documentaries. One exception is Reeves (1999), who found that propaganda films that were consistent with previously held views had more impact on viewers than propaganda films that were inconsistent with audience members' preconceptions.

Little work has been done, however, on the use of documentary video/film by activists engaged in social movements, such as the abolition of the death penalty. A notable exception is Whiteman (2004), who studied the relationship between documentary films and several social movements seeking reform, including a documentary that pushed for better public housing in North Carolina, one that exposed social and environmental hazards linked to mining in Wisconsin and how that documentary was used by environmental groups, and how labor activists used a documentary on textile production in the southeastern United States that examined a bitter and violent strike in the 1930s that had long been neglected as a political resource. From this analysis, Whiteman developed a coalition model of political impact to better understand the role of documentary film designed to promote social justice issues. According to this model, the impact of an activist documentary is best studied by examining its development, production, and distribution stages, something that past research had neglected. Whiteman also contended that past research employed an "individualistic model" that focused on the influence of film documentaries on individuals' attitudes and behaviors, and he argued, instead, for the need to study the broader influence of documentaries on reforms and policies being sought by social movements.

Keeping Whiteman's (2004) goals in mind, this chapter examines the development, production, and distribution stages of the video documentary to save Joe Amrine's life and help stop the use of the death penalty in the United States. This video documentary was guided by an emergent grounded theory derived from the use of a constant comparison process to analyze ethnographically gathered data (interviews with individuals and focus

groups conducted with over 40 activists, field notes from participant observation, and printed materials from activist organizations) about advocacy
communication (McHale, 2004). This practical, middle-range perspective
identified communication forms used by activists, the intended audiences for
this communication, the perceived functions of this communication, and the
factors that influence such communication. In particular, the perspective
identified video as an especially effective tool of social action for reaching the
general public, other activists, politicians, and the media. The grounded theory revealed that video potentially can achieve a variety of functions, including educating people, mobilizing advocates, aiding lobbying efforts, and
facilitating media coverage. This theory also revealed that video/film has particular characteristics—such as multiple cues, language variety (e.g., formal
vs. casual or the source characteristics of interviewees vs. a narrator), and a
personal character (e.g., humanizing the topic by showing the individual
human beings involved)—that contribute to its effectiveness in reaching and
motivating audiences. These aspects of the activist communication perspective convinced me that production of a video documentary could be useful
in the fight to save Amrine and in the larger antideath penalty movement.

BACKGROUND ON AMRINE'S CASE

Description and analysis of the production of *Unreasonable Doubt: The Joe
Amrine Case* is a story of a personal journey for me. I am appreciative of the
opportunity to have been deeply involved in a battle that had significant
ramifications for Amrine and for Missouri and that became a victory for
people who fought so hard to save Amrine. My personal and political views
influenced my involvement in and perception of the relevant events. In particular, my view that the death penalty is unethical because the policy uses
my tax dollars to kill people has influenced my participation in the political
sphere. My decision to study and support antideath penalty advocates is
based on my belief in free expression in a democracy. I embrace that subjectivity and attempt to mine my emic understanding of the experience for
knowledge that only one who has turned "native" might possess.

Joe Amrine was on death row for a crime he did not commit. In 1979,
he began serving a 7-year sentence for robbery and check forging, a crime to
which he plead guilty. In 1985, while serving time in Jefferson City
Correctional Center in Missouri, Amrine was implicated by three inmates in
the murder of another prisoner, Gary Barber. Despite the testimony of a
prison guard and two prisoners who identified someone else as having committed the crime, Amrine was tried and sentenced to death for that murder.
Following the trial, the state's three major witnesses all said they lied at
Amrine's trial and never actually saw Amrine fatally stab Barber.

Before I became involved with the battle to save Amrine's life, I was immersed in the Missouri antideath penalty community and the midwest regional antideath penalty advocacy movement. As part of my research on the antideath penalty, universal healthcare, and environmental advocacy movements for the theory of communication activism I was developing (McHale, 2004), I was devoting much time to participant observation of the antideath penalty community. I had a working relationship as an activist and scholar with several key members of that community in Missouri who later would contribute to the battle to save Amrine's life. Eight months before I became involved with Amrine's case, I hosted at my home a group of people called Journey of Hope, who have lost loved ones to murder but publicly oppose the death penalty. I also began work with that group on a video documentary about Sister Helen Prejean, the author of the book *Dead Man Walking* (1993), who was portrayed by Susan Sarandon in the Academy award-winning film adaptation of that book. I was trained in film production at New York University and had worked as a professional video producer for the University of Missouri at Columbia (MU) for a short period of time before entering MU's communication doctoral program. I also had previously directed and produced several short video projects. My background and involvement in these activities provided me with opportunities to forge strong relationships with several people who would be involved in the fight to save Amrine, especially Jeff Stack, the legislative coordinator of Missourians Against the Death Penalty.

Throughout the fight to save Amrine from execution, there was a strong relationship between the video documentary we were making and those involved in other ways with the antideath penalty movement. Certainly, the video documentary was a political tool for the movement; at the same time, the movement helped to draw attention to the video documentary and the influence of the documentary was tied to the existence and mobilization of this movement. In this, as in other cases, documentary videos/films seeking to promote social reform and change likely will have more influence if they are linked to the larger mobilization of social activists with respect to the issue on the table. This has been brought to the fore in the work of those associated with the Media Research and Action Project, who emphasize the significance of the links between researchers, activist media outlets, journalists, and social movements (see Ryan, 1991; Ryan et al., 1998), although these scholar-activists do not directly speak about documentary video/film projects per se (for the potential impact of documentary in social/political movements, as previously noted, see Whiteman, 2004). Coordination between the documentary production team, supporters of Amrine, his legal defense team, his family, the local church community, and antideath penalty advocates throughout the state of Missouri was an important part of the campaign to save Amrine, as shown in the preproduction, production, postproduction, and distribution of the documentary.

CREATION AND DISTRIBUTION OF THE VIDEO DOCUMENTARY

The video project first involved researching and crafting our cinematic approach in the preproduction and production stages. The effort then entailed postproduction and editing, followed by exhibition showings of the video and other promotional activities.

Preproduction

At the time I heard about Amrine's case, I was a graduate student instructor in MU's Department of Communication and directing a short video documentary about Sister Helen Prejean's visit to Missouri. I was working on this documentary with Ryan Wylie, an ex-student of mine who was pursuing his undergraduate degree in communication. Wylie heard about Amrine's case from members of the university's chapter of Amnesty International. He arrived at my home one evening in December 2000 for an editing session and mentioned that Amrine's case might make a strong topic for a video documentary. I asked him to get any information Amnesty International had about the case, the most important of which proved to be an unpublished manuscript written by two Webster University (St. Louis, MO) students that made a compelling case for Amrine's innocence (Muzslay & Ketchum, 1999).

After reviewing the relevant information about Amrine's case, Wylie and I agreed that we would produce the video documentary together, with me directing it and him serving as assistant director and editor. I set up an appointment for Wylie and me to meet Sean O'Brien, Amrine's attorney, and a small group of antideath penalty advocates who were working on Amrine's behalf.

Wylie and I met O'Brien at a pizza parlor that is a campus landmark at MU and what would be the location of Amrine's first meal after he left prison. O'Brien was a considerate and charismatic lawyer who worked for the Public Interest Litigation Clinic, an organization that provides legal services to those accused of serious crimes but who lack the resources to fund their defense. O'Brien had won a case before the U.S. Supreme Court several years earlier on behalf of a death row inmate that exonerated him. He carried himself with the poise, determination, humility, and gumption of someone who was working in the spirit of advocacy for social justice. At the meeting, I explained to him that I had read the story about Amrine written by the Webster University students, and then asked him, "What are the flies in the ointment?" as I wanted to know the counterfactuals—specifically, what witnesses or evidence suggested that Amrine actually committed the crime. He answered that he could not find any evidence or witnesses that indicated Amrine was guilty. O'Brien explained that of all the murder cases he had worked on, this was the one that he thought most warranted reversal. He was very persuasive and left me with the impression that Amrine likely was innocent.

At that meeting, O'Brien gave us videotaped depositions conducted with Randall Ferguson and Jerry Poe, two of the three primary witnesses at Amrine's trial. I was emotionally moved when I returned home and viewed these depositions. Consistent with the theory of advocacy communication on which I was working, video is more personal than written communication, and the nonverbal cues displayed by and the appearance of immediacy (the human presence) in the statements of these two men were more emotionally compelling than the print communication I had read on the case (the manuscript by the Webster University students). After seeing the videotaped recantations of these two witnesses in Amrine's case and contemplating my emerging theory of advocacy communication, I realized that a documentary about Amrine's case potentially could be useful for persuading other activists, the general public, and public officials that Amrine's execution would be unjust. I made it a personal goal to deliver edited pieces of the depositions to Bob Holden, the Governor of Missouri. I, thus, decided to produce a video documentary about Amrine's case.

The emerging theory of advocacy communication that I was working on revealed that if advocates make it easy for journalists to cover a story, it more likely will receive coverage. By providing video footage about Amrine's case, particularly to television news reporters, I believed we could get attention focused on the case, which had received no television or newspaper coverage in mid-Missouri. Whether this communication activism actually would help Amrine was irrelevant in my decision to produce and direct the video documentary. I believed that the documentary simply was a good thing to do (ontologically), not because it might have positive consequences, and Wylie and Dan Huck, another former student and another producer of the video, felt the same way.

My decision to create the video entailed more preproduction, production, and postproduction work. It also required money from my significant other, Dr. Kim McHale, who was an Assistant Professor of mathematics at Columbia College, a small, liberal arts college in Columbia, MO. As a graduate instructor, my salary was under $8,000; consequently, we relied on her income to produce the documentary, and she was, therefore, the de facto executive producer. We, thus, personally funded the production of the video documentary and subsequently distributed it for the cause for the cost of a copy of the video. Many other people also donated their time and energy (especially Wylie and Huck), and we were granted access to equipment through MU's Department of Communication, for which we are appreciative.

Further research was necessary before drafting the script for the video documentary. O'Brien sent me a number of legal documents, including transcripts of depositions from other people involved in the trial, such as the prosecutor, additional witnesses, and jurors, and O'Brien's legal motions. I then conducted an extensive media search about the case and found archived articles from local newspapers on the murder, trial, and sentencing. I also found a short piece about the trial published in *Newsweek* ("They're on Death Row," 2000), which was important because it featured a photograph of Amrine. I believed that a shot of the article in the video documentary would add to our credibility, for if *Newsweek* had raised questions about the case, the general public, other activists, media personnel, and government officials might be inclined to think that our position had merit.

In the preproduction stage, we also had to make arrangements to use available video footage that was relevant to the case. For example, Jim Theabuat, a filmmaker in Kansas City, had footage of the Jefferson City Correctional Center, the prison facility where the murder happened; footage of the Potosi State Correctional Center, the prison in which Amrine was being held (because Missouri had discontinued executions in Jefferson City and moved them to the Potosi facility); and even footage of the room in which he would be executed. We solicited Theabuat's help, and he offered the footage to us for inclusion in the video documentary.

Scripting documentary is a more recursive process than writing many other types of scripts, such as television programs or dramatic films, because documentaries usually are restricted to what actually happened as captured on videotape or film rather than what can be dramatically created or recreated. In televisual production, a script usually is completed and shooting schedules are generated based on the shots in the script. In documentary production, however, the initial script is a shot "wish list," and footage is gathered with the understanding that additional footage might be needed as the shots on the wish list are whittled down. Simply put, the makers of documentary cannot plan on gathering footage that is exactly what they want; they must work with the footage they get. As Walters (1994) suggested, "In the true documentary, in contrast to programs that are re-creations, the sequences cannot be scripted in detail in advance; they can only be loosely planned" (p. 449). Footage of what actually happened is logged as the best selections are noted.

We used a computer-editing system to capture and label good shots that conveyed important information. The best shots then were slotted into the script using the label of the captured video clip. This labeling process makes editing relatively easy, because the editor, Wylie, could go to the appropriate computer file to find the clip with the same label as the one used in the script at the appropriate spot. The development of the script then gave rise to what shots were needed. In this case, after logging between 20-30% of the footage at our disposal, I crafted a general developmental plan for the documentary and placed the name of the captured video clips into the appropriate places in the script. As shots were slotted into the script, we became aware of additional shots and interviews that were needed. This necessitated further preproduction work, including conducting additional research (e.g., gathering interview contact information) and making arrangements for further interviews and shooting plans.

The preproduction process also was influenced by the antideath penalty activists in Missouri. We relied on a leading activist in Missouri to provide additional background on the case and give us ideas about things we might want to include in the documentary. Consistent with Whiteman's (2004) work, the preproduction process energized those few activists already fighting on Amrine's behalf. In particular, it helped to mobilize Amrine's family. His family had not been very active in the battle before we started the preproduction process but the knowledge that some MU students were producing a video documentary on his case increased the family's desire to fight to save Joe, including getting interviews with Amrine's sister and brother. The role of the documentary in encouraging people to become more active on Amrine's case continued during the production phase.

Production

The difference between preproduction and production is less distinct in video/film documentary than with other types of media programming because of the dependence in documentaries on occurrences that are video-taped or filmed as they happen. Once I structured a tentative shooting schedule, we confirmed taping plans with the principals involved and made arrangements for locations. Even the construction of the shooting schedule was flexible, with plans amended to accommodate participants and locations.

MU was a supportive environment for the production, dissemination, and promotion of the video documentary about Amrine's case. The university and its Department of Communication offered logistical support for the project; in particular, equipment and technical knowledge provided by Mike Atkins, the director of the video-production facilities at the Academic Support Center, was instrumental in completing the documentary. Fred Ross, a faculty member in the Department of Physics and a computer technician, also helped to upgrade my home computer so that editing could be done there. Former students of mine also played key roles in running cameras, providing technical support, and in completing, disseminating, and promoting the documentary. As previously noted, the efforts of Wylie and Huck, in particular, were indispensable to the completion of the project.

Initially, in the production stage, a number of interviews had to be conducted. First, there were two jurors from the original trial who subsequently had changed their mind about the guilty verdict and had stated in post-trial depositions that they believed the jury had made a mistake in Amrine's trial. The one whom we felt was most compelling was the jury foreperson (whose name is being withheld at his request). I contacted him and asked if he would be willing to be videotaped in an interview. He vehemently declined, saying he was tired of talking about the case. He had stated in several court depositions that the jury made the wrong decision, and he claimed that if saying that did no good, he did not see how our efforts would help. The second juror, Larry Hildebrand, agreed to be interviewed for the documentary. In fact, Hildebrand seemed relieved to get another opportunity to speak about the case; I sensed that he felt guilty about how the jury deliberations had gone and appreciated the opportunity to communicate his feelings in another venue. We set up a shooting date and interviewed him in my home office. The footage from that interview was compelling and became an important part of our final product.

I also wanted to give those on the other side an opportunity to share counterfactuals of which we were not aware. This decision was linked to my commitment to provide balance in the video documentary rather than a desire to include conflict in the narrative. Research also suggests that audiences may be more receptive to a presentation that offers arguments from both sides of an issue (see e.g., Allen, 1998). The first prosecutorial voice we sought was the Missouri Attorney General Jay Nixon, who, in November 2001, had requested that the Missouri Supreme Court set a date for Amrine's execution. We arranged a meeting with Tim Holsti, a spokesperson for Nixon. Wylie and I met with Holsti at the Attorney General's office to videotape an interview. We gave him every opportunity to explain why Amrine should be executed, despite no remaining witnesses or evidence, but surprisingly, he merely made a legalistic argument and said that the courts had found Amrine guilty, ruled subsequently that he had received a fair trial, and, according to the law, Amrine should be executed. We thought that officials at the Attorney General's office might have knowledge about some evidence or witnesses we did not know about but they did not.

Another important prosecutorial voice we wanted to include was that of Judge Thomas Brown, who was the original prosecutor in Amrine's murder trial and now was a presiding judge in Cole County, the jurisdiction of Gary Barber's murder, the man Amrine was accused of killing, and the location of Amrine's 1985 trial for that murder. I called Judge Brown on the telephone to inquire about his willingness to answer some questions on videotape. Initially, he was adamant in his refusal to participate; however, during the course of the conversation, I told him about the information we were planning to include in the documentary, and he began to explain how we were wrong about the case. I suggested that we needed him to explain on videotape how our thesis of Amrine's innocence was incorrect. With that in mind, he finally agreed to be interviewed, and we arranged a meeting in his chambers.

The interview with Judge Brown was tense and I could tell he was not enjoying it. Surprisingly, Brown could cite no evidence or witnesses that we had not considered besides an allusion to confidential informants and access to information through means that could not be introduced in court. At one point, I mentioned that one of the witnesses, Randall Ferguson, had said that prison officials knew he was being sexually abused by other prisoners and that they promised him protection against this abuse if he testified against Amrine. At that point, Judge Brown became very upset and accused me of journalistic sensationalism for suggesting, which I never had, that there was a conspiracy against Amrine. In the end, however, Brown never presented a cogent argument for Amrine's execution, although his most compelling statements as to why the execution should proceed were included in the final version of the documentary.

Another prosecutorial voice we desperately sought was that of Captain George Brooks, a primary investigator in the murder investigation and now a captain in the Cole County Sheriff's Department. Randall Ferguson said in our interview with him that Brooks knew of his sexual abuse. Ferguson said that when he was interviewed by Brooks during the initial 1985 investigation, Brooks shut off an audiotape recorder and said that he could protect Ferguson from abuse if Ferguson would testify against Amrine. We planned on including Ferguson's statement in the documentary, but felt a responsibility to give Brooks an opportunity to respond to the charge. I talked to Brooks on the telephone once, outlined our project, and shared Ferguson's accusation, but Brooks declined the opportunity to comment. We also showed up at Brooks's office to give him another chance to respond, but he would not see us. Brooks later killed himself in January 2005, one month after Amrine filed suit against Brooks for investigatory impropriety.

One of the most difficult aspects of the production process was getting access to Amrine from officials at Missouri's Department of Corrections and at the Potosi Correctional Facility where he was being held. Prison officials gave several reasons why we could not interview Amrine, mostly related to security concerns. In an effort to get around these obstacles, a student at MU who possessed press credentials (and, therefore, was allowed to bring a video camera into the Potosi prison), but who was not involved in this video documentary production process, agreed to interview Amrine and allow us to use the footage. However, because Amrine was behind glass and could only communicate to the reporter through an intercom telephone receiver, the audio signal on the video footage was unusable. Without acceptable footage of Amrine, we could not complete the documentary.

Sean O'Brien thought of a way to get me into the prison with a camera. He argued to prison officials that Amrine had a right to speak to the governor through a video as part of his right of review. Prison officials subsequently agreed that we could meet with Amrine in a room where we could properly videotape him and capture the audio. A date was arranged, but unfortunately, when that date arrived, we were refused the promised access to Amrine. O'Brien and I met Amrine in a small room with a glass partition and had to speak with him through a telephone receiver. Luckily, this room was equipped with a small slot through which a prisoner and his or her lawyer could pass legal papers. I took the cover off of a small lavaliere (a lapel microphone) and smashed it with my heel until it could fit through the slot. Fortunately, the microphone still worked and the interview went well, producing much footage that would be very important in the final version of the documentary.

We also had written into the script a variety of needed *b-roll shots* (video shots, also called *inserts* or *cut-aways*, which can be used under the voice-over or interview to increase the visual variety within the story) that included locations, maps, and a few dramatic recreations of actions referred to in the documentary. In the editing process, we would cut to these shots to visually reinforce the words being spoken, as well as to provide some variety, for we did not want the documentary to simply be a series of talking heads. There has been some controversy over the inclusion of dramatic recreation in documentary (see, e.g., Walters, 1994). The rise of *cinema verite* (the emphasis in video/film on actuality and on the role of the makers of a documentary in a situation rather than their *representation* of reality) has lessened the use of director reconstruction of what may have happened (Bruzzi, 2000). In view of this controversy, I decided to keep such recreations to a minimum, including only two small clips in which we recreated events. The first clip involved crafting a weapon that met the exact specifications of the murder weapon as described in court documents and including a shot of it when the weapon was mentioned. The second clip involved dramatically recreating prison officials destroying original testimony from witnesses. I believed that these two instances did not distort the narrative and added valuable visualization for two important aspects of the case.

Postproduction

Editing is the central aspect of postproduction. One of the communicative powers of video, as with film, is its ability to juxtapose images and sound, with the arrangement of the shots creating a cumulative meaning and effect that transcends the individual images and sounds. Technology also has made the editing process easier; advances in editing and special effects software enabled us to craft the finished product in several rooms in my home that we dubbed "the editing suite," after we doubled the amount of memory on one of my home computers and updated the editing software. Wylie, as the editor, did most of the actual arrangement of video clips into a unified whole in accordance with the plans I had developed in the script. Huck was responsible for generation of the graphics and other effects used in the video documentary, such as superimposition of multiple shots in one frame and all computer-generated fonts. Wylie and Huck spent many hours editing the final product, with me observing, making sure that they kept to the script and giving them my opinion on hundreds of editing choices.

The completion of the video documentary added energy to activists fighting to save Amrine and increased their morale, as was the case to a more limited extent during preproduction, which is consistent with Whiteman's (2004) findings. The few activists who had been working on the case felt validated by the existence of the documentary. After the release of the documentary, Vera Amrine, one of Joe's sisters, told me that family members may have had doubts about Amrine's guilt, but when they heard that we were making a documentary, they felt more motivation to get involved. "You guys don't even know Joe," Vera Amrine said. "If you guys are fighting for him, we sure need to be." The family would prove to be a valuable resource during promotion and exhibition of the documentary, as we could count on between 10 and 15 of them showing up at most events.

Promotion and Exhibition

Our largest battle came after we actually finished the video documentary in terms of showing it at as many venues as possible and promoting all of the events that accompanied its exhibition. I was in a unique position as I was finalizing the previously mentioned approach for understanding advocacy communication that outlined available forms, functions, potential audiences, and factors that influenced activists' use of such communication. This grounded perspective emerged from the analysis of the qualitative data collected (Glaser & Strauss, 1967), with meanings attributed to the use of various communication media by over 40 regional activists being the most important data for the development of the theory that informed the promotion and exhibition of the video documentary.

This qualitative research involved the search for *emic knowledge* (an understanding of events from the perspective of those who live them) as opposed to *etic knowledge* (knowledge gathered from an outsider observing a scene) (Lindlof & Taylor, 2002). Thus, ethnographic methods of data collection and qualitative analysis of those data (using the process of constant comparison) guided our promotion of the video documentary, with emerging typologies from the grounded theory of communication advocacy providing informal checklists of possible communicative actions to take to advance Amrine's case through the promotion and exhibition of the documentary. For instance, the perspective suggested that using a wide variety of media is effective for promoting activists' messages. Accordingly, I crafted e-mails to activists, public officials, and media personnel; worked with other activists who had knowledge of graphic design to produce, copy, and distribute fliers; sent press releases to media personnel via fax; made arrangements for interviews with radio, television, and newspaper reporters; promoted showings of the video at group meetings of associated activists; sent information about showings to associated groups and organizations so that their newsletters would announce them; and organized protests and press conferences (including inviting speakers, making logistical arrangements with government officials responsible for protest locations, and ensuring that posters about Amrine's case would be present at the protests).

This perspective also made me consider communication with the audiences that activists had identified as being important. I tried to make sure activists from a number of groups and organizations, government officials, and media managers and reporters knew about our activities. I also considered the possible functions of such communication and did my best to make sure that the distribution, exhibition, and promotion of the documentary were designed to perform these functions. I, thus, continually checked our promotion and exhibition strategies against the perspective that emerged from my ethnographic research and, in turn, these strategies helped to hone that perspective.

The theory of advocacy communication suggested that activists thought any and all available means of communication should be used to promote an advocacy position. In accordance with that precept, I did whatever I could to help activists who supported Amrine to travel throughout Missouri and present the documentary in a variety of venues, such as on college campuses and in community meeting rooms and churches. The most important audiences were the governor, legislators, and judicial officials because they actually could help Amrine; consequently, protests were organized and events were held to get copies of the video documentary to these audiences. Activists throughout the state also used the video as a tool to mobilize other activists who could help, and many activists reported that they had seen the documentary in various locations. Between February 2002 and April 2003, the documentary was shown on at least 10 university campuses, at three film festivals, in three urban theaters, and was broadcast throughout Missouri, Arkansas, and Kansas on a regional religious television network that was owned and managed by a pastor who opposed the death penalty and had been involved in several previous capital punishment cases. We also received a grant from the Tides Foundation (a foundation that opposes the death penalty) to produce 500 duplicates of the documentary. A member of the Western Missouri Coalition Against the Death Penalty initiated the grant and sent a copy of the video documentary to every senator and representative in the Missouri state legislature.

We also labored to increase the media's attention on Amrine's case; for instance, before each showing, I delivered press releases and communicated with editors and reporters to procure news coverage locally, regionally, nationally, and internationally. Ultimately, the video documentary was covered by the Associated Press, mentioned on National Public Radio, and portions were featured on British Broadcasting Corporation television.

Our experiences from this video project show that the media in the United States, although driven mostly by the priority of corporate profit, contain space for messages of social justice. Advocates, however, must possess the knowledge, skills, and gumption necessary to take advantage of these opportunities. Effective use of media outlets, thus, was a key part of our campaign strategy. Television news organizations in Kansas City, Columbia, and St. Louis covered the story a number of times, particularly when events were arranged in conjunction with the documentary, such as showings or other events. In the Jefferson City market, the state capital, there were at least 22 television news stories on the case, all of which used pieces of the documentary in their coverage. In at least two instances, all three area television stations covered stories related to Amrine's case and the documentary in their 5:00 p.m., 6:00 p.m., 10:00 p.m., and morning news programs. All of these stories depicted Amrine's guilt as questionable and his imminent execution as potentially unjust.

The first thing I did any time I had an idea for an event was to consult with members of the Missouri antideath penalty community. Before screenings and other events were announced to the media, logistical arrangements were made with antideath penalty activists (such as the most appropriate dates and times for the event, where the event was to be held, whether we had permission to use that location, and who was responsible for the public address system or video-projection equipment). As described in McHale (2004), arrangement of such logistical details requires use of various forms of communication, including interpersonal, group, and electronic communication. Advocates have to talk to each other about activities; this is done through face-to-face interaction and group meetings, and augmented with communication through the internet.

Although the term "media event" may have a negative connotation to some people because of the perception that this type of event has no value other than to attract the media's attention, the phrase does highlight the idea that the media usually do not cover simple statements of position (activists simply stating or issuing an opinion on an issue usually will not receive media attention). The media, however, will air opinions in conjunction with the coverage of an event. An event that is designed to attract media coverage, therefore, must have significance beyond simply getting such coverage. In fact, events that are meaningful and significant in the sense that they have an influence on people with or without media coverage will be judged by the media to be authentic and likely will be afforded coverage (McHale, 2004). The best events also have news value and visual elements that make them conducive for media coverage and possess inherent value for those who attend. Screenings of the documentary provided all of these characteristics.

As we exhibited the documentary, we used any and all available venues. Artistic cinema houses in Columbia (MO) and Kansas City were valuable venues for exhibition that generated press coverage of the screenings, the documentary, and Amrine's case. The documentary also was shown in nontheatrical settings, including churches and city/community meeting rooms. The first showing, on February 22, 2002, was a screening at the Rag Tag Theater in Columbia, with other screenings throughout the state soon following. Apart from these screenings, other events included the broadcast of the video documentary on the 8-channel religious broadcasting network mentioned previously, a rally on the state capital steps and delivery of the documentary to the governor's office, and a press conference at the state capital where we delivered to the governor's office petitions and legal briefs from university student organizations across the state of Missouri in support of Amrine. The documentary also was featured at two regional video/film festivals, one in St. Louis and the other at the Kansas Film Festival, where it received a second-place award.

Once the appropriate details about events were confirmed, we crafted messages about them for the media. The use of press releases and press kits reduced the amount of work for news directors and reporters by making these events easier to cover. These communication tools save journalists time and effort, and save their news organizations money. Activists, unfortunately, often neglect these simple techniques when seeking news coverage, but they have been shown to be very effective by public relations professionals, who often work for groups or organizations with power and resources. Information ancillaries, such as press releases and press kits, increase accessible knowledge on a topic for reporters (Gandy, 1982). I wrote the press releases for the events approximately 2 weeks before the events were scheduled. The first paragraph of the press releases contained comprehensive leads (information that explained who was doing what, where, and when), with subsequent paragraphs containing information in descending order of importance. These two features are essential aspects of the inverted pyramid news story form, a press release convention with which, among other conventions, advocates responsible for media relations should be familiar. The secondary information, which contained background about the case and the video documentary, as well as quotes from me as its director and producer, could be cut and pasted in other press releases. The press releases regularly were updated with information about previous events.

Although written a few days earlier, I first sent press releases to media outlets approximately 10 days before scheduled events. I wanted the media personnel responsible for deciding what stories would be covered (generally, the assignment editor or news director) to become familiar with the case, our efforts, and our position on Amrine's case. Ten days would have been too early to send the press releases if they were the only releases sent out, but I sent them again 4-5 days before the event, as well as the day before the event. I knew I ran a risk that if too many press releases were sent, news directors and assignment editors could feel pestered, but I thought that if the events were worthy and the people responsible for the day's news agenda knew about them, they would send reporters to cover these events regardless of whether they felt pestered.

One of the relevant findings that emerged from my study of advocacy communication was that many media outlets have become accustomed to receiving press releases via fax and that this is the easiest way to assure that information will be routed to those responsible for assigning stories to reporters. Delivery through fax also was very convenient and inexpensive once we had access to computer equipment, software, and contact information (McHale, 2004). I had bought a fax program several months before for other advocacy activity. I gathered all of the fax contact telephone numbers for local, regional, and national news organizations. To continue to remind relevant public officials of our efforts, I entered their fax numbers into our list, and when I needed to send out press releases, I could address them to the whole list, hit the send button, and over 25 fax machines would receive a copy of the release within a few minutes. The computer fax capability allowed me to do this in much less time than I would have had to spend with a traditional fax machine and much less time and money than would have been required if I delivered the press releases through the U.S. mail. I also could have e-mailed the press release to journalists, but then they would be required to print a copy of it. With computer fax capabilities, I knew there would be a hard copy of our message in the offices of media outlets.

Putting together a press kit also was a useful promotional tool for our advocacy efforts. I always gave the reporter a press kit during an interview. In a folder with the name of the video documentary on the front, I enclosed a copy of the documentary, the latest press release, a promotional flier, a short description of the video, my contact information, and other articles that had been written about the documentary (e.g., "A Film to Save a Life," 2002; Brown, 2002a, 2002b, 2002c; Detrick, 2002; Feldstein, 2002; Kidd,

2002; Marshall, 2002), which provided additional information for reporters and added legitimacy to our effort by showing not only that we were professional in our approach but that other news organizations deemed the project worthy of coverage.

To gain television news coverage, the most important part of the press kit was the documentary itself, because access to video that can be used by reporters as b-roll can increase the chances that a story will be featured on television news programs. Because the documentary included interviews with the key witnesses and other principal characters in the case, television reporters could use that footage rather than having to go out and gather new footage themselves. The lesson here is that advocates should do as much work for reporters as possible to increase the chances that their story will be covered. Providing reporters with access to these visual elements, in this case, facilitated television news coverage.

We also created a web page that provided a description of the documentary, a visual graphic of a promotional poster, ordering information, a link to Sean O'Brien's office so that people could get more information about the case, and a link to the Missouri governor's office so that people could send him their opinion about the case (and I used that link to contact the governor's office approximately once a week for several months). Several weeks after the initial release of the documentary, the Communication Department at Illinois State University (ISU), where I would begin work as an Assistant Professor the following August, designed an additional web page through which the video documentary could be viewed online in several formats, giving a much wider audience the opportunity to see it.

The promotion and exhibition of the video documentary was dependent on antideath penalty advocates in Missouri, and all events we initiated or joined were coordinated with those advocates, consistent with Whiteman's (2004) work. Our project, thus, was linked to the efforts of movement activists, which significantly aided the promotion and exhibition of the documentary. Events in St. Louis were cosponsored by the Eastern Missouri Coalition Against the Death Penalty, and events in Kansas City were cosponsored by the Western Coalition Against the Death Penalty and personnel from Sean O'Brien's office in Kansas City. Antideath penalty activists initiated many of the showings around Missouri, including additional screenings in Springfield, Joplin, and Jefferson City.

Promotion and exhibition of the documentary energized activists working on Amrine's case, and their efforts energized us. In particular, MU's American Civil Liberty Union's (ACLU) chapter became more active once the video came out. For example, at the first showing in Columbia, Amnesty International and Missourians Against the Death Penalty both had information tables at the event, and Amnesty International members started a petition drive in which those who opposed Amrine's execution signed a letter that was sent to the governor. The efforts of these advocates fueled our desire to fully maximize the promotional value of the documentary for educating the public about this case.

Effects

In November 2002, the Missouri Supreme Court reconsidered its previous decision not to hear Amrine's case. This was an unprecedented move, as the Missouri Supreme Court had never before reviewed a death sentence with a last-minute *habeas corpus* petition. Amrine and his lawyer, O'Brien, have commented that the publicity about the case generated by the video documentary may have persuaded the court to re-examine the case. Although Amrine had exhausted the normal appeal process, the court reviewed the case again. The Missouri Supreme Court held a public hearing in February 2003. During the hearing, the lawyer from the Missouri Attorney General's office argued that because Amrine had received a fair trial, the Supreme Court had no right to overturn the conviction. When pressed by the judges, the representative from that office said that the question of Amrine's innocence was irrelevant. O'Brien claimed he knew, at that point, Amrine's sentence would be overturned. On April 29, 2003, the Missouri Supreme Court released Amrine due to insufficient evidence.

There is evidence, if only anecdotal, of the impact that the video documentary had in saving Amrine's life. In the end, our efforts to gain media coverage were an important catalytic factor in the coverage of Amrine's case by the media and influenced the subsequent interest expressed in the case by the public and by the Missouri Supreme Court. The documentary, according to O'Brien, "did help to draw enough attention to get the court to take another look at the case" (cited in Blose, 2004, p. 10). O'Brien further explained to the press, "That documentary inspired a lot of people to look at the case and write the Governor and it inspired newspapers to start reporting on the case. It changed the whole dynamic" (cited in Blose, p. 11). O'Brien also said that he believed the video documentary influenced the Missouri Supreme Court's decision to review the case and that:

> The influence was to make the courts look at the case, because courts are concerned about how their judgments will appear in the public. For them to sit back silently and let Joe be executed would have created a public backlash. (cited in Heitzman, 2003, p. A10)

Amrine reiterated this view, stating in a published interview, "I couldn't get the public awareness before it [the video]. It did a world of good for me" (cited in Richardson, 2003, p. A1). Amrine repeatedly has stated that he believes the documentary had an impact on his release; for instance, he claimed that "prior to the documentary, I didn't have a lot of support. I had a little, but not as much as after the [documentary]. It saved my life" (cited in Youngs, 2003, p. 1). The battle to save Amrine involved the convergence of a number of voices, with activists and ordinary citizens raising their voices to demand justice in this case. The video documentary was a crucial factor in encouraging and supporting these voices.

LESSONS LEARNED ABOUT COMMUNICATION ACTIVISM

This chapter has described an example of communication activism informing and being informed by efforts to free an innocent man from a wrongful death sentence. There are several lessons about communication activism that can be learned from this experience. First, activism should be done not only to get results but, more simply, because it is the right thing to do. Our video documentary production team did not embark on this journey only for results (Amrine's release); we believed we had a responsibility to speak out, whatever the result. Honestly, I was skeptical that we could play a role in reversing a decision of the Missouri criminal justice system. However, if I had turned my back on the truth, especially in light of our communication abilities and access to communication resources that could make the project a reality, I felt I would not be fulfilling my democratic responsibility. Although it may be idealistic, citizens in a democracy have a responsibility to speak out against injustice when they see it. We all have different communication strengths and abilities, and the ideal of participatory democracy is that we should use those resources to speak out when our eyes have been opened to failures of our government to honor its humanitarian potential. To treat another person, even a convicted criminal, as I would wish to be treated is not special; it is what we need to do to call ourselves human beings. If Joe Amrine had been executed, we would have produced a video documentary that would have made a compelling case that a man innocent of a murder had been killed by the state, which would be valuable in the larger battle to ensure that innocent people are never executed and would have increased awareness that there always is a risk of killing innocent people when we rely on state-sanctioned murder as a response to crime (see Sunwolf, Volume 1). Fortunately, the people of Missouri did not, in this case, execute an innocent man.

Second, scholars need to take advantage of available resources for engaging in communication activism. University environments can provide much support to scholars who seek to make a positive difference in their communities. In general, MU was supportive of our efforts. We had access to the necessary equipment and personnel with specialized computer skills and other requisite knowledge, and the opportunity to work with students was helpful. We even received an award for the production of the documentary from the Peace Studies program at the university. If there were groups or administrators who opposed our activism, we did not hear from them. In the end, the video documentary garnered much positive media attention for the university and its Department of Communication.

After I began my first tenure-track position at ISU, the project was recognized as a combination of creative research activity and community service. Fellow faculty members and the chairperson of ISU's Communication Department were very supportive of the effort, although on at least one occasion, a fellow professor quipped that he hoped my continuing efforts to encourage video documentary to free those who had been wrongfully accused did not lead to freeing inmates who "shouldn't be free." Overall, however, the university environments in which I worked supported our effort and appreciated the publicity generated from the project. Activist scholars, thus, should take advantage of available resources and try to generate positive media coverage for the university in which they work.

A third lesson learned from this project was that activists should make it as easy as possible for news organizations to cover activists' issues. In this case, press releases, press kits, and the video documentary itself helped news managers and reporters to do their job. Another aspect of this lesson is that crafting effective sound bites makes reporters' jobs easier. If advocates offer several terse statements that reveal the heart of the matter rather than talking in long, meandering sentences, reporters will have better quotes at their disposal and not have to shift through statements to get quotable comments. This is just another example of the need for advocates to become media savvy by considering how reporters work and making their job easier.

A fourth lesson from this project is that the nature of a particular media market may be conducive (or disadvantageous) to a campaign for advocacy of social justice issues. In our case, Columbia is located 35 miles from Jefferson City, the state capital, which meant that every time we were able to gain media coverage, we also were getting coverage where state officials could see it. In addition, because this media market is smaller than the markets in the two largest cities in the state (St. Louis and Kansas City), it may have been easier to compete with other potential news items.

A fifth lesson is that when a case is as clear as was Amrine's case, it may be easier to persuade people to take note and become involved than in cases that are not so obvious. To me, the truth was simple and compelling: A man was about to be executed for a crime despite no witnesses or evidence against him. With a proposition that clear, the video documentary and resulting communication activism merely exposed the situation. I believe that even those who were in favor of the death penalty had a difficult time supporting Amrine's execution. The lesson is that activists should highlight the strengths of their cases.

Sixth, this project demonstrated that the theory of advocacy communication (McHale, 2004) and similar scholarship can inform an advocacy campaign (see, e.g., Goodman, 2003; Ryan, 1991; Ryan et al., 1998), and this interaction between communication scholarship and activism offers many lessons for communication scholar-activists. The recursive nature of this research and video production can be useful for others seeking to study activism at the same time that they assist activist efforts. Lessons were learned about the production and distribution of a video documentary, sharing information, coordinating activists' efforts, working with representatives from news outlets, and organizing lobbying efforts. The lesson here is that *praxis* (the combination of theory, research, and practice) is an effective way to engage in activism.

Another valuable lesson from this work supports Whiteman's (2004) contention that scholarship needs to emphasize the possibilities for video/film documentaries to have broad social influence rather than considering such effects solely within an individualistic framework (e.g., effects on individuals' beliefs, attitudes, and values). For instance, the impact of documentaries must be considered as one of a number of factors that can influence governmental action. Unfortunately, past research has neglected the potential influence of video/film documentary production, distribution, and exhibition on society. I have tried to address these issues in this research, and the result is a more organic picture of how video/film documentary can influence public policy.

One of the most important lessons from this experience is that the production and exhibition of a video/film documentary can be useful in the fight for social justice if there are links made between the documentary and a larger social justice movement. In this instance, there were extensive links between our work on the documentary and the movement against the death penalty in Missouri. Although I mentioned this connection at several points throughout this chapter, a key theme of the lessons that can be learned is that the influence of the documentary *Unreasonable Doubt: The Joe Amrine Story* was very much tied to the work of this social justice movement. Documentaries such as this one will have the most impact when all aspects of production, distribution, and exhibition are coordinated with the larger topical social movement. In many ways, I was not an "independent" video documentary producer/director but, rather, an activist rooted in a broader collective social justice effort.

Finally, every project has elements that could have gone better and much can be learned from these instances. In our case, one of the mistakes that we made was not having more personnel involved with the final stages of postproduction of the video documentary. For instance, an adequately staffed video production should have a sound editor whose responsibility includes checking that all the audio levels are consistent throughout the final video. The editor, assistant editor, and I assumed this responsibility, but it is preferable to have someone do this that has some distance from the arduous and detailed task of actually editing the documentary. We would have been well served to find and solicit the help of qualified personnel to help us with this task at the last stage of production. Although the sound was acceptable, variations in the audio levels between shots could be distracting. Although I likely am overly critical of this aspect of the documentary because I worked on it and viewed it so many times, variations in the audio levels in the initial version of the video documentary were disappointing to me.

CONCLUSION

In this chapter, I explored the use of video/film documentary as a form of communication activism designed to aid in preventing the execution of an innocent man. I identified how a theory about activist communication was useful in the preproduction, production, postproduction, exhibition, and promotion of this documentary, and helped to generate some important effects that can be attributed to this documentary. For instance, I would not have produced the documentary if the emerging theory on which I was working had not indicated that video can have an impact on viewers that other communication forms might not. All of our efforts related to the promotion of the documentary were influenced by transferable findings about how advocates communicate for particular purposes and to particular audiences. I also outlined some lessons learned from this experience about communication activism. The video documentary and the media attention it generated were an important factor in the battle to save Amrine's life, complementing and supporting the growing voices that demanded that Amrine be granted justice. Our experiences, thus, show that video/film production is an important form of communication activism that can assist marginalized members of society to secure political and social reform in the quest for social justice.

The story of the fight to save Amrine from execution is, as in all cases of activism, one of *gumption*, a word of old Scottish origin that refers to activists' will to advocate and their enthusiastic enactment of advocacy communicative *praxis* — action in the public realm or *polis* informed by theory and research. I was fueled by the injustice of Amrine's impending execution and my belief that our video production team and other Amrine supporters could effectively communicate the startling truth of his innocence. Gumption, thus, drove the battle to save Amrine, as is necessary in all advocacy efforts.

POSTSCRIPT

During the battle to save Amrine after the release of the video documentary, I either videotaped or had someone videotape relevant events, including protests, screenings, legal officials wrangling with decisions about how and when to release Amrine, and his joyous release and homecoming. I also secured permission to use television news footage about the case from several stations, which included footage of the Missouri Supreme Court hearing that led to Amrine's release. This footage has been crafted into a second documentary that was funded partially by the European community through an organization called Hands Off Cain (dedicated to fighting against the death penalty). In August 2004, Danny Glover committed to providing the voice-over for this second part of the story and his narration was recorded in New York City in October 2004. The video documentary, *Picture This: A Battle to Save Joe* (McHale, Wylie, & Huck, 2005), was completed in May 2005 (available from Hampton Press, and includes the *Unreasonable Doubt* documentary). *Picture This* has been screened at more than 50 venues, at the meeting of the United Nations Human Rights Commission in Geneva in April 2005, and was included in the 2005 Amnesty International On-Campus Film Festival. Hopefully, the second installment of our video documentary on the battle to save Amrine will help to promote the cause of abolishing the use of the death penalty in the United States.

REFERENCES

A film to save a life. (2002, May 7). *The Maneater*, p. 18.

Adorno, T. (1991). *The culture industry: Selected essays on mass culture.* New York: Routledge.

Allen, M. (1998). Comparing the persuasive effectiveness of one- and two-sided messages. In M. Allen & R. W. Preiss (Eds.), *Persuasion: Advances through meta-analysis* (pp. 87-98). Cresskill, NJ: Hampton Press.

Bandura, A. (1971). *Psychological modeling: Conflicting theories.* Chicago: Aldine-Atherton.

Barnouw, E. (1993). *Documentary: A history of the non-fiction film* (2nd rev. ed.). New York: Oxford University Press.

Blose, C. (2004). Lights, camera, activism. *Mizzou, 92,* 10-11.

Bohn, T. (1977). *An historical and descriptive analysis of the "Why we fight" series.* New York: Arno Press.

Brown, W. (2002a, February 22). Film probes death row inmate's case. *Columbia Missourian*, pp. A1, A9.

Brown, W. (2002b, March 7). Filmmakers challenge proposed execution. *Columbia Missourian*, p. A9.

Brown, W. (2002c, March 8). Group protests Amrine sentence. *Columbia Missourian*, p. A1.

Bruzzi, S. (2000). *New documentary: A critical introduction.* New York: Routledge.

Detrick, C. (2002, February 22). Filming for freedom. *The Maneater*, pp. 12-13.

Durkheim, E. (1933). *The division of labor in society* (G. Simpson, Trans.). Glencoe, IL: Free Press. (Original work published 1902)

Feldman, S., & Sigelman, L. (1985). The political impact of prime-time television: "The Day After." *Journal of Politics, 47,* 557-578.

Feldstein, M. J. (2002, February 17). Grad student's film explores murder case. *Columbia Daily Tribune*, p. A1.

Fiske, J., & Hartley, J. (1978). *Reading television.* London: Methuen.

Fromm, E. (1976). *To have or to be?* New York: Harper & Row.

Gandy, O. H., Jr. (1982). *Beyond agenda setting: Information subsidies and public policy.* Norwood, NJ: Ablex.

Gerbner, G. (1999). Cultivation analysis: An overview. *Mass Communication & Society, 3-4,* 175-194.

Glaser, B. G., & Strauss, A. L. (1967). *The discovery of grounded theory: Strategies for qualitative research.* Chicago: Aldine.

Goodman, S. (2003). *Teaching youth media: A critical guide to literacy, video production, and social change.* New York: Teachers College Press.

Hall, S. (1982). The rediscovery of "ideology": Return of the repressed in media studies. In M. Gurevitch, T. Bennett, J. Curran, & J. Woolacott (Eds.), *Culture, society, and the media* (pp. 56-90). New York: Methuen.

Heitzman, L. (2003, September 23). Amrine, filmmaker revisit case. *Columbia Daily Tribune*, p. A10.

Hovland, C. I., Janis, I. L., & Kelly, H. H. (1953). *Communication and persuasion: Psychological studies of opinion change.* New Haven, CT: Yale University Press.

Janis, I. L., Hovland, C. I., Field, P. B., Linton, H., Graham, E., Cohen, A. R. et al. (1959). *Personality and persuasibility.* New Haven, CT: Yale University Press.

Katz, E., & Lazarsfeld, P. F. (1955). *Personal influence: The part played by people in the flow of communications.* Glencoe, IL: Free Press.

Kidd, E. (2002, February 20). Filmmakers try to do the right thing. *Scene Magazine*, p. 11.

Klapper, J. T. (1960). *The effects of mass communication.* Glencoe, IL: Free Press.

Lasswell, H. D. (1935). *World politics and personal insecurity.* New York: Whittlesey House, McGraw-Hill.

Lazarsfeld, P. F., & Merton, R. K. (1948). Mass communication, popular taste, and organized social action. In L. Bryson (Ed.), *The communication of ideas, a series of addresses* (pp. 32-58). New York: Institute for Religious and Social Studies.

Lenart, S., & McGraw, K. (1989). America watches "Amerika": Television docudrama and political attitudes. *Journal of Politics, 51,* 697-712.

Lindlof, T. R., & Taylor, B. C. (2002). *Qualitative communication research methods* (2nd ed.). Thousand Oaks, CA: Sage.

Lippmann, W. (1922). *Public opinion.* New York: Harcourt, Brace.

Marcuse, H. (1964). *One-dimensional man: Studies in the ideology of advanced industrial society.* Boston: Beacon Press.

Marshall, S. (2002, March 8). Three local filmmakers leave no doubts in documentary about Amrine. *The Missourian,* p. 8.

McCombs, M. E., & Shaw, D. L. (1972). The agenda-setting function of mass media. *Public Opinion Quarterly, 36,* 176-187.

McHale, J. P. (2004). *Communicating for change: Strategies of social and political advocates.* Lanham, MD: Rowman & Littlefield.

McHale, J. P. (Producer/Director), Wylie, R. (Producer/Editor), & Huck, D. (Producer/Assistant Editor). (2002). *Unreasonable doubt: The Joe Amrine case* [Videotape/DVD].

McHale, J. P. (Producer/Director), Wylie, R. (Producer/Editor), & Huck, D. (Producer/Assistant Editor). (2005). *Picture this: A fight to save Joe* [Videotape/DVD]. (Available from Hampton Press)

Muzslay, L., & Ketchum, C. (1999). *Amrine on death row despite questionable evidence.* Unpublished manuscript.

Nichols, B. (1981). *Ideology and the image: Social representation in the cinema and other media.* Bloomington: University of Indiana Press.

Nichols, B. (1991). *Representing reality: Issues and concepts in documentary.* Bloomington: Indiana University Press.

Nichols, B. (1994). *Blurred boundaries: Questions of meaning in contemporary culture.* Bloomington: Indiana University Press.

Noelle-Neumann, E. (1984). *The spiral of silence: Public opinion, our social skin.* Chicago: University of Chicago Press.

Prejean, H. (1993). *Dead man walking: An eyewitness account of the death penalty in the United States.* New York: Random House.

Reeves, N. (1999). *The power of film propaganda: Myth or reality?* New York: Cassell.

Richardson, S. (2003, September 21). Freed inmate to make grateful visit to ISU. *The Pantagraph,* p. A1.

Ryan, C. (1991). *Prime time activism: Media strategies for grassroots organizing.* Boston: South End Press.

Ryan, C., Carragee, K. M., & Meinhofer, W. (2001). Theory into practice: Framing, the news media, and collective action. *Journal of Broadcasting & Electronic Media, 45,* 175-182.

Ryan, C., Carragee, K. M., & Schwerner, C. (1998). Media, movements, and the quest for social justice. *Journal of Applied Communication Research, 26,* 165-181.

Schramm, W. (1954). *The process and effects of mass communication.* Urbana: University of Illinois Press.

Schramm, W., Lyle, J., & Parker, E. B. (1961). *Television in the lives of our children.* Stanford, CA: Stanford University Press.

They're on death row. But should they be? Five cases where there may be big questions. (2000, June 12). *Newsweek,* p. 26.

Tönnies, F. (1940). *Fundamental concepts of sociology (Gemeinschaft und gesellschaft)* (C. P. Loomis, Trans.). New York: American Book. (Original work published 1887)

Walters, R. L. (1994). *Broadcast writing: Principles and practices* (2nd ed.). New York: McGraw-Hill.

Whiteman, D. (2004). Out of the theaters and into the streets: A coalition model of the political impact of documentary film and video. *Political Communication, 21,* 51-69.

Youngs, J. (2003, September 19). Amrine, activists speak out at rally. *The Maneater,* p. 1.

6

SPECTRUM WARS

Bridging Factionalism in the Fight for Free Radio

Ted M. Coopman

University of Washington

In the winter of 1999, the micro radio movement was in disarray. Throughout the 1990s, advocates of low-power (100 watts and under) community radio had fought an escalating war with the Federal Communications Commission (FCC) and incumbent broadcasters for access to the airwaves. The movement had expanded from its anarchist collectivist origins to include churches, community groups, right and left libertarians, and a host of others who were fed up with the state of U.S. media and had decided to do something about it. Apparently exhausted from the conflict and the accompanying bad print and television publicity, the FCC had acted on a petition for the legalization of low-power FM (LPFM). With the proposed rulemaking,[1] the FCC changed from enemy to reluctant ally. This created schisms within the micro radio movement, with the newer, more moderate members embracing the idea of legalization, but the anarchist pioneers of the movement, who had been fighting the FCC through the electronic civil disobedience of pirate radio, railing at the idea of licensing and the restrictions it would bring. Despite this split, all those involved agreed that a poorly conceived service would be far worse for all parties than outright prohibition. The question was how such a diverse, dispersed, and under-funded coalition of activists and community groups could come together to counterbalance the well-financed influence of the broadcasting lobby and ensure the creation of a functional LPFM service.

This chapter recounts my experiences in helping to create the Joint Statement on Micro Radio (JSMR) as part of the public comment period on the rulemaking for an LPFM service. The FCC is the government agency responsible for regulating telecommunications, including radio. One way the FCC formulates policy is by accepting petitions that suggest the modification, elimination, or creation of new regulations. The FCC conducts its own research and, if the staff and the Commission itself concur that the changes are justified, opens a rulemaking to ask for public comment. The rulemaking on LPFM was one of the first made accessible online via the Electronic Comments Filing System (ECFS). This system greatly improved access and resulted in a then-record 3,000 comments. This marked a significant change, as previously comments usually were filed only by affected industries and some public-interest organizations. Public comments are designed to argue not only for rejection, acceptance, or expansion of a rulemaking proposal but also to influence specific, often technical, details on how a particular policy functions. The devil, as they say, is in the details, and technical and organizational requirements can have huge ramifications for how a policy is implemented and functions.

The goal of the JSMR was to form a united front to advocate for specific technical and ownership restrictions for LPFM that would ensure it was accessible to the widest variety of communities, allow for the maximum number of new radio stations, require local ownership and control, and not fall prey to consolidation by large, deep-pocketed organizations. Several key movement participants who were collectively aware of what was needed for a successful radio service (myself included) believed that a document signed by all the major parties would carry more weight with regulators and clearly illustrate our solidarity.

The obstacle to cooperation on JSMR was an ideological division within the broader micro radio movement that centered on extra-legal radio stations having to go off the air to be eligible for a license, amnesty for those whose stations already had been shut down by the FCC, and the creation of a commercial, in addition to a noncommercial, LPFM license. These issues were emotionally charged and created a lot of animosity among participants. The challenge, therefore, became how to convince stakeholders to reserve controversial demands for their individual comments and come together on the many important technical issues that could make or break a new LPFM service.

I became involved with micro radio in 1993 while pursuing my master's degree in mass communication. My first serious forays into scholarship and activism, thus, were concurrent in the sense that I was educated in the ways of media activism and academe at the same time. My object of study soon became my political passion as I embraced the goals of this emerging movement. In many ways, the development of the movement, my scholarship, and my activism matured simultaneously, and this parallel development provided me with some insights into the role of the activist scholar. Furthermore, I found myself in a unique position within the movement as an "in-outsider," in that I was considered to be a participant but had exterior motives as a researcher. As I explain in this chapter, I was able to use my experience to make a unique contribution to the micro radio movement—the JSMR. I begin with a brief historical overview of the micro radio movement, followed by a discussion of emergent social movement networks and distributed communicative practices within the movement. I then discuss the process of developing the JSMR. I conclude the chapter by exploring some issues involved in doing activist research and sharing some final thoughts.

A BRIEF HISTORY
OF THE MICRO RADIO MOVEMENT

Community activist Mbanna Kantako coined the term "micro radio" (also known as free radio, or low-power radio), and his small low-power Springfield, IL station, put on the air in 1986, is widely considered to be the first station of the micro radio movement (Shields & Ogle, 1992). To Kantako and the other micro radio activists who followed him, micro radio meant radio that was community based, had free-form content, and was free of government oversight. Micro radio was needed because, at that time, the FCC did not grant FM licenses for radio stations under 100 watts.[2]

Micro radio remained a minor phenomenon until 1990, when activist anarchists embraced the concept in the wake of what they saw as the first Gulf War media debacle. Micro radio pioneer Stephen Dunifer, with the help of the National Lawyers Guild, launched a court challenge to the FCC's ban on low-power radio in an effort to begin to democratize media in the United States.

Dunifer was one of a growing number of "extralegal" radio activists across the United States engaging in what they saw as "electronic civil disobedience." Self-described anarchists ran a majority of the stations, arguing that if they could operate without interfering with other broadcasters, they should be able to broadcast without the restraint of government-issued licensing or oversight of content and political activity. These low-power radio broadcasters objected to the FCC's right to control access to the broadcast spectrum and challenged the constitutionality of broadcast regulations in court. Because they were not interested in obtaining licenses and saw the FCC as a corrupt tool of corporate media, micro radio broadcasters did not consider filing for a rule change on the prohibition of low-power radio (Coopman, 1999, 2000a, 2000b; Walker 2001).

Dunifer's legal challenge (*U.S. v. Dunifer*, 1995/1998) managed to survive long enough in federal court to set off an explosion of unlicensed radio activism to "seize the airwaves." Operating under the belief that the pending court case offered some protection from federal enforcement of broadcast regulations, and excited by the possibility of starting their own community radio stations, the number of low-power radio stations created by activists mushroomed. This was evidenced by the increased demand for transmitter kits, heightened FCC enforcement activity, and more activity on micro radio web sites and listservs (Anderson, 2003; Walker, 2001). The effect was that diverse groups of co-conspirators—from church and community groups to libertarians—joined the anarchists who started the movement (Coopman, 2000b). Although they shared the belief that mainstream media disenfranchised their views, many of the new members of this ad hoc movement did not share the anarchists' distaste of licensing or distrust of the FCC. Although most of these participants supported purely noncommercial radio, others argued that the issue was that media conglomerates had frozen out small entrepreneurs and agitated for commercial LPFM (Coopman, 2000a, 2000b; Walker, 2001).

Most of the more politically moderate community stations went off the air in fear of the FCC following the ruling against Dunifer in federal court, which held that he had no "official standing" to challenge FCC rules and, hence, the merits of his challenge were never heard (Coopman, 2000b). Although this ruling left the movement in some disarray, it did not alleviate the pressure on the FCC, which had been fighting a losing battle to shut down unlicensed radio stations for most of the 1990s (Coopman, 1999). Between 1997 and 1998, the FCC raided 44 radio stations (Anderson, 2003); however, the FCC claimed to have shut down, either through warnings or equipment seizures, over 250 radio stations in 1998 alone. In that year, the FCC estimated that there were 300-1000 unlicensed radio stations in operation (Curtius, 1998).

As the community group radio stations went off the air and the conflict between the FCC and free radio hardliners raged, a group of liberal advocates sensed that the government's resolve was wavering. This was evidenced by increasingly bad print press, rising expenditures in enforcement, pressure from religious and community groups relayed through their representatives, and the increasing likelihood that a court might find the whole regulatory system invalid. In 1997, advocates submitted a petition for a legal low-power radio service.

EMERGENT SOCIAL MOVEMENT NETWORKS

The micro radio movement is a new variant of social movements enabled by technological and social trends that developed during the 1990s. The nature of social movements has evolved and diversified since the 19th century, with social movements both affected by, and creating, broad societal and technological changes. Traditional labor and class-based, or "old," social movements diversified into "new" social movements, and different models of collective action sprung up in Europe and the United States. *New social movements* simply refer to social movements that arose after World War II and whose foci tended to be on issues that cut across traditional class lines (Eyerman & Jamison, 1991; Melucci, 1996). Eyerman and Jamison's (1991) model of "cognitive *praxis*" of social movements is at once an attempted synthesis of European and U.S. theories of collective action and a new conceptual framework for social movement analysis. Process based, this analysis focuses on the creative role of consciousness and cognition that transforms groups and individuals into social movements. From this perspective, collective action is a process that opens up spaces in which new types of knowledge and experience can emerge. Eyerman and Jamison identified three dimensions within their study of the environmental movement that articulate its cognitive *praxis*: cosmological, technological, and organizational.

The *cosmological dimension*, the most important dimension, articulates a movement's "world-view," its "historical meaning," "utopian mission," or "emancipatory aims" (Eyerman & Jamison, 1991, p. 68). This worldview is intertwined with a movement's identity. The issue of media democracy, the visceral as opposed to legal trope of free speech, and the idea of freeing the airwaves for use by the people clearly are the core of the micro radio movement's cosmology. As Eyerman and Jamison (1991) found, a worldview often only becomes manifest when opposition forces its articulation. The aggressive response of the broadcasting lobby and the FCC certainly provided a counterforce that helped to solidify the micro radio movement's cosmology.

The *technological dimension* involves the practical articulation of a movement. In this case, this was the "utopian" (Eyerman & Jamison's, 1991, term) embrace of technology to meet the movement's ends. Unfortunately, history shows that technologies have a tendency to increase rather than decrease social control (Beniger, 2003). Moreover, in this instance, it really is not possible to discuss this dimension as separate from the *organizational dimension*, the way a movement gets its message across. The technology of the internet has an explicit organizational structure. The utopian technologies are progressively less expensive computers, the internet, or, more specifically, e-mail, listservs, web sites, and the corresponding ability to organize and exchange information at little or no cost (for a more detailed discussion of the effects of the internet on the micro radio movement, see Coopman, 2000c). The use of these technologies clearly is in line with the same technological developments as described in the environmental movement by Eyerman and Jamison (1991). Organizationally and technologically, the micro radio movement is distributed and nonhierarchical. Individuals and groups have affinity relationships based on common goals and immediate needs and desires (for a discussion of affinity groups, see Palmer, Volume 1). In this way, the micro radio movement is a collectivity that closely resembles the anarchist sensibility (Epstein, 2001) exhibited by many activist groups over the last decade, which, considering the origins of many of the free radio stations, is not surprising.

Melucci (1996) theorized on the new iteration of collective action that springs from individuals' experience, as well as from collective experience. In complex societies, he saw a trend toward social movements manifesting and organizing in the form of networks. Conflicts increasingly involve individuals' identities and their ties to the uses and distribution of resources, as opposed to broader-based labor or class issues. In such an environment, collective action becomes a product of the beliefs and aspirations of the actors involved. Melucci recognized that "in the last 30 years, emerging social conflicts in complex societies have not expressed themselves through political action, but rather have raised cultural challenges to the dominant language to the codes that organize information and shape social practices" (p. 8). From such a perspective, everyday life and the individual become intertwined with collective action, which increasing avoids or ignores political frameworks. Although the micro radio movement eventually moved into a more traditional confrontation with the FCC, it made this transition under duress. Fundamentally, the movement had more to do with the anarchist practice of setting up autonomous zones (Bey, 1991) and seizing abandoned property through "squatting" than with seeking redress from the state. The impetus was to take action outside the system as opposed to petitioning government for redress, the latter being what eventually transpired despite the best efforts of the micro radio movement's founders.

The micro radio movement, thus, is an example of a social movement as a network. Although most of the research in social movement networks focuses on transnational movements, this national movement shares many of the same characteristics (see Arquilla & Ronfeldt, 2001; Gerlach, 2001; Hass, 1992; Keck & Sikkink, 1998; Tarrow, 1998, 2003). In fact, Tarrow (1998, 2003) believed that these global movements represent a "scale shift" from domestic or national to international social movements grounded in interpersonal social networks. Tarrow (1998) also found that those who are kept informed and stay in contact with other members of a social movement are more likely to stay active and interested in a particular social cause. As Tarrow (2003) explained, "diffusion/emulation and brokerage/coalition" are elements of transnational contention and scale shift; comparatively, "diffusion involves the transfer of information along established lines of interaction while brokerage entails the linking of more unconnected social sites" (p. 32). These processes foster the development and sharing of successful tactical and strategic repertoires, actions that have been proven to work (Tarrow, 1998; Tilly, 1975).

The micro radio movement exhibits these characteristics. The effectiveness of the movement largely is due to its ability to manage constantly shifting participation and the allocation of scare resources; these resources include intelligence about opponents, technical and organizational information, and mutual support and reinforcement. Multiple methods of interaction nourish the political and social diversity of the movement. The internet connecting traditional media and interpersonal networks enables the diffusion of novel ideas, as well as the introduction of new resources and, thereby, enhances "the strength of weak ties" (Granovetter, 1973, 1983), which are comprised of acquaintances and contacts that allow access to information and resources outside individuals' current social circles. These inherent characteristics made feasible organization and action on projects such as the JSMR.

The micro radio movement closely resembles Gerlach's (2001) segmented, polycentric, and networked (SPIN) organizations. These affinity networks are comprised of "many diverse groups, which grow and die, divide and fuse, proliferate and contract" and have "multiple, often temporary, and sometimes competing leaders or centers of influence" (Arquilla & Ronfeldt, 2001, p. 289). These groups form a "loose, reticulate, integrated network with multiple linkages through travelers, overlapping membership, joint activities, common reading matter, and shared ideals and opponents" (Arquilla & Ronfeldt, pp. 289-290). Multiple contact points and distributed infrastructures make these networks highly resilient. Gerlach envisioned SPIN networks as movement networks—overtly political and ideologically focused. Arquilla and Ronfeldt primarily were concerned with networks of groups rather than individuals; however, their "all-channel-network" model, "where everybody is connected to everybody else" (p. 8), is an accurate graphic representation of the micro radio movement. Moreover, Arquilla and Ronfeldt's interpretation of social network analysis clearly placed "interpersonal and relational properties," or "social capital," as the "interesting" factor in network participation (p. 318; see also Herman & Ettema, this volume). In the JSMR, my social capital and that of other agitators played a direct role in our ability to negotiate with different factions and dictated the way that negotiations were organized.

To further understand how the micro radio network evolved, I developed the concept of a "dissentwork" (Coopman, 2005). A *dissent network*, or *dissentwork*, is a network of individuals that emerges as an alternative, or in opposition, to entrenched hierarchical organizations or systems. Residual communication infrastructures from mediated and interpersonal contacts provide the foundation of an emergent dissentwork. In the West's information- and communication-pervasive society, people's exposure to divergent information is ever-expanding. People participate in communities that are extensions of the physical world or wholly virtual (Bell, 2001; Correll, 1995; Watson, 1997). As time progresses, these connections become denser and interconnected. For instance, the density of connections that the micro radio movement had were quite robust after 6 years (1993-1999) of struggle.

Certain robust information cascades through these connections until it reaches a critical point and creates potentially observable effects. *Memes*, broadly construed as rich concepts or ideas that resonate with people's lifestyles and form the building blocks of culture that help people to assemble their reality, much like a gene is a building block of life (Blackmore, 2000; Brodie, 1995), and information cycle through these connections and can resonate with certain individuals. Given time and opportunity, individuals act on the information, which can manifest a dissentwork. Dissentworks, thus, are emergent manifestations of resistance and action based on an unofficial consensus among participants on what is reasonable/unreasonable or just/unjust, a consensus that is enabled and magnified by digital technology. Although face-to-face (FtF) interactions or old media, such as print and broadcasting, also are potential elements of a dissentwork, the instantaneous nature and low cost of digital communication act as the catalyst of a dissentwork and make the potential effects more profound and widespread (Coopman, 2005).

I argue that the micro radio movement is a dissentwork. The micro radio movement, although still largely intact, has folded itself into a large media democracy meta-movement that has grown to include the Independent Media Center (or IMC movement), media and press reformers and critics, and groups that support community media.[3] It has further diversified into those who support the development of legal LPFM stations, others who still operate and support extra-legal stations, and some who work actively on reform of broadcast regulations. These groups and individuals, for the most part, continue to interact through established distributed communicative practices.

DISTRIBUTED COMMUNICATIVE PRACTICES

The first free radio stations were mainly anarchist collectives. Epstein's (2001) examination of anarchism and the antiglobalization movement found many of the same characteristics that were manifest in the free radio movement years earlier. This parallelism is not surprising because these same tendencies became fixtures in many activist circles beginning in the early 1990s. Epstein called this an anarchist "sensibility," or what I term "practical anarchism." *Anarchism*, in the context of free radio, is a commitment to a particular organizational structure and egalitarian ethic, or what Epstein called "politics of the moment" (¶ 1), more than anything else.

In many ways, this view is reminiscent of Scott's (1985) concept of "everyday resistance," in which resistance to domination, in any form, usually comes from a myriad of small acts rather than through full-scale confrontation. As Scott observed, "In light of a supportive subculture, risk is reduced by large-scale complicity" (p. 35). Scott described everyday resistance as "a social movement with no formal organization, no formal leaders, no manifestoes, no dues, no name, and no banner" (p. 35). Everyday resistance is tactical, as opposed to strategic and calculated, and usually is based on immediate gains. Over time, individual grievances have the potential to become collective grievances and individual tactical acts, in turn, "circle back to influence consciousness" (Scott, p. 38). The free radio movement followed this trajectory with individual anarchist collectives running extra-legal radio stations that were involved in their communities. These anarchists came from the ranks of other activist groups and brought their social action orientation with them. These activists teamed up with other groups and invited into the movement all those who shared their collective grievances. As a movement, these distributed and diverse groups proved hard for authorities to deal with (Coopman, 1999). The involvement of a wider sector of society bought individual free radio stations a certain amount of collective cover.

Everyday resistance represents a dissentwork-like social movement structure, as described in Bleiker's (2000) concept of "transversal dissent." He argued, based on an examination of the collapse of East Germany, that rather than distinct organizationally driven phenomena, dissent is evolving into a myriad of small acts that reach a critical mass where emergent collective action takes place. The interlaced social networks that appeared in the confined geography of the German Democratic Republic, therefore, were analogous to the distributed networks of the micro radio movement. A similar effect was seen in the 2001 People Power 2 revolt in the Philippines (Rheingold, 2002).

Anarchist free radio collectives, thus, emerged from a variety of pre-existing activist groups with anarchist sensibilities. A primary part of these sensibilities involved consensus decision making (see Palmer, Volume 1).

Achieving consensus, in spirit if not in practice, is central to the collective structure in anarchist free radio stations. Activist and free radio web sites, such as the "Anarchism in Action" section on Radio4all.org, as well as Foodnotbombs.net and Consensus.net, explore consensus decision making and all its variations; indeed, many members of the media democracy movement consider Consensus.net the ultimate resource online. Although there are many decision-making techniques, the concept of consensus is central to the culture of these radio stations. The similar philosophies that activists bring to these stations from other anarchist groups create an atmosphere in which members share decision-making styles that maximize the opportunity for cooperation (Sager & Gastil, 1999). The close interactions and common experiences of members further create a culture that maintains a collectivist atmosphere (Kennedy, 1998; Monroe, 2001).

Even as the free radio movement spread to encompass groups and individuals with different philosophies and ideologies, this mode of consensus decision making persisted. In particular, the commitment to consensus was not the result of a mass conversion to anarchist philosophy but to the technical and logistical demands of a distributed and leaderless national movement. The distributed and often asynchronous nature of the internet encouraged distributed and asymmetrical decision making. Burke (1997) argued that *power*, defined as one actor's ability to control resources that another person desires, is not inherent in any position within a network. The desire Burke identified is not in gaining advantage but in participation, finding that "power is dependent on both the network structure and the nature of the identities positioned in that network" (p. 149); thus, power is negotiated. This negotiation illustrates the nature of the interaction between the position (node) and the actor (identity) in understanding power. In her research on the Holocaust, Monroe (2001) found that moral and ethical reciprocity and trust existed between self-identified network members. That is, for Jewish rescuers, versus bystanders or Nazi sympathizers, personal relationships and social networks were better predictors of individuals' action than were religion or other cultural factors. Once one self-identifies in a particular category, the tendency is to extend equity across all members. In the case of the micro radio movement, requests for assistance or offers of help on the Micro Radio Network (MRN) listserv, for instance, usually were taken at face value, as participants were fellow movement members.

The relationship between participants in the micro radio movement is founded on the constructs and exercise of identity, the motivation for participation, and the functionality of the micro radio movement dissentwork. The power of a dissentwork rests in the conflation of distinct identities into coordinated action for perceived self- and group benefit. That power is exercised and self-reinforcing in the sense of affecting people's ability to participate, validation of their identity, and their belief that action will result in desired outcomes. In this case, participants with differing ideologies found commonalties within the context of a larger goal—access to the airwaves.

Although local action and coordination between participants were facilitated through FtF interaction, regional and national deliberation and coordination were achieved through computer-mediated communication (CMC). van Dijk (1996) articulated a useful bridge between explorations of democracy and CMC, arguing on the most basic level that CMC, or information and communication technology (ICT) in his terminology, offers a technology of freedom that fundamentally could alter traditional group decision making. Although van Dijk's analysis is directed primarily at the larger political functions of democracy and their applications, it is relevant in this context, for the level of participation and wide-ranging discussions on the rulemaking by movement participants would not have been possible without CMC. These discussions informed the smaller deliberation on the JSMR, whose participants were so geographically distributed that the logistics of communicating would have been so difficult and expensive that the negotiations never would have taken place. Furthermore, the national cohesion of the micro radio movement would have been much more problematic without the use of CMC.

Generally, CMC discussions take longer to accomplish the same amount of work in a given time frame and participants make fewer remarks when compared to FtF communication (Bordia, 1997), which is most likely due to the mediated nature of online discussion. However, Bordia (1997) found that CMC and FtF groups were similar in the overall time period used to complete a task, the number of remarks made (including task-related comments), and the ability of these groups to successfully complete their tasks. CMC groups outperformed FtF groups on idea generation, as well as reduced individuals' production blocking (the tendency to obstruct) and their apprehension of their peers' evaluation. Moreover, CMC groups also were superior in their ability to increase in size, with no decrease in individual productivity, and showed greater equality in member participation and reduced normative social pressure. This scaling ability of CMC was evidenced by the rapid expansion and diversity of the micro radio movement coinciding with its increased effectiveness. Furthermore, social norms on the MRN listserv were emergent rather than imposed, due to the inability to discipline participants, although this environment largely was influenced by the listserv operators' unwillingness to intervene to impose rules. For instance, dyadic exchanges were taken off-list unless they could be linked to broader member concerns. Where CMC fell short was in regard to socioemotional interaction. The unavailability of social cues and the extended time needed for CMC versus FtF communication made incidental talk less likely to occur. The lack of such cues also resulted in more uninhibited behavior in CMC groups, which, depending on the behavior, could be a positive or negative attribute of reduced normative social pressure. The various ways of communicating and interpreting social cues on the MRN listserv certainly reflected this, as participants' tendencies to "read" messages from specific individuals in a positive or negative light, although an impediment at times, could be used as an advantage. For example, a comment or suggestion by a member of a particular activist group might automatically be dismissed or perceived as a slight by an ideological opponent, whereas another participant not affiliated with that group could reframe this original post by offering a more nuanced interpretation of the poster's intent or otherwise legitimating the comment by engaging it. These negotiated discourses became a listserv norm.

Postmes, Spears, and Lea (2000) found that, as in FtF groups, CMC group norms emerge over time. Moreover, supplemental FtF interaction among CMC group members had a minimal impact on the development of these norms, especially compared to "the emergent normative influence in the use of technology" (Postmes et al., p. 364). In addition, they found that the salience of social identities became greater over time with distinct groups. Therefore, within the context of a CMC group, long-term interaction should result in the increased ability of members to note social cues within messaged texts. Different relationships and ways of interacting between specific individuals on the MRN listserv became evident over time, and the often-coarse language or put-downs were no longer perceived as negatives. On one occasion, I sent a personal e-mail to a participant about a particularly strong rebuke being unhelpful to the group discussion, and he informed me that he had known the person in question for years and, therefore, that person knew not to take being called a "fucking idiot" personally.

Paccagnella (1997) found in his ethnographic study of open virtual communities that "people can build personal relationships and social norms that are absolutely *real* and meaningful even in the absence of physical, *touchable* matter" (p. 2). Rafaeli and Sudweeks (1997) discovered that "CMC is an experiment in social integration and democratic participation" (Introduction, ¶ 2), in that it is a new medium in which interaction is negotiated and recontextualized. In their study of large online groups, Rafaeli and Sudweeks argued that the "documented presence of interactivity in the behavior of these groups is both evidence for their reality, and a mechanism for their formation" (Discussion, ¶ 2). Furthermore, although interactivity was both absent and present in this CMC environment, Rafaeli and Sudweeks asserted that FtF groups also exhibit the tendency to fall in and out of interactivity. The dynamics of online interaction combined with preexisting organizational tendencies made the cognitive level and speed of communication and decision making possible for the micro radio movement. Having participated in both FtF and virtual discussions of issues affecting the movement, neither seemed more "real" or valuable to participants.

These factors all came into play when the movement was faced with the issue of specific coordinated action within the constraints of the FCC LPFM rulemaking. Whereas opportunistic tactical actions, protests, and resource exchanges gave participants a good deal of flexibility with opponents and other challenges, the direct interaction with a government regulatory agency within the context of this narrowly defined proceeding was a different matter. This is what the micro radio movement faced in January 1999 with the surprise announcement of a rulemaking for a low-power radio service.

IT'S THE JOINT: HANGING TOGETHER OR HANGING SEPARATELY

In 1997, the Amherst Alliance and Richard Harrison each filed a petition requesting the creation of a low-power radio service, and, in 1998, the FCC opened these petitions for public comment. A radio broadcast engineer, Roger Skinner, then filed another petition for such a service that was folded into the general FCC comment period. The Amherst Alliance is a relatively small but nationally distributed media reform organization that advocates for government policies intended to foster greater diversity of ownership and programming in the media. The Committee for Democratic Communication (CDC) filed a successful extension request for more public comments, and The National Association of Broadcasters (NAB), the main lobbying group for television and radio broadcasters in the United States, later requested and received another extension. The initial comment period ended in the fall of 1998. In general, public interest in micro radio was high, with over 20,000 inquiries on LPFM flooding the FCC in 1998 alone. Still, few in the movement thought that these petitions could overcome the objections of the powerful broadcasting lobby, and many believed that any proposed LPFM service would be so flawed as to be dead on arrival (Anderson, 2003).

On January 28, 1999, the FCC adopted MM Docket No. 99-25 as a rulemaking for the creation of a LPFM service. The MRN listserv had been especially active around the first of that year as it became apparent that the FCC was seeking an armistice in the radio wars of the previous decade. After a long, hard year of FCC raids and increasing strife within the micro radio movement, this rulemaking was met with both relief and suspicion. Many moderate participants welcomed any positive recognition by the FCC and the chance that they might be able to obtain a license and either get on the air or return to the airwaves. Even the edgiest radio anarchists wondered what it would be like to not have to worry about an interagency SWAT team crashing through their studio door. Although the movement as a whole was united in members' desire for access to the airwaves, how that access would manifest was open to interpretation. The do-it-yourself (DIY) anarchist and libertarian core of the movement renounced the concept of licensing as unwarranted government intrusion, seeing a license as a contract with the government that restricted freedom and content—essentially requiring a license to dissent. Many movement members desired squatters' rights to any open radio spectrum, perhaps including a simple registration system, to prevent the FCC from allocating their frequency space; others were more pragmatic and would settle for the chance at a license that did not cost the hundreds of thousands of dollars in engineering and attorney fees normally required to get a full-power station on the air.

Movement members' reactions ranged from calls to redouble the mobilization to seize the airwaves through electronic civil disobedience and force a full FCC capitulation to embracing the FCC as a new ally against incumbent broadcasters and gladly accepting what the agency was willing to offer. A small group of us saw the FCC's move as a potential catastrophe. I had remarked on the MRN listserv years earlier that the most effective step the FCC could take was the creation of a new radio service that would split the micro radio movement, consume all of the unoccupied radio spectrum, and eliminate any legal cover or recourse for radio activists. Worse still, if the FCC did not impose ownership restrictions, the same media giants who ruled the airwaves would consume the scraps on which the pirates had been living. The potential of the LPFM rulemaking to split the movement became evident in the FCC's "grace period" for extra-legal broadcasting, with operational unlicensed stations being given until February 23, 1999 to shut down; if these stations went dark, the operators would not have their activities used to prevent them for consideration as future licensees.

Don Schellhardt had been a member of MRN, as well as the practical (if not official) leader of the Amherst Alliance. Together with Nickolaus and Judith Leggett, he filed one of the petitions that instigated the LPFM rulemaking procedure. According to the Amherst Declaration of September 17, 1998 (see http://www.amherstalliance.org/declaration.html), the Alliance's goal was a low-power radio service comprised of both commercial and noncommercial stations. This placed the Amherst Alliance at odds with many members of micro radio movement, such as the National Lawyers Guild and micro radio pioneer Dunifer, who saw commercialization of the airwaves as one of the evils against which the movement was fighting. Schellhardt believed that his aspirations to resuscitate mom-and-pop commercial radio could coexist with the desires of the noncommercial radio advocates. The existence of extra-legal micro radio stations that used advertising and the realization that noncommercial radio (especially evangelical networks) could be just as predatory and monopolistic as commercial radio bolstered his position. Schellhardt approached the movement through the MRN listserv and opened a dialogue in February 1999 with this in mind.

Although larger issues, such as corporate control of 95% of the U.S. media, continued to flare up on the MRN listserv, the discussions quickly turned toward consideration of pragmatic action regarding technical problems, ownership protections, local content, and defense against broadcasting interests. Although there were many points of agreement, several major stumbling blocks emerged, or what Schellhardt referred to on the listserv as "poison pills." These stumbling blocks, especially the commercial element of the LPFM service and an amnesty for pirates who had continued broadcasting, formed wedges between factions and often resulted in acrimonious discussion.

> To the extent that the commission is today considering simply a lower tier of commercial broadcasters we strongly disagree.
>
> —Press Release by the CDC and the
> National Lawyers Guild (January 28, 1999)

> I am a capitalist, but I love my neighborhood.
>
> —Bill Doerner
> (Post on MRN Listserv, February 4, 1999)

Two weeks into the discussion, Schellhardt ceased arguing the commercial radio service issue. A crucial founding element of the Amherst Alliance was the desire for members to own, operate, and make a modest living from small commercial radio stations dedicated to promoting local businesses. Seeking reciprocity from other movement members, the Amherst Alliance endorsed noncommercial, nonprofit stations as part of the overall service. However, anticapitalists and critics of commercial radio excess still were staunchly opposed to any type of commercial LPFM and, consequently, it was difficult to get support behind the Amherst Alliance when the majority involved in the debate saw the current problem as too much commercial radio. Participants said they thought that the "commies" in Amherst would be good stewards, but they also expressed skepticism that other licensees would be so trustworthy. The terms "commies" and "non-commies"—advocates favoring and rejecting commercial LPFM, respectively—were descriptors I created as a joke for a listserv post in an attempt to cool down the rhetoric. These ironic, humorous, and non-pejorative terms for the different factions resonated with many listserv members and often were used during these deliberations. Any possibility of accommodation on the issue

ceased at the end of February when the CDC announced that it was organizing a collective filing for noncommercial advocates. The rejection of a dual
service was a bitter blow to the Amherst Alliance, whose members saw it as
an effort to cut them out of LPFM.

> I think that the work that you all are doing has reached its most impor-
> tant stage—but I do think that the credibility in D.C. that you seem to
> value so much would not be so credible if the above-mentioned stations
> and others had not put their asses on the line, turned "pirate radio" from
> a clandestine hobby into a political movement, and put this issue on the
> national map.
>
> —Shawn Ewald
> (Post on the MRN Listserv, February 4, 1999)

> At the same time, we will ALSO be saying that Times Have Changed—
> and the moral rationale for civil disobedience has now been eroded by
> the FCC's new display of open-mindedness.
>
> —Don Schellhardt
> (Post on the MRN listserv, February 6, 1999)

Just as the Amherst Alliance believed that the rejection of a commercial
component was tantamount to death, the free radio pioneers saw the refusal
of the Amherst Alliance to back full unconditional amnesty as a slap in the
face to those who had advanced the movement to this point. The Amherst
Alliance supported amnesty for previously interdicted, as well as extra-legal,
stations that went off the air by the putative February 23, 1999 deadline.
Moreover, it felt that an "electromagnetic ceasefire" was in order and that
this would demonstrate that micro radio advocates were not just rabble but
a movement that could be negotiated with in good faith. However, most of
those involved with the movement over many years had lost faith in the
process or the FCC as a trustworthy party. These members thought that the
only trump card they held was the ability to put extra-legal stations on the
air. If stations went dark, the FCC would no longer feel any pressure to act
quickly and, they argued, this would slow down the process. With no presence on the air, community support would wane and activist broadcasters
would lose focus and disperse. Many activists, thus, saw the Amherst
Alliance's position as highjacking a movement they had painstakingly built
over years of struggle and at great personal cost.

Hopelessly at odds over commercial LPFM and amnesty, the main two
factions went their own way in responding to the FCC rulemaking. Each
worked to gain external allies and craft its respective filing. There was some

discussion of purging "commies" on the MRN listserv or starting a "non-commie" list, but it was decided that the MRN listserv still represented a good place to keep in touch and informed.

> A joint agreement is something we ALL AGREE on. (If we wanted to file a joint DIS-agreement we would have it out this evening.) It is not important right now what we DO NOT agree on, only what we DO agree on.
>
> —Ted M. Coopman
> (Post to MRN listserv, March 7, 1999)

I had supported the idea of some type of collective statement from the movement as a whole, as I was convinced that a joint statement would carry considerable weight with the FCC commissioners or, in a worst-case scenario, compelling evidence in a court challenge. However, it became apparent that some issues could not be overcome and that different factions within the broader micro radio movement would file their own rulemaking comments. It also was apparent that Schellhardt would be unable to pull together the major factions, as his affiliation with the Amherst Alliance had "tainted" him in the eyes of many. After reviewing the listserv discussions, I concluded that two sets of comments, those of Petri Dish of the Prometheus Radio Project and those of the Amherst Alliance, were the most coherent and organized. I stripped out the poison pills and reconciled these two documents. I agonized over whether to add my preferences in this new document, but ultimately decided only to apply my knowledge of federal regulations, First Amendment law, and FCC culture in modifying or adding material. On March 5, 1999, I posted the first draft of this document to the MRN listserv and asked for feedback. Schellhardt responded first by personal e-mail, laying out, as was his tendency, an exhaustive analysis of my draft. Based on his response, it was apparent that the most difficult aspect of my work would be to reconcile the position of the noncommercial wing with that of the Amherst Alliance. I now was well aware what was palatable for the "non-commies"; it now was a matter of selling it to the Amherst Alliance.

The MRN listserv is an open forum, and the listserv operators kept us updated on lurkers from the government and the radio industry. Postscript comments to the enemies in our midst became standard fare in listserv discussions. Generally, sensitive items were discussed off-list. The general consensus, however, was that spies could lurk all they wanted, as they could not stop us anyway. However, Schellhardt always was conscious of security and suggested that we keep detailed negotiations off the listserv, so that any lurkers would view the movement as divided and any group statement would be a surprise. This concern would be validated when the NAB included out-of-context excerpts from MRN listserv posts, including one of my own, in its rulemaking comments.

A consistent voice of reason and a lighting rod for some of the more vociferous anarchists on the MRN listserv was Jesse Walker, an associate editor at the libertarian magazine *Reason*, who would later write a university press-published alternative history of U.S. radio (Walker, 2001). Walker enjoyed wide access to a variety of political and social milieus and offered a thoughtful and consistent left-libertarian perspective. I attempted to enlist him as a signatory to the JSMR, but he demurred, choosing to limit his endorsement to his own comments. He did, however, support my overall strategy and provided consistent and valuable technical and philosophical advice to me during the drafting of the joint statement. His understanding of communication policy, law, and history provided a double-check on my knowledge and perspectives, and having another "expert" outside the factional divides was critical to the negotiation process.

The JSMR was a technical vehicle for an ideological statement. The ideals of local media access and control and general media democracy had to be distilled into a technical argument that would appeal to the staff and Commission members at the FCC. Despite different interpretations of these concepts, the underlying ideals cut across all factions. With the help of Walker, my contribution was to craft language that skirted potential regulatory or constitutional conflicts and ground the arguments in practical requirements to meet our goals. This often meant backing into positions that would have a result we desired, without overtly stating our position on the issue, as well as forecasting loopholes and trying to plug them. Language and word choice reflected the administrative and regulatory culture we were attempting to reach. It was not a matter of pushing our agenda on the agency so much as pulling our agenda out of the FCC in such a way as to make it part of its agenda as well. It is crucial to understand that most of the FCC (like many three-letter government agencies) is comprised of civil servants, lawyers, and engineers, many of whom were (by and large) sympathetic to the creation of the proposed LPFM service. In many ways, we needed to give the regulators the tools to make the case for us.

Through the spring of 1999, I worked with Schellhardt to prune and fine-tune the JSMR. The CDC group comments were debated daily on the MRN listserv, making the position of the noncommercial wing of the movement readily apparent. Between Schellhardt and me, we brought several smaller groups into the JSMR discussion; these included Americans for Radio Diversity (ARD) out of Minneapolis (MN), Prometheus Radio Project, Radio Free Richmond (VA), and the Michigan Music is World Class! Campaign headed by Green Party members Tom and Sue Ness. Known to us as *Jam Rag* (their publication), Tom and Sue Ness and their staff had organized a powerful grassroots statewide movement in support of LPFM. Between these groups and the CDC, I emerged as the "honest broker" (in Schellhardt's words) who moved between all sides producing and distributing the evolving drafts. The pressure was intense. I feared that we would not have enough time to circulate the JSMR to collect signatures from movement members and supporters in time for the initial public comments deadline of April 12, 1999. Fortunately, problems with the FCC's new online filing system pushed back that date. The comment period again was delayed, over the objections of the Amherst Alliance, to August 2, 1999, in response to the NAB extension request. These delays turned out to be crucial to the success of the JSMR. My plan had been to go public with the major parties already signed on, as I thought that this would lead other groups and individuals to add their support as well. Moreover, it would solidify the JSMR as a completed document and, thereby, head off further debate from other parties that might endanger the brokered agreement, a real danger given that many parties still were fixated on the major sticking points between factions.

Drafts of the JSMR were flying between the Amherst Alliance and the CDC. With the exception of one phone call to Phil Tymon, a movement activist and lawyer working with the CDC, all exchanges were conducted via email. The technical and wording differences were resolved by early July 1999, the CDC and the Amherst Alliance signed on, and the JSMR was publicly released on the MRN listserv.

The final version of the JSMR reflected both a response to elements within the proposed rulemaking and inclusion of elements that the movement considered to be critical. The document was designed to transfer as much power as practical to communities and protect against the consolidation that had so negatively affected full power radio through a variety of technical and ownership restrictions. These restrictions often were mutually self-reinforcing and structured so that a central theme, such as local control, was advanced even if some elements were rejected. For example, we opposed (successfully) the creation of the largest class of LPFM, 1,000 watts. Setting the limit at 100 watts would allow for more stations. A 100-watt station has a smaller contour (signal reach), which concentrates focus on more specific constituent communities. Smaller reach reduces the utility of a station to incumbent broadcasters, both as an acquisition or cooptation target and as a competitive threat. Moreover, ownership is restricted to those living within the contour, and cross-ownership with other media or multiple-station ownership would be prohibited (another success, at least in the short term). This feature was designed to increase responsiveness to community concerns. Finally, time sharing and locally based conflict resolution between applicants and stations were encouraged. Other provisions included a restriction on transferring licenses, a "use it or lose it" provision to ensure frequencies were utilized, and a rule barring LPFM stations from being used as translators (rebroadcasting another station's signal).

The Micro Radio Masses Vote

> We, the undersigned organizations and individuals, representative of a wide spectrum of micro radio advocates, strongly believe that the items contained in this Joint Agreement are essential to the success of any Low Power Radio Service. Individual signatories may hold differing views concerning many aspects of the proposed rulemaking and will file individual comments as well as signing this agreement. The absence of items or issues in this agreement is not meant to imply or indicate any specific stance by any of the signatories. This agreement simply states aspects of the proposed rulemaking that are of such importance that they cut across all ideological lines and are accepted as essential to the fair and proper creation of a Low Power Radio Service.
>
> —Preamble to the JSMR

Support by the CDC and the framing of the JSMR presentation as an additional, as opposed to a primary, group comment were the two factors that made the JSMR palatable to most of the movement participants. Support for the JSMR started slowly, but quickly built momentum as the August 2, 1999 deadline loomed. Tom Ness and his crew hit the streets of Michigan to collect signatures. Despite declarations that a comment without amnesty for extra-legal broadcasters would be a nonstarter for certain listserv members, most of those groups and individuals saw the value of the JSMR and signed on. The most notable of these was the A-infos Radio Project/Radio4all collective headed by Lyn Gerry and Shawn Ewald (the MRN listserv operators) and the Prometheus Radio Project. Interest in the JSMR remained high, even after the first deadline passed, and two supplements (which allowed the addition of more signatures) to the JSMR were filed later that month, which included the Micro Empowerment Coalition (MEC), and initial signatories, such as Prometheus and the CDC, and added the voice of Fairness and Accuracy in Reporting (FAIR).

Ultimately, 31 organizations representing 13 states and 97 individuals from 17 states signed the JSMR. Perhaps more importantly, many of the organizational signatories also filed individual comments, which had the net effect of reinforcing key elements that cut across the different filings. The willingness and ability of the parties to come together was a testament to the social action possibilities unleashed through new communication technologies, as well as the power of emergent coalition affinity networks.

Epilogue

Countermobilization by the NAB previously had focused on pushing the FCC to crack down on unlicensed stations and in exaggerating technical concerns, such as signal interference. Much to the surprise and disgust of micro radio advocates, National Public Radio (NPR), despite diplomatic efforts, came out in opposition to any LPFM service. NPR cited concerns over the crowding on the reserved section of the FM band where most noncommercial stations are located and interference with the Reading Services to the Blind, which was a carrier signal that piggybacked on a station's primary signal and was picked up by a special receiver. The FCC found no credible interference issues, or as the activists would say, other than interference with monopoly control and incumbent broadcasters' bottom line.

When it became apparent that the FCC would proceed with some type of low-power service, incumbent commercial broadcasters managed, oddly aligning themselves with many free radio activists, to remove any commercial uses. The pressure partially was removed from NPR when the now fully noncommercial service was allowed on frequencies in both the reserved and nonreserved parts of the FM band. Incumbents who still had underlying epistemological issues with this new service focused their concern on the use of third-adjacent channels to create new space for LPFM stations.[4] Briefly, adjacent channels on either side of a station's frequency are reserved space to prevent interference between stations. These buffers are relics of the limitations of 1960s-era broadcast technology. However, broadcasters were loath to give up any spectrum space that had potential uses.

Despite opposition from the NAB and NPR, the FCC created a LPFM radio service in 2000. Although the FCC has the reputation of being a "tool" of industry, this varies among administrations, with William Kennard's tenure as Commissioner being marked by hostility with incumbent broadcasters on the LPFM issue (Opel, 2004). Failing to curtail use of third-adjacent channels, incumbent broadcasters sought relief from allies in Congress.

Incumbent broadcasters' heavy lobbying over signal interference concerns resulted in the U.S. Congress scaling back available frequencies by 70%, which was a direct result of the repudiation of FCC technical expertise by incumbents and the related demand that third-adjacent protections be preserved. The ironically titled Radio Broadcasting Preservation Act (RBPA), which put restrictions on the frequencies that the FCC could use for LPFM, made it into law as a rider on an Omnibus Spending Bill in late 2000 (Stavistsky, Avery, & Vanhala, 2001). Such flexing of corporate muscle over turf, profits, and regulatory control presents the greatest countermovement-style threat to media reformers (Hamilton, 2004). Despite the RPBA, KCJM-LP, the first LPFM station, went on the air June 21, 2001 in Alexandria, LA.

As of March 2005, the Federal Communications Com-mission (2005) listed 371 licensed LPFM stations.

As part of the RBPA, Congress ordered an independent interference study and, in 2003, the MITRE Corporation (2003) validated the claims made by the FCC and by LPFM advocates, finding no interference issues with this new service. In fact, the decision to employ MITRE backfired on LPFM opponents. The rather conservative FCC plan for the opening of third-adjacent channels was outdone by MITRE's finding that the second-adjacent channel should be opened as well. This irony was not lost on the previously disparaged FCC engineers (personal communication, November 15, 2004). The MITRE findings, combined with public outrage over media ownership limits (McChesney, 2004), boded well for a possible expansion of LPFM.

There were two parties that managed to bring the issue of community radio and LPFM to the forefront of national media policy: the micro radio pioneers, who put the original pressure on the FCC through electronic civil disobedience; and the Amherst Alliance, which sensed that the time was right to approach the FCC and set the rulemaking process in motion. Ironically, these two groups were the big losers in the eventual LPFM service. The poison pills of commercial LPFM and amnesty for pirates eventually were too hard for the FCC to swallow, and these were not included in the final rules. The blanket ban on pirates holding LPFM licenses eventually was overturned for being too broad (*Ruggiero v. FCC*, 2002), but it made little difference to most extra-legal stations because they rejected the idea, as well as the accompanying restrictions imposed by licensing. The Amherst Alliance continues to fight for media reform and has been active and effective on the issues of digital audio broadcasting conversion (IBOC) and media-ownership controls. Dozens, if not hundreds, of extra-legal free radio stations continue to broadcast and scores more come and go. However, the major effect has been the increased level of public awareness of media issues, as exemplified by the massive and unexpected groundswell of public outrage against the easing of media consolidation rules in 2003 (McChesney, 2004).

The issue of whether the creation of the LPFM service was a successful outcome of the micro radio movement is debatable (Hamilton, 2004). Certainly, the creation of LPFM in its current form was not the intent of the micro radio pioneers. These activists saw any license and the resulting restrictions as an abdication of personal freedom. Many of these activists, although generally supportive of the new service, rejected licensing and continued to broadcast in violation of federal law. Hamilton (2004) argued that rather than a threat to existing broadcasters, the new LPFM service has been embraced and used to further the end of incumbents. Moreover, he contended that the FCC action served more to debilitate the potential of the movement than validate it. I, as well as other activists, expressed this fear as early as 1995. In fact, I had remarked on the MRN list that the fastest way to shut us down was to start licensing stations. It was abundantly clear to us all that a poorly designed LPFM service was a worse threat than the status quo. In fact, a voiced concern was that such a service be designed to protect the open spaces in which the extra-legal stations operated. Interestingly enough, the intervention of incumbent broadcasters, resulting in the RBPA, ensured the dominance of extra-legal stations in urban areas by banning LPFM stations from the adjacent channels in which many of the unlicensed stations operate. The potential of these adjacents was brought home in 2002 by a mass Reclaim the Media action in Seattle, where 13 extra-legal stations were put on the air, all on second-adjacent channels.

Even so-called successful movements rarely get everything they want, and the micro radio movement is no exception. As Hamilton (2004) admitted, LPFM represents a long struggle for media equity and democracy. What the micro radio movement did accomplish is spark a larger media democracy movement, deal the first defeat to incumbent broadcasters since the creation of public radio, introduce a wide and diverse cross section of U.S. Americans to the power and passion of community media, and embolden extra-legal stations to maintain their radical critique.

LESSONS LEARNED ABOUT COMMUNICATION ACTIVISM: THE SCHOLAR-ACTIVIST DIALECTIC

Evaluating one's effect on a movement over the course of a decade is challenging. In retrospect, the two most significant impacts that I had on the movement was that of an expert and broker (Tarrow, 2003). Offering technical expertise in arcane areas, such as institutional behavior, political processes, or regulatory schemes, is the most overt way a scholar can contribute to a movement. Although any expertise I possess in matters of broadcasting regulation and history or media law were objectively helpful in the micro radio movement activities, in general, and crafting the JSMR, in particular, my initial role as an in-outsider proved to be of greatest utility. Because I joined the movement as a researcher, I belonged to no existing group or faction and, thus, had no ideological baggage. I did not shy away from taking stands, sometimes radical, on certain issues. However, the initial perception of me by other movement members as a nonaligned participant persisted. This, I believe, partially was due to my researcher's tendency to closely read and analyze e-mails and listserv posts looking for patterns. I became somewhat of a broker (Tarrow, 2003) by identifying overlaps in polarized exchanges and using these overlaps to build bridges or, in certain cases, to reframe positions and arguments in a more palatable manner. Furthermore, at times, some parties simply were unwilling to accept ideas from certain participants, even to the point of habitually deleting their listserv posts. In these cases, simply hearing it from another source was sufficient.

Mische (2003) described how the complex interaction of participants and ideas in an emergent and fluid network requires that a central theme of a movement be malleable enough to "read" in different contexts. She described "identity qualifiers" as cues given off to indicate the operational elements of participants' identity and affiliation at a particular moment; "temporal cuing" as the narratives that participants use to describe themselves that also project an image as a potential ally or productive partner; "generality shifting" as the sliding up and down the scale of abstraction depending on the audience—that is, the shifting of inclusiveness scales to build selective solidarity; and "multiple targeting" as the creation of a message that plays well, if differently, to a variety of constituencies. In a diverse and complex movement, such as micro radio, the fluidity of interactions crossed all these areas. The framing of a particular issue or concept and the language used were keys to connecting with participants and brokering between factions. This negotiation was especially complex, given that several of Mische's (2003) communicative strategies needed to be deployed in a single message going to a general audience. The ability to reframe, abstract, and identify patterns are important skills that academics can use to aid communication within a movement.

The ability to shift interaction methods (Mische, 2003) fluidly is particularly prevalent in CMC. Postmes et al. (2000) discussed how norms in a CMC environment emerge over time. Moreover, in an open CMC environment, such as the MRN listserv, formal enforcement of particular interaction rules is a useless exercise. In turn, Paccagnella (1997) found that relationships built in virtual environments also can be every bit as real as those built in physical space. What this means is that real, productive relationships can be fostered via new communication technologies. The technical benefits of e-mail or web sites as fast and efficient ways to organize action, share resources, and transmit information are obvious; less obvious is the interactive benefit of creating a space where no particular group controls the turf, the loudest and the most aggressive cannot dominate the conversation, and everyone, at least potentially, has an opportunity to speak. The lack of social cues has been seen as a negative for CMC (Postmes et al., 2000), but often the lack of physicality can be a benefit. On a listserv, a heated exchange between two participants becomes a side discussion instead of stopping all communication. Furthermore, it requires a little more premeditation and thought to make a hasty comment when a person is required to type it out, rather than just opening his or her mouth. FtF interaction is, and likely will continue to be, a crucial element of any collective action. However, in broad and diverse coalitions, a little virtual space can allow for relationships to develop incrementally and may blunt what may be counterproductive visceral reactions to visual characteristics.

Participants in the micro radio movement consistently describe it as a social movement, often referring to it as "the movement." Broadly, it could be considered a "new social movement," as much as the term lacks utility. It certainly can be described using Eyerman and Jamison's (1991) cognitive *praxis* model or Melucci's (1996) challenge to dominant social codes. The peaking or emergence of micro radio as a social movement and its "success" with the creation of LPFM, followed by the submergence of the preexisting network, also fall under Melucci's (1996) theoretical framework. Moreover, putting extra-legal stations on the air where the technocratic FCC and incumbent broadcasters claimed there was no room illustrated their irrationality and partiality. This also created a symbol of resistance that was picked up by the print press (Opel, 2004). Furthermore, one certainly could see the initial victory of Dunifer over the FCC in Federal Court to be a moment of "cognitive liberation" (McAdams, 1982), in which there emerged a sense that not only could something be done to address the problem with the media (McChesney, 2004) but that there was a possibility of success. The issue is not whether the micro radio movement was a movement or a new social movement but the utility of describing it as such; this is the impetus (or impetuousness) of my work on dissentworks (Coopman, 2005).

Micro radio, or media reform for that matter, is not a mass movement in comparison to the environmental or even the most recent antiwar movements. McAdams (1982) seemed to prefer the term "insurgency," and I think this might best describe micro radio. The utility in recognizing the difference is in the comparison of size versus distribution. The key here is that digital communication technologies fostered the cognitive liberation of a movement that otherwise might never had the critical mass to form and recognize itself. The momentum to spread from a relatively isolated political demographic to a broader ideologically diverse movement would not, in my opinion, have been possible without the internet (Coopman, 2000b, 2000c). The organizational mass and infrastructure to project power with little or no funding, elite support, or vanguard is a direct result of unique properties and social conditions present beginning in the last decade of the 20th century. The properties of the micro radio movement, as described here, are, at least, a new variant of a new social movement in the previously described power of distributed communicative practices, and perhaps even a new phenomenon in the unintended/unconscious cooperation and participation of some of the parties involved. A bold statement perhaps, and one I will seek to examine in detail in another venue after further theoretical development. However, the issue is not the rejection of the new social movements model, as much as the argument that a finer tool might be useful in investigating movements such as micro radio.

The noted theorist C. Wright Mills (1959) described sociology as the ability to see the connection between private troubles and public issues. In this sense, scholars and activists have much in common. Moreover, both academe and social movements, in a general sense, as well as with respect to their component parts, are distinct and often rarified environments. Negotiating the distinct culture of a movement or activist group can be daunting. As Petri Dish of the Prometheus Radio Project put it, the "wing-nut factor" always must be taken into account. Activist milieus can be chaotic and dynamic, and they often attract diverse people. Most activist veterans are adept at negotiating their physical and relational environments. I found that observing older hands as they negotiate their environment yielded invaluable lessons.

As McAdams (1982) noted, there is a tendency to lionize the activists we study and ignore the unpleasant or unflattering aspects of individuals or movements. This is a particularly dangerous pitfall for a scholar who fully participates in and does research on a social movement. Writing about one's comrades in an honest fashion and with critical analysis has proven to be a problematic task, and I admit that I have had only moderate success. My only advice here is, as both a scholar and an activist, to keep one's goals and priorities straight and remember why one is doing what he or she is doing and one's responsibilities to both the movement's goals and aspirations, as well as to those of the academy. The dialectic tension between these two worlds is both challenging and rewarding. Success is sweet; failure, at times, dramatic; and consequences potentially dire. The effort is, I think, an important and worthwhile one not only for academe and activism but for society as well.

My journey through the ongoing rigors of learning to be an activist and scholar has irrevocably shaped my perceptions. For good or ill, separating the two now is difficult. This has caused no little difficulty in both of these worlds; this includes the perception of ulterior motives in one arena and of potential bias in the other. The most plausible option is a rigorous and radical critique of the process of both scholarship and activism. My friend and colleague Andy Opel (2004) rather generously identified me as a "movement intellectual" within the micro radio movement. Reviewing my actions through the lens of his analysis has been a sobering experience and provided some insight into the probable reactions to my work by fellow free radio activists. It would seem that scholarship and activism, especially at the same time, are not for those of faint heart or queasy stomach.

CONCLUSION

The micro radio movement developed over the course of the 1990s and continues to operate in many forms. Although broadly falling into the category of a new social movement, this particular movement appears to deviate in interesting ways, mostly tied to the impact of new communication technologies. The increased availability of new media technologies, especially the internet, over the course of the growth of the movement appeared to have a major impact on the evolution of communication strategies and processes that have been observed in studies of computer-mediated communication. The impact of such communication, in comparison to face-to-face interaction only, allowed for a much more widespread and even distribution of resources and magnified the impact of key debates and discussions. Organizational coordination without central direction or control to a degree that was required to compete with established institutions would not have been possible without the aid of these technologies. Although the measure and level of success of the movement probably depends on one's position and predisposition, the fact that such widespread opposition could develop and be maintained over the long term and ultimately lead to systemic change is a success.

Any study of activism or social movements is problematic. Detailed research and analysis can be used to aid a movement, legitimize its grievances to elites or the public, or to focus the efforts of authorities on social control or repression. Ultimately, each scholar must weigh the consequences of his or her research. However, social movement research is a critical aspect of understanding our social world.

The JSMR is something of which I am proud. However, I realize that it really is a rather small thing in comparison to the sacrifice and accomplishments of many media activists. What it does show is that it is possible to reach across ideological divides and set aside personal agendas to achieve a common good. It is something we did and can do again. It is the potential to work together beyond our immediate self-interests to build a better world.

NOTES

1. A *rulemaking* is a process in which external petitioners, the current administration, or the FCC itself proposes new regulations. Such a process starts a series of public comment periods in which interested parties respond to the proposed new rules and to others' comments on those rules. The end result usually, but not always, is a new regulation. The Commissioners themselves make the final decision. This process can take years to accomplish.
2. The FCC is empowered to regulate telecommunications, including broadcasting in the electromagnetic spectrum, which is considered to be public property and a limited resource. This gives the FCC power to require certain rules, ranging from banning obscenity to ownership restrictions. Licenses are required that act as long-term leases of spectrum space. Broadcasting without a license is illegal and can lead to fines or imprisonment. The FCC eliminated this type of low-

power broadcasting in 1978 at the behest of the Corporation for Public Broadcasting and National Public Radio. These organizations argued that low-power broadcasting was an inefficient use of the spectrum. This ruling, combined with federal deregulation, had the practical effect of putting FM broadcasting licenses beyond the reach of a vast majority of the population (Soley, 1999; Walker, 2001).

3.   The Prometheus Radio Project is an excellent example. This organization began with members of a shutdown free radio station in Philadelphia and developed into a collective that helps LPFM stations to get on the air. Organization members filed a successful appeal to halt the implementation of new FCC ownership rules in 2003 (Caruso, 2003).

4.   Room for LPFM was created by removing third-adjacent channel interference protections. Every radio station has space around the channel it occupies that serves as a buffer to keep other stations from interfering with its signal. For example, a station at 90.7 FM has what is called a "co-channel" that consists of its assigned frequency of 90.7. The "first adjacent" for this station covers 90.7 to 90.9, the "second adjacent" covers 90.7-91.1, and the "third adjacent" extends from 90.7 to 91.3. Adjacent channels also extend in the same manner on the other side of the co-channel: 90.5 and so forth. These standards were set in place in 1963; at that time, radio transmission technology did not allow for placing stations any closer to each other (Coopman, 2002).

REFERENCES

Anderson, J. (2003). *The history of LPFM: Part 1*. Retrieved September 10, 2003, from http://www.diymedia.net/feature/fhistlpfm.htm

Arquilla, J., & Ronfeldt, D. (Eds.). (2001). *Networks and netwars: The future of terror, crime, and militancy*. Santa Monica, CA: Rand.

Bell, D. (2001). *An introduction to cybercultures*. New York: Routledge.

Beniger, J. R. (2003). Who shall control cyberspace? In L. Strate, R. L. Jacobson, & S. B. Gibson (Eds.), *Communication and cyberspace: Social interaction in an electronic environment* (2nd ed., pp. 59-69). Cresskill, NJ: Hampton Press.

Bey, H. (1991). *T.A.Z.: The temporary autonomous zone, ontological anarchy, poetic terrorism*. Brooklyn, NY: Autonomedia.

Blackmore, S. (2000). *The meme machine*. New York: Oxford University Press.

Bleiker, R. (2000). *Popular dissent, human agency, and global politics*. New York: Cambridge University Press.

Bordia, P. (1997). Face-to-face versus computer-mediated communication: A synthesis of the experimental literature. *Journal of Business Communication, 34*, 99-120.

Brodie, R. (1995). *Virus of the mind: The new science of the meme*. Seattle, WA: Integral Press.

Burke, P. (1997). Exchange theory: An identity model for network exchange. *American Sociological Review, 62*, 134-150.

Caruso, D. B. (2003, September 9). *Former radio pirates enjoy victory against FCC: New restrictions may give a new voice to public broadcasting*. Retrieved

September 10, 2003, from http://www.thetimesonline.com/articles/2003/09/11/business/business/86d2a9c696f06f2d86256d9d006c7d3f.txt

Coopman, T. M. (1999). FCC enforcement difficulties with unlicensed micro radio. *Journal of Broadcasting & Electronic Media, 43*, 582-602.

Coopman, T. M. (2000a). Dunifer v. the FCC: A case study of micro broadcasting. *Journal of Radio Studies, 7*, 287-309.

Coopman, T. M. (2000b). Hardware handshake: Listserv forms backbone of national free radio network. *American Communication Journal, 3*(3). Retrieved February 1, 2003, from http://acjournal.org/holdings/vol3/Iss3/articles/ted_coopman.htm

Coopman, T. M. (2000c). High speed access: Micro radio, action, and activism on the internet. *American Communication Journal, 3*(3). Retrieved February 1, 2003, from http://acjournal.org/holdings/vol3/Iss3/rogue4/highspeed.html

Coopman, T. M. (2002, November). *Lies, damn lies, and statistics: Congress, selective science, and the destruction of low power radio.* Paper presented at the meeting of the National Communication Association, New Orleans, LA.

Coopman T. M. (2005). Dissentworks: Agency, identity, and emergent dissent as network structures. In M. Allen & M. Consalvo (Eds.), *2nd internet research annual* (pp. 107-122). New York: Peter Lang.

Correll, S. (1995). The ethnography of an electronic bar: The Lesbian Café. *Journal of Contemporary Ethnography, 24*, 270-289.

Curtius, M. (1998, March 5). Defiant pirates ply the radio airwaves—pretrial ruling prevents FCC crackdown. A leading outlaw broadcaster hails the decision. *Los Angeles Times*, p. 1.

Epstein, B. (2001). Anarchism and the anti-globalization movement. *Monthly Review, 53*(4). Retrieved August 20, 2002, from http://www.monthlyreview.org/0901epstein.htm

Eyerman, R., & Jamison, A. (1991). *Social movements: A cognitive approach.* University Park: Pennsylvania State University Press.

Federal Communications Commission. (2005, March). *FM query search results for licensed LPFM stations.* Retrieved March 20, 2005, from http://www.fcc.gov/fcc-bin/fmq?state=&serv=FL&vac=3&list=2

Gerlach, L. P. (2001). The structure of social movements: Environmental activism and its opponents. In J. Arquilla & D. Ronfeldt (Eds.), *Networks and netwars: The future of terror, crime, and militancy* (pp. 289-310). Santa Monica, CA: Rand.

Granovetter, M. (1973). The strength of weak ties. *American Journal of Sociology, 78*, 1360-1380.

Granovetter, M. (1983). The strength of weak ties: A network theory revisited. *Sociological Theory, 1*, 201-233.

Hamilton, J. (2004). Rationalizing dissent: Challenging conditions of low-power FM radio. *Critical Studies in Media Communication, 21*, 44-63.

Hass, P. (1992). Epistemic communities and international policy coordination. *International Organization, 46*, 1-35.

Keck, M. E., & Sikkink, K. (1998). *Activists beyond borders: Advocacy networks in international politics.* Ithaca, NY: Cornell University Press.

Kennedy, J. (1998). Thinking is social: Experiments with the adaptive culture model. *Journal of Conflict Resolution, 42*, 56-76.

McAdams, D. (1982). *Political process and the development of Black insurgency, 1930-1970*. Chicago: University of Chicago Press.

McChesney, R. W. (2004). *The problem of the media: U.S. communication politics in the twenty-first century*. New York: Monthly Review Press.

Melucci, A. (1996). *Challenging codes: Collective action in the information age*. New York: Cambridge University Press

Mills, C. W. (1959). *The sociological imagination*. New York: Oxford University Press.

Mische, A. (2003). Cross-talk in movements: Reconceiving the culture-network link. In M. Diani & D. McAdam (Eds.), *Social movements and networks: Relational approaches to collective action* (pp. 258-280). New York: Oxford University Press.

MITRE Corporation. (2003, May). *Experimental measurements of the third-adjacent channel impacts of low-power FM stations (Vol. 1: Final Report)*. Retrieved March 21, 2005, from http://www.mitre.org/work/tech_papers/tech_papers_03/caasd_fm/caasd_fm_v1.pdf

Monroe, K. (2001). Morality and a sense of self: The importance of identity and categorization for moral action. *American Journal of Political Science, 45*, 491-507.

Opel, A. (2004). *Micro radio and the FCC: Media activism and the struggle over broadcast policy*. Westport, CT: Praeger.

Paccagnella, L. (1997). Getting the seats of your pants dirty: Strategies for ethnographic research on virtual communities. *Journal of Computer-Mediated Communication, 3*(1). Retrieved March 3, 2003, from http://www.ascusc.org/jcmc/vol3/issue1/paccagnella.html

Postmes, T., Spears, R., & Lea, M. (2000). The formation of group norms in computer-mediated communication. *Human Communication Research, 26*, 341-371.

Rafaeli, S., & Sudweeks, F. (1997). Networked interactivity. *Journal of Computer-Mediated Communication, 2*(4). Retrieved March 3, 2003, from http://www.ascusc.org/jcmc/vol2/issue4/rafaeli.sudweeks.html

Rheingold, H. (2002). *Smart mobs: The next social revolution*. Cambridge, MA: Perseus.

Ruggiero v. FCC, 2002 U.S. App LEXIS 9065 (D. C. Cir. May 2, 2002).

Sager, K. L., & Gastil, J. (1999). Reaching consensus on consensus: A study of the relationships between individual decision-making styles and use of the consensus decision rule. *Communication Quarterly, 47*, 67-79.

Scott, J. C. (1985). *Weapons of the weak: Everyday forms of peasant resistance*. New Haven, CT: Yale University Press.

Shields, S. O., & Ogle, R. M. (1992, March). *Black liberation radio: A case study of the micro–radio movement*. Paper presented at the meeting of the Popular Culture Association, Louisville, KY.

Soley, L. (1999). *Free radio: Electronic civil disobedience*. Boulder, CO: Westview Press.

Stavistsky, A., Avery, R., & Vanhala, H. (2001). From class D to LPFM: The high-powered politics of low-power radio. *Journalism & Mass Communication Quarterly, 78*, 340-354.

Tarrow, S. (1998). *Power in movement: Social movements and contentious politics* (2nd ed.). New York: Cambridge University Press.

Tarrow, S. (2003, February). *The new transnational contention: Organizations, institutions, mechanisms.* Paper presented at the "Globalization" Seminar, Duke University, Durham, NC.

Tilly, C. (1975). *From mobilization to revolution.* Reading, MA: Addison-Wesley.

U.S. v. Dunifer, No. C94-03542 CW, slip op (9th Cir. June 16, 1998).

van Dijk, J. A. G. M. (1996). Models of democracy: Behind the design and use of new media in politics. *Electronic Journal of Communication, 6*(2). Retrieved January 28, 2003, from www.cios.org/getfile/DIJK_V6N296

Walker, J. (2001). *Rebels on the air: An alternative history of radio in America.* New York: New York University Press.

Watson, N. (1997). Why we argue about virtual community: A case study of Phish.net fan community. In S. G. Jones (Ed.), *Virtual culture: Identity and communication in cybersociety* (pp. 102-132). Thousand Oaks, CA: Sage.

7

A COMMUNITY CONFRONTS THE DIGITAL DIVIDE

A Case Study of Social Capital Formation Through Communication Activism

Andrew P. Herman

State University of New York at Geneseo

James S. Ettema

Northwestern University

Community-based organizations are vital assets for lower income communities, confronting such issues as substance abuse prevention and treatment, healthcare availability, job training, and housing. In the course of their work, these organizations undertake many communication-related activities that strengthen the bonds within the community, as well as build bridges linking the community and its residents to the larger society and its resources. In particular, ever-changing communication technologies constantly offer new possibilities for amplifying the effectiveness of these organizations and, in turn, empowering their communities. Despite these possibilities, however, many community-based organizations, like many individual households in their neighborhoods, find themselves separated from the rest of society by the digital divide (National Telecommunications and Information Administration, 1999).

The Neighborhood Communication Project examined in this chapter worked in a lower income urban community to address the digital divide through the sharing of technical expertise among community-based organizations. The objective was to help small neighborhood groups create both social capital (networks of useful relationships) and intellectual capital (leadership and problem-solving capacities). The project was a partnership of Northwestern University, as represented by the authors, along with other faculty and students, and a community-based organization (hereafter referred to as the CBO). The CBO is located in a Chicago neighborhood in which about 9 out of 10 residents are African American and 1 in 4 live below the poverty level. The CBO began in the 1980s as an affiliation of community groups formed to advocate for the preservation of healthcare institutions in the neighborhood, but over the years its activities expanded to include health, education, and economic development initiatives. The CBO had a core staff of about five people, but its paid employees could range up to a dozen or more when larger funded projects were in progress. A large corporation's charitable foundation provided financial support for the Neighborhood Communication Project.

Over its 3-year life span, the project evolved into an expertise-sharing resource that worked in some way with about 50 community groups and small businesses. Research conducted by the project partners at the beginning of their work indicated that even small groups in the neighborhood had gained access to basic computer technology for functions such as record keeping and word processing. At that point, they most needed access to expertise, including internet skills. In response to this need for a new type of grassroots leadership, the project created and funded the role of a community technology coordinator. Drawing on the theory of asset-based community development, as outlined later, the idea of a community technology coordinator recognized that if this community had a great need, it also had a great capacity to meet that need. Thus, the job of the coordinator was to broker relationships between organizations that could facilitate technology strategy development, staff training, web site creation, grant proposal development, and other tasks.

Accounts of this project could certainly include the byline of the community technology coordinator, as well as the CBO's director and its specialist in research and training, among others, for they were all truly "authors" of the project. The authors whose names appear on this chapter want to offer an appreciative account of the hard work and creativity of our community-based colleagues, an account that those individuals would have been too modest to offer themselves. Yet, reluctantly, we do not refer to those individuals, the project, or even the community by name because of the sensitivity of some material that follows. Nonetheless, whenever "we" or "our" appears in what follows, the authors mean to gratefully acknowledge our project partners.[1]

Although the CBO was very experienced in community development and commanded a broad range of activist skills, we were relatively new to communication activism in the community context and, consequently, our role in the project was as often that of student as teacher. Nonetheless, we tried to make ourselves useful by supporting the work of the project in a number of ways. One avenue of support was financial. We leveraged the relationship between the university and the project's funder by devising a proposal that allowed the foundation both to honor its philanthropic commitment to the university and pursue its interest in educational and developmental applications of technology. We managed relations with funders throughout the project, including administration of budgets and preparation of regular reports to the foundation, as well as to the community.

Another avenue of support was conceptual. We designed and analyzed the survey research that began the project. This research brought to bear the ideas of asset-based community development theory to assess the needs and map the assets of the community and, in turn, set the conceptual foundation for the work of the community technology coordinator. We also mentored the community technology coordinator in these ideas, culminating in his admission to a university graduate program.

Other avenues of support included directing the talents of university students toward accomplishing some of the tasks identified in the survey research—most successfully, a web site for community organizations and businesses—and channeling information about government and foundation grant opportunities to the community listserv. One more avenue of support might best be characterized as symbolic, although the CBO personnel assured us that this form of support was not inconsequential. An example was a tour of the university for high school students from the community, organized by Herman. For some students, this was not only the first time that they had an opportunity, for instance, to create music in a digital laboratory but the first time that they had ventured so far—both geographically and psychologically—from their inner-city neighborhood.

Our account of the project begins by introducing key concepts that guided our communication activism. The conceptual overview sets the context for a narrative account of the project that highlights some of the struggles and victories that we all experienced. Quantitative data collected at the end of the project then provide an alternative perspective on these experiences. We conclude the chapter by looking back on this experience for some lessons learned about communication activism.

KEY CONCEPTS GUIDING
OUR COMMUNICATION ACTIVISM

From its inception, we approached this project primarily as an opportunity for community action and only secondarily as a setting for social research. Nonetheless, it was a project informed by theory. The concept of asset-based community development (ABCD), as articulated by McKnight and his associates at Northwestern University's Institute for Policy Research, views communities first and foremost as rich with assets rather than rife with problems (Kretzmann & McKnight, 1993; McKnight, 1995, 1997; www.northwestern.edu/ipr/). This approach to social action recognizes the need for outside assistance to many communities, but it insists on the centrality of a community's inherent capacities in any plan of action. Thus, ABCD is "internally focused," emphasizing the agenda-building and problem-solving resources of individual citizens, neighborhood groups, and community institutions, such as education, healthcare, and local government (Kretzmann & McKnight, 1993, p. 9). In turn, ABCD is "relationship driven," recognizing that to channel community capacities successfully, connections must be nurtured among citizens, groups, and institutions. At this point in the conceptual development of our project, the idea of "social capital" becomes crucial.

Coleman (1988) famously described *social capital* as the value that inheres in the structure of relations among actors. Theorists of social capital, such as Gittell and Vidal (1998) and Putnam (2000), make an important distinction between relationships that bond and those that bridge. *Bonds* are close personal relationships that, according to Putnam (2000), are "inward looking and tend to reinforce exclusive identities and homogeneous groups" (p. 22). These relationships provide necessary support from family, friends, and perhaps communities defined by ethnicity, religion, or other social factors. At the same time, however, these bonds can be restrictive, discouraging individuals from moving beyond their immediate social enclaves or disallowing outsiders from joining bonded groups (Portes, 1998; Woolcock, 1998).

Whereas bonds reinforce relationships that may already exist, *bridges* open exclusive, homogeneous networks to advantageous relationships that otherwise would not exist (Briggs, 1998; Fernandez, Castilla, & Moore, 2000; Wood, 1997). Thus, bridges open new contacts with information sources and new avenues of support. Burt (1997) defined social capital "in terms of the information and control advantages of being the broker in relations between people otherwise disconnected in social structure" (p. 340). Such brokers make connections that span what Burt characterized as "structural holes" in interpersonal networks. In turn, they gain resources, often in the form of intellectual capital, which would otherwise be unobtainable.

For networks of social relationships to yield their value, they must be governed by certain social norms—especially *generalized reciprocity*, or the expectation that others will reciprocate services rendered (Adler & Kwon, 2000; Coleman, 1998). Putnam (1993) argued compellingly for the importance of generalized reciprocity with evidence that the strength of this norm is a factor that distinguished the more and less socioeconomically successful provinces of Italy. To succeed, reciprocity, in turn, demands *trust* (Fukuyama, 1999). Although theorists of social capital, such as Coleman and Putnam, view trust as a variation on the idea of norms that govern social structure, scholars of psychology and communication are more likely to understand trust as a characteristic of interpersonal relationships. For example, the useful interpersonal model of trust proposed by Rempel, Holmes, and Zanna (1985) emphasizes three relational components: (a) *predictability* reflects a rational assessment of how another person will act in the future; (b) *dependability* references a psychological state of reliance on, and perhaps vulnerability to, another; and (c) *faith* is a person's belief that another will "come through" for him or her. As we show, reciprocity and trust are important issues in the particular setting of our project.

If, as Coleman (1988) argued, social capital is value that inheres in relationships, much of the theoretical and empirical work that followed did not consider the communication processes that actually constitute these relationships. Beyond an appreciation of reciprocity and trust, the sociological understanding of social capital typically leaves relational communication in an unopened black box (see, e.g., Adler & Kwon, 2000; Fukuyama, 1999; Putnam, 1995; for counter-examples, see Briggs, 1998; Edwards & Foley, 1998). Some social capital theorists argue that the black box need never be opened (Greeley, 1997), but as communication theorists and activists, we cannot agree. We, thus, see our project as an opportunity for communication theory to add perspective on the structure of relationships in which social capital inheres. The theoretical concerns in the study of relational communication—including self-disclosure (e.g., Altman & Taylor, 1973; Dindia, 2002; Sias & Cahill, 1998; Taylor & Altman, 1987), social similarity (e.g. Burgoon, 1992; Yun, 2002), trust (e.g., Millar & Rogers, 1987; Pearce, 1974; Rempel et al., 1985), and social support (e.g., Albrecht, Adelman, & Associates, 1987; Albrecht, Burleson, & Sarason, 1992; Fischer, 1982)—all have a place in the study of social capital. In turn, these concepts can contribute to more sophisticated strategies for community action.

Thus, our project, as a practical endeavor in communication activism and community development, was given intellectual life by a few key theoretical concepts. We thought of the mandate issued by *asset-based community development* to build community capacity for self-help as a process of constructing *bridges* that could span *structural holes*. We thought of the *social capital* that inheres in these relationships as value that could be "cashed in" for *intellectual capital* in the form of technological expertise. We thought of *social interaction* as the means to realize this potential value. Finally, we thought of *trust* as essential to that interaction, even if we did not appreciate its full importance until the conclusion of the project when we debriefed with our partners who had worked every day in the neighborhood to help create it.

MAPPING COMMUNITY ASSETS

People often have come into this neighborhood "to help," but as one of the project participants stated bluntly, "There are a number of issues that those people must confront and one is trust." This participant, an information technology manager in a large social service agency, would prove himself to be a dependable source of expertise throughout the project, but the issue of trust first had to be addressed to his satisfaction. As he explained, "A lot of times when people in the community see a new face come in, they'll ask, 'What's he trying to get out of it?' It has to be a two-way street."

Building an initial bridge to the community, rather than gathering resources to bring across that bridge, often is the greater problem according to the information technology manager:

> A lot of resources are there. A lot of the time, government or other agencies will offer the resources. Unfortunately, what happens is that, like the carpetbaggers who used to go into the South, the resources end up in the hands of people who are not directly or closely related to the community. So all the money is spent, all the equipment is purchased, and all the training is done, but it doesn't hit the people who need it.

He went on to tell a story about a university (not ours, we are relieved to say) that secured a large grant to provide technology training to community groups, "except their ties to the community weren't so great." The university found that community colleges were needed as bridges. "The university said to the community colleges, 'We've got the money, we've got the capacity, but you can bring in the community groups,'" he recalled. "It worked out pretty well because they had the foresight to recognize that they couldn't tap into the community as well as other people could."

Our project began with one important bridge already in place. Over a number of years, the university and the CBO had partnered on a number of funded projects. The CBO director and her staff had generously opened doors in their community to students seeking internships, as well as to researchers seeking data. Indeed, the CBO's resident specialist in research and training, who characterized bridging—bonding as a continuum rather than as a dichotomy, suggested that the relationship between the CBO and university had developed into a bond thanks, in large measure, to the work of McKnight and his colleagues. Whether bridge or bond, the project could approach its first task with a history of reciprocity between the partners.

A task central to ABCD is research, but research understood not as an analysis of social problems or even an assessment of human needs but, rather, as a mapping of existing community assets. In our project, of course, technical know-how was the community asset of central interest, and the project partners began their work with a survey of those assets administered under the auspices of the CBO research staff. The CBO's specialist in training and research, a PhD-trained social scientist with many years of community development experience, was adamant that if we wanted information, we could not just go into the community and take it. As the information technology manager said, "It has to be a two-way street." With this in mind, the partners trained and paid community residents to conduct the fieldwork for the study.

The specialist and another CBO staff member began the survey research late in 1998 by interviewing neighborhood residents to serve as paid project staff. Three of the chosen residents, who were designated as research managers, had all received interviewer training in previous projects and used those skills to gain at least part-time employment. Three other of the chosen residents, newcomers to survey interviewing, completed approximately 30 hours of training over the next several months. In training sessions, the specialist masterfully presented interviewing skills in readily accessible terms: reading the questions as written but paraphrasing as needed, showing interest in what the respondent said but limiting feedback to a few appropriate terms, and so forth. The specialist also elicited comments about the survey questionnaires to be used, both to be certain that the researchers-in-training understood their form, content, and purpose and that those of us from the academic world understood what the form, content, and purpose would mean to respondents. We admit without embarrassment that there often was a great deal of homework for us to do in the form of questionnaire revision after these training sessions.

The interviewers began work by talking to block captains in the CBO-sponsored block club and then moved on to interviews with community group leaders, who were the primary focus of the project. These interviews focused on individual and organizational levels of expertise in information and communication technology, as well as access to, and actual use of, that technology. Knowing that the act of measurement often affects that which is measured, we wanted these interviews to help move issues surrounding the digital divide (such as the need for community technology centers) higher on the group leaders' agendas. "Those interviews," said the CBO's specialist, "did get people talking to each other."

Before reviewing the results of this research and the action plan that emerged from it, we pause to consider the interviewer training as an outcome of, rather than merely an input to, the project. For the three research managers who had previous experience, the project was additional, gainful employment that enhanced their marketable skills. As the specialist said, "They grew with it." As for the interviewers who had no previous experience, we offer a few judiciously chosen, but poignant facts that speak to the dedication of the CBO and the realities of life in its home neighborhood. Several of the interviewers-in-training seemed (at least to us) simply to fade away. Three, however, completed the training. Two remained with the project long enough to conduct many of the interviews with block captains and group leaders, even as they both worked at their recovery from substance abuse, and one of them, a sometime cleaning woman, became a full-time assistant to the community technology coordinator after the asset mapping was completed. Not long after, however, the other member of the interviewer team suddenly died. "That death really pulled her down, but she hung in [the project] for several years," said the specialist of the surviving member of the team. Finally, however, the surviving member was separated from the organization for cause. "This was the longest period of productive work in her life," concluded the specialist, who always viewed life in a sympathetic but clear-eyed way, "but the project didn't save her."

ASSETS OF A (DIGITALLY) DIVIDED COMMUNITY

The asset-mapping interviews with the leaders of the 23 organizations constituting the core of the CBO's network of affiliates provided a picture of an urban U.S. community at a particular moment in the history of the digital divide—the turn of the 21st century. Analysis of these groups belies any simplistic distinction between technological "haves" and "have-nots." Nearly all community groups had access to some technological assets; even the smallest groups had, at least, basic computer equipment that they used for management and communication functions, such as mailing lists. Three-quarters of the group leaders, especially those in larger organizations, rated their computer equipment as contributing "a great deal" (as opposed to "some" or "not much") to their organizations. When asked to comment on their ratings, the leaders who said their computer equipment contributed something less than "a great deal" each seemed to have a situation-specific issue in mind. For example, a 40-person social service agency rated its equipment as contributing only "some" to its work because it recently had networked with city government and was struggling to incorporate the technology into its work of giving and receiving client referrals.

Thus, these community groups were not abject "have-nots." Although some smaller groups relied on donated computer equipment, most had a recurring budget for equipment, and although some group leaders barely qualified as computer literate, they or someone in the organization could at least accomplish basic tasks. This certainly is not to say that any of the leaders were satisfied with their technology-related assets, as all of them readily could identify specific training, staffing, or equipment needs. Nonetheless, the interviews made it clear that the differences between the groups in terms of training, staffing, and equipment constituted a digital divide *within* the community. This was precisely the problem—and the opportunity—the project intended to address. The community had needs but also capacities.

The interviews also revealed that these groups brought a great deal of knowledge into their community. When asked to list the types of information that their groups disseminated to clients or members, about half the leaders cited housing, health, and substance abuse treatment, and more than one leader also mentioned economic development, employment, education, recreation, and public safety. Because few households in the community had internet access, public information was disseminated primarily via meetings and print. Only a few groups offered community residents direct access to information technology or training, although several groups aspired to do so. All leaders pointed to a lack of such access as a problem, although most of them did not have well-developed conceptions of what should be offered.

For these community groups, the internet remained an information-retrieval tool more than a multiway communication medium. About two-thirds of the groups had access to the internet and to e-mail. The leaders of about half the groups with access (i.e., one-third of all studied) reported that this technology was contributing "a great deal" to the work of their organizations, primarily through increased information-gathering efficiency. These leaders typically characterized that contribution as faster, easier access to information they probably would have retrieved in some other way, such as information from the Centers for Disease Control about HIV, AIDS, and violence prevention strategies. There was, however, little mention of participation in discussion groups or other, more fully interactive, online activities.

Only about one-quarter of the community groups had a web site of their own or were working on developing one. However, belief in the value of a web site ran very high both for those with sites and for those who had yet to develop one. Among the expected (or at least highly desired) functions were not only sharing information with the community but also influencing public officials, increasing public support for the organization, and expanding the organization's membership base. These expectations and hopes raised concerns about an expectations gap between what is desired from information and communication technology and what is likely or even possible for a small organization to gain from that technology. Nonetheless, creation of an internet presence for these small groups seemed essential.

In retrospect, these interviews yielded one more crucial fact, even if that fact was not clear to us at the time: Many community groups wanted to upgrade their organizational capabilities and provide public access to technology, but none of them viewed technology or technical expertise as central to their mission or identity in the community. Ironically, this view facilitated the work of the project by helping to preclude turf battles between the groups that we hoped would participate. As the CBO's specialist in research and training observed:

> Community-based organizations are territorial because resources are scarce and that turns people who should be allies into enemies—who has the ear of the alderman and so on. This made it harder for our project, which focused on groups, to take off than a project that went directly to community members. On the other hand, did any groups own technology as a topic in the community? Probably not.

From the specialist's point of view, "the community undermines itself in terms of lack of trust due to competition." That competition is most keen for foundation grants and government contracts in their service area, as well as media attention that can validate a group's efforts in the eyes of those funders. Such competition, however, is not unlimited. "Relationships among community groups are like siblings," the specialist concluded. "Trust for what? For the most basic issues of survival—yes; for resources and media attention—no."

The information technology manager, who always was willing to share his know-how, was well aware of this territoriality:

> I was talking with my CEO one time about the network [of project participants] and what we were doing. He was concerned about the amount of resources we were bringing to the table as compared to what others are bringing to the table. I convinced him that it would only help all of us. He said, "OK, if you feel that strongly about it, then just go ahead and do it."

The manager's attitude throughout our project, in his own words, was, "Let's not worry about territory and this contract versus that contract. So what's important is that we keep this on a working level rather than the CEO level."

THE COMMUNITY TECHNOLOGY
COORDINATOR AS LEADER

This was the uneasy context in which the project partners agreed to create the role of community technology coordinator: Groups varied greatly in technological sophistication even as they all struggled to keep up with technological change. Moreover, groups jealously guarded their access to resources even as they remained allies in their fight for life. Based on the asset-mapping research we had conducted, we concluded that more than access to technology and even to technological expertise, the priority should be access to trusted technological *leadership*. The title initially attached to this leadership role was "community knowledge organizer." Although this title referenced two important dimensions of the envisioned role—community organizing and knowledge management—the more euphonious phrase "community technology coordinator" eventually was adopted. The basic task assigned to the coordinator was to help participating groups locate and utilize information and communication resources in a way that enhanced not only their organizational efficiency but also their community-building effectiveness.

What did this intended exercise in social and intellectual capital formation mean in actual practice? For larger and more sophisticated organizations, the coordinator could play a role that readily would be recognized as "knowledge management" in the corporate world: promotion of strategic thinking about information resources, for instance, and dissemination of information to those who need it, when they need it. For example, the director of research for a successful housing rehabilitation organization said:

> As a result of participating in the project, we took a closer look at technology needs both internally and from the community's perspective. It has been a catalyst and a milestone in making us think about the digital divide. We have been able to build capacity in terms of knowing what resources are available, such as funding, web sites, community technology centers, technology projects, etc. The project has enabled us to make strong connections with various technology-oriented companies and organizations. As a result, we have collaborated to submit several proposals for bridging the digital divide.

In contrast, given the needs of the smaller and less sophisticated community groups, the coordinator's information technology knowledge management functions often were the more elementary activities of the "IT guy." A sampling of the coordinator's log entries from the first year of his work (i.e., the second year of the project) makes clear the importance of this function in addressing the divide between the larger and smaller groups:

- Set up computers and established e-mail accounts for the staff of a small youth center
- Established e-mail accounts for the staff of a neighborhood advocacy group
- Discussed technology for small businesses at a meeting of the neighborhood business association (and helped repair computers while there)
- Consulted on internet and computer-based activities for children with the staff of a Head Start center
- Consulted on development of a community technology center and a web site with the staff of a neighborhood elementary school
- Regularly sent e-mails about grant opportunities, upcoming meetings, and so on to all participating organizations.

Even if this consulting was elementary—or perhaps *because* the problems and solutions often were elementary—it had an important community-building function. The administrator of the small youth center concluded, "If we had not joined the Neighborhood Communication Project, I would not know how to use the internet. I feel more comfortable about my use of technology."

In the second year of the coordinator's work, the community-organizing aspect of the role emerged more fully as the coordinator placed particular emphasis on sustaining the community's technical capability through training. He organized a series of workshops open to all community group leaders under the rubric of "Our Community's Response to the Digital Divide." As the following sample of topics suggests, these sessions exemplified the coordinator's efforts to construct bridging relationships that could span structural holes and exchange social capital for intellectual capital:

- Technology Grant Writing Workshop, a 2-part event featuring the director of information technology for a Chicago-area university and a representative of the Inner City Computing Society
- City of Chicago CivicNet, featuring representatives from the Metropolitan Planning Council and the city of Chicago speaking about opportunities for community groups created by the city's development of a fiber-optic infrastructure called CivicNet

- Community Technology Strategic Planning, featuring the director of information technology for a large suburban hospital and the community technology coordinator
- "How Can I Become a Technology Professional?," another 2-part event featuring, among others, a telecommunications network manager, a software developer, and a public relations manager for a telecommunications company
- Technology Resource Tour and Luncheon, featuring visits to a number of newly created community technology centers in the neighborhood

This last event was another of those "symbolic" activities, as mentioned previously, that was important in terms of raising consciousness about assets within the community. Three months prior to the event, six organizations began planning this demonstration of how far the neighborhood had come in terms of access to technology and learning opportunities. When the area's U.S. congressional representative was persuaded to attend, the state representative and the Chicago council member who represented the neighborhood also accepted an invitation. This, in turn, brought the people the project really wanted to reach: about 150 community group leaders, educators, and business people who were interested in touring the community technology centers that had sprung up in a church basement, a school library, and the commons room of a rent-subsidized apartment building. After lunch and the inevitable remarks of the politicians, the attendees watched *Virtual Technology Resource Tour*, a videotape produced by three teenagers.

We are certain that this event was empowering for many members of the community even though we did not measure members' increased awareness or changed attitudes. Thus, we have only a "success story" to tell—a mere anecdote to those for whom social-scientific duty always is understood in quantitative terms. Be that as it may, here is the conclusion to the story. After dessert and the last speech, the community technology coordinator stood in the sunshine on the steps of the elegant old city park pavilion at which the luncheon was held and watched as parents and teachers came to pick up the 50 or so teenagers who had attended. "This was eye-opening," an attendee said shaking his hand. "I had no idea any of that existed here."

We do not attempt to provide a comprehensive account of the coordinator's activities, which also included much technology-related work with neighborhood youth and the captains of the large and active block club sponsored by the CBO. We do, however, pause to consider the lessons learned from one other activity. The research conducted in the first year of the project revealed that only about one-quarter of the community-based organizations had a web site of their own, but their belief in the value of a web site ran very high. With this in mind, the project set out in the first year of the coordinator's work to give the community a greater presence on the internet. Working with university students, the coordinator launched a web site that offered community groups and small businesses the opportunity to present statements of mission, directories of activities and services, and other information.

The goal was to become the go-to web site for information *about* the neighborhood *for* the neighborhood, and, to some extent, that goal was met. Providing another success story, an administrator of the Illinois Employment and Training Center said:

> Before joining the Neighborhood Communication Project, we had no knowledge of the many community-based organizations that are located in the area. We have changed our agenda as a result of the project and its web site. We are now focusing our attention on placing job applicants in positions that are available in the community rather than referring them to jobs located in the suburbs.

Over the next 2 years, the coordinator and a university graduate student serving as webmaster worked to increase the value of the site by introducing a search engine and then adding more information about community groups and businesses based on the search terms that visitors used. However, a plan for undergraduate student volunteers to create and maintain a development-oriented discussion forum and a youth-oriented neighborhood news service on the site faltered. For small community groups, the promise of help from undergraduate volunteers is "made to disappoint," according to the CBO's specialist for training and research. Group leaders must expend considerable effort planning and structuring the tasks to be accomplished by volunteers. Moreover, the time needed for those tasks often is extensive. "The time needed is measured in days not hours—which students just don't have," she said, concluding that the schedules and agendas of community groups and students just do not mesh very well. Then again, we probably could have tried harder with this.

THE COMMUNITY TECHNOLOGY COORDINATOR AS A SUCCESS STORY

When we recount the project's success stories, such as they may be, in ways that place the community technology coordinator at the center of the action, we are giving credit where it is due. The success stories are his, even if not his alone, and his place in them reveals the challenges of learning to work in community development. He came to the project with youthful enthusiasm from his undergraduate studies at a well-regarded college. With a liberal arts degree, he had no more than the average level of computer literacy for someone of his age and educational background. Thus, he scrambled to learn technology skills from short courses and self-directed study, as well as from the mentoring of the experienced information technology manager who is quoted throughout this chapter.

It also is important to know that although the coordinator is an African American raised in Chicago, he was not from the neighborhood in which the project worked. As he explained:

> I grew up thinking of [project's home neighborhood] as just a destitute ghost town. So, since I've been here it's blown my mind—the beauty of this area of the city, not only the people but the institutions and resources that are here. It's so funny to find out, coming from the other side of town, that people who grew up here thought the same way about my side of town.

"He needed to learn the particulars of the neighborhood," said the CBO's specialist in training and research about the coordinator's first days on the job, "and he needed to look through the labels that often are applied to people there—'gang member' and so on." The most important lesson to be learned by any newly arrived community development practitioner, according to the specialist, is to "listen to people." This may be an obvious lesson, but probably more so to the veteran of many projects than to the recent college graduate. In any case, the coordinator did listen to those he sought to help, as well as those who sought to help him. "He came from an elite school, which gave him the confidence to bridge to Northwestern University," said the specialist. From those of us at the university, he acquired the conceptual vocabulary of community development. From the senior leadership of the CBO, particularly its director who had built her organization from scratch, he absorbed the street smarts of community leadership. As is the tacit nature of street smarts, they proved difficult for the coordinator to articulate. When we interviewed him at the conclusion of the project and asked what he had to learn to succeed in his role, he replied, "How to deal with people—politicians, academics, community leaders." When asked what he had learned from his boss, the CBO director, he said simply, "Everything."

Whatever else may constitute the street smarts of community leadership, they certainly include the cultivation and communication of trust among groups and individuals. Thus, the success stories and the coordinator's role in them inevitably return to that theme. For even the most mundane technology consulting tasks, trust is at a premium, as powerfully conveyed in an interview with the director of a new and struggling technology center in the neighborhood. The value of predictability, dependability, and, ultimately, faith in others powerfully emerge from the director's account of the first meeting with the coordinator. The director, like the coordinator, was a young African American just learning the skills necessary to succeed in both technology training and community development. This account, which we have declined to edit into a more politically correct version, begins with the director's desperate need for help networking the equipment in the fledgling center:

> When I met [the coordinator] I said, "I have to tell you this before we even go any farther, that anytime I deal with a brother I get disappointed. And I am so fed up with it. If you can do the job, do it. If you can't, get out, because I don't have patience for that headache anymore."
>
> I told him that I dealt with one brother who claimed to be a pastor. He came in and he just caused a whole lot of headaches. I let him go. I dealt with another brother with the same name as his [the coordinator's]. I came to find out he was an alcoholic. Every time he got his paycheck, he disappeared. He had to go. I dealt with another brother who was a womanizer. He messed up with all of the residents in the building.
>
> I said to [the coordinator], "You know, my head is full and I am waiting. I don't know whether to trust you or what, so you need to be very straightforward with me. I need to know what you can do and what you can't do because I'm very skeptical of brothers."

The coordinator had "bridged" to the director through a mutual friend and, hence, he was not entirely unknown. The director decided to take a risk but, at the same time, to put the coordinator to the test. As she explained:

> I had a job that I wanted done and I said, "This is a job that I want done. This is the one I have. I don't have anymore, so either take it or leave it." I said, "Go in there and see if you can give me an estimate." And he went in there and said he could do it for cheaper than I thought. . . . So, you know, when he said that I was, like, "Oh no!"
>
> Then he said, "The other thing is that I need to work after hours because of my other work. I have to work the whole night long." And I was very skeptical. Would everything be gone? But I gave him the keys and he said, "Tomorrow morning when you come in, everything will be working."
>
> I was, like, "You're kidding. You know I'm getting tired of that." But when I came in, the computers were all connected and they were all working. I was so impressed. He is for real.

The director summarized the working relationship with the coordinator that developed over the course of the project in these terms:

> We are able to do things more efficiently. I trust [the coordinator] a lot because he does what he says he will do, and that's what we need here in the neighborhood. If you don't have that trust, you cannot work with anybody, because you don't know whether they really care about what they're doing or whether they will deliver. And because we have the same vision, I'm able to give him the keys and just say, "Go in there on the weekend and just do whatever you have to." I know that he will really do what needs to be done.

As the director's reference to "the same vision" implies, a history of pre-dictability and dependability matured into a bond of trust. At the same time, the director's overall account points toward the role of social similarity, self-disclosure, and other relational psychological and communication variables in the development of trust and reciprocity. We soon turn to a quantitative analysis of the role of such factors in this activist project, but the director's account speaks eloquently of the importance of communicative behavior to the development of usable social capital.

BRIDGING, BONDING, AND BROKERING

As our success stories have indicated, the community technology coordinator was an effective technology consultant and trainer, as well as advocate for the participating groups. The basic concept of the project, however, was that the coordinator would create opportunities for others to consult, train, and advocate—and not try to do it all himself. He was well schooled in the idea of social capital as a communication process, and when we interviewed him at the conclusion of the project, he paid homage to the key concept of brokering productive relationships:

> I think that as the community technology coordinator, my work in helping people to communicate with one another helps us to achieve our goal. If you can't communicate with one another, then . . . you can't work together; you can't unite; you can't coalesce—all those good words.

He went on to indicate, even if implicitly and modestly, that the working together, uniting, and coalescing depended heavily on his efforts:

> I'm just the person who tries to bridge between people. I do that by building relationships with people not only here in the community but relationships in other organizations, people who work with the city, people who work in business. I think that is the primary reason I can do

the things that I do now. I've built strong relationships with a core group of people.

The principles of ABCD direct attention to a community's capacity for self-help, but they do not blind us to the reality of community needs. Because needs for technical information and expertise were so great among the less sophisticated groups and the demands so great on the more sophisticated groups and their leaders, the coordinator had to do if not all, then much. We do, of course, have examples of relationships that the project helped to form but then developed on their own; for instance, the connection between the director of a small substance abuse prevention organization and faculty members of Northwestern University's Medical School or the arrangement for a community college to provide technology training to the staff of a social service agency, who, in turn, would provide training to families with foster children. As the information technology manager of that social service agency (the same manager who has appeared as a hero in previous success stories) concluded, "None of this would be in place if the Neighborhood Communication Project hadn't been pulling all of these groups together."

Even so, the project's success in brokering relationships that did not require the coordinator's constant care remains a question. Rather than continuing to pile on the anecdotes, we turn to quantitative data gathered from project participants using a mixed-methods approach (see Creswell, 2003). These methods included the in-depth interviews conducted with group leaders that yielded the comments quoted throughout this chapter. They also included an extensive self-administered questionnaire completed by the leaders addressing the communicative behaviors related to social capital in the context of their groups. Although 33 group leaders agreed to fill out the questionnaire, 14 actually returned it. This sample size and response rate typically elicits an apologetic reference by researchers to "exploratory analysis," but a turnout rate of 42% is very good for events in our neighborhood. Even though our analysis of these data must be limited to zero-order correlations and other simple statistical procedures, the results turn out to be unequivocal, even dramatic, on a number of key points.

Seeking Technical Assistance Drove Communication Among Participants

Self-reported levels of giving technical assistance to others ($M = 1.85$ on a 4-point scale) and seeking assistance from them ($M = 1.92$) were similar (see Table 7.1 for the means of all key variables). However, assistance giving was much less strongly related to the number of communication partners that

Table 7.1.   Statistics of Key Variables

Key Variables	M	SD	Scale Range
Seeking Technical Assistance	1.93	.74	4 point
Providing Technical Assistance	1.85	1.00	4 point
Number of Technology Partners	1.86	.77	3 point[a]
Technical Assistance Received	2.00	.71	4 point
Organizational Technical Efficacy	3.79	.85	5 point
Personal Technical Efficacy	3.62	.95	5 point
Overall Level of Communication	1.31	.48	2 point[a]
Social Support/Mutual Assistance	3.00	1.37	5 point
Social Similarity Index	3.43	.70	5 point
Self-disclosure Index	3.49	.99	5 point
Trust Index	4.25	.40	5 point

Notes. For all means presented, a lower score represents "less" of the item being measured.
[a]Original scales were collapsed for a more even distribution of the data.

project participants regularly consulted about technology, $r = .26$, as compared to assistance seeking, $r = .70$.[2] This difference became even more dramatic when leaders' perceptions of their organizations' technical efficacy were controlled, in which case, assistance giving was unrelated to the number of communication partners, $r = -.06$, whereas assistance seeking remained positively and strongly related, $r = .67$. Thus, group leaders may (or may not) have given assistance regardless of whether their network was larger or smaller, but when they needed assistance, they turned to a larger group. All of these findings are consistent with the idea that the need to get help, a need that could be pressing whatever the level of technical efficacy within an organization, drove network formation and use. On the other hand, the ability or desire to give help did not drive communication, perhaps reflecting the fact that these leaders, especially those with technology skills, were extremely busy with the tasks of their groups. (One leader calculated 132 hours of work during an 88-hour pay period.) With everyone so busy, were any needs for expertise actually met?

Networks Did Have Value as Social Capital

The best report card on the project available from these data was the self-report of technical assistance actually received in the course of the project.

The average rating was exactly 2.00 on a 4-point scale (SD = .71), which meant that the project was "somewhat valuable" for "getting assistance regarding information and communication technologies." Although this overall rating was not as high as we would have liked, this assessment did reveal some interesting complexities. Specifically, assistance actually received was strongly correlated with the number of partners in the network, r = .62, as well as with the overall level of communication with other project participants, r = .49. Causal direction remains an open question, of course, but this is the best quantitative evidence that we have of social capital accumulation in the project and the importance of communication among participants in unlocking the value of network contacts. Simply put, more interactions meant more positive results.

Social Capital Was Not the Same Thing as Social Support

A question designed to elicit the group leaders' sense of mutual assistance ("How often do you help one another with technical problems?") correlated much more strongly with giving assistance, r = .61, than with seeking assistance, r = .22. Hence, the concept of "help one another" seemed to mean giving help much more than receiving it. Moreover, the correlation of social (i.e., mutual) support with assistance actually received was negligible, r = .06, further indicating that helping one another was really a one-way street. Did this reflect the reality of the digital divide within a community where mutual support was not yet possible, thus requiring the community technology coordinator and a few others to "do it all"? The information technology manager thought not. "There are a lot of people in this community who understand technology," he said, reaffirming the central assumption of the project. "The problem is that we don't know each other." Whether there really were enough people who understood technology for the idea to work remains an open question. In any case, it is clear that many participants' networks were better characterized as information-seeking resources than as information-sharing cooperatives.

Differences Between More and Less Technologically Sophisticated Organizations Probably Did Not Lessen

Technical assistance received was not related to personal technical efficacy, r = .02, indicating that leaders already rich in expertise did not necessarily get richer, but assistance received and organizational efficacy were somewhat more strongly related, r = .30. We might seek refuge in the argument that, given the small sample, a correlation of this size lacks statistical signif-icance. However, these data certainly do not allow us to argue that we helped to close the digital divide among organizations within the communi-ty, even if most participants received some benefit from the project. Whether this outcome was inevitable or whether a different strategy might have reduced the differences between more and less sophisticated groups remains another open—and pressing—question.

Communication Across Dissimilarity Remained a Challenge

Bridges promise contacts with new and different types of people. Therefore, if bridges really are built in the course of network formation, larger social networks will exhibit less similarity among their members than smaller net-works. Our data indicated that the size of the network was unrelated to an index measuring the average social similarity between the leaders and their network partners, $r = .06$. Thus, these data did not show a clear bridging effect; a larger network may, or may not, have been similar to the leader. At the same time, however, average social similarity was negatively, but only very weakly, related to assistance actually received, $r = -.15$, which suggests that, at least, assistance could be obtained without regard to social similari-ty. Moreover, when the overall level of communication among leaders and their networks was controlled, the relationship between social similarity and assistance actually received became strongly negative, $r = -.50$. In line with the idea of bridging, this correlation is evidence of the value of diversity, as participants received more assistance when their network included dissimi-lar partners, although the effect occurred only when the amount of commu-nication among partners was controlled. Hence, dissimilarity had value, but only if communication could somehow occur. To both social capital theo-rists and communication activists, this result should affirm the importance of communication processes to social capital formation and use.

Self-Disclosure Did Not Produce a Similarly Dramatic Effect

With the overall amount of communication controlled, an index measuring leaders' average level of self-disclosure to network partners showed no rela-tionship with assistance actually received, $r = .05$. However, self-disclosure remained part of the story, as it did correlate with assistance seeking, $r = .49$, and that relationship was unaffected when either organizational or personal technical efficacy was controlled. This finding suggests that self-disclosure may have been something more than simply a plea for help. Self-disclosure may always be an inevitable by-product of networking, but in this setting, it also may have been a "social penetration" strategy for seeking assistance (Altman & Taylor, 1973).

Trust Among Communication Partners Was High

Unlike self-disclosure, a measure of trust was unrelated to assistance seeking, $r = -.03$. Trust also was unrelated to assistance actually received, even with the overall amount of communication controlled, $r = -.16$. The absence of relationships most likely reflected the high mean on the trust measure (4.3 on a 5-point scale), which we would expect to suppress the possibility of larger correlation coefficients. To those with expertise in survey measurement, this result might be taken to mean that some other measure of trust, one that yields greater variation, should be used in future research. Perhaps, however, it means, instead, that the issue of trust was, in fact, resolved—at least enough to seek and receive assistance from others among these particular people in this particular time and place and on this particular topic.

LASTING OUTCOMES AND LESSONS LEARNED ABOUT COMMUNICATION ACTIVISM

The qualitative and quantitative findings converge to suggest that the Neighborhood Communication Project was more an information-dissemination system than the expertise-sharing cooperative originally envisioned by the project partners. The community technology coordinator did create many opportunities for community groups and their leaders to help each other, but the coordinator (both the role and the person) was synonymous with the project. With his departure from the CBO, the group leaders saw the project as coming to an end, even though many valuable technology-oriented relationships had been formed.

What remained? New community technology centers that offer points of public access to equipment and training is one answer. When the project began, five locations for public access to technology existed in the neighborhood; when it ended, there were, by the coordinator's count, 17 locations. Although we cannot know exactly how much credit the project can take for this outcome, we can say that the project did help to focus attention on the need for these centers and to find some of the resources necessary to conceive and develop them. As the CBO's specialist for training and research said, "The project created the right environment through the university's attention to the issue of technology. In particular, it was a catalyst to growth [of the CBO] in terms of technology." Indeed, as the project was ending, the CBO was finalizing plans for a 50-computer technology center as one component of a newly constructed social service facility.

At the same time, the community technology coordinator was finalizing his personal plans. "When I came to the project, I wasn't long out of school and the project provided the motive and the opportunity to learn about technology," he said, "but when the grant ran out, I had to decide what to do." He decided to start a business. "The project helped me to see technology as in-demand and important, and it helped me to see a demand among small not-for-profits that the project couldn't meet." At the time of our last interview with him, the coordinator was completing both his university graduate studies and the application process for minority contractor status with the city and county governments. "He sees himself as an entrepreneur now," said the CBO's specialist for training and research. "He learned the community well enough to know where the business might be." One way to sustain gains—a way that is economically meaningful in this job-poor neighborhood—is to build them into a business.

In our last interview with the CBO's specialist for research and training, she concluded that, simply by focusing the attention of the CBO and the community, in general, on issues of technology at a receptive moment, the project had made its most useful intervention. She felt the project's moment had begun to pass when more organizations in the community recognized information and communication technology as both an organizational imperative and an issue of social justice. Indeed as this chapter was being written, clergy across Chicago neighborhoods were campaigning for more widely available, high-speed internet service at lower cost.

Here, then, is one lesson of our project with regard to communication activism that is specifically intended to address the digital divide. One sort of divide—for example, the difference in the social importance attached to the issue—may close but others soon open, driven by the availability of newer technology, the demand for higher levels of expertise, and the reality of harder problems to solve (e.g., Ettema, 1984; Light, 2001). Simply by promoting a higher standard of technological sophistication among community groups, the project helped to redefine the nature and amount of help that was needed to "catch up." As many activists have come to know well, the digital divide is at once fascinating and frustrating.

With this in mind, it is not surprising, although still disappointing, to conclude that the particular digital divide motivating our project, the divide *within* the community among groups' levels of technical efficacy, apparently did not close in the course of the project. The most desperately needed asset—technical expertise—was comparatively scarce in this community. Moreover, the holders of that asset were individuals who sometimes were at odds with others in their group about sharing the asset. As the information technology manager observed, groups sometimes worried about the amount of resources they were bringing to the table as compared to other groups. Assets were stretched thin and unevenly distributed, making reciprocity problematic. The quantitative data indicated that those seeking assistance were able to get help, but the data also suggested assistance was not equally shared, as those in the best positions to seek and use it got more of it.

These factors challenged asset-based community development ideals. Here, then, is a second lesson of our project with regard to communication activism that subscribes to those ideals: The needed asset must, of course, actually exist in the community, and those who control it must share it. Sharing intellectual assets, such as technical expertise, is the very meaning of social capital. The concept of social capital, in turn, emphasizes the norms of trust and reciprocity, and those concepts, in turn, emphasize the importance of social interaction. Asset-based community development, in short, requires effective communication.

This project does, indeed, show that social interaction was essential to unlocking the value of social capital. Even if the project did not create a cooperative for sharing expertise and social support, it did promote productive social interaction and, in turn, the dissemination of useful information. Although the project may not have equalized access among community groups to the asset of technical expertise, it did demonstrate the role of communication in capitalizing on that asset by whomever was in a position to use it. More specifically, the quantitative data showed that assistance actually received was related to the number of communication partners and the overall level of communication with those partners. Moreover, higher levels of communication could overcome social dissimilarity to give and receive that help. Without communication, technical expertise would have remained locked away. The project, thus, helped the community's own activists make a set of keys.

The conclusion that higher levels of communication could overcome social dissimilarity in the giving and receiving of assistance points us, once again, to the issue of trust. Therein lies another lesson of our project—a lesson that may well apply to communication activism in general. Although the quantitative data do not show a relationship between level of trust and the seeking or receiving of help, the people we interviewed insisted that trust was important, and our quantitative data do indicate that trust was present among project participants. Certainly we can say that our experience was an exercise in the development of trust. We acknowledge that, as social scientists, we initially were worried about turning over the research process to trained but neophyte interviewers. However, we learned that the data were not simply there for the *taking* (more usually and neutrally referred to as *collecting*); rather, the data must be given to us by the community. We also worried about turning over the responsibilities of the community technology coordinator's role to a recent college graduate with little formal training in information and communication technology, but we learned that with enthusiasm and commitment the other skills would follow. Although these lessons seem specific to our particular project, we take them to be lessons in gaining and maintaining the spirit of activist research.

CONCLUSION

Community leaders and communication activists must be prepared to confront an ever-changing digital divide created by new information and communication technologies and the increased expertise needed to master them. In this chapter, we presented a case for asset-based community development, as well as social and intellectual capital, as useful concepts for leaders and activists in this confrontation with an important issue of social justice. We also showed how these concepts interlock with the relational communicative behavior of leaders and activists. We conclude that productive use of community assets and the formation of social and intellectual capital demand skilled communication. To understand these behaviors and skills is the challenge for communication research and to use that research in service to the community is the excitement of communication activism.

NOTES

1. We can at least thank several Northwestern University faculty members by name. They are John McKnight, Professor Emeritus of Communication Studies, and Paul Arntson, Professor of Communication Studies, who provided conceptual guidance and practical support. Thanks also to Patrick McMullen, the graduate student in Communication Studies who served as webmaster. "Neighborhood Communication Project" is a pseudonym in which "Neighborhood" is substituted for the name of the particular Chicago-area community.

2. On the self-administered questionnaire, respondents anonymously listed and then answered questions about the communication partners that they consulted regarding technology. The number of partners was collapsed into three categories that yielded a more normal distribution: small (one person consulted), medium (2-6), and large (7 or more). The number of partners consulted was strongly correlated with self-reports by leaders of their overall level of communication during the project as measured on a 4-point scale, $r = .82$. With an $N = 14$, correlation coefficients of $r = .46$ are statistically significant at the $p = .05$ level and $r = .62$ at the $p = .01$ level (one-tailed test).

REFERENCES

Adler, P. S., & Kwon, S. (2000). Social capital: The good, the bad, and the ugly. In E. L. Lesser (Ed.), *Knowledge and social capital: Foundations and applications* (pp. 89-115). Boston: Butterworth-Heinemann.

Albrecht, T. L., Adelman, M. B., & Associates. (1987). *Communicating social support.* Newbury Park, CA: Sage.

Albrecht, T. L., Burleson, B. R., & Sarason, I. (Eds.). (1992). Approaches to the study of communication, social support and helping relationships [Special issue]. *Communication Research, 19*(2).

Altman, I., & Taylor, D. A. (1973). *Social penetration: The development of interpersonal relationships.* New York: Holt, Rinehart and Winston.

Briggs, X. (1998). Doing democracy up-close: Culture, power, and communication in community building. *Journal of Planning Education and Research, 18,* 1-13.

Burgoon, J. K. (Ed.). (1992). Chautauqua: The role of communication in the similarity-attraction relationship [Special section]. *Communication Monographs, 59,* 164-212.

Burt, R. S. (1997). The contingent value of social capital. *Administrative Science Quarterly, 42,* 339-365.

Coleman, J. S. (1988). Social capital in the creation of human capital. *American Journal of Sociology, 94,* S95-121.

Creswell, J. W. (2003). *Research design: Qualitative, quantitative, and mixed methods approaches* (2nd ed.). Thousand Oaks, CA: Sage.

Dindia, K. (2002). Self-disclosure research: Knowledge through meta-analysis. In M. Allen, R. W. Preiss, B. M. Gayle, & N A. Burrell (Eds.), *Interpersonal communication research: Advances through meta-analysis* (pp. 169-185). Mahwah, NJ: Erlbaum.

Edwards, B., & Foley, M. W. (1998). Civil society and social capital beyond Putnam. *American Behavioral Scientist, 42,* 124-139.

Ettema, J. S. (1984). Three phases in the creation of information inequities. *Journal of Broadcasting, 28,* 383-395.

Fernandez, R. M., Castilla, E. J., & Moore, P. (2000). Social capital at work: Networks and employment at a phone center. *American Journal of Sociology, 105,* 1288-1356.

Fischer, C. S. (1982). *To dwell among friends: Personal networks in town and city.* Chicago: University of Chicago Press.

Fukuyama, F. (1999, November). *Social capital and civil society.* Paper presented at the International Monetary Funds Conference on Second Generation Reforms, Washington, DC. Retrieved July 2, 2003, from http://www.imf.org/external/pubs/ft/seminar/1999/reforms/fukuyama.htm

Gittell, R., & Vidal, A. (1998). *Community organizing: Building social capital as a developmental strategy.* Thousand Oaks, CA: Sage.

Greeley, A. M. (1997). Coleman revisited: Religious structures as a source of social capital. *American Behavioral Scientist, 40,* 587-594.

Kretzmann, J. P., & McKnight, J. L. (1993). *Building communities from the inside out: A path toward finding and mobilizing a community's assets.* Evanston, IL: Northwestern University, Institute for Policy Research.

Light, J. S. (2001). Rethinking the digital divide. *Harvard Educational Review, 71*, 709-733.

McKnight, J. L. (1995). *The careless society: Community and its counterfeits.* New York: Basic Books.

McKnight, J. L. (1997). A 21st-century map for healthy communities and families. *Families in Society, 78*, 117-127.

Millar, F. E., & Rogers, L. E. (1987). Relational dimensions of interpersonal dynamics. In M. E. Roloff & G. R. Miller (Eds.), *Interpersonal processes: New directions in communication research* (pp. 117-139). Beverly Hills, CA: Sage.

National Telecommunications and Information Administration. (1999). *Falling through the net: Defining the digital divide.* Washington, DC: U.S. Department of Commerce.

Pearce, W. B. (1974). Trust in interpersonal communication. *Speech Monographs, 41*, 236-244.

Portes, A. (1998). Social capital: Its origins and applications in modern sociology. *Annual Review of Sociology, 24*, 1-24.

Putnam, R. D. (with Leonardi, R., & Nanetti, R. Y.). (1993). *Making democracy work: Civic traditions in modern Italy.* Princeton, NJ: Princeton University Press.

Putnam, R. D. (1995). Bowling alone: America's declining social capital. *Journal of Democracy, 6*, 65-78.

Putnam, R. D. (2000). *Bowling alone: The collapse and revival of American community.* New York: Simon & Schuster.

Rempel, J. K., Holmes, J. G., & Zanna, M. P. (1985). Trust in close relationships. *Journal of Personality and Social Psychology, 49*, 95-112.

Sias, P. M., & Cahill, D. J. (1998). From coworkers to friends: The development of peer friendships in the workplace. *Western Journal of Communication, 62*, 273-299.

Taylor, D. A., & Altman, I. (1987). Communication in interpersonal relationships: Social penetration processes. In M. E. Roloff & G. R. Miller (Eds.), *Interpersonal processes: New directions in communication research* (pp. 257-277). Beverly Hills, CA: Sage.

Wood, R. L. (1997). Social capital and political culture: God meets politics in the inner city. *American Behavioral Scientist, 40*, 595-605.

Woolcock, M. (1998). Social capital and economic development: Toward a theoretical synthesis and policy framework. *Theory and Society, 27*, 151-208.

Yun, K. A. (2002). Similarity and attraction. In M. Allen, R. W. Preiss, B. M. Gayle, & N. A. Burrell (Eds.), *Interpersonal communication research: Advances through meta-analysis* (pp. 145-167). Mahwah, NJ: Erlbaum.

PART II

Performing Social Change

8

CATALYZING SOCIAL REFORM THROUGH PARTICIPATORY FOLK PERFORMANCES IN RURAL INDIA*

Lynn Harter
Ohio University

Devendra Sharma
California State University, Fresno

Saumya Pant
Arvind Singhal
Ohio University

Yogita Sharma
Texas A&M University

On a hot July afternoon in the village of Abirpur of India's Bihar State, as the radio played old Hindi songs and the cows grazed along the monsoon-drenched paddy fields, Usha and her six friends gathered under the banyan tree to discuss their dilemma. How could they convince their parents to allow them to attend the week-long participatory theater workshops in the village of Kamtaul, located 20 miles away?

---

*We thank the following individuals and organizations for their collaboration, support, and help with conducting the present research project: David Andrews and Kate Randolph of Population Communications International (PCI), New York; Gopi Gopalakrishnan, Neelam Vachani, Pankaj Kumar Singh, Akhilesh Kumar Sharma, Anil Kumar, Sushil Kumar, and Virendra Pratap Singh of Janani in Patna, India; Pundit Ram Dayal Sharma, Himanshu Saini, Vishnu Sharma, Sangeet Sharma, and Indu Sharma of Brij Lok Madhuri; and P. N. Vasanti, Mumtaz Ahmed, Chetna Verma, Alok Shrivastav, and the team of field researchers at the Centre for Media Studies, New Delhi, India. This research was supported by a grant from PCI to Ohio University.

This chapter tells the story of the participatory theater workshops and performances that we initiated and co-facilitated in the Indian State of Bihar in the summer of 2003, highlighting the struggles faced by young, village-based girls like Usha, who previously had never dared to step out of their communities. Workshops participants came from four villages, including Usha's village of Abirpur in Bihar's Vaishali District, and from the villages of Kamtaul, Madhopur, and Chandrahatti in Bihar's Muzzaffarpur District. The participatory theater project was created as part of a larger study to assess the outcomes of an entertainment-education Indian radio soap opera called *Taru* in India's Bihar State. Authors Singhal and D. Sharma both were intimately involved in the conceptualization, design, and implementation of the larger *Taru* entertainment-education evaluation project (see Singhal, Sharma, Papa, & Witte, 2004).

In this chapter, we focus on one important part of this project—the participatory theater workshops and performances conducted in July 2003. We begin by describing the social landscape of India, in general, and Bihar State, in particular. We then situate the participatory theater workshops and performances within the larger historical context of our previous interventions in Bihar, followed by a discussion of our theoretical perspectives and a description of the participatory theater project and its theoretical and practical outcomes. We conclude the chapter with some reflections about our communication activism.

THE SOCIAL LANDSCAPE
OF INDIA AND BIHAR STATE

India is one of the largest and most culturally diverse democracies in the world. Although India has achieved significant gains in its agricultural, industrial, and service sectors since its independence from Great Britain in 1947, poverty and inequality have abated more slowly than expected, despite government-sponsored rural-development initiatives and increased involvement of nongovernment organizations with local citizens (S. Kumar, 2002; Singhal & Rogers, 2001). A great disparity also exists in levels of social development across the various Indian states. The State of Bihar, which lies in the northern, Hindi-speaking belt of India, is both the most rural state and, based on economic and social indicators, the poorest.

Districts Muzzaffarpur and Vaishali in Bihar State, where the four villages of our intervention are located, ranked very poorly among all 590 districts of India on the Reproductive Health Composite Index in the 2001 national census (Population Foundation of India, 2002). In Muzzaffarpur, the male literacy rate, for instance, is 60% and the female literacy rate is

35%, with 54% of girls married before the age of 18. The district's total fertility rate is 5.1, with a 25% contraceptive prevalence rate (CPR). Only 31% of children in Muzzafarpur are completely immunized and 81% of them are underweight. District Vaishali fares no better: Its male literacy rate is 64% compared to the female literacy rate of 38%, approximately 63% of girls are married before the age of 18, the district's total fertility rate is 5.0 and the related CPR is 24% among all eligible couples, only 22% of children are completely immunized, and 51% of the children are underweight (Population Foundation of India, 2002).

The caste system is highly entrenched in rural Bihar (as in most of India), embodying a complex system of hierarchically arranged social differentiation among people (Harriss-White, 2003).[1] The caste system simultaneously unites and divides various groups of people, but its most salient feature is mutual exclusiveness, with each caste regarding the other castes as separate communities. Akin to the privileges that come from being a member of a higher caste, the "good life" in Bihar seems to be designed mostly for men. A son's birth is celebrated as a joyous occasion, whereas a girl's birth is viewed as a burden by her family. Sons usually attend schools, whereas daughters tend to housework and care for younger siblings. When a girl is ready for marriage, her family will have to pay *dowry*—a bride price (in cash and/or material goods)—to the groom's family. Once married, it is the *dharma* (or "duty") of the wife to serve her husband, in-laws, and children (Jung, 1987; Pande, 2003).

HISTORICAL CONTEXT
OF CURRENT INTERVENTIONS

Within this societal context, since February 2002, we co-initiated (with villagers and rural health practitioners [RHPs]) a series of participatory interventions designed to assist local groups and community members in these four villages of India's Bihar State to secure social and political reform. Specifically, folk performances were held in February 2002 across these four villages to promote listening to the entertainment-education radio serial *Taru* produced by All India Radio (see Photograph 8.1). *Entertainment-education* (E-E) is the process of purposely designing and implementing a media message to both entertain and educate (e.g., to increase audience members' knowledge about a social issue, create favorable attitudes toward change, and shift social norms) (Singhal & Rogers, 1999). *Taru* (named after the woman protagonist) was a 52-episode E-E radio soap opera, broadcast in the northern, Hindi-speaking region of India from February 2002 to February 2003. The purpose of *Taru* was to raise consciousness about the

Photograph 8.1. Some 800 people attended the folk performance in Madhopur Village to promote listening to *Taru*. This performance, staged in February 2003, a few days before *Taru* began broadcasting, resulted in the formation of several *Taru* listening clubs. (Source: Authors' personal files)

value of gender equality, small family size, reproductive health, and caste and communal harmony (Singhal et al., 2004). A primary function of the folk performances, carried out a week prior to the broadcast of *Taru* and attended by 800-1,000 people in each location, was to prime the message-reception environment for the radio serial, encouraging audience members to tune in to it.

D. Sharma[2] scripted these pre-broadcast *Taru* folk performances in the *nautanki* genre (a popular musical folk theater form of Northern India), using a *nat* and *nati* (male and female narrators) to engage the audiences. The folk performances were sponsored by Ohio University with help from Janani[3] and the Centre for Media Studies. A folk song introduced the themes and characters of *Taru*. The folk performance was customized to the local Bihar milieu (including use of local colloquial expressions, costumes, and props) in 2-day workshops with members of Rangkarm, a local theater group in Patna, the capital of Bihar State.

Key aspects of the *Taru* storyline, especially its first few episodes, were dramatized in the folk performances to generate the audience's interest in listening to the forthcoming broadcasts. All of these folk performances ended with an open competition for audience members in which radio transistors (with a sticker of *Taru*'s logo) were awarded to self-selected groups of young women, young men, and families who correctly answered questions based on the performance of the drama. These groups then were formalized into *Taru* radio-listening clubs. In each village, at least four listening groups, each comprised of 6-8 members, were established. Each group received an attractive notebook (with a *Taru* logo), and group members were encouraged to discuss with others in their village the social themes addressed in the serial, relate the emplotments and characters to their personal circumstances, and record in their journals any decisions or actions they took as a result of being exposed to *Taru*.

A qualitative study[4] of these four villages in Bihar—Abirpur, Kamtaul, Madhopur, and Chandrahatti—indicated that a *Taru* fever has since taken hold in these villages (Singhal et al., 2004). Discussions of *Taru* among listening group members have led directly to several community initiatives to secure social reform. For instance, in Kamtaul Village, an adult literacy program for *dalit* village women was launched, and several early marriages (of underage girls) were stopped. In Abirpur Village, male and female members of *Taru* listening groups, after 7 months of discussion and deliberation, collectively started a school for underprivileged children, inspired by a similar act role modeled by Neha, a character in the radio serial. Such mixed-sex collaboration was previously highly uncommon in Bihar's villages and faced strong resistance from certain community members. However, these groups' collective zeal, coupled with strong support from the highly respected local RHP, made the establishment of the school possible. As of mid-2003, some 50 children had attended this 2-hour afternoon school 6 days a week (see Photograph 8.2).

Photograph 8.2. An open-air school for underprivileged children in Village Abirpur that was established by Abirpur's *Taru* listening club members after being inspired by Neha, one of the radio serial's characters, who engaged in a similar deed. (Source: Authors' personal files)

In July 2003, authors Pant, D. Sharma, and Y. Sharma returned to Bihar (under the direction of Singhal and Harter) to organize participatory theater workshops for members of *Taru* listening clubs from each of the four villages. The interventions were carried out in collaboration with Brij Lok Madhuri. The week-long workshops were designed to empower each group and its members to develop participatory theatrical performances to capture their individual- and group-listening experiences in relation to *Taru* and their concomitant attempts to secure political and social reform in their respective villages. These folk performances then were staged for village members to bring participants' narratives into the realm of public discourse.

THEORETICAL FRAMEWORK

The dialogic theorizing of Brazilian educator Paulo Freire (1970, 1994, 1998) and its application by Augusto Boal (1979) in the global movement called the *Theater of the Oppressed* served as the theoretical backdrop against which our interventions were crafted. Underscoring Freire and Boal's work is the assumption that the greatest challenge facing activists is the need to understand, appreciate, and respect the knowledge of people's lived experiences as expressed in their vernacular. Freire, best known for his classic book *Pedagogy of the Oppressed* (1970), argued that most political, educational, and communication interventions fail because they are designed by "technocrats" who seldom take into account the perspectives of those to whom the interventions are directed. No intervention that is truly empowering, Freire argued, can remain distant from those who are disenfranchised. Like Freire, we believe that the authentic potential of activism begins with the lived experiences of involved participants (see also the writings on communication and social justice by Frey, 1998; Frey, Pearce, Pollock, Artz, & Murphy, 1996).

Freire (1970) critiqued the mechanistic "banking" model of education and activism, in which "deposits" of knowledge are made in the minds of audiences, and offered, instead, proposals for democratic problem-solving interventions (see Rich & Rodríguez, this volume). Freire started from a position of faith—faith that people can develop discursive consciousness about their material and social circumstances, a process he called *consientizacao*. By positioning oppressed individuals as "subjects" rather than "objects," a Freireian perspective acknowledges that these individuals can and should participate in the transformation of their economic, social, and political domination. As agents who act on and transform the world, individuals must perceive the reality of their oppression not as a static entity that cannot be changed but as a limiting situation that they can transform. Freireian methods to accomplish these goals incorporate critical reflection, dialogue, participation, autonomy, democratic decision making, and problematization.

Freire's work draws attention to what it means to be at the periphery or center of the tenuous relationship between the "colonizer" and the "colonized." As Freire (1970) argued, "Revolutionary leaders cannot think *without* the people, nor *for* the people, but only *with* the people" (p. 131). Throughout our intervention process in Bihar, we were conscious of the potential and tendency to "inscribe" or impose our activist agenda within the local community. Rather than penetrating the cultural context of our participants irrespective of their potentialities, we conceptualized our role as working *with* (not *for*) participants to organize efforts to resist oppressive ideologies, patterns, and practices. Sensitized to the importance of dialogical pedagogy/intervention, our primary goal was to create space in the form of participatory theater for community members to *name* their world in order to transform it. Instead of dislodging the oppressed from one reality to "bind" them to another, we sought to make it possible for participants to narrate their experiences, create alternatives to dominant scripts for how to enact public and private roles, and rehearse such "counter-stories" on a public platform (Nelson, 2001).

Inspired by the writings of Freire, Brazilian theater director Boal (1979) developed the *Theatre of the Oppressed* (TO), an international movement that uses theater as a vehicle of participatory social change. Underscoring Boal's work is the assumption that all theater is ideological in that it reproduces or resists value-laden practices and patterns. As such, theatre, directly or indirectly, entertains, educates, informs, influences, and incites action. Boal's techniques of TO, based on Freireian principles of dialogue, interaction, problem posing, reflection, and conscientization, are designed to activate spectators to take control of situations rather than passively allow things to happen to them. The goal, therefore, is to transform passive spectators into actors in charge of dramatic action. The human body, the source of sound, as well as movement, is the means of producing theatre; thus, embodiment is the means of producing transformation. Through controlled bodily actions, a passive observer becomes an active protagonist (see Rich & Rodríguez, this volume)

Boal (1979) argued that most marginalized individuals are spectators of public affairs rather than active agents because of fear of their oppressors. To begin the transformation to an active agent, he developed a series of theatrical exercises to ferret out internalized oppression. In particular, he emphasized the importance of exercises that "undo" participants' muscular structures—the way they walk and talk—to raise people's consciousness about how their body structure, gait, and voice embody an oppressed/oppressor relationship. For instance, when peasants are granted space to act as landowners, their physical bearings change (e.g., posture), reflecting the ideologies associated with their new roles (Singhal, 2004). Boal provided numerous exercises designed to increase individuals' awareness of their body, including deformations suffered because of the type of work they perform. These exercises are particularly crucial to the process of transformation given that human beings are so conditioned to linguistic expression that their body's expressive capabilities are underdeveloped and unconscious. Although Boal described a series of useful techniques to be used by facilitators in helping spectators to become active agents, we argue that such techniques must concomitantly take into account local cultural members' modes of expression, including ways of doing theater.

Within such a culturally infused context, participants can use the tools of theater (e.g., character development and emplotment) to acquire new ways of knowing reality and sharing that knowledge with others. TO is a form of "rehearsal theater" for people who want to give voice to their experiences and discover new ways of fighting against oppression in their daily lives. By rehearsing, and potentially accepting or rejecting, solutions to articulated problems, participants have opportunities to "try out" counter-narratives. The theatrical act, by itself, is a conscious intervention, a rehearsal for social action based on a collective analysis of shared problems of oppression. Participatory theater, however, potentially embodies a process of participation that is empowering both as a *means* (for involved agents) and an *end* (in terms of potential structural outcomes generated). In the case of Bihar, India, we used Freire and Boal's work as sensitizing concepts in the facilitation of participatory "folk" theatre, song, and poem performances.

DESCRIPTION OF THE PARTICIPATORY THEATER WORKSHOPS AND PERFORMANCES

The participatory theater workshops were facilitated over a 3-day period (July 24-26, 2003) from 9:00 a.m. to 5:00 p.m. in the village of Kamtaul. The public performances of the subsequent plays were enacted in all four villages on July 27 and 28, 2003. Kamtaul was chosen as the site of the workshops because it is somewhat centrally located among the four villages and has a 3-room *panchayat ghar* (the local self-government community center), with a 35 x 30 meter yard that provided space for multiple rehearsals (see Photograph 8.3). In addition, the RHP of Kamtaul, Sheilendra Singh, is a progressive and locally influential person, who later became a regular listener of *Taru* (his daughter, Vandana, was a leader in Kamtaul's *Taru* listening club).

A month before the workshops began, Pant, D. Sharma, and Y. Sharma worked on location with Janani officials, RHPs (like Singh), prospective

Photograph 8.3. A participatory theater rehearsal in progress in Kamtaul's *panchayat ghar.* Each day, several dozen bystanders watched the theater workshops proceedings. (Source: Authors' personal files)

participants, and participants' parents to plan the logistics for the intervention. Activities involved hiring a production executive for the theater workshops, professional video and still camerapersons to document the workshops and performances, caterers to provide meals to participants, drivers and busses to transport participants, and professionals who managed stage materials and props, including an audio-amplification system. In addition, Pant, D. Sharma, and Y. Sharma, supported by local opinion leaders, negotiated the granting of permission by parents so that their children could participate in the workshops and performances.

Fifty members of *Taru* listening groups from across the four villages took part in the participatory theater workshops and performances. Participants ranged in age from 9-27 years old, with 25 female and 25 male participants.[5] The workshops opened with D. Sharma orienting participants to the week-long activities, followed by a speech by Manoj Maharaj, the RHP of Abirpur Village, endorsing the theater project. Participants then were organized into two "adult" groups (ages 15-27) and one children's group (ages 9-14). In forming these groups, care was taken to ensure that they had mixed-gender and mixed-village representation.

During the first 3 days of the workshops, participants developed skills in script writing, character development, costume and set design, voice projection and body control, and acting and singing. Two folk artists, Rajiv and Dheeraj, from the local theater group Rangkram, along with Pant, D.

Sharma and Y. Sharma (all of whom had previous training in theater, especially D. Sharma), provided initial direction for the workshops.
Participants first were asked to introduce themselves by telling a story
about their lives—a story situated in the context of their families and communities. Although a few participants initially were reluctant to share stories (girls were shier than boys) or had difficulty understanding what
counted as a "story," a rich collage of narratives quickly emerged within
each group. The facilitators urged the group members to identify common
themes among their stories and start to create a "meta-story" that could be
used to develop a performance script.

   Throughout the workshops, participants engaged in vocal exercises to
enhance their speech volume and breath control (e.g., singing songs and
shouting collectively). Participants also engaged in a series of body movement exercises (e.g., yoga and stretching exercises) to increase their awareness of their body and its potential as a tool of performance (see Photograph
8.4). Collectively, these exercises helped to build team spirit and deepen
friendships among participants and decreased participants' social awkward-
ness during the performances. Female participants, in particular, learned to
relax their bodies in front of men and use their bodies for public expression.
Traditionally, Indian women are taught to be docile in public; they are
expected to keep their voice low and be passive in bodily movement (R.
Kumar, 1993). Furthermore, the woman's body is considered sacred, and its

Photograph 8.4. Participants of the theater workshops engage in physical
and vocal exercises in preparation to play their respective roles. (Source:
Authors' personal files)

sanctity is preserved by limiting public exhibition. Workshop exercises challenged these cultural conventions and, as a result, increased females' self-confidence and willingness to perform in public and, ultimately, offered females a way to be comfortable with their body without dishonoring it. For example, in an interview conducted with a participant after the performances, Usha Kumari discussed her impressions of the first day:

> First, I did not know how to behave with the workshop participants. They were all strangers to me and I felt shy. In my village, I am not shy, as I know all the boys and girls. However, it was different now, as these boys were not my brothers but strange men. Slowly, I felt comfortable in their presence as we did a number of physical exercises together. That helped in identifying with one another. Soon, all of the participants became my good friends. I hope I can keep in touch with all of them.

Pant, D. Sharma, and Y. Sharma encouraged participants to create performances centered around self-identified social issues, using their own vernacular, personal stories, and master narratives of their communities. In sum, the "means of production" of the theater workshops and subsequent performances rested primarily with the participants. All aspects of performance—from role development to preparation of the stage—were co-created by participants. For example, in making a decision about how to construct the stages, groups of young boys from each village were recruited to bring a dozen *takhats* (flat wooden beds) from their homes to create raised platforms for the performances. On another occasion, in the village of Chandrahatti, the ground on which the wooden platform stage was constructed was uneven, and a group of workshop participants promptly brought tools from their homes and created a level ground.

During the workshops, participants created three separate plays (for a summary of the scripts, see the Appendix). The negotiation of emplotments was not an easy task for all the groups. For example, one of the groups decided to construct a script on the problems of child marriage and dowry. The following excerpt from D. Sharma's fieldnotes illustrates the democratic evolution of this script construction and captures Boal's (1979) vision of encouraging traditional "spectators" to actively wrestle with the potentialities and pitfalls of diverse solutions:

> Participants evolved the scripts after countless revisions of drafts and after much discussion amongst group members. One specific incident is illustrative of this process. The ending of the play on dowry and child marriage was not perceived as realistic by many group members. In the initial plot, as the wedding was underway, the father of the groom was demanding dowry from the bride's family, and the groom was refusing

to accept dowry. For some young women, this solution seemed unrealistic. For hours, the whole group debated about how the play should end. After many revisions, a solution was reached that was agreeable to all. An additional scene was added between the groom and his friends prior to the wedding to establish the groom's character as idealistic and sympathetic toward women. Further, the wedding scene was modified. A confrontation occurs between the father and son at the beginning of the wedding in which the father ultimately gives in to the son's wishes to protect the prestige of his family, which would surely be damaged if the son walked away from the alter. The rehearsals for the play started after a whole day of discussion!

The 3-day workshops were followed by 2 days of public performances. No professional actors were used in the performances; instead, participants served as cast members, directors, and set managers. Performances were promoted in advance through word-of-mouth channels, capitalizing on the contacts of the local RHPs, as well as those of family members and friends of the workshops participants. Prior to the start of the performances, live folk and popular songs were played on the loudspeaker to generate attention among villagers. Each play was publicly performed in each of the four villages for audiences that ranged in number from 300-500 people. Interspersed with the plays were a folk dance, some songs, and a poem—all initiated and created by the participants. In each village, we situated the performance site in an open area that was easily accessible to residents. In most cases, villagers provided tarpaulin sheets or mats on which audience members sat. Importantly, we strategically positioned women at the front of the audience, with men clustered behind them, and, in so doing, subverted the dominance usually exerted by men on such occasions (see Photograph 8.5). Many women who were not allowed to leave their home (e.g., young married women) watched from the terrace of their home. When space ran short, onlookers perched themselves on trees or terraces to view the performances (see Photograph 8.6).

All of the workshops and performances were videotaped. Throughout the workshops, Pant, D. Sharma, and Y. Sharma took extensive fieldnotes. In addition, the three scripts were translated from Hindi to English. After completing the workshops, D. Sharma, Pant, Y. Sharma, and Singhal (who attended the folk performances), as well as trained interviewers from the Centre for Media Studies in New Delhi, conducted in-depth interviews with workshop participants, participants' family members, and audience members. In conducting these interviews, we were particularly interested in how people accounted for their experiences and, in so doing, situated themselves and others in relation to the social order of this particular context. The interview protocol included questions about whether and how individuals experienced empowerment through the participatory theater project, challenges

Photograph 8.5. Women and girls sit in front as a folk performance unfolds in the village of Chandrahatti. (Source: Authors' personal files)

Photograph 8.6. Spectators perched on a rooftop watch a performance in the village of Abirpur. The banner with the *Taru* logo says, "Listener club members of *Taru* present a cultural performance." (Source: Authors' personal files)

and emotions experienced by participants and audience members, and if, when, and where communication about the project took place among interviewees' social networks. A total of 62 in-depth interviews were conducted, audiotaped, and later transcribed into English for analysis. In addition, a letter we received from one of the participants was transcribed from Hindi into English. We triangulated data from these sources to document several theoretical and practical outcomes of the participatory theater workshops and performances.

THEORETICAL AND PRACTICAL IMPLICATIONS OF OUR COMMUNICATION ACTIVISM

Competing views of community are inscribed and enacted through cultural performances and, consequently, illustrate ways in which cultural performances negotiate communal identity politics. Indeed, the concept of "community" possesses no fixed, stable referent but, instead, is a contested concept whose meaning is continuously negotiated in and by cultural performances and other symbolic forms (see Adelman & Frey, 1997; Shepherd, 2001). Like other scholars interested in performance for the purpose of promoting social change (e.g., Conquergood, 1988; see Rich & Rodríguez, this volume; Walker & Cunningham, this volume), we assume that a reciprocal relationship exists between cultural performance and the constitution of community, such that communities not only produce but are produced by cultural performances. Cultural performances inscribe community by inserting into circulation particular interpretations of community, through both *description* (i.e., the past and the present) and *prescription* (i.e., the future). As explained next, agents of the participatory theater interventions in Bihar developed counter-narratives that resisted dominant community identities and created social networks characterized by social capital. At the same time, we witnessed the synergistic possibilities that can emerge from multilayered, participatory E-E initiatives. Collectively, these outcomes illustrate the theoretical and practical implications of our communication activism and its heuristic potential.

Counter-Narratives

Narratization is a means of structuring experience (including temporally envisioning outcomes); hence, narration is a strategy used to achieve envisioned ends (Burke, 1969; Wittgenstein, 1953). Indeed, a chief characteristic of narrative is its ability to render understanding by connecting (however unstably) parts to a constructed configuration or a social network of relationships comprised of symbolic, institutional, and material practices (see Sunwolf & Frey, 2001). Narrative theorizing provides a particularly fruitful framework from which to address the discursive understandings through which subjectivities/identities are constructed (Somers, 1994). Individuals orient to their life worlds, in part, by way of diverse stocks of knowledge that are social in origin. In that light, participatory theater serves as a particularly rich site to explore the (re)construction of identity (individual and communal) through *counter-narratives*, which Nelson (2001) described as emplotments that discursively reconfigure disempowering elements of the existing social order as articulated by and based on the lived experiences of individuals.

The people who participated in these theater workshops and performances discovered a vocabulary for composing their personal stories, connected their stories to other participants' narratives, and spun out alternatives to the dominant societal scripts affecting their lives. Participants' scripts identified *master narratives*, what Foucault (1973) referred to as cultural "truths" based on "global" or "unified" knowledge that often serve to sustain the status quo by involving individuals in its service (e.g., making them "docile bodies" or helpless personae caught in the problem). For instance, the participatory theatre performance scripts recognized the powerful forces of dowry and the caste system as impinging on participants' daily routines and relationships. Concomitantly, through the participatory theater workshops and performances, we glimpsed story threads of resistance to dominant narratives based, in part, on what Foucault termed "local popular" or "indigenous" knowledge.

For some of the theater workshop participants, the performances reinforced existing counter-narrative mindsets and provided a public forum to express these privately held convictions. For instance, one participant argued, "Everyone in the village knows that dowry is a problem but they will not do anything about it." The workshops and performances allowed for the expression of these inner voices using villagers' own cultural dialects (specifically, folk theater). Another participant, Didi, stated:

> I am almost 17 years old and I know the kind of pressure I am facing with marriage. But after listening to *Taru* and having you here in the village, I feel confident to fight and not let my parents come under any pressure.... I am happy that my village saw the plays and realized that we were not doing anything wrong.

In other cases, the performances represented an "awakening" of discursive consciousness about social inequities. For some participants, especially the children, these workshops and performances were among their first opportunities to reflect on their social, political, and material life circumstances. Regardless of the layers of social consciousness that we witnessed among participants, the performances collectively served to rearticulate roles and scripts for community life by constructing, maintaining, reinforcing, and renegotiating relationships among community members.

Participatory theater is unique in its simultaneous (re)construction of personal identity and cultural critique. Although performing autobiography, in one sense, is something we accomplish daily, in public performances, such as the participatory theater interventions described here, participants selected bits and pieces of their lived experiences to share with audiences—creating a pastiche of observations and characters both real and imagined. One participant, Soni, shared during an interview:

> When Saumya *didi* [sister] asked me to tell a story about my life or my village, I thought of several episodes but wasn't sure if they are appropriate for the occasion. Then when I heard other participants highlight significant issues in their lives, I felt confident to share my story with the group. I belong to a very poor family as my father and my brother are unemployed. My mother manages to feed us on food that we grow. My dream is to study and change our monetary situation by getting a job. But I hope that my parents will not marry me before I can accomplish my dream. I shared this with the group and felt comforted by their empathy. I felt that we were a team and my dream can get fulfilled!

Participants, thus, simultaneously performed self and culture and, in so doing, offered an often caustic social critique viewed and sanctioned by the community as entertainment because it was articulated in folk theater form. Through performing their marginality, participants resisted the hegemonic power and privilege that shape their public and private lives and, as argued by Bruner (1987), "in the end we become the autobiographical narratives by which we 'tell about' our lives" (p. 15).

In a true Freireian (1970) spirit, the interventions encouraged workshop participants to engage in narrativizing about their concrete situations and provided a public platform through which to *tell* their narratives. By telling their stories, people legitimize their experiences, construct alternatives to dominant scripts, strategize their roles in emplotments, and prepare themselves for resistance to change. Not to "tell" is to limit the empowering possibilities of our narrative capabilities. The witnessing of such narratives on the part of audience members also can lead to *consientizacao*. One audience member said of the performance play that she observed, "It motivates the villagers to *think* on *dowry* issues." Ultimately, the telling of counter-narratives, understood as rehearsals for social change, can lead to action. Indeed, as Boal (1979) argued, "Perhaps the theatre is not revolutionary in itself; but have no doubts, it is a rehearsal of revolution" (p. 155).

Social Networks

Strong social networks were created among participants through this participatory theater project, networks that have remained intact and grown stronger since we left Bihar. The social capital developed through these networks holds promise for ongoing grassroots efforts directed toward social change (see Herman & Ettema, this volume). Putnam (1995, 2000) referred to *social capital* as connections among individuals, and the norms of reciprocity and trustworthiness that arise within those connections, that facilitate coordination and cooperation for mutual benefit. He argued, as have other social capital theorists (e.g., Esman & Uphoff, 1984), that social capital is both a private and public good. Our lives are made more productive by social ties, and social connections are important for the "rules of conduct" (read: ideological meaning formations) that they sustain.

An important element of social capital, albeit rarely articulated or theorized, is friendship. Rawlins's (1992) treatise illustrated how friendships, as cultural categories and sources of imagery about social being, are central to the challenges, satisfactions, and dramas of social configurations during one's life. "At any juncture," explained Rawlins, "we can celebrate or critique friendship for its role in shaping an individual's immediate experiences of self, others, and society in living life's configured and interpenetrated moments to their fullest" (p. 273).

In the intervention described here, theater participants emphasized the value of friendships formed through the workshops and performances. One participant, Meera, shared in an interview:

> I am glad to see the people who did this project and some of my friends who had come from other places. I didn't know them earlier but during the program, we became good friends. I wish to meet them again.

Another theater participant, Lakhendar, said:

> From the very beginning, I felt comfortable in Kamtaul. I knew we were going to meet strangers, but I trusted you to take us somewhere safe and good for our sisters. Seeing the other participants, they looked like us and behaved like us . . . they were equally lost (laughter). But I know that now we have a relationship forever. We will definitely invite them to our village and introduce them to our family.

As these quotes show, among other benefits, networks of interaction broadened participants' sense of self, developing the "I" into the "we," and enhanced their awareness of the benefits of a co-constructed communal life.

At the end of the week-long workshops and performances, several participants in the village of Abirpur created a drama club to continue using forms of folk theater and dance for social change. The following is an excerpt from a focus group interview conducted with them about the newly formed drama club:

Mahesh:	It has become very important that we continue acting in such plays.
Kiran:	I really enjoyed it.
Saumya: (Researcher)	Why do you think it is important?
Anuj:	Well, we saw how many people came to watch our show. They stood in the sun to see us. I believe if we do more, we will have more viewers.
Sukhi:	And it was fun.
Saumya: (Researcher)	What was fun?
Benu:	Meeting other people. It was like a holiday.
Saumya: (Researcher)	Would you do these performances again with other people?
Ramesh:	No, first we have to create our own group identity. We have to show our community in Abirpur and Salaempur that we have learned from you and others how to do the shows . . . and then we will show it to other villages outside ours.
Uma:	And we will show them that girls can also be important and useful.
Saumya: (Researcher)	So what kind of plays will you do?
Sukhi:	We want to do religious plays, some musicals . . .
Uma:	We have to do plays that are engaging . . . maybe have some music in them and then some social issues . . . like we did.
Saumya: (Researcher)	Would you like to organize into a group?
Manu:	Yes. . . . Let us call us *Taru Natya* (Drama) club.

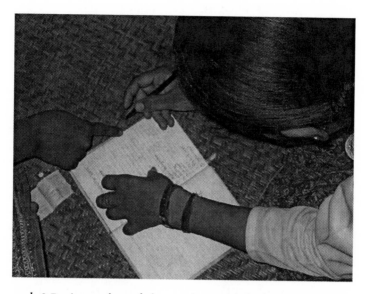

Photograph 8.7. A member of the newly established *Taru* Drama Club in the village of Abirpur signs its constitution. (Source: Authors' personal files)

In the village of Abirpur, members of the drama club created and signed a constitution (see Photograph 8.7), elected both male and female officers, and created and performed a socially charged play on August 15, 2003, India's Independence Day of celebration. Participants also created a *Taru* cricket club and organized tournaments in eight villages. The social capital generated through these social networks, thus, holds promise for influencing participants' (and others') public life and private prospects.

De Tocqueville (1835/1956), commenting on the propensity for civic engagement in the United States, focused attention on the unprecedented potential for social networks to make democracy work. Neo-Tocquevillean scholars have unearthed a wide range of empirical evidence illustrating how norms and networks of civic engagement relate to the quality of public life and the performance of social institutions (for a review of literature, see Putnam, 2000). As Putnam (1995) argued, "For a variety of reasons, life is easier in a community blessed with a substantial stock of social capital" (p. 67). The social networks created through this participatory theater project represent efforts of participants—men and women alike—to mobilize solidarity, alter the self-identified disempowering elements of their communities, and make democracy work.

Multilayered and Participatory Entertainment-Education Initiatives

Like the participatory theater projects in Hmong refugee camps facilitated by Conquergood (1988) and the Westerville Prison theater project coordinated by the University of Natal (Young-Jehangeer, 2002), the interventions discussed in this chapter illustrate how E-E scholarship and practice can benefit by consciously incorporating dialogic, participatory processes in designing, producing, and assessing social change interventions. E-E initiatives typically rely on media vehicles to tackle issues of development and social change (Jacobson 2002; Singhal, 2004), leaving little room for the dynamic dialogic pedagogy espoused by Freire (1970) and Boal (1979). The participatory process of creating and implementing public performances among members of *Taru* listening clubs illustrates how synergistic possibilities for social action emerge when E-E radio broadcasts are strategically integrated with community-based group listening and participatory theatre. The use of folk theater, which, by its nature, facilitates intense communication between performers and audience members, coupled with the radio serial and listener groups, represents a truly "multilayered" entertainment-communication intervention.

Many participants, when asked during interviews we conducted with them, described the benefits of multilayered E-E interventions with participatory components. One young girl, Pramod, said:

> After listening to *Taru* and having you here in the village, I feel confident to fight and not let parents come under any pressure. I have seen Usha *didi* and how she has resisted pressure from community, so I am quite sure I can do so too.

Another participant, Ashish, commented:

> *Taru* has changed our lives. We have started breathing a different air. She [*Taru*] has not only helped us by being our friend but has helped us to break the silence with our fathers. . . . I am so thankful to *Taru* and to you who have also made a difference by coming here. . . . You are just like *Taru* for us.

Over the past 2 years, our experiences working with the women, men, and children of Bihar lead us to conclude that the field of communication and social change can be theoretically and practically enriched through the blurring of boundaries between distinct models and approaches to communication interventions (see also Morris, 2003). By integrating participatory elements within traditional E-E initiatives, assumptions about the nature of communication evolve from the vertical processing of information transmission from the knowledgeable to the less knowledgeable to a horizontal dialogic interaction as the catalyst for individual and community empowerment. Although some development projects give lip-service to the notion of participation, the theater workshops and performances highlighted in this chapter represent genuine grassroots participation and control over content decisions and outcomes.

LESSONS LEARNED ABOUT COMMUNICATION ACTIVISM

At the crux of our work is a vision of *social justice*, described by Frey et al. (1996) as "engagement with and advocacy for those in our society who are economically, socially, politically, and/or culturally underresourced" (p. 110). Our goal was (and continues to be) to work with the women, men, and children of Bihar, India, to first identify oppressive grammars, practices, and patterns, and then through performances, to reconstruct those discursive patterns in more socially just ways. These participatory theater efforts can best be described, therefore, as social justice activities, guided by dialogic theorizing and enabled and constrained by structural forces (e.g., social, temporal, historical, and material).

Perhaps the most important lesson we learned about communication activism was the importance of honoring and respecting local traditions coupled with paradoxically challenging some of those customs. One month prior to the workshops, D. Sharma went to Bihar to logistically prepare for the interventions. As previously mentioned, one of our biggest challenges was gaining the permission of parents for their daughters to participate in the workshops and performances (as exemplified in the dilemma that Usha and her friends faced in the opening paragraph to this chapter). Socially, it is not customary for Indian girls and young women to speak (let alone perform) in the public sphere, nor do girls leave their respective villages until marriage. At the same time, families depend on young women to perform necessary daily household chores (e.g., preparing and serving meals). For these reasons, parents generally were not supportive of allowing their daughters to participate (despite overwhelming enthusiasm on the part of the daughters).

Encountering such parental resistance, D. Sharma reframed the workshops and performances as a "cultural program." In Indian high schools, functions are organized on certain days of national importance (e.g.,

Independence Day and Gandhi's birthday). As part of these celebrations, students (both boys and girls) often perform for the entire village population. The rhetorical repositioning of the intervention as a cultural program successfully persuaded some parents to give their consent for their daughters to participate. However, we still experienced widespread resistance from village elders who believed that young unmarried women should stay at home and not publicly "exhibit" themselves on stage.

The presence of Pant and Y. Sharma (both women) in the field prior to the workshops, as well as the support of key opinion leaders (e.g., RHPs), were instrumental in securing female participation in this participatory theater project. For example, Pant stayed with the family of the village RHP in Abirpur for several weeks prior to the start of the workshops. Through her networking with local opinion leaders, including the RHP and his sister Usha, she established credibility with other families in Abirbur. She initiated conversations with parents, allowing them to express their concerns about their daughters' participation in the workshops and performances. Parents were concerned about how other members of the community would perceive their daughters as a result of participating in public performances, perhaps perceiving them as "immoral" and "loose." Pant, thus, had to delicately validate their fears and simultaneously encourage them to "trust" their daughters and the fieldworkers. The following excerpt comes from Pant's fieldnotes:

> Although I successfully persuaded some parents to allow their daughters to participate, I did so from a place of respect—respect for their desire to protect their daughters by keeping them within the boundaries of the community. I was not there to dishonor their pride. My role was to illustrate the possibilities of the workshops for parents. I relied on my ability to re-frame the issues at hand, hopefully making "participation" on the part of their daughters "possible." But, I respected parents' decisions to not let daughters participate. In the course of a conversation, if I felt I was pushing the boundaries too much, I would pause and let the villagers continue the conversation and find and implement their own solutions.

Eventually, a gathering in Abirpur of all participants' parents was organized to talk about these issues. As rapport between the fieldworkers (and their mission) and parents was solidified, an environment of trust emerged that eventually led to the participation of the 25 young women and girls from the four villages.

During the workshops, tensions abounded between time and logistical constraints and accomplishing the goals of the workshops. Ideally, we wanted to provide participants with the space and time they needed to debate ideas about social problems and their potential solutions, but we only had 3 days to prepare participants for their public performances. Consequently, at times, we had to "push" them to finalize the script, conduct the rehearsal, and complete the set design. Due to time constraints, participants tended, in some cases, to script simple solutions for complex societal problems (e.g., dowry and gender inequality). Given the difficulty we encountered in gaining parents' permission for their daughters to participate, however, it would not have been feasible to extend the length of the workshops. Ultimately, we sacrificed some complexity in the "problem-posing process" (Freire, 1970) to create social networks among participants and lay the foundation for future efforts toward change.

Another limitation of the theater project was a lack of caste diversity among participants. How deep or wide a social innovation spreads, as articulated by diffusion theory (Rogers, 1995), depends, in part, on the types of social networks that are tapped into by interventionists and researchers. The majority of these participatory theater workshop participants were members of a higher caste; only a handful of them were from lower castes. The homogeneous nature of participants was due, in part, to our recruitment methods that relied on preexisting connections with local RHPs, all of whom were high-caste Brahmins who resided primarily in high-caste villages. The relative lack of caste diversity among participants is no doubt related to the high-caste status of the RHPs. Individuals in lower castes usually live in remote areas not as approachable for fieldworkers (i.e., no walking paths), and although individuals in the lower caste did reside on the fringes of these villages, they were not easily accessible to us as fieldworkers. Village norms also warrant that lower caste people come to high-caste or village public areas but not the other way around. Consequently, we believe our communication activism was more effective in challenging oppressive gender roles than caste roles, although it did create the conditions for workshop participants (mostly high caste) to wrestle with caste issues and enact stage-based rehearsals to address them in the future. Given the raised consciousness of higher caste individuals in these villages, and given that they already have begun to rehearse and enact caste-based storylines, the stage is set for ongoing consciousness-raising about caste inequities. We know that many workshop participants (e.g., Vandana and her mother Kamtaul) currently are intervening with literacy classes for lower caste and other disadvantaged people.

It is an exciting and challenging task for us to develop more effective strategies for increasing diverse participation in future projects. To accomplish this goal, our (present) higher caste workshop participants are uniquely positioned to orchestrate the involvement of their lower caste counterparts because they are strong advocates for intercaste harmony in their villages, feel collectively efficacious to take on new challenges, and are socially networked at the village level to involve lower caste individuals in future projects. One potential strategy for increasing caste diversity among participants is to cultivate contacts/relationships with opinion leaders within lower caste communities in an effort to gain their support for the project and, therefore, gain access to existing social networks within communities.

Finally, we realized the historical and culture-bound nature of communication activism. Boal (1979) urged active participation on the part of audience members to realize the full potential of the Theater of the Oppressed. The audience, according to Boal, should be fully aligned with the actors and become part of the performative experience (see also Mienczakowski, 2001; Mienczakowski & Morgan, 2001). Freire (1970), however, cautioned that the content of dialogues, which presuppose action, must be carried out at the stage where the participants are in their struggle for liberation. Interventions and social change, thus, should vary in accordance with historical/cultural conditions and the level at which the oppressed perceive reality. In a Freireian spirit, we argue that action researchers and fieldworkers must gauge and engage the "readiness" of people to accept new ideas and defy traditional norms. In the case of these participatory theater interventions, we consciously chose not to fully engage audience members as "active spectators" during the performances (e.g., audience members asking questions during and after the presentation), for we did not feel confident in performance participants' ability to respond to free-flowing audience participation or our ability to facilitate such a conversation. We had promised parents that we would protect their daughters, and we were not confident in being able to control potential hostilities had we encouraged active participation by audience members. It was a huge accomplishment to bring young men and women from Indian villages together to participate in the performances—counter-narratives that defied norms and broke from conventions. Thus, these theater interventions laid the groundwork for future projects that can more fully realize Boal's vision of active audience-spectatorship.

We did, however, conduct postperformance interviews with audience members and they overwhelmingly indicated support for the performances. One viewer, Sunita, exclaimed, "I liked everything from the beginning 'til the end." Although most viewers expressed support for the various performances, one man, Kulawati, indicated that he would not let his daughter participate and explained, "There is nothing wrong in participation but we do not approve this. House is more important than all this. Men in society are not same, all have different views, and its not necessary that all should approve this." Having workshops such as these followed by performances demonstrates tremendous ground-based support. It is not surprising, however, that some villagers, like Kulawati, wondered why "outsiders" engaged in mixed-gender workshop activities, including allowing young girls on stage.

CONCLUSION

The ways in which we construct our sense of being are increasingly performative in nature (Denzin, 1995), as narrative links quite well to, for instance, discipline and surveillance (including self-monitoring), and equally well to character-based identifications and narrative sequencing. From this perspective, the participatory theater interventions described in this chapter represent an ensemble of stories told by participants about themselves; narratives inevitably marked by and articulations of wider economic, political, and social structures. The work of Freire (1970) and Boal (1979) transforms a once-understood aesthetic experience (i.e., entertainment) into a medium for engaging people politically.

Issues of gender inequities, dowry, and caste as performed by participants represent deeply entrenched social, political, and economic problems — systemic issues that are difficult to change overnight. Although we do not claim that the 1-week participatory theater workshops and performances have corrected these social ills, they provided a first-time opportunity for young men and women from four villages of Bihar State in India to work together and voice their concerns — on stage, with a microphone — in front of their parents, elders, and other community members. In the context of rural Bihar, such actions represent important steps toward securing social, cultural, and political reform. In that sense, the workshops and performances represent important rehearsals for securing social and political change. By providing a space for participants to performatively engage in sense making about their lived experiences, this communication intervention revealed important intersections between deeply personal and autobiographical accounts, broader hegemonic cultural narratives, and counter-narratives that offered alternative visions for individual and community identities. We strongly believe that the web of friendships created through this project, both within and across the four sites where this intervention was carried out, will continue to work toward social reform in these villages.

✣ ✣ ✣ ✣

With a little help and support from us, but mainly through their own courage and resolve, Usha and her six friends in Abirpur Village took part in the participatory theater workshops in Kamtaul Village. There they met Vandana, a resident of Kamtaul Village and an avid listener of *Taru*, as well as several dozen other *Taru* listening club members. Collectively, they engaged in social activism and justice with the following hope (as expressed in a letter sent to us by Vandana after the performances):

One day, society's darkness will disappear
One day, flowers of happiness will bloom
And, the lamp of enthusiasm will glow!

APPENDIX: DESCRIPTION OF STORYLINES

Play 1 (Children's Group)

The play is based on two interrelated stories, both of which focus on issues of gender inequality. In the first story, Rajeev's daughter attends school and is harassed by the neighborhood boys because they believe girls should stay at home. The girl complains to her parents. Rajeev, although supportive of her daughter's education, is portrayed as a weak man who decides to withdraw her from school as he fears social opposition. But his wife is a strong woman, and with the help of her two sons, she is able to convince her husband to continue their daughter's education. In the second story, Chandni (the protagonist of the play) wants to study, but her father does not allow her to go to school. In his opinion, only sons should get educated. He is confident of his three sons' future success and provides them with ample educational opportunities. But Chandni's mother supports Chandni's education against her husband's will. Time passes and one day Chandni's father has an accident and becomes paralyzed. He looks to his grown sons for support, but they are portrayed as "good for nothing" and are unable to help. Meanwhile, Chandni has done very well in her studies and has a good job. She supports her family in the aftermath of her father's accident. Chandni's father realizes his mistake and repents. He asks the audience not to repeat his mistake and to give their daughters equal opportunities to succeed.

Play 2 (Adult Group)

The play was scripted on the basis of a real-life event. Inspired by the character of Neha in *Taru*, who opens a school for "untouchables," teenage boys and girls in the village of Abirpur started a school for less privileged children. They make this decision after much discussion and deliberation in their listeners' club. They overcome many difficulties, including social opposition and lack of material infrastructure, to establish the school. In their school, they give free pen-and-paper supplies to the poor children from their own pocket money. During class sessions, discussions about women's empowerment, dowry, and small family size also take place. This play also effectively relied on humor to bring its message home.

Play 3 (Adult Group)

Sharma and Mishra arrange the marriage of their son and daughter without consulting their children. Mishra's daughter is against this marriage because she is too young and wants to finish her studies before getting married. Sharma's son also tells his father that it is illegal to marry an underage girl. Father and son have a confrontation, and the son separates from the father. To save face, Sharma promises Mishra a marriage between his younger son, Ratneshwar, and Mishra's daughter. Mishra agrees. After 4 years, Mishra reminds Sharma of his promise. Meanwhile, Sharma's younger son has been admitted to an engineering college and has bright career prospects. Sharma tells Mishra that he wants a huge sum of money for dowry. Mishra is shocked but finally agrees to fulfill Sharma's demands. Wedding preparations begin. When Ratneshwar comes back from his college to get married, his friends tell him that his father is taking dowry in his marriage. Ratneshwar is furious and confronts his father on this issue. Sharma very cunningly assures Ratneshwar that he will not take dowry. Ratneshwar is very happy and agrees to get married. But at the wedding, Sharma again demands dowry. Everybody is stunned, but the bride Vandana is very bold. She declares that she will not marry in a family that is greedy for dowry. Seeing her boldness, Ratneshwar falls in love with her. He clearly tells his father that if he insists on the dowry, he will leave home and never return. Sharma, afraid of losing face in front of the whole community, abandons his demand for dowry. He goes through a change of heart and appeals to the audience members to not take dowry. He urges them to remove this social ill from Indian society.

NOTES

1. Although there are many layers of caste-based segmentation among Hindus in India, there exist four main caste categories, arranged in a hierarchy. The Brahmans, mainly comprised of temple priests, represent the highest caste. The next highest caste is the Kashatrias, the warriors and rulers, followed by the Vaisias, the landlords and traders in society. The lowest in the caste hierarchy are the Shudras, members of the peasant class and those engaged in menial occupations. Among the Shudras, at the very bottom of the caste pit, are the "untouchables," mainly scavengers and waste handlers. A person, whether a man or a woman, is born into one of these castes and his or her social position, thus, is fixed by heredity, not by personal or professional accomplishments.
2. Sharma is also Creative Director of Brij Lok Madhuri, an organization dedicated to using Indian folk forms to promote social change. He was closely involved in the programming aspects of *Taru* as a member of the advisory committee formed by PCI. He co-facilitated script-writing workshops in New

Delhi and then worked closely with many of the writers of *Taru* to ensure the integration of key issues in the storylines of the serial.

3. Janani is a Patna-based organization that has networked over 25,000 RHPs in the State of Bihar, India. Janani served as a ground-based collaborator for the on-air *Taru* radio initiative; its RHPs promoted the program and provided service delivery on the ground to support the radio soap's reproductive health messages.

4. By May 2003, researchers from the Centre for Media Studies in New Delhi and Singhal and D. Sharma had made eight rounds of visits to these four villages, spending over 70 days in them. Various techniques of data collection were employed, including over 50 in-depth individual and focus group interviews, participant observation, note-taking, and photograph and video documentation. In addition, over 20 listening group members' diaries from these four villages currently are being translated and transcribed for thematic analysis.

5. Although we set out to recruit an equal number of male and female participants, the outcome of equal gender distribution of participants occurred spontaneously and coincidentally as we navigated our way through the difficulty of gaining the permission of parents and transporting participants to the location of the workshops.

REFERENCES

Adelman, M. B., & Frey, L. R. (1997). *The fragile community: Living together with AIDS*. Mahwah, NJ: Erlbaum.

Boal, A. (1979). *The theater of the oppressed* (C. A. McBride & M-O. L. McBride, Trans.). New York: Urizen Books.

Burke, K. (1969). *A grammar of motives*. Berkeley: University of California Press.

Bruner, J. (1987). Life as narrative. *Social Research, 54*, 11-32.

Conquergood, D. (1988). Health theater in a Hmong refugee camp. *Drama Review: A Journal of Performance Studies, 32*, 174-208.

Denzin, N. K. (1995). *The cinematic society: The voyeur's gaze*. Thousand Oaks, CA: Sage.

De Tocqueville, A. (1956). *Democracy in America* (R. D. Heffner, Ed.). New York: New American Library. (Original work published 1835)

Esman, M. J., & Uphoff, N. T. (1984). *Local organizations: Intermediaries in rural development*. Ithaca, NY: Cornell University Press.

Foucault, M. (1973). *The birth of the clinic: An archeology of medical perception* (A. M. S. Smith, Trans.). New York: Pantheon Books.

Freire, P. (1970). *Pedagogy of the oppressed* (M. B. Ramos, Trans.). New York: Herder and Herder.

Freire, P. (1994). *Pedagogy of hope: Reliving* pedagogy of the oppressed (R. R. Barr, Trans.). New York: Continuum.

Freire, P. (1998). *Pedagogy of freedom: Ethics, democracy, and civic courage* (P. Clarke, Trans). New York: Rowman & Littlefield.

Frey, L. R. (1998). Communication and social justice research: Truth, justice, and the applied communication way. *Journal of Applied Communication Research, 26,* 155-164.

Frey, L. R., Pearce, W. B., Pollock, M. A., Artz, L., & Murphy, B. A. O. (1996). Looking for justice in all the wrong places: On a communication approach to social justice. *Communication Studies, 47,* 110-127.

Harriss-White, B. (2003). *India working: Essays on society and economy.* New York: Cambridge University Press.

Jacobson, T. L. (2002). Participatory communication for social change: The relevance for the theory of communicative action. In P. J. Kalbfleisch (Ed.), *Communication yearbook* (Vol. 27, pp. 87-123). Thousand Oaks, CA: Sage.

Jung, A. (1987). *Unveiling India: A woman's journey.* New Delhi, India: Penguin Books.

Kumar, R. (1993). *The history of doing: An illustrated account of movements for women's rights and feminism in India, 1800-1990.* New Delhi, India: Kali for Women.

Kumar, S. (2002). Gains and stagnation in Bihar and Andhra Pradesh. In D. Narayan & P. Petesch (Eds.), *From many lands* (pp. 147-180). Washington, DC: Oxford University Press and the World Bank.

Mienczakowski, J. (2001). Ethnodrama: Performed research—Limitations and potential. In O. Atkinson, A. Coffey, S. Dalamont, J., Lofland, & L. Lofland (Eds.), *Handbook of ethnography* (pp. 468-476). Thousand Oaks, CA: Sage.

Mienczakowski, J., & Morgan, S. (2001). Ethnodrama: Constructing participatory, experiential and compelling action research through performance. In R. Reason & H. Bradbury (Eds.), *Handbook of action research: Participative inquiry and practice* (pp. 219-227). Thousand Oaks, CA: Sage.

Morris, N. (2003). A comparative analysis of the diffusion and participatory models in development communication. *Communication Theory, 13,* 225-248.

Nelson, H. L. (2001). *Damaged identities, narrative repair.* Ithaca, NY: Cornell University Press.

Pande, M. (2003). *Stepping out: Life and sexuality in rural India.* New Delhi, India: Penguin Books.

Population Foundation of India. (2002). *District profile: Bihar.* New Delhi, India: Author.

Putnam, R. D. (1995). Bowling alone: America's declining social capital. *Journal of Democracy, 6,* 65-78.

Putnam, R. D. (2000). *Bowling alone: The collapse and revival of American community.* New York: Simon & Schuster.

Rawlins, W. K. (1992). *Friendship matters: Communication, dialectics, and the life course.* New York: Aldine de Gruyter.

Rogers, E. M. (1995). *Diffusion of innovations* (4th ed.). New York: Free Press.

Shepherd, G. J. (2001). Community as the interpersonal accomplishment of communication. In G. J. Shepherd & E. W. Rothenbuhler (Eds.), *Communication and community* (pp. 25-36). Mahwah, NJ: Erlbaum.

Singhal, A. (2004). Entertainment-education through participatory theater: Freirean strategies for empowering the oppressed. In A. Singhal, M. Cody, E. M. Rogers, & M. Sabido (Eds.), *Entertainment-education and social change: History, research, and practice* (pp. 377-398). Mahwah, NJ: Erlbaum.

Singhal, A., & Rogers, E. M. (1999). *Entertainment-education: A communication strategy for social change.* Mahwah, NJ: Erlbaum.

Singhal, A., & Rogers, E. M. (2001). *India's communication revolution: From bullock carts to cyber marts.* Thousand Oaks, CA: Sage.

Singhal, A., Sharma, D., Papa, M. J., & Witte, K. (2004). Air cover and ground mobilization: Integrating entertainment-education broadcasts with community listening and service delivery in India. In A. Singhal, M. Cody, E. M. Rogers, & M. Sabido (Eds.), *Entertainment-education and social change: History, research, and practice* (pp. 351-374). Mahwah, NJ: Erlbaum.

Somers, M. R. (1994). The narrative constitution of identity: A relational and network approach. *Theory and Society, 23,* 605-649.

Sunwolf, & Frey, L.R . (2001). Storytelling: The power of narrative communication and interpretation. In R. Robinson & H. Giles (Eds.), *The new handbook of language and social psychology* (2nd ed., pp. 119-135). New York: Wiley.

Wittgenstein, L. (1953). *Philosophical investigations* (G. E. M. Anscombe, Trans.). Oxford, England: Blackwell.

Young-Jehangeer, M. (2002, May). *Working from the inside-out: Drama as activism in Westerville female prison.* Paper presented at the International Conference on Convergence: Technology, Culture, and Social Impacts, University of Natal, Durban, South Africa.

9

A PROACTIVE PERFORMANCE APPROACH TO PEER EDUCATION

The Efficacy of A Sexual Assault Intervention Program*

Marc D. Rich

José I. Rodríguez

California State University, Long Beach

Susan stands center stage with her eyes focused straight ahead. She appears to be in a state of crisis. There are 10 people surrounding her, all audience members who have agreed to create physically frozen images/statues on stage. One image is directly behind her, pointing at Susan's face and yelling, "This is all your fault." Another image, down stage left and a few feet from Susan, is shrugging her shoulders and saying, "Nobody will ever believe you." A third image is seated directly in

*The authors gratefully acknowledge the contributions of Jennifer Page, Rachel Hastings, and Lisa Lindsay.

front of Susan, hands over bowed head, whispering, "If he loves you, it isn't really rape." A constellation of these images surrounds Susan, all frozen in place and repeating lines that might be going through a woman's head after surviving a sexual assault. The lines, all designed to create doubt and fear in Susan's mind, blur into a choir of antagonistic voices. When the scene ends, the facilitator holds the silence for a few seconds before asking the audience members to explain what they have just witnessed. A number of hands are raised and the dialogue begins.

This scene is part of a sexual assault intervention program utilized by interACT, a university-based performance troupe under the direction of Marc Rich since 2000. The program was developed in response to the high incidence of sexual assault on college campuses, which, as Simon (1993) noted, "is now at near epidemic proportions" (p. 289). *Sexual assault* can be defined as "forced sexual aggression or contact with or without penetration against a victim" (Black, Weisz, Coats, & Patterson, 2000, p. 589). The impact of sexual assault and postassault trauma has gained significant attention from contemporary researchers because, as Resick and Schnicke (1992) explained, "sexual assault is a major life-threatening, traumatic event from which many victims never fully recover" (p. 4; see also Crabtree & Ford, Volume 1). The statistics regarding the number of women who have been raped or sexually assaulted are staggering. According to Black et al. (2000), "24-50% of women have been or will be sexually assaulted during their lives" (p. 589). In the weeks, months, and years following sexual assault, survivors may experience depression, anxiety, suicidal thoughts or attempts, and poor self-esteem (Butterfield, Barnett, & Koons, 2000). The most common serious effect of sexual assault is Post Traumatic Stress Disorder (PTSD): In the first week after a sexual assault, 94% of women will meet the criteria for a full diagnosis of PTSD; 90 days after the crime is committed, 47% of survivors still meet those criteria (Resick & Schnicke, 1992).

Date or acquaintance rape is especially prevalent among college students "because they live in communities where many factors related to date or acquaintance rape, such as age, alcohol use, and rape-tolerant behavioral norms, converge" (Holcomb, Sarvela, Sondag, & Holcomb, 1993, p. 159). In a frequently cited study, Koss, Gidycz, and Wisniewski (1987) found that 27% of college women had experienced rape or attempted rape, 25% of college men were involved in some form of sexual aggression, and 8% of men since the age of 14 had raped or attempted to rape a woman. Men who participate in fraternities or organized sports are most likely to assault women, with an astounding 35% of men in fraternities reporting forcing someone to have sex with them (Bohmer & Parrot, 1993). Although males may know that raping a woman is wrong, they "choose to do it because they know the odds of being caught and convicted are very low" (Bohmer & Parrot, p. 21).

In the vast majority of college rape situations, the survivor knows the assailant. According to Mann, Hecht, and Valentine (1988), "Date rape is such an epidemic on college campuses across the nation that more college women are now raped by dates and boyfriends than by strangers" (p. 269). The result, in addition to the serious physical and psychological impact that rape has on college students, is that "many women who are assaulted drop out of school" (Bohmer & Parrot, p. 1).

To address this epidemic, several sexual assault intervention models have been developed, implemented, and evaluated on college campuses. The majority of these models, however, are didactic, typically consisting of lectures, videotapes, or traditional theatrical performances, and, therefore, are consistent with passive learning models. For example, Lanier, Elliot, Martin, and Kapadia (1988) conducted a study in which audience members were exposed to six didactic, scripted scenes that illustrated concepts, such as the use of alcohol in date-rape scenarios and the notion that going to someone's home is not an agreement to have sex. In another didactic intervention program designed by Hanson and Gidycz (1993), participants were provided with information regarding rape statistics, watched a videotape illustrating variables related to sexual assault, and viewed a second videotape highlighting ways to prevent sexual assault. Although these intervention programs show statistically significant results, they are not aligned with proactive models that engage the audience to facilitate personal agency and social change.

One particular intervention model that recently has grown in popularity on college campuses (Raynor, 1993), and is the subject of this study, is *peer education*, which involves students taking an active role in the education of their cohorts. In peer education, students may, among other activities, present information in a formal or informal manner, perform in educational plays, or serve as mentors to their peers. According to Black et al. (2000):

> The effectiveness of peer education stems from the fact that peer educators convey information and communicate with their contemporaries in ways that professionals cannot. Most importantly, peer educators live among their constituents, have access to students, and are privy to students' personal lives. (p. 593)

Although peer-education programs are popular, unfortunately, such programs typically remain didactic and focus entirely on debunking rape myths without regard for what happens to a woman after she is assaulted. It is common for peer educators to promote an inactive audience role by using lectures, traditional performances, and films/videos. In a critique of this approach, Frankham (1998) argued that most peer troupes employ these "very didactic teaching methodologies," and, as a result, peer educators often are "disappointed by the level of participation on the part of those being 'educated'" (p. 183). Although didactic programs may help to debunk rape myths and disseminate information about sexual assault, audience members are not challenged to prevent assaults or taught how to comfort a woman who is victimized. Most peer-education programs, thus, lead audience members to remain passive rather than encourage them to take an active stance.

Because of their tendency to perpetuate an educational climate in which students are passive learners, Freire (1993) referred to didactic modes of instruction as "banking education" because "the students are depositories and the teacher is the depositor. . . . The scope of action allowed to the students extends only as far as receiving, filing, and storing deposits" (p. 53). Freire called, instead, for a more dialogic approach to education, a "problem-posing education" in which multifaceted, student-centered problems are posed by instructors and students who are critically engaged in the learning process. As Freire explained:

> Whereas banking education anesthetizes and inhibits creative power, problem-posing education involves a constant unveiling of reality. The former attempts to maintain the submersion of consciousness; the latter strives for the emergence of consciousness and critical intervention in reality. Students, as they are increasingly posed with problems relating to themselves in the world and with the world, will feel increasingly challenged and obliged to respond to that challenge. (p. 62)

The call to develop and employ dialogic, problem-solving approaches to education has been taken up by performance studies scholars, who are interested in "the process of dialogic engagement with one's own and others' aesthetic communication through the means of performance" (Pelias, 1992, p. 15). As noted by Stucky and Wimmer (2002), "One characteristic of performance studies pedagogy is its emphasis on embodiment. . . . A substantial development in performance studies pedagogy has been a consistent attention to enactment, to experiential learning in the classroom" (p. 3). This experiential learning through performance places the audience in an active rather than passive role, for, according Pelias and VanOosting (1987):

> The level of audience participation within any theatrical event may best be seen on a continuum from inactive to proactive. When defined as "inactive" . . . the audience's task is simply to receive what is given. . . . "Active" audience members' imagination flesh out the skeletal suggestions of a performer. . . . The next level of participation might be described as "interactive." At this point, both performers and audience

are seen as coproducers, each contributing to the artistic event. . . . At the far end of the continuum, the audience might be identified as "proactive." Given this maximum participation, status of performer is conferred on all participants. (p. 227)

The interactive and proactive end of the performance studies continuum is consistent with Freire's (1993) problem-posing pedagogy. In both problem-posing pedagogy and proactive performances, students and audience members are challenged to assume an active role in their learning. Furthermore, instructors in problem-posing classrooms, and facilitators in proactive performances, seek to democratize the learning experience by providing a safe space for dialogic exchanges.

By democratizing the learning experience through the creation of a safe space for dialogic exchanges via performance, performance potentially serves the purpose of promoting social change. As Cohen-Cruz (2001) explained, it is "the crucial interaction of art and social circumstances that renders an activist theatre project efficacious" (pp. 95-96). There, thus, exists in theatre and performance studies a rich history of scholar-artists dedicated to facilitating social change. As Kushner (2001) noted, "American artists have been working for social change for many decades, whether the issue was labor, civil rights, poverty, disarmament, women's rights, gay/lesbian liberation, homelessness, AIDS, cultural diversity, or commercial globalization" (p. 64). Performance as a means for enacting social change, which stands in contrast to didactic, disembodied pedagogical techniques, "entails a shift of emphasis from product to process [that] . . . decenters, destabilizes, undermines, and deconstructs any view of a 'finished world' that is given to us for passive consumption" (Conquergood, 1986, pp. 38-40). Proactive performances, thus, fundamentally are a form of activism in which audience members use theatre to fight oppression and promote social change.

Although proactive performances for the purposes of promoting social change have been employed for many years, and the theoretical reasons for why they potentially work are well understood, researchers to date have not measured the outcomes of such performance-based activist activities. The purpose of this chapter, therefore, is to assess the outcomes associated with a peer-education intervention that fosters a proactive performative audience stance for the purpose of promoting social change. Specifically, we explore the efficacy of the proactive sexual assault intervention program utilized by interACT. We use the terms *interACT scene* and *interACT performance* interchangeably to refer to the enactment (by trained actors) of a potential sexual assault episode, and the likely aftermath of that situation. This scene or performance is deemed a proactive intervention because the audience members actively participate in the unfolding situation, on stage, with the actors. This interACT scene is the centerpiece of our intervention program.

Having conducted this specific sexual assault scene over 75 times on and off our college campus, we are committed to using proactive performance as a prevention strategy not only because of its potential for reducing sexual assault but also because this approach is situated within the larger context of performance as activism for social change. Although we have witnessed qualitative changes in audience members (our target group) and received ongoing positive feedback from them, we are interested in more formally assessing the efficacy of this program. Therefore, this study attempts to measure proactive performance from a quantitative perspective. Because this study represents the first attempt to quantify such effects, we opted not to compare the efficacy of proactive performance to another pedagogical modality (e.g., a lecture, video, or didactic performance focusing on sexual assault). Hence, we are not concerned at this stage with whether this method is the most efficacious means of peer education; instead, we are most interested in discovering what theoretically relevant outcomes are connected with social activist theatre and potential ways to measure the impact of participatory performance on audience members.

In the next section of this chapter, we provide a brief overview of Boal's social activist theatre and how it informs interACT's intervention. We then describe our research study and offer quantitative research evidence that suggests the efficacy of our sexual assault prevention program. We conclude the chapter with lessons learned about proactive performance as communication activism.

AUGUSTO BOAL'S SOCIAL ACTIVIST THEATRE

Boal's (1979, 1992, 1995) work first garnered international attention after the publication of *The Theatre of the Oppressed* (TO), a book in which he critiqued Aristotelian theatre, which is the basis for contemporary theatre produced in traditional settings, as being inherently oppressive and elitist. Boal argued that Aristotelian theatre separated spectators (the people) from the actors (the elite) and taught audience members that going against the status quo would have dire consequences. By shattering the imaginary fourth wall separating audience members from actors, and placing theatre in the hands of the people, Boal believed that "spect-actors" could use dramatic techniques to better themselves and their sociopolitical standing; as Boal (1979) explained, "The barrier between actors and spectators is destroyed: all must act, all must be protagonists in the necessary transformations of society" (Foreword).

Boal (1979) argued, in particular, that *catharsis*, a device used in Aristotelian plays, purges audience members of their desire to initiate social change because:

> The character follows an ascending path toward happiness, accompanied empathically by the spectator. Then comes a moment of reversal: the character, with the spectator, starts to move from happiness toward misfortune. . . . The character recognizes his error . . . [and] through the empathic relationship . . . the spectator recognizes his own error . . . his own anticonstitutional flaw. . . . The character suffers the consequences of his error, in a violent form, with his own death or with the death of loved ones . . . . The spectator, terrified by the spectacle of the catastrophe, is purified of his hamartia [anticonstitutional flaw]. (p. 37)

Hence, through empathizing with the protagonist and her or his tragic life, spectators are purged of their desire to fight against the status quo, which leads to a feeling of catharis. For Boal, Aristotelian theatre, thus, is a coercive mechanism designed to disempower people and teach them to stay passive in the face of oppression.

In contrast to Arisotelian theatre, when a protagonist in Boal's theatre is treated unfairly, audience members are encouraged to take the stage and attempt to break the oppression. On the continuum developed by Pelias and VanOosting (1987), Boal's TO techniques, which can be used with scripted scenes and traditional plays or in an improvisational manner to create scenarios based on audience members' stories, are proactive and represent the highest level of audience involvement. Similar in nature to Freire's (1993) concept of "participatory education," Boal believes that people should use the theatre to empower themselves. According to Schutzman and Cohen-Cruz (1994a), "Influenced by Paulo Freire's dialogic philosophy of education, Boal's vision is embodied in dramatic techniques that activate passive spectators to become spect-actors—engaged participants rehearsing strategies for personal and social change" (p. 1).

The nature of the work created by Boal and Freire were both shaped by the political landscape of their home country (Brazil), and TO is a natural extension of Freire's pedagogy of the oppressed. During lectures and workshops, Boal consistently has spoken of Freire's influence on TO. For Freire, the classroom is a politicized space of potential liberation; for Boal, the theatre, when democratized, enables spect-actors to rehearse for real-life scenarios within the relatively safe confines of the theatre.

Although Boal's earliest work was used as a "rehearsal for revolution," following his imprisonment, torture, and subsequent exile from Brazil for creating plays that were considered dangerous by an oppressive military regime, he began to develop additional techniques that are more therapeutic than his original work (The Rainbow of Desire) and oriented toward enacting political change (Legislative Theatre). In particular, he began to consider psychosocial issues, such as fear, depression, and emptiness, and, consequently, "began to realize the depth of pain these oppressions produced"

(Schutzman & Cohen-Cruz, 1994a, p. 4). In response to what he called "cops in the head," internalized oppressors linked to external antagonists and overt power structures, Boal (1995) developed a series of psychosocial performance techniques, known as "The Rainbow of Desire," "to discover how these cops got into our heads, and to invent ways of dislodging them" (p. 8). Even his most psychosocial techniques, however, are designed to move from the individual to the group level and from the local to the global perspective. For example, a woman who begins a performance by focusing on a specific man who sexually harassed her may come to understand the broader implications of a male-dominated society in which women are oppressed in a variety of ways by various antagonists.

Boal's techniques have been used in educational, communal, and therapeutic contexts throughout the world, and a number of scholars have documented the use of these techniques in those contexts. As examples, a 1990 edition of *The Drama Review* contained two articles by Boal (1990a, 1990b) and articles about Boal's work by Cohen-Cruz, Cohen-Cruz and Schutzman, and Taussig and Schechner. Similarly, Schutzman and Cohen-Cruz's (1994b) text, *Playing Boal: Theatre, Therapy, Activism,* provides case studies, as well as cross-cultural aspects, of Boal's techniques, and a sequel, *A Boal Companion: The Joker Runs Wild* (edited by Cohen-Cruz and Schutzman, 2006). A number of contemporary scholar-artist-activists also have discussed Boal's impact on their understanding of performance and social change (Alexander, 2001; Fung, 2001; Paterson, 2001). For instance, in response to traditional performances at a conference on HIV and AIDS, Jones (1993) noted that "the focus on educating the audience lacked an essential action step" (p. 23) and suggested, as a remedy, that the more proactive approach offered by Boal would "move the traditionally passive theatre audience into an active posture" (p. 24). Practitioners also have described using Boal's techniques in the specific contexts of "privileged" classrooms (McConachie, 2002) and healthcare environments (Brown & Gillespie, 1997) and with new police recruits (Telesco, 2001) and homeless youth (Westlake, 2001). Given this understanding of Boal's philosophy, techniques, and impact, we turn to a description of the interACT scene.

THE INTERACT PROACTIVE PERFORMANCE

The interACT scene begins with three college men, one of whom is Jeremy, enjoying a night of drinking and fun. When the conversation shifts to Jeremy's girlfriend, Susan, and accusations are made by the other men about his inability to "keep her in check," tempers quickly flare. Three women, including Susan, enter the scene, and Jeremy starts to ask pointed questions about Susan's whereabouts and attire. Susan tries to respond, but Jeremy becomes increasingly agitated and verbally aggressive. After asking everyone to leave the apartment, Jeremy becomes even more antagonistic toward Susan. He critiques what Susan is wearing, accuses her of flirting with other guys, and reprimands her for making him look bad in front of his friends. The scene ends with Jeremy grabbing Susan's arm and exclaiming, "This will never happen again."

The second scene begins the next day, with Susan explaining to her friends that Jeremy "forced himself" on her after they left the apartment. One of her friends becomes quite emotional, urging Susan to go to the hospital immediately and then press charges against Jeremy. The second friend says that Susan is acting like a "drama queen" and subsequently blames her for making Jeremy angry.

Following these first two scripted scenes (lasting approximately 10 minutes in total), four proactive scenes are created with the audience. The first scene (described in the opening of this chapter) is based on Boal's (1995) notion of "cops in the head" and involves audience members identifying and embodying the negative voices that are present in Susan's head after she is assaulted. After 8-10 voices are identified, the audience members create a constellation of images around Susan. If audience members believe that they are representing a dominant, loud voice in Susan's head, they stand close to Susan; softer voices are spread out across the stage. All of the voices begin speaking at once, enabling audience members to better understand why women often are so confused after an assault, and why friends need to demonstrate compassion and empathy toward them.

The second and third proactive scenes utilize Forum Theatre, Boal's fundamental strategy for inducing audience participation. In Forum Theatre, a scene in which a protagonist is oppressed or unable to achieve her or his objectives is performed, either scripted or not, in its entirety. The scene then is performed again with audience members replacing the protagonist and attempting to change the outcome of the performance. Forum Theatre typically generates a boisterous audience response as audience members are able to watch their peers come face-to-face with difficult antagonists. The goal of Forum Theatre is not to arrive at the "perfect solution" but, rather, to generate a set of assertive communication strategies that potentially can be utilized in real-life situations. In the first Forum, audience members replace one of Jeremy's friends in an attempt to prevent the sexual assault and, therefore, the second scene from occurring. During the second Forum, audience members replace Susan and try to get a more compassionate response from her friends. As audience members become more assertive, the antagonists become increasingly problematic. Hence, Forum Theatre encourages audience members to enact multiple interventions. In the final proactive scene, audience members replace Susan's friends and make an effort to be more patient and understanding with her. This scene is quite challenging because Susan is convinced that she is somehow at fault or that nobody will believe her if she reports the assault to the authorities. Thus, audience members are faced with actual challenges of enacting behaviors that are empathic and helpful within the context of a highly charged human drama.

Following the performance, information sheets are passed out to the audience that include rape statistics and rape crisis phone numbers. The interACT scene has been performed for high school and college students, nonprofit organizations, and populations that include adults in drug and alcohol rehabilitation centers and juveniles in prisons. Most audiences consist of approximately 40 members; however, the scene has been done for as few as 10 people, and as many as 800. Having performed this scene over 75 times on and off campus, we believed we were making a positive impact as evidenced by audience members' participation and their willingness to discuss sexual assault after participating in the performance. By designing a study to measure the efficacy of the performance, we hoped to learn more about the value of the interAct program and, more generally, the potential efficacy of proactive performance methods as communication activism.

THEORETICAL RATIONALE FOR STUDY AND RESEARCH QUESTIONS

Three theoretical perspectives germane to communication research helped to guide this study. First, the Elaboration Likelihood Model (ELM; Petty & Cacioppo, 1986) was used to explicate the potential role of value-relevant involvement and issue-relevant thinking in audience members' responses to the interACT scene. Second, the affective learning model (Rodríguez, Plax, & Kearney, 1996) was employed because it explains the role of affective and cognitive learning in the college classroom. Third, the egoistic and altruistic models were used because they illuminate the role of comforting communication in interactions that involve responses to distressed others (Stiff, Dillard, Somera, Kim, & Sleight, 1988). Each of these theoretical perspectives is explained next.

The Elaboration Likelihood Model: Involvement and Issue-Relevant Thinking

According to the ELM, there are two general routes to persuasion: the central (systematic) and peripheral (heuristic). When processing a persuasive message via the central route, individuals are said to engage in *issue-relevant thinking*, which, according to O'Keefe (1990), occurs when people attend to and reflect on the issues embedded in a message, a process termed *elaboration* (Petty & Cacioppo, 1986). Petty and Cacioppo argued that this process of elaboration is central to the ELM. To do this type of thinking, persons must have the capacity and motivation (involvement) to think about the issue in question.

One form of involvement connected with issue-relevant thinking is *value-relevant involvement*, which Johnson and Eagly (1989) defined as "the psychological state that is created by the activation of attitudes that are linked to important values" (p. 290). Once important values and attitudes are activated, people generate specific thoughts (e.g., favorable or unfavorable views of the issue) that are influenced, at least partially, by the strength or quality of the arguments presented in a persuasive message. For instance, the ELM predicts that strong arguments (defined as logical and persuasive) should lead to the generation of favorable thoughts, which then should lead to persuasion in the direction the source intended. Conversely, weak arguments should lead to the generation of unfavorable thoughts and little or no persuasive effects.

When processing via the peripheral route, individuals are said to engage in little or no issue-relevant thinking. In this mode of processing, persons rely on simple decision rules or mental heuristics, such as the attractiveness or credibility of the source. Put another way, persuasion via the peripheral route occurs without scrutinizing the quality of the arguments presented in the message and, generally, is more short-lived than persuasion via the central route.

Using the conceptualization of value-relevant involvement, along with the predictions of the ELM (Petty & Cacioppo, 1986), we argue that individuals who report high levels of value-relevant involvement are more likely to engage in issue-relevant thinking than individuals who report low levels of value-relevant involvement. Hence, if an audience member cares about an issue, he or she is more likely to reflect or think seriously about that issue. Regarding the efficacy of the interACT performance, we argue that the negative depictions of aggressive behavior and insensitive comments in the scripted scenes might induce greater value-relevant involvement in audience members than in individuals who are not exposed to the scripted scene. Hence, focusing audience members' attention on negatively valenced consequences that are likely to occur if assertive action is not taken during a sexual assault episode should induce this high level of value-relevant involvement. With this heightened level of value-relevant involvement, audience members may be more likely to engage in issue-relevant thinking about sexual assault. For this reason, questions regarding audience members' value-relevant involvement, as well as their issue-relevant thinking, are central to understanding and determining the potential impact of these two variables on other theoretically relevant outcomes (e.g., perceived argument quality and subsequent attitude change). With this goal in mind, the following research questions were posed:

> RQ1: Does the interACT performance have an impact on audience members' value-relevant involvement and issue-relevant thinking?
>
> RQ2: Is audience members' value-relevant involvement related to their issue-relevant thinking?

Affective Learning Model: Affective and Cognitive Learning

According to Rodríguez et al. (1996), "*Affective learning* [italics added] has been conceptualized as a process involving the acquisition or modification and maintenance of positive or negative attitudes toward the subject or teacher" (p. 295). Rodríguez et al. showed that affective learning is an important predictor of *cognitive learning*, defined as the self-perception of how much one has learned (Richmond, McCroskey, Kearney, & Plax, 1987).

Rodríguez et al. (1996) further argued that instructional behaviors, such as teacher immediacy (teachers' display of warmth and caring toward students), increases student affective learning, which leads to cognitive learning. Put another way, the relationship between empathic instructional behaviors and cognitive learning is mediated by affective learning. We were interested, therefore, in discovering if the proactive and empathic qualities stressed by the interACT performance induced affective learning and subsequent cognitive learning. Consistent with this objective, the following research questions were advanced:

> RQ3: Does the interACT performance have an impact on audience members' affective and cognitive learning?
>
> RQ4: Does audience members' affective learning impact their cognitive learning?

Altruistic and Egoistic Models: Comforting Communication

Communication scholars increasingly have become interested in the comforting messages that individuals engage in to assist distressed others (see, e.g., Burleson, 1983, 1984; Burleson & Samter, 1985). According to Stiff et al. (1988, p. 210), *comforting* involves individuals responding with helpful behaviors, such as listening or "saying the right thing," when they are in the presence of an emotionally distressed other.

Stiff et al. (1988) explained the production of comforting messages using two theoretical perspectives. The *altruistic model* argues that other-oriented or selfless motivations to comfort distressed others originate from a desire to improve the condition or state of the distressed individual. In contrast, the *egoistic model* claims that the motivation to comfort distressed others arises from self-centered or solipsistic predispositions, such that people comfort distressed others not out of concern for the other person's welfare but, instead, for the purpose of meeting their own ego needs as helpers. Although we are not interested in the motivation to comfort per se, we find these explanations helpful in understanding the potential role of comforting in the distressing aftermath of sexual assault. For this reason, a final research question was posed to assess participants' willingness to comfort in response to the interACT scene:

RQ5: Does the interACT performance have an impact on audience members' willingness to comfort sexual assault survivors?

METHODS

Participants

Four hundred fifty-eight participants were recruited from two sections of the same introductory, mass lecture communication course at a large urban U.S. university. Students from these two sections (an 11:00 a.m. and 12:30 p.m. section) were randomly selected to participate in one of the two conditions, with a comparable number of participants in each condition ($n = 228$-230). A total of 458 students participated in the study during a regular class period. There were 162 males and 296 females; 270 freshmen, 105 sophomores, 59 juniors, and 24 seniors; and participants ranged in age from 17-32, with an average age of 19.12 years. As a group, ethnic minorities accounted for approximately 56% (the majority) of this sample, with 201 Anglos, 124 Asians, 96 Lationa/os, 28 African Americans, and 9 others/declined to state ethnicity. Participation was voluntary, and no incentive or reward was offered. Rich, as a skilled facilitator, was responsible for introducing the interACT performance, setting up the proactive scenes, and encouraging audience members to come on stage with the peer educators.

Design and Procedures

This study constituted a quasi-experiment using a random selection, posttest-only, control group design, with an experimental condition (the interACT scene) and a control condition (a lecture/demonstration).[1] In the experimental condition, participants first were told that the researchers were interested in "getting your opinions and reactions to a peer-education demonstration," and then were exposed to the proactive performance by interACT. Following the performance, participants were asked to report their levels of value-relevant involvement, affective learning, cognitive learning, issue-relevant thinking, and willingness to comfort. Before participants were dismissed, the purpose of the study was explained in detail.

In the control condition, participants listened to a lecture and demonstration on how to use a web-based instructional program germane to the course content.[2] The lecture demonstrated (via a live online hook-up) how to use this program to access course assignments, course notes, exam results, and general course information. Following this presentation, participants were told that the researchers were interested in "getting your opinions and reactions to a demonstration," as well as their evaluation of other relevant campus issues (e.g., sexual assault), and participants completed the same instruments administered to the members of the experimental group. Before participants were dismissed, the purpose of the study was explained in detail.

Instrumentation

To test the dimensionality of all of the measures, we analyzed these data using the form of confirmatory factor analysis (CFA) developed by Hunter and Gerbing (1982) and operationalized in Hamilton and Hunter's (1991) CFA computer program, which provided the output presented in this section. Consistent with this type of CFA analysis, three criteria were used to evaluate items: (a) item content, (b) internal consistency (whether items measuring the same underlying construct relate to one another in the same way), and (c) parallelism (whether items measuring the same underlying construct relate to other variables assessed in the study in a similar manner). This procedure showed that the measurement model for each instrument (the number of items or indicators per instrument) varied. Specifically, CFAs resulted in the retention of three items on the following scales, which had 4-5 original items: comforting, affective learning, and cognitive learning. The measurement models for the other instruments were unchanged and, consequently, all of the original items were maintained. Results of the tests for internal consistency, parallelism, and reliability are summarized next. In all cases, participants responded to the items using a 5-point Likert scale (1 = *Disagree Strongly*, 5 = *Agree Strongly*), with higher scores reflecting more of the variable assessed. Coefficient alpha was used to estimate reliability.

Involvement. The value-relevant involvement scale was comprised of four items: (a) "I care about the issues presented in the demonstration," (b) "The topic of the demonstration was important to me," (c) "I care about the issues presented in the demonstration," and (d) "The topic of the demonstration was valuable." This scale passed the test for internal consistency, with factor loadings ranging from .66 to .92, items were parallel, total test for flat $\chi^2(33) = 4007.38$, $p < .001$, and the reliability of this scale was .76.

Affective learning. To measure affective learning, participants reported the degree to which they liked the demonstration with regard to three items: (a) "I liked the demonstration," (b) "The demonstration was pleasing," and (c) "I enjoyed the demonstration." This scale passed the test for internal consistency, with factor loadings ranging from .76 to .96, items were parallel, total test for flat $\chi^2(33) = 182.48$, $p < .001$, and the reliability of this scale was .86.

Cognitive learning. To assess cognitive learning, participants reported the degree to which they learned something from the demonstration with regard to three items: (a) "I learned from the demonstration," (b) "The demonstration taught me something," and (c) "The demonstration was educational." This scale passed the test for internal consistency, with factor loadings ranging from .84 to .89, items were parallel, total test for flat $\chi^2(33) = 281.68$, $p < .001$, and the reliability of this scale was .79.

Issue-relevant thinking. To measure issue-relevant thinking, participants reported the degree to which the demonstration caused them to think, with the scale comprised of four items: (a) "The demonstration caused me to think," (b) "The demonstration caused me to reflect," (c) "The demonstration caused me to ponder," and (d) "The demonstration caused me to contemplate." This scale passed the test for internal consistency, with factor loadings ranging from .75 to .93, items were parallel, total test for flat $\chi^2(33) = 154.48$, $p < .001$, and the reliability of this scale was .90.

Comforting. To assess this final variable, participants reported their willingness to comfort someone who has been sexually assaulted with regard to three items: (a) "I can comfort a person who has been sexually assaulted," (b) "I could comfort someone who has been sexually assaulted," and (c) "I know how to comfort someone who has been sexually assaulted." This scale passed the test for internal consistency, with factor loadings ranging from .66

to 1.00, items were parallel, total test for flat $\chi^2(33) = 189.39$, $p < .001$, and the reliability of this scale was .84.

RESULTS

We computed independent sample *t*-tests, as well as correlation coefficients and linear regression analyses to provide an estimate of the effect sizes for these variables. We believe that reporting both the significance and magnitude of effects is important for two reasons. First, given that significance tests are influenced greatly by sample size, an effect may be statistically significant but relatively trivial in terms of magnitude, as determined by the correlation size. Thus, we report effect sizes to be able to identify weak and strong effects. Second, for meta-analytic reasons, we report effect sizes so that future researchers may be able to compare these results with similar studies on performance as communication activism.

The independent sample *t*-tests showed that audience members in the interACT condition ($M = 16.41$, $SD = 3.05$) reported higher levels of value-relevant involvement than those in the control group ($M = 15.74$, $SD = 3.12$), $t(455) = 2.33$, $p = .02$, $r = .11$. In the interACT condition, linear regression analyses showed that the impact of value-relevant involvement on issue-relevant thinking was significant and substantial, $t(227) = 9.08$, $p < .001$, $r = .52$. In addition, individuals in the interACT condition ($M = 13.61$, $SD = 1.81$) reported higher levels of affective learning than those in the control group ($M = 10.92$, $SD = 2.61$), $t(456) = 12.83$, $p < .001$, $r = .52$. Respondents in the interACT condition ($M = 17.68$, $SD = 3.90$) also reported higher levels of cognitive learning than those in the control group ($M = 15.67$, $SD = 3.24$), $t(456) = 6.00$, $p < .001$, $r = .27$. In the interACT condition, linear regression analyses showed that the impact of affective learning on cognitive learning was significant and substantial, $t(227) = 6.56$, $p < .001$, $r = .40$. Audience members in the interACT condition ($M = 16.51$, $SD = 3.40$) also reported higher levels of issue-relevant thinking than those in the control group ($M = 11.79$, $SD = 3.87$), $t(456) = 13.85$, $p < .001$, $r = .54$. Finally, individuals in the interACT condition ($M = 13.93$, $SD = 2.18$) reported higher levels of willingness to comfort than those in the control group ($M = 11.63$, $SD = 2.80$), $t(450) = 9.76$, $p < .001$, $r = .41$.

DISCUSSION

In this study, we examined theoretically relevant outcomes associated with the interACT performance about sexual assault. The results showed that the participants exposed to this performance, in comparison to control group participants exposed to a lecture and demonstration, found the performance to be more involving, enjoyable, educational, and thought-provoking, and reported a greater willingness to engage in comforting behaviors with someone who has been sexually assaulted. These results have important implications for the efficacy of proactive performance as communication activism. Most importantly, the significant and substantial outcomes connected with the interACT scene demonstrate empirically the efficacy of this performative intervention. These results, however, also need to be understood in relation to the limitations of this study.

Implications

The proactive performance scene may be aptly suited to leading audience members to see the importance of sexual assault by presenting an embodied, interactive human drama. The embodied nature of this process is novel and unexpected because students, especially in educational contexts, are accustomed to more didactic presentations, such as lectures. In our view, the novelty of praxis[3] demonstrated by the performance not only punctuates the perceived importance of sexual assault but also casts the performative and ultimately transformational elements of this craft on center stage where they belong.

The transformational elements of performance activism may be explained, at least partially, by exploring how the effects of issue-relevant thinking with regard to sexual assault are driven by novelty and task importance. For instance, research shows that a variety of contextual factors affect the likelihood of issue-relevant thinking; two of these conditions are the importance of a task and exposure to unexpected message content (Maheswaran & Chaiken, 1991). We believe that the interACT scene provides both of these contextual features, with the relatively unexpected mode of message presentation (the interACT scene), which dramatizes the importance of sexual assault, inducing issue-relevant thinking. Although these two features could be induced in a variety of other ways (e.g., by presenting anecdotal or statistical evidence didactically), we believe that they lend themselves efficaciously to proactive, performance-based interventions, such as the interACT scene.

Also of interest is the fact that both cognitive and affective learning were affected in a significant and substantial manner by the interACT scene. Moreover, affective learning influenced cognitive learning in a manner consistent with previous research (Rodríguez et. al., 1996). These findings are important because they illustrate that a pedagogical modality that is performance based (the interACT scene) and not didactic can influence these bottom-line instructional goals. Put another way, these results demonstrate that nontraditional, performance-based social activism can lead to important and theoretically relevant learning outcomes. These findings are of particular import considering that traditionally, the teacher has been cast in the all-important, antecedent position of power in the causal chain that leads to cognitive learning (Richmond et al., 1987; Rodríguez et al., 1996). In light of this traditional approach to learning, our findings with regard to affective and cognitive learning are refreshingly seditious. Indeed, this study shows that self-perceived learning can occur when the traditional teacher role is "absent." This finding bodes well for future efficacy studies of nontraditional, performance-based approaches to communication activism.

In terms of comforting women who have been sexually assaulted, this investigation has significant theoretical implications for future research on performance for social change, as well as applied value. In the interpersonal literature, for example, comforting has been linked theoretically to prosocial characteristics, such as empathy (Burleson & Samter, 1985; Stiff et al., 1988). Specifically, Stiff et al. (1988) showed that when individuals understand (engage in perspective taking) and care about the welfare of another person (demonstrate empathic concern), they are more likely to comfort that person. This result was explained using the altruistic model, with other-oriented motivation as a key predictor of such comforting behavior. In contrast, individuals are less likely to comfort another when they experience emotional responses similar to the distressed other (emotional contagion), a result that was explained using the egoistic model, with self-centered motivation being the key predictor of the lack of engaging in comforting behavior. Given these two results and corresponding explanations, we speculate that because willingness to comfort as a result of exposure to the proactive performance was high in this study, participants were operating from a more altruistic than egoistic motivation.

Within the context of social change and sexual assault, these potential causal chains may explain why individuals do or do not comfort distressed others in the aftermath of sexual assault. In this way, empathy and comforting may be useful within the context of performance-based sexual assault interventions by providing theoretically meaningful conclusions about social change in this specific domain of inquiry. Thus, for theoretical reasons, it would be highly fruitful to further investigate the relationship between empathy and comforting within the context of performance-based sexual assault interventions.

Second, from an applied perspective, future research may help scholars, practitioners, and performance artists to create and enact a model of relevant constructs (specifically, perspective taking, emotional contagion, empathic concern, and comforting) that facilitate the increased demonstration of prosocial behavior in encounters that involve potential sexual assault. With this knowledge in hand, the research process potentially could go in a number of important directions. For example, if we learn that the interACT scene, or others similar to it, generate empathic concern on the part of audience members, we could begin to map the specific processes that lead to comforting behaviors in potential sexual assault episodes and identify potent prevention variables (e.g., empathic concern and perspective taking). Moreover, by mapping these processes, we may discover that some intervention models do not facilitate empathic concern and, consequently, suffer in terms of efficacy. These interventions then could be reshaped to account for the role of empathy in facilitating prosocial behaviors, such as comforting, in the aftermath of sexual assault. These types of adjustments based on research evidence would yield a well-informed model of performance-based communication activism regarding sexual assault.

The role of value-relevant involvement also was significant, but the size of the effect ($r = .11$), reflected in mean differences, was not large. This result may be explained by the fact that the control group was exposed to a lecture and demonstration germane to course content (the use of web-based instructional software); hence, student involvement seems reasonable, as the topic was personally relevant to students and aligned with their values/needs (e.g., getting a good grade in the course). For these reasons, the results simply may demonstrate that when compared to highly relevant instructional topics, the interACT scene may not be deemed as engaging as topics that are perceived as low in value-relevant involvement (e.g., a lecture students deem to be irrelevant). Viewed from this perspective, the results for involvement may be seen as consistent with what would be expected when an audience is exposed to more "natural" control conditions, as opposed to sterile ones (e.g., an irrelevant lecture) or no stimulus at all (e.g., students simply filling out the posttest measures).

The results related to value-relevant involvement also may be attributed to the specific content or wording of the instrument used to measure this variable. We created a measure of value-relevant involvement aligned with traditional definitions of ego-involvement (i.e., issue involvement or personal relevance). Johnson and Eagly (1989), however, argued that different types of involvement have different types of effects in persuasion research. Specifically, in their meta-analysis, Johnson and Eagly identified three types of involvement. In addition to value-relevant involvement, *impression-relevant involvement* refers to a person's desire to express socially appropriate attitudes and *outcome-relevant involvement* refers to the degree to which an individual believes that an attitude object is related directly to her or his personal goals. Johnson and Eagly demonstrated that "with outcome-relevant involvement, high-involvement subjects were more persuaded than low-involvement subjects by strong arguments and less persuaded by weak arguments" (p. 305). Research participants, thus, were not persuaded as much in conditions of value or impression-relevant involvement as they were in out-come-relevant conditions.

Based on Johnson and Eagly's (1989) work, outcome-relevant involve-ment may be better suited than value-relevant involvement for measuring the impact of the interACT scene. More specifically, outcome-relevant involvement has been linked with persuasive outcomes in studies that induce accountability for judgments (Chaiken, 1980) and enhance the importance and consequences of behavior (Maheswaran & Chaiken, 1991). Because the interACT scene makes both of these issues salient (i.e., accountability and consequences), we suspect that a measure of outcome-relevant involvement may prove more fruitful than focusing on value-relevant involvement. Interestingly, however, value-relevant involvement had a significant and substantial effect on issue-relevant thinking ($r = .52$) and, therefore, seemed to be a strong predictor variable in this study. Regardless of the particular form of involvement measured in the future, outcomes related to accounta-bility and consequences may be particularly important to assess in perform-ance-based models of communication activism.

Limitations

Although this project revealed some substantial findings regarding the effi-cacy of proactive performance models, there are several significant limita-tions to this study that must be acknowledged. The first limitation stems from the use of a quasi-experimental design. One could argue that other fac-tors may have caused these results because we used intact or cohort groups and did not measure them beforehand, and the results, therefore, could be due to the unique characteristics of these groups. Although this may be the case, we attempted to address this concern in several ways. First, every attempt was made to minimize threats to internal validity. For example, the data were collected at the same time period, meaning that there is little to no reasonable effects to be expected with regard to maturation, history, and mortality. Second, the participants came from quite large cohort groups ($n = 228$-230), and they were recruited from a large general education course that services a richly diverse student population, including African American, Latina/o, Asian American, Anglo, and other ethnic groups. Our sample also was diverse in terms of age, class standing, and sex. Thus, idiosyncratic group differences that might have a significant impact on the results with small samples (typical in traditional psychological research) are not as likely in the present study, meaning that a threat in terms of selection also is unlikely.

A second limitation of the study is that we do not know what specific features of the interACT scene produce the observed effects. One could argue, for example, that the effects observed in the study simply are a function of a change in presentational format (a lecture and demonstration vs. a performance). One also could argue that the observed effects are caused simply by the presentation of sexual assault material in one condition and not in the other; in other words, we would get the same results if participants experienced a lecture or other didactic pedagogy about sexual assault. Given the current data, there is no way of assessing the validity of these potential, alternative interpretations. We do, however, feel confident that the effect sizes reported in the study—(a) $r = .11$, value involvement; (b) $r = .52$, value-relevant involvement and issue-relevant thinking; (c) $r = .52$, affective learning; (d) $r = .27$, cognitive learning; (e) $r = .40$, affective and cognitive learning; (f) $r = .54$, issue-relevant thinking; and (g) $r = .41$, comforting—are of a large enough magnitude to merit serious consideration and further exploration. We also feel confident that we demonstrated that the interACT scene affected theoretically relevant outcome variables in a manner consistent with previous research (e.g., Petty & Cacioppo, 1986; Rodríguez et. al., 1996). We think that these latter results are significant given that this project is the first attempt at quantifying Boal's techniques in action. For this reason, we believe that questions regarding ambiguous causal attribution and message features can be answered best by future research that directly compares performance-based interventions with more didactic approaches to communication activism.

The third limitation of the study concerns the difficulty of measuring behaviors and behavior change with regard to sexual assault. Like most studies on this topic, we did not measure actual behavior or behavior change but, rather, participants' perceptions of their involvement, issue-relevant thinking, cognitive learning, affective learning, and comforting. Even if we attempted to measure behavior in the present study (e.g., asking audience members to count the adaptive or functional intervention behaviors they observed during the scene), we do not know what a person would do during an actual sexual assault scenario. We decided to accept this limitation and attempted to assess outcomes based on participants' responses to an interactive, audience-centered simulation of a scene that could lead to sexual assault, as well a scene depicting the aftermath of dating violence.

One could argue that the absence of behavioral data is problematic because the impact of the interACT performance on observable behavior is empirically "unknown." This claim, although potentially valid from the limited perspective of the data presented here, is shortsighted within the larger context of the qualitative dynamics of proactive performance, as well as the currently undefined or latent quantitative dimensions of this phenomenon. Simply put, actual observers of the interACT performance probably would be reluctant to report that supportive behavior was not observed or that no change in behavior (i.e., from unhelpful to helpful) was witnessed during the performance because they see members of the audience coming up on stage and intervening effectively numerous times during the scripted scenes. Indeed, observers of the interACT performance could be asked to count the number of times they observed a participant come on stage and change one of the characters' or his or her own behavior from unhelpful to helpful.[4] Although this specific type of behavioral data was not collected in the study, that does not mean that supportive and effective actions were nonexistent in the interventions that were attempted on stage by participants during the scripted scenes. On the contrary, supportive and effective behaviors were present; they simply were not documented empirically. Given these limitations, the conclusions of this study might best be characterized as tentative, yet highly encouraging. One of our major goals in this preliminary study was to collect quantitative data and demonstrate that performance outcomes could be measured efficaciously. With this goal in mind, our study may be viewed as a humble first step in a long-term plan of programmatic research.

LESSONS LEARNED ABOUT PERFORMANCE AS COMMUNICATION ACTIVISM

From this study of proactive performance, we learned pragmatic and philosophical lessons about communication activism. From a pragmatic perspective, we note that Boal's techniques originally were conceived as a tool for revolutionary practice with homogenous populations, who usually can come to a consensus about their oppressive conditions. In contrast, we work with a heterogeneous population of students who may or may not be aware of issues related to sexual assault. Hence, there naturally is little agreement among members of this population about the dynamics of sexual assault, and a lack of clarity about who the oppressors are in the scenes. For example, it is not unusual for students to initially empathize with the boyfriend (Jeremy) and state that he basically is a good guy who gets "riled up" by his antagonistic friend. It is tempting in these moments to fall into a didactic teaching mode and explain to students why they are "wrong." We have learned, however, that audience interventions best illuminate the true nature of the characters.

Second, participatory education can be messy, and a skilled facilitator is needed to ensure that the performance does not become too convoluted. Facilitating proactive performance is a unique skill because one needs to understand theatrical techniques, be comfortable facilitating discussions about controversial topics, and be able to project a level of energy and enthusiasm that fosters an interactive environment. When opportunities for graduate students to facilitate these programs have been provided, a rigorous facilitator training program is needed. To meet this goal, we have recruited graduate students during their first semester of study to work with interACT.

Third, preparing to do proactive performance is a time-consuming task. As Uno (2001) explained in his discussion about the essential aspects of performance and social change, "The first [essential aspect] is paradoxically the easiest and the hardest: being present over a long period of time, enough to establish a commitment and continuum as the work moves forward" (p. 71). This study represents the culmination of 5 years of research and development. Over that period, we have learned that interACT performers need time to learn the scripted scenes, become proficient in improvisational skills, and learn about sexual assault. When students audition for interACT, they understand that they are signing on for a 1-year commitment. Because interACT consistently has a number of returning students, new members typically do not perform until their second semester in the troupe. We believe it is problematic to perform proactive scenes without being knowledgeable about sociopolitical issues. In the worst-case scenario, peer-education groups can perpetuate the very attitudes they are attempting to change. Although interACT attracts students who are committed to social change, many of them still initially hold beliefs that are counterproductive to confronting the problem of sexual assault. We believe it is unethical and, quite frankly, disingenuous to put students on stage who believe, for instance, that women somehow are at fault for their victimization. Students, thus, prepare to perform by learning about sexual assault through reading essays, attending lectures, keeping journals, and rehearsing the scenes during the semester before participating in a performance.

In addition to the pragmatic lessons learned, we were faced with philosophical issues as well. As the first researchers who have attempted to quantitatively measure Boal's techniques, we have come to understand that some performance scholars are not in favor of such research. For example, Jackson (1995) argued that:

> As far as I know, no one has yet attempted any follow-up study after a [Boal] workshop: such an initiative would probably be doomed to failure, as we are often dealing with unquantifiable changes which resist statistical analysis; the observable changes are qualitative. (p. xxiv)

In a similar vein, Schutzman (2003) stated that "I find the efficacy yardstick disturbing and inappropriate in realms of art (and I believe that Theatre of the Oppressed lies there fundamentally)" ("Post Workshop Reflections," ¶ 4). It is understandable that these and other performance studies scholars are reticent about embracing the positivist model because performance practitioners are most interested in embodied methodologies—most notably,

ethnography, phenomenology, and autobiographical and performative writing—and quantitative studies can reduce the body to numerical data and,
thereby, render it invisible.

Considering the perceived binary distinction drawn between quantitative and more embodied methodologies, perhaps it is not surprising that
scholars in performance studies may view quantitative researchers as the
"other," a position that may be warranted but limits dialogue—and possibilities—nonetheless. We believe that quantitative analysis need not be conflated with positivism, and that there is great potential for using both quantitative and qualitative methods to explore performance efficacy. In fact, as
Bavelas (1995) explained, the "Yin and Yang" of these diverse modes of
inquiry can be complementary:

> The set of quantitative versus qualitative research is usually constructed
> as consisting of only two elements in a relationship of opposition. . . .
> These differences are socially constructed, and to the extent that we
> insist on maintaining them, we will severely limit the number of
> approaches we can invent to explore our common interests. (pp. 51-52)

Although we are sensitive to the concerns of our performance studies
colleagues, we ultimately concluded that the heuristic value of measuring
performance efficacy, combined with the opportunity to potentially reduce
sexual assault, outweighed the potential downfalls. For scholar-artists who
facilitate proactive performances, it may be useful to consider the impact of
these techniques using quantitative measures to know whether this pedagogy facilitates sociopolitical change. As performance studies scholar Park-
Fuller (2003) argued, "Community action research must include the gathering of hard data on which we can base our claims" (p. 290).

We are deeply interested in employing a variety of methodological techniques—both qualitative and quantitative—to discern the impact of the
interACT program. In direct response to Schutzman's (2003) argument that
art and efficacy should not be conflated, Logan (2003) noted:

> My view is that art—like any symbolic action—is inherently efficacious
> in that it somehow influences an audience who experiences it. I believe
> this is inescapable. Thus, I believe that where TO lies is not an either/or
> proposition, it is both art and politics, that we need not choose between
> these poles of an imagined continuum. ("Expanding the Boundaries of
> Jokering; Kudos and Some Cautions," ¶ 5)

We agree with Logan's assertion and argue that the prohibition in performance studies against using quantitative methods is an arbitrary one.

What emerges in our work is a third worldview—a space where quantitative research and performance *praxis* meet to enact and assess a perspective of social change and activism in everyday life. From this perspective, the objective stance of quantitative assessment combines with the intersubjective and embodied experience of proactive performance. These two worldviews, thus, can coexist in a dialectical tension, such that each provides a profound perspective that can be discerned only by holding both of them in awareness. This "holding in awareness" of two supposed alternative truths is the core element of a third worldview that leads to communication activism and social change as informed by these two complementary truths. Perhaps most interestingly, by employing this worldview, our work has produced quantitative results that demonstrate the types of effects that performance scholars have known intuitively all along—showing that "the proof is in the pudding."

CONCLUSION

Considering the devastating impact that sexual assault has on college campuses, proactive peer-education programs are worth implementing and evaluating. After conducting a study on a traditional prevention model, Borden, Karr, and Caldwell-Colbert (1988) concluded that "didactic [sexual assault] training is insufficient to change attitudes. This study would support the need to introduce new, more dynamic, vivid interactive program formats to enhance the desired effects of consciousness raising, attitude change, and empathy toward rape" (p. 135). The interACT performance is one such attempt to employ a proactive performance to change people's attitudes and behaviors toward sexual assault and those who are victims of it.

One week after a recent interACT performance, we were contacted by two audience members, who revealed that a close friend of theirs had been sexually assaulted, and that they knew how to respond appropriately as a direct result of the interACT performance. We also have heard from numerous audience members who have intervened in situations that could have led to a sexual assault. We contend that the feedback we have received from audience members who respond in proactive ways to prevent sexual assault and help sexual assault survivors are not isolated incidents but, rather, a validation of the findings of this study.

Kushner's (2001) quote provides a nice frame for considering the potential of performance as communication activism to promote social change: "Art is not merely contemplation, it is also action, and all action changes the world, at least a little" (p. 62). When students are challenged to become communication activists, to be proactive and prevent sexual assault during an interACT performance, it is our great hope that they will be transformed into agents of change in their community.

NOTES

1. We employed intact group assignment (Campbell, 1969), in which one of two aggregate sample groups rather than individual participants were randomly "selected" for exposure to the interACT scene, and the other aggregate group was exposed to a lecture/demonstration. Random selection was operationalized by assigning each group a number (1 for the 11 a.m. section and 2 for the 12:30 p.m.), and then drawing these numbers from a hat. The first number drawn represented the group exposed to the interACT scene; the next number referenced the lecture/demonstration group. We did not employ random assignment at the individual participant level because the logistics of randomly assigning 458 students to two conditions would have presented several challenges that we wanted to avoid. For instance, students potentially would be required to come to class at an hour other than their regularly scheduled class time, creating scheduling conflicts for some students because they had another class at that hour. Equally important, students may have become confused about or forgot what time they were supposed to show up because their randomly assigned time was inconsistent with their habitualized class schedule. The likely results of these problems would have been a lower overall sample size and a potential validity threat related to selection because students would self-select out of the study for reasons beyond our control (e.g., scheduling conflicts, confusion, and forgetfulness).

2. This type of control condition was used because it is consistent with the vast majority of control conditions employed in the research on sexual assault reviewed for the purposes of conducting this study (e.g., Black et al., 2000; Borden et al., 1988; Frazier, Valtinson, & Candell, 1994; Holcolmb et al., 1993; Lanier et al., 1988). By using this type of control condition, the results from this study can be generalized most efficaciously to the existing body of literature on sexual assault.

3. This term is used in a manner consistent with dialectical materialism, which postulates that comprehension, prognostication, or forecasting of life events is determined primarily through enactment or behavioral practice instead of deduction (Reese, 1993). From this perspective, *praxis* is defined as "action in the world for a specific purpose, or goal-directed activity" (Robins, Schmidt, & Linehan, 2004, p. 34).

4. One reason we did not ask audience members to report "perceived" behavior change in these ways is because we were under enormous time constraints. The class sections used in our sample met for only 50 minutes, and the interACT scenes took up all of that time. Furthermore, we had to pass out and collect over 200 questionnaires in a timely manner for each section. Thus, we had to ask the participants to stay an extra 10 minutes to complete the posttest measures. Given these time constraints, we decided to keep the measures as short as possible.

REFERENCES

Alexander, B. (2001). Theater inside. *Theater, 31*(3), 80-82.

Bavelas, J. B. (1995) Quantitative versus qualitative? In W. Leeds-Hurwitz (Ed.), *Social approaches to communication* (pp. 49-62). New York: Guilford Press.

Black, B., Weisz, A., Coats, S., & Patterson, D. (2000). Evaluating a psychoeducational sexual assault prevention program incorporating theatrical presentation, peer education, and social work. *Research on Social Work Practice, 10,* 589-606.

Boal, A. (1979). *Theatre of the oppressed* (A. Charles & M. O. Leal-McBride, Trans.). New York: Urizen Books.

Boal, A. (1990a). Invisible theatre. *Drama Review, 34*(3), 24-34.

Boal, A. (1990b). The cop in the head: Three hypotheses. *Drama Review, 34*(3), 35-42.

Boal, A. (1992). *Games for actors and non-actors* (A. Jackson, Trans.). New York: Routledge.

Boal, A. (1995). *Rainbow of desire: The Boal method of theater and therapy* (A. Jackson, Trans.). New York: Routledge.

Bohmer, C., & Parrot, A. (1993). *Sexual assault on campus: The problem and the solution.* New York: Lexington Books.

Borden, L. A., Karr, S. K., & Caldwell-Colbert, A. T. (1988). Effects of a university rape prevention program on attitudes and empathy toward rape. *Journal of College Student Development, 29,* 132-136.

Brown, K. H., & Gillespie, D. (1997). We become brave by doing brave acts: Teaching moral courage through the Theater of the Oppressed. *Literature and Medicine, 16,* 108-120.

Burleson, B. R. (1983). Social cognition, empathic motivation, and adults' comforting strategies. *Human Communication Research, 10,* 295-304.

Burleson, B. R. (1984). Age, social-cognitive development, and the use of comforting strategies. *Communication Monographs, 51,* 140-153.

Burleson, B. R., & Samter, W. (1985). Individual differences in the perception of comforting messages: An exploratory investigation. *Central States Speech Journal, 36,* 39-50.

Butterfield, M. I., Barnett, L., & Koons, C. R. (2000). *Victim to victory: A survivor group for women veterans who have experienced sexual trauma.* Durham, NC: Women Veteran's Comprehensive Health Center.

Campbell, D. T. (1969). Reforms as experiments. *American Psychologist, 24,* 409-429.

Chaiken, S. (1980). Heuristic versus systematic information processing and the use of source versus message cues in persuasion. *Journal of Personality and Social Psychology, 39,* 752-766.

Cohen-Cruz, J. (1990). Boal at NYU: A workshop and its aftermath. *Drama Review, 34*(3), 43-49.

Cohen-Cruz, J. (2001). Motion of the ocean: The shifting face of U.S. theatre for social change since the 1960s. *Theatre, 31*(3), 95-107.

Cohen-Cruz, J., & Schutzman, M. (1990). Theatre of the Oppressed with women: An interview with Augusto Boal. *Drama Review, 34*(3), 66-76.

Cohen-Cruz, J., & Schutzman, M. (Eds.). (2006). *A Boal companion: Dialogues on theatre and cultural politics.* New York: Routledge.

Conquergood, D. (1986). Between experience and meaning: Performance as a paradigm for meaningful action. In T. Colson (Ed.), *Renewal & revision: The future of interpretation* (pp. 26-59). Denton, TX: NB Omega.

Frankham, J. (1998). Peer education: The unauthorized version. *British Educational Research Journal, 24,* 179-194.

Frazier, P., Valtinson, G., & Candell, S. (1994). Evaluation of a coeducational interactive rape prevention program. *Journal of Counseling and Development, 73,* 153-158.

Freire, P. (1993). *Pedagogy of the oppressed* (rev. ed.; M. B. Ramos, Trans.). New York: Continuum.

Fung, A. (2001). How participatory theater can improve deliberative politics. *Theater, 31*(3), 67-68.

Hamilton, M., & Hunter, J. (1991). *CFA.* Unpublished computer program for conducting confirmatory factor analysis, East Lansing, MI.

Hanson, K. A., & Gidycz, C. A. (1993). Evaluation of a sexual assault prevention program. *Journal of Consulting and Clinical Psychology, 61,* 1046-1052.

Holcomb, D. R., Sarvela, P. D., Sondag, A., & Holcomb, L. C. (1993). An evaluation of a mixed-gender date rape prevention workshop. *Journal of American College Health, 41,* 159-164.

Hunter, J. E., & Gerbing, D. W. (1982). Unidimensional measurement, second-order factor analysis and causal models. In B. M. Straw & L. L. Cummings (Eds.), *Research in organizational behavior* (Vol. 4, pp. 267-320). Greenwich, CT: JAI Press.

Jackson, A. (1995). Introduction. In A. Boal, *Rainbow of desire: The Boal method of theater and therapy* (A. Jackson, Trans., pp. xviii-xxvi). New York: Routledge.

Johnson, B. T., & Eagly, A. (1989). Effects of involvement on persuasion: A meta-analysis. *Psychological Bulletin, 106,* 290-314.

Jones, J. (1993). Personalizing HIV personal narratives: An aesthetic and political imperative. In F. Corey (Ed.), *HIV education: Performing personal narratives: Proceedings of a conference funded by the U.S. Centers for Disease Control and Prevention and Arizona State University* (pp. 175-197). Tempe: Arizona State University.

Koss, M. P., Gidycz, C. A., & Wisniewski, N. (1987). The scope of rape: Incidence and prevalence of sexual aggression in victimization in a national sample of higher education students. *Journal of Consulting and Clinical Psychology, 55,* 162-170.

Kushner, T. (2001). How do you make social change? *Theatre, 31*(3), 62-93.

Lanier, C. A., Elliott, M. N., Martin, D. W., & Kapadia, A. (1998). Evaluation of an intervention to change attitudes toward date rape. *Journal of American College Health, 46,* 177-180.

Logan, C. (2003). Presence and absence in online performance: Configurations in the problematics of access. *American Communication Journal, 6*(3). Retrieved August 20, 2003, from http://www.acjournal.org/holdings/vol6/iss3/responses/logan.htm

Maheswaran, D., & Chaiken, S. (1991). Promoting systematic processing in low motivation settings: Effect of incongruent information on processing and judgment. *Journal of Personality and Social Psychology, 61,* 13-25.

Mann, C. A., Hecht, M. L., & Valentine, K. B. (1988). Performance in a social context: Date rape versus date right. *Central States Speech Journal, 39,* 269-280.

McConachie, B. (2002). Theatre of the Oppressed with students of privilege: Practicing Boal in the American college classroom. In N. Stucky & C. Wimmer (Eds.), *Teaching performance studies* (pp. 247-260). Carbondale: Southern Illinois University Press.

O'Keefe, D. J. (1990). *Persuasion: Theory and research.* Newbury Park, CA: Sage.

Park-Fuller, L. (2003). Audiencing the audience: Playback Theatre, performative writing, and social activism. *Text and Performance Quarterly, 23,* 288-310.

Paterson, D. (2001). The TASC is: Theater and social change. *Theater, 31*(3), 65-66.

Pelias, R. J. (1992). *Performance studies: The interpretation of aesthetic texts.* New York: St. Martin's Press.

Pelias, R. J., & VanOosting, J. (1987). A paradigm for performance studies. *Quarterly Journal of Speech, 73,* 219-231.

Petty, R. E., & Cacioppo, J. T. (1986). *Communication and persuasion: Central and peripheral routes to attitude change.* New York: Springer-Verlag.

Raynor, A. (1993). The value of peer education on the college. In F. Corey (Ed.), *HIV education: Performing personal narratives: Proceedings of a conference funded by the U.S. Centers for Disease Control and Prevention and Arizona State University* (pp. 17-22). Tempe: Arizona State University.

Reese, H. W. (1993). Contextualism and dialectical materialism. In S. C. Hayes, L. J. Hayes, H. W. Reese, & T. R. Sarbin (Eds.), *Varieties of scientific contextualism* (pp. 71-105). Reno, NV: Context Press.

Resick, P. A., & Schnicke, M. K. (1992). Cognitive processing therapy for sexual assault victims. *Journal of Consulting and Clinical Psychology, 60,* 748-756.

Richmond, V. P., McCroskey, J. C., Kearney, P., & Plax, T. G. (1987). Power in the classroom VII: Linking behavior alternation techniques to cognitive learning. In M. L. McLaughlin (Ed.), *Communication yearbook* (Vol. 10, pp. 574-590). Beverly Hills, CA: Sage.

Robins, C. J., Schmidt, H., III, & Linehan, M. M. (2004). Dialectical behavior therapy. In S. C. Hayes, V. M. Follette, & M. M. Linehan (Eds.), *Mindfulness and acceptance: Expanding the cognitive-behavioral tradition* (pp. 30-44). New York: Guilford Press.

Rodríguez, J. I., Plax, T. G., & Kearney, P. (1996). Clarifying the relationship between teacher nonverbal immediacy and student cognitive learning: Affective learning as the central causal mediator. *Communication Education, 45,* 294-305.

Schutzman, M. (2003). Joker runs wild. *American Communication Journal, 6*(3). Retrieved August 30, 2003, from http://www.acjournal.org/holdings/vol6/iss3/schutzman/index.html

Schutzman, M., & Cohen-Cruz, J. (1994a). Introduction. In M. Schutzman & J. Cohen-Cruz (Eds.), *Playing Boal: Theatre, therapy, activism* (pp. 1-16). New York: Routledge.

Schutzman, M., & Cohen-Cruz, J. (Eds.). (1994b). *Playing Boal: Theatre, therapy, activism.* New York: Routledge.

Simon, T. (1993). Complex issues for sexual assault peer education programs. *Journal of American College Health, 41,* 289-291.

Stiff, J. B., Dillard, J. P., Somera, L., Kim, H., & Sleight, C. (1988). Empathy, communication, and prosocial behavior. *Communication Monographs, 55,* 198-213.

Stucky, N., & Wimmer, C. (2002). Introduction. In N. Stucky & C. Wimmer (Eds.), *Teaching performance studies* (pp. 1-29). Carbondale: Southern Illinois University Press.

Taussig, M., & Schechner, R. (1990). Boal in Brazil, France, and the USA: An interview with Augusto Boal. *Drama Review, 34*(3), 50-65.

Telesco, G. (2001). Theatre of the recruits: Boal techniques in the New York Police Academy. *Theatre, 31*(3), 55-61.

Uno, R. (2001). How do you make social change? *Theatre, 31*(3), 62-93.

Westlake, E. J. (2001). *The children of tomorrow*: Seattle Public Theatre's work with homeless youth. In S. C. Haedicke & T. Nellhaus (Eds.), *Performing democracy: International perspectives on urban community-based performance* (pp. 67-79). Ann Arbor: University of Michigan Press.

10

NARRATIVE AS COMMUNICATION ACTIVISM

Research Relationships in Social Justice Projects

Deborah Cunningham Walker

Coastal Carolina University

Elizabeth A. Curry

CASA (Community Action Stops Abuse)

When they talk about CASA or the project, Deb and Elizabeth use the words "we, our, or us," not "them or they."

Deb and Elizabeth are part of CASA because they understand us. They get it.

Lots of people study domestic violence, but they were the first researchers interested in us, the workers. We felt validated because university researchers thought what we did was important, and they asked us to help them understand our work.

They didn't lecture us; they listened to us.

These are some of the staff's observations about our participation in the University Community Initiative (UCI) Project, a grant-funded research collaboration between Community Action Stops Abuse (CASA) and the University of South Florida's (USF) Communication and Sociology Departments. CASA is a community service organization located in St. Petersburg, FL that advocates for victims and survivors of domestic violence by providing both emergency assistance and long-term support. USF is a large, metropolitan, state-supported university that seeks to connect with its surrounding community by forging partnerships designed to assist with social problems.

Like the mermaid songs that M. Gergen (1992) theorized—distinct, yet blended; unique, yet familiar—the voices of those involved in the UCI Project also have merged "so that each, in its own special timbre, lends to the harmony of the whole" (p. 127). Utilizing narrative vignettes linked by observation and analysis, we demonstrate the use of narrative as communication activism, theorizing this work as an example of K. J. Gergen's (2000) idea of "poetic activism." Poetic activism challenges us to develop creative methods of analysis, presentation, and dissemination of research results. Perhaps most importantly, poetic activism offers researchers the opportunity to approach the research relationship itself "poetically," so that the partnerships created within a research project also can serve as effective change agents. Therefore, the process, as well as the product, of a research project can generate social reform.

Activism means changing the way people think, understand, and act. It implies action or involvement on the part of all participants, including researchers, as a means of effectuating social change. There are several aspects of communication activism that comprise our project; they include the establishment of a CASA/USF internship program, participation in each other's development activities, and the production of a booklet of narratives used as a funding, lobbying, and recruiting tool. However, in this chapter, we focus on the most important and foundational element of this multilayered, activist project: developing a research relationship that shifts the paradigm away from one of expert academics providing assistance to a needy community toward one that privileges a collaborative, engaged relationship between university and community partners, changing the model from charity outreach to social justice engagement.

To explicate the relational characteristics of this communication activism, we first offer a brief overview of CASA and the UCI Project and then provide our theoretical and methodological frameworks. We then present a narrative colloquium that explains and models the engaged research relationship we struggle to enact. We conclude the chapter with lessons learned about the development and maintenance of such a research relationship. We briefly discuss many of our interventions within the UCI Project, but we frame these interventions as being dependent on revisions to all participants' understanding of the research relationship.

COMMUNITY ACTION STOPS ABUSE (CASA)

CASA is a member of the National Coalition Against Domestic Violence (NCADV), a local, state, regional, and national coalition that supports "community-based, nonviolent alternatives" for recently and previously battered women and their children. The NCADV believes that:

> Violence against women and children results from the use of force or threat to achieve and maintain control over others in intimate relationships, and from societal abuse of power and domination in the forms of sexism, racism, homophobia, classism, anti-Semitism, able-bodyism, ageism and other oppressions. NCADV recognizes that the abuses of power in society foster battering by perpetuating conditions which condone violence against women and children. Therefore, it is the mission of NCADV to work for major societal changes necessary to eliminate both personal and societal violence against all women and children. (National Coalition Against Domestic Violence, n.d., ¶2)

Domestic violence transcends gender; victims can be homosexual or heterosexual men, as well as women, although CASA contends that this is primarily a women's issue. According to the Riley Center (n.d.), a domestic violence shelter managed by the St. Vincent de Paul Society in San Francisco, 95% of domestic violence victims are women. The U.S. Bureau of Justice (1993) found that females are victims of domestic violence four times as often as are males, and the American Medical Association estimated that over four million women per year are victims of severe assaults by boyfriends and husbands (Glazer, 1993). These statistics are not surprising considering that, according to Women's Rural Advocacy Programs (n.d.), domestic violence is the number-one reason for women's emergency room visits each year; 25% of all reported crime is wife assault.

CASA's (2000) vision is a community without violence—to "make home a safe place." Founded in 1977, CASA actively partners with other community agencies to reach a variety of disenfranchised and disadvantaged groups whose members have been battered, including the deaf community, gay and lesbian couples, and the elderly. The organization consists of a shelter, a community outreach building that includes administrative offices and a thrift store, two transitional housing complexes, a legal advocacy office at the county courthouse, a youth community center, and various other satellite service providers, such as a visitation center and legal aid offices. CASA is staffed by over 50 full- and part-time employees and hundreds of volunteers who do everything from knitting blankets to raising thousands of dollars annually.

THE UCI PROJECT

For the past 3 years, our research has supported CASA's mission to advocate for social change by providing community education, outreach support, crisis intervention, and safe environments for survivors of domestic violence and their children. Our involvement with CASA began by chance, much like any other relationship. Marcie Finkelstein, the director of the Center for Engaged Scholarship, a think tank located at USF that specializes in identifying and funding university-community partnerships, met CASA's executive director, Linda Osmundson, at a dinner party. Linda mentioned to Marcie that CASA had been involved in many research projects with university researchers, but CASA's staff members felt that they had not benefited from those experiences. She indicated that researchers often arrived unannounced and at inconvenient times, disrupted the work schedule, required the completion of endless forms, and then often left without even sharing any of their research results with the CASA community. Linda expressed feeling "ripped off" by what she perceived as self-serving academics who cared nothing for CASA or its increasingly difficult battle against domestic violence.

Marcie offered to introduce Linda to some researchers at USF who would design a research project *with them* instead of *for them*, utilizing narrative and other interpretive methods of analysis, with a shared goal of promoting community action to stop abuse. These introductions grew into the UCI Project—a university-community collaboration consisting of CASA staff members and academics from a variety of disciplines: communication, psychology, sociology, women's studies, mass communication, and human resources. As doctoral candidates in USF's Department of Communication, we were invited onto the project because of our interests in narrative, social action research, and activism.

The UCI Project partners decided to engage in a long-term, comprehensive, participatory ethnography that employed interactive interviews to collect narratives told by paid and unpaid workers at CASA about their experiences of working in the field of domestic violence. We hoped that by nurturing an understanding of the complexities of working within a community service organization, we might assist our community—legislators, funders, and the public at large—as it sought to understand the complexities of the social problem of domestic violence.

The UCI Project grant had the following goals:

1. Establish a collaborative relationship between CASA and USF and document the process of developing the project as a collaborative university-community group partnership.
2. Conduct an ethnographic study of CASA, emphasizing the ways that staff, volunteers, and former shelter residents tell their stories and engage in sense-making in their professional and personal lives.
3. Study the use of stories by staff and volunteers at CASA to communicate domestic abuse as a social problem and dispel misunderstandings about it in the wider community.
4. Assess the feasibility of a volunteer program between CASA and USF; if advisable, develop an action plan to recruit students who would volunteer at CASA for USF course credit.
5. Produce a booklet of stories to be used locally, statewide, and nationally with victims, families, community groups, volunteers, scholars, and related agencies in reframing domestic violence in our society.

One of the goals of the UCI Project that seems especially noteworthy was our hope to dispel widespread cultural misunderstandings, or "collective representations" (Loseke, 1987, 1992), that affect perceptions of domestic violence within our society. Some of these collective representations include conflicting "gender narratives" (Wood, 2001) that condemn a woman for failing to leave an abusive situation and simultaneously condemn her for failing to "stand by her man"; the requirement that victims comply with prevalent cultural scripts (Baker, 1996), such as filing police reports or participating in therapy; existing "folk notions" (Baker, 1996; Loseke, 1987, 1992) affirming an "acceptable" level of violence in intimate relationships; and victims' frequent refusal to conform to collective representations as a way of retaining power within a powerless space (Baker, 1996; Hegde, 1996; Lempert, 1997; Murray, 1988). As Cacho-Negrete (2000) summarized, "Nobody wants to be identified as a battered woman, because battered women are held responsible for their abuse" (p. 18).

All of the UCI Project goals have been exceeded. The collaborative relationship between CASA and USF has grown to include partnered community events and active participation in each other's work and mission. Over 40 CASA staff members have been interviewed, and their stories have been compiled into a booklet that has been successfully used as a development, rhetorical, and recruitment tool. Almost 2,000 copies of the booklet, *Many Faces, Many Voices Working Against Domestic Violence, The CASA Story of Stories* (Curry & Walker, 2002), have been sold or gifted for fundraising, outreach, and education. An internship program has been established, and more than 20 USF undergraduate students have received course credit for volunteering at CASA. We have embraced CASA's vision of a community without domestic violence, and we believe the UCI Project has contributed to that vision.

THEORETICAL AND METHODOLOGICAL FRAMEWORKS

Social Action Research

It was significant that the first goal of the UCI Project addressed relationship and community building. As partners, we understood that the goals, tasks, and products of this project would depend on the development and maintenance of a reflexive relationship among all project participants. This understanding is central to the social action and feminist epistemologies that framed this research project. According to Greenwood and Levin (1998), social action research involves participants and researchers co-generating knowledge through collaborative communication processes in which all participants' contributions are taken seriously, treating the diversity of experiences and capacities of the participants as crucial resources in the development and implementation of a research project.

Feminist Epistemologies

The salient characteristics of social action research embody many of the principles of feminist methodology, and because CASA is, after all, an organization embracing and espousing a feminist-fueled gender movement—the battered women's movement—ways of knowing and being in the world as articulated by some feminist writers were important for grounding this project. For example, feminist standpoint theory argues that because "subordinate groups must know how to survive in their oppressor's world, plus know their own reality" (Dankoski, 2000, p. 4), their understandings of those realities are more complex, rich, and varied than those of the dominant group. This epistemology, although recognizing that women's perspectives often spring from diverse politics, ethnicities, and special interests, advocates methodologies that seek to "build unity, solidarity, and sisterhood" (Weil, 1996, p. 201). Weil (1996) theorized "an action framework for feminist community practice" (p. 203) that builds on "feminist values" (p. 201), such as nurturance, caring, recognition of each individual's dignity and worth, and a sense of responsibility for each other. Ceglowski (2000), Gatenby and Humphries (2000), Swigonski (1993), and Tillman-Healy (2001, 2002) stressed the development of close relationships within a research project that are based on mutual trust, disclosure, and ethics. Considering that we had been invited into CASA expressly as a response to dissatisfactions emerging from its members' participation in other research projects, we knew it was important to honor and privilege their understandings, methodological preferences, and ways of knowing.

Research Relationships

Literature on reflexive research relationships emphasizes interpersonal communication and the importance of listening to those who are participants or partners in the research. Boundaries blur in the interplay between researchers and research participants (Ceglowski, 2000; Ellingson, 1998; Ellis & Berger, 2002; Ellis & Bochner, 2000; Ellis & Flaherty, 1992; Jorgenson, 1999; May & Patillo-McCoy, 2000; Milburn, Wilkins, & Wilkins, 2001). Jorgenson (1999) stressed the need to recognize such relational contexts in research when she wrote about the communicative process involving reciprocal perspective taking between researcher and respondents. During our UCI Project, a critical question was, "How do they see researchers and us as researchers?," especially because the domestic violence workers told us from the start that they had negative perceptions of researchers. At the same time, we struggled with trying to understand what it is like to work against domestic violence. Thus, a collaborative research project becomes "an expression of relationships among persons" (K. J. Gergen & Gergen, 1999, p. 78).

Narrative as Poetic Activism

We theorize that both the research relationships developed and the tangible results of the UCI Project are representative of K. J. Gergen's (1994, 2000, 2001) ideas of relational responsibility, generative theory, and poetic activism. Gergen proposed that researchers must look at the context of how human beings are related and interdependent. This idea of relational responsibility suggests that we must value process as much as product, as engagement is continuous and reflexive. Generative theory posits that action and discourse are integrally linked. Talk becomes our most effective change agent, for discourse leads to social action (see Adams, Berquist, & Galanes, Volume 1; Jovanovic, Steger, Symonds, & Nelson, Volume 1). Language and engagement, however, do not solely constitute poetic activism; reflexivity, impetus for social change, and community also contribute to the development of poetic activism, assisting in the creation of a methodology that is simultaneously tangible and ephemeral.

Summary

The challenges within this project have been complex and multilayered. Community-based action research ultimately becomes a search for meaning, which moves us away from competitive, power-driven processes toward more cooperative ways of knowing. These new models require humility, care, and equity (Ansley & Gaventa, 1997; Stringer, 1999). During the UCI Project, we attempted to enact these qualities and values. In the remainder of this chapter, we share some of the lessons learned during the project using specific examples, reactions of our co-researchers and colleagues, and our reflections. We also share episodes of assessment, evaluation, and metacommunication. Throughout the project, we have created opportunities for CASA and USF participants to discuss the research process and review the progress of the project. These opportunities for sense-making have included luncheons, interactive interviews, project meetings, multiple local and state presentations, a National Communication Association conference panel that included the executive director of CASA, and a university colloquium on the research relationship that featured two staff members from CASA. These were times when we were actively engaging in communication activism poetically, which enabled us to create project products, including the successful internship program and narrative booklet of stories.

We have found that both engaged scholarship and social justice depend on relationships involving time, trust, and respect. To operationalize these relational characteristics, we plan to address the challenges and successes of the UCI Project with respect to the following themes: (a) maintaining an empathetic stance as we learned from collaborative partners; (b) suspending assumptions about the "other"; (c) dialogic, active listening; (d) coping with vicarious trauma in a crisis-oriented setting; (e) discussing the process by engaging in metacommunication with co-researchers; (f) developing ties and on-site involvement; and (g) issues with leaving the site.

We envision the narratives emerging from this project—the stories within the booklet, as well as the stories emerging from the project—as bringing about political and social reform. Our experiences during the past 4 years have confirmed that these stories have served to change perceptions—those of the politicians and lobbyists attempting to enact social justice; the clerks, attorneys, and judges charged with administering social justice; and the community members and donors supporting and funding social justice. We theorize this project—our work together with CASA and CASA's work alone—as examples of K. J. Gergen's (2000) idea of poetic activism, work that generates theory and constitutes meaning in a relational manner.

COLLOQUIUM OF CO-RESEARCHERS

This section of the chapter presents our lessons learned within the narrative framework of a university colloquium we presented about the UCI Project called "Developing the Research Relationship." The narrative we have constructed is based on extensive fieldnotes we took during this colloquium, numerous conversations among all of the colloquium participants as we processed the event, presentations and papers that resulted from the exchanges during and about the colloquium, and our co-researchers' review of this chapter. The colloquium panel was initially designed as a presentation to the university community about our research relationship with CASA staff members. When we expanded the panel to include two staff members from CASA who actively participated in the research project, it became an *enactment* of our relationship as co-researchers. The panel demonstrated a relational experience as part of our continuing relationship. It also provided an occasion for reflexivity about action research; as Weick (1995) maintained, "Research and practice in sensemaking needs to begin with a mindset to look for sensemaking, a willingness to use one's own life as data, and a search for those outcroppings and ideas that fascinate" (p. 191).

This colloquium and chapter are examples of using narrative to achieve academic sense-making, storied examples of sense-making about an occasion of sense-making; consequently, we present a type of metasense-making of reciprocal reflexivity among the researchers involved and our university community of students and faculty. The narrative is intended as a complex example of the interplay between individual and social activities that demonstrate the importance of social action research as a relationship. Finally, the narrative is an example of our vision of K. J. Gergen's (2000) idea of poetic activism, one of the foundational theories for our work. We invite the reader to engage the following narrative framework, which includes events of the colloquium and flashbacks to events throughout the project. In the concluding section of the chapter, we summarize the meanings we have come to understand and the lessons we have begun to learn about the importance of the development of "poetic" research relationships to promote social justice for victims and survivors of domestic violence; their advocates, activists, volunteers, and fieldworkers; and the communities affected by this significant social problem.

Coming Together

The hallway erupts in a cacophony of voices and bodies as afternoon classes empty. Students with backpacks flow in both directions. Some stop to talk
in clusters, creating traffic jams. Toni, a doctoral student in USF's
Department of Communication, waves and steps to the side as students
surge around us. "Hey, Deb, Elizabeth! I'm looking forward to your colloquium this afternoon. The flier says that a couple of the panelists are coming from CASA. That should be really interesting. Not sure it's been done
before, at least since I've been here."

Elizabeth responds, "The original idea was for Deb and me to talk about
developing the research relationship. Since we position the CASA staff as
our co-researchers, not just participants, we decided we should invite them
to be part of the panel."

Deb jumps in, "Yeah, it will be lively because they've had really negative experiences before with researchers. Today, they'll have an audience of
academics and researchers they can talk back to."

Deb and Elizabeth walk a few steps down the hall to the small lecture
lab, and Deb begins to organize the informational brochures about CASA
that they intend to distribute to the audience. Elizabeth glances at the clock.
"I'm a bit worried about Judy and Clarissa. I hope they can find our building. You know, parking is a nightmare."

"Even though I sent them maps and parking passes, I know they'll be
nervous. You finish arranging the chairs; I'll go downstairs and watch for
them." Deb hustles down the stairs. The room begins to fill with students
and professors, and soon the room is full. A few minutes later, Deb shep-
herds Judy and Clarissa from CASA into the room. Elizabeth hugs them.
They huddle together for a few minutes and then settle into the chairs
arranged panel style in front of the audience.

Colloquium Part I: Why Did You Let Us In?

Elizabeth serves as panel moderator, introducing the panelists and then
proposing, "Many of you have heard us discuss parts of this project in our
classes. The handout we gave you has more detailed information about the
UCI Project, but the key to our presentation lies in the project's first goal:
establishing a collaborative relationship between CASA and USF and documenting that process. All the other goals depended on the establishment
of the research relationship. Today, we propose three broad areas of discussion: (a) preconceptions about research, or, why did you let us in? (b)
what were our milestones as we began to build trust? and (c) what would

we do differently? We'll be sharing lessons learned about collaborative research that seeks to secure justice not only for a social issue but also for project participants, and, hopefully, we'll stimulate discussion because this topic is critical to everyone's work. So today, in keeping with our pledge to listen, we've asked our CASA partners to begin the panel. Clarissa, could you tell the audience why you let us into the site and your first impressions of us?"

Clarissa begins, "We just love Deb and Elizabeth now. Deb isn't afraid to get dirty; she sorts laundry, cooks, stocks the pantry—whatever needs doing. Elizabeth is the listener; she comes to visit, brings us chocolate, cookies, or pizza, and just listens. Now I don't want to offend you because you are all researchers, but at CASA, we didn't have very good opinions of university folks. Our experiences with researchers had not been good—until Elizabeth and Deb." Some of the audience members chuckle at her candor.

Judy follows up, "Frankly, we have felt used by other researchers. They come with long surveys, lots of questions, and we spend hours of our time on the project, and then they leave, and we never hear from them again! I don't know how the rest of you work, but Elizabeth and Deb treated us with respect. They weren't pretentious. They used their first names. They were dressed nicely, but casually. They went to the CASA volunteer training and committed to spending lots of time with us. Elizabeth would talk with us and tape record our long, rambling conversations, full of thoughts and ideas. Then lo and behold, she would pull it all together and bring us a report, a paper, a story. Now some parts of the papers are a little boring to us, but the stories are great." Again, the audience laughs. "Elizabeth would ask us to read what she wrote, and whether she had gotten it right. She would describe us so well we could just see ourselves!"

Clarissa looks over at Elizabeth and says in a subdued voice, "And they were both human. I remember when Elizabeth cried at our first meeting when she told us about her friends who had been abused. Then we all knew that she could really feel the pain, that there was empathy." Clarissa looks at Elizabeth again, checking to see if it is okay that she told the audience about the tears. She continues in a more animated voice, "We all remember our first meeting so well! We had lots of questions and concerns. Deb took notes, and Elizabeth talked more. They watched as CASA staff members talked; they really looked at us and seemed to listen so intently. They acknowledged people who spoke and, at one point, told us what they had written, like a summary. They even laughed. You know what was the thing that closed the bond, the superglue to the whole thing? They said, 'We want to learn about you. We want you to tell us how we can learn about what it's like to work against domestic violence, what it's like to volunteer.' Wow! We weren't used to that approach."

Colloquium Part II: Building Trust

"One of the important developments in this unfolding research relation-ship," observes Elizabeth, "seems to have been building trust." She shifts in the metal folding chair. "Especially in light of your negative experiences with previous researchers, and given the sensitive and confidential nature of your work, could we talk a little bit more about why you trusted us?"

Clarissa leans forward with a big smile, clasping her hands together, eager to contribute. "You got it!" She looks at the audience. "In the field of domestic violence, we talk about folks who get it and folks who don't get it. Some people just can't understand why a woman doesn't leave her abuser or may seem to instigate her batterer . . ."

"At CASA, we believe these common cultural misconceptions are all forms of victim blaming," chimes in Judy. "The question people should ask is, 'Why does a man beat and emotionally abuse someone he says he loves?' Most researchers don't get it, but we didn't have to fight with Deb and Elizabeth about our core philosophies and mission. They got it!"

Deb warms at the praise, but feels a bit uncomfortable, too. She doesn't want the audience to assume that they have engaged too much in the rela-tionship and not enough in research. At the same time, however, she embraces the subjectivity of the relationship. Deb comments, "Elizabeth and I have talked about different ways of realizing you've achieved a bit of trust, a bit of community, on-site. We've talked about the differences between 'trust as a moment' and 'trust over time,' for example."

Elizabeth jumps in. "For me, I was able to monitor trust levels through a series of little moments. When I was first invited to stay for lunch, for example, or when I was no longer asked to leave the room during a crisis call or conversation with a child abuse investigator, or being asked to have a smoke with Judy." Judy laughs, coughs, and nods.

"I was also able to see 'moments' of trust develop," Deb agrees, "such as being given the house master keys, for example, when working in the pantry or closet. I vividly remember the day I walked up to the shelter and was immediately buzzed in without having to identify myself through the security intercom—things like that. For me, however, trust seemed to be a more gradual process than spontaneous 'moments' of event, especially at the shelter. Little by little, it seemed, people took more to me, spoke more open-ly around me. . . ." Deb silently reflects on her time at the shelter:

After stocking the pantry all morning, I join the staff for lunch. Bonnie, the house manager, interrupts the low, constant hum of conversations and hops up to turn up the radio. Whitney Houston fills the room. "Lemme sing for you all!" she says, lip-synching while holding her Snapple bottle up like a microphone. "Oooooh, Herman!" she drawls her husband's name out sexily, and we all burst out laughing. "This is for you, Herman," she cooes, as she moves her hips suggestively. We all howl.

Judy nods toward me and says softly to Bonnie, "Remember, we have company."

Bonnie says, "Oh, right," and begins to straighten up.

"Oh, no, keep singing," I implore, eager to become one of the group. Bonnie sits back down, but she smiles at me and starts telling us about Herman's habit of giving things pet names. "What is it about men that they have to name all their body parts?" I ask, raising my eyebrows to look suggestive. All the girls laugh, and Bonnie says, "Oh, Herman's name for that is Mr. Pop-up. 'Course, it never pops up when I want it to!" We all scream with laughter.

"Betcha' it never comes when you want it to, either?" I lewdly suggest. More shrieks of laughter. "No pun intended," I add dryly to hoots and giggles. Bonnie wipes tears of laughter from her eyes and says, "You know what I'm talkin' 'bout, girl!" After we calm down and resume eating, Judy leans over and says, "You have to excuse us. We're a little crazy. When you do what we do, you have to be."

"How did you all find the time to do all this?" Toni asks from the audience. Murmurs of agreement ripple through the room. Elizabeth and Deb smile at each other. It is a challenge, among many others, that they have discussed quite frequently.

Colloquium Part III: Processing Problems

"It's hard," Elizabeth and Deb agree. "Managing time and negotiating schedules were major challenges."

"It was one of the staff's main concerns about the project," interjects Judy. "We were worried that accommodating researchers would be difficult, not only from a time standpoint but from the standpoint of confidentiality, too."

"You see," Clarissa again leans forward. "We work in a crisis environment. We may schedule an appointment or interview with you, and have every intention of keeping it, but then things might just explode. We might get several crisis calls all at once; we might have walk-ins, police drop-offs, emergency pick-ups. . . . Like today, we were later coming here than we planned to be because a mother abandoned her baby at the shelter." The audience members shift uncomfortably in their chairs, their faces show mixed emotions, and the room grows quiet. "We don't know if that mother is alive or dead. We don't know where she is now. Maybe her abuser found her or maybe she is trying to escape. She knew the baby was safe at the shelter; maybe that's why she left the baby—to protect the baby from the abuser. But we can't keep that baby." Clarissa pauses.

Judy continues, "This morning shelter workers had to call DCF (Florida's Division of Children and Families) to transport that baby to foster care. We know that the mother will probably lose her rights to the baby because of the abandonment. We must follow the law, but it breaks your heart too. Staff members were upset, shelter residents were upset, and it involved lots of paperwork! So then we look at the clock, and it's time to come here, so we go tearing up the interstate to get here. First thing when we walked in that door, we told Elizabeth and Deb about it, not as an excuse but because we wanted them to know. We knew they could understand what that event meant to the staff."

"We've learned to approach the project with flexibility because of situations like Judy and Clarissa just described," muses Elizabeth. "We found the assumption on the part of previous researchers that the research participants had to alter their schedules to accommodate that of the researchers a bit, well, presumptuous . . . maybe arrogant. Who were we to assume that our needs should supersede those of families in crisis?"

"But then how is it possible to complete a research project in one semester?" asks one of the new doctoral students in the audience.

"It's not," Deb asserts flatly. "There's no way to propose it, get it approved, conduct it, analyze it, write about it, and present it in one semester."

Elizabeth softens Deb's candor. "But you can write the proposal for it one semester, and begin orientation and data collection in another. This began as a year-long grant project and has extended into several years."

"That brings up another challenge," Deb adds, "getting out. The next time I engage in a long-term project like this, I'll have very clear guidelines for ending it. It's a tough balance to achieve: You want to be involved and have a long-term relationship, and you develop a sense of responsibility toward the organization. . . ." She pauses. "But after awhile, you are forced to move on, or things occur that make it difficult to sustain that level of commitment."

"Mmmmm, I can see where that would be challenging," says Judy. "I knew Deb was writing her dissertation and attending a lot of conferences and that Elizabeth was the primary caretaker for her chronically ill mom and still meeting consulting obligations, but I had no idea how crazy the drive between St. Petersburg and USF in Tampa is."

"But it's funny," Elizabeth interjects, "because CASA became sort of a refuge for me . . ."

"It made us feel good to go there . . ." Deb interrupts, "I would often complain about having to go, but then when I got there, everyone was so nice . . ."

"And they'd make you feel so good," adds Elizabeth.

"That's when I'd feel guilty about feeling resentful," Deb says, taking her glasses off and rubbing her eyes, feeling hesitant about bringing up a sensitive issue, but deciding that it is important to demonstrate frank disclosure in this colloquium about research relationships. "Guilt and resentment, actually, were always difficult emotions for me to negotiate as I continued volunteering. For example, when I began volunteering at the legal advocacy office at the courthouse, I found out I had to pay $40 to attend a mandatory training session. I got a parking ticket because the advocate who was supposed to relieve me was late, so I'd feel angry, then guilty about my anger. I'd also get angry at the clients. I'd try to tell myself that the people I was trying to help were battered, bruised, traumatized, resentful, and defensive, but I'd still be left feeling like some of them were just plain nasty."

"Well, some of 'em are just plain nasty, just like all folks, no better, no worse," Judy says sympathetically. "You just can't take it personally."

"I know, but still, I'd think to myself if one more woman puts her hand up in my face. . . . Then I'd feel so guilty for being so impatient and insensitive," Deb allows her thought to trail away.

"It's okay to feel resentful and impatient sometimes," Clarissa says softly.

"But even worse, Deb, was your fear for the clients' safety, your vicarious traumatization," observes Elizabeth. Elizabeth remembers Deb's hysterical phone call after she had a particularly challenging day volunteering at the courthouse:

"E, I can't stop crying! I wish I could just quit. This isn't for me. I don't have the patience or sensitivity for this kind of work, plus I'm scared all the time." Deb sobs the words out.

"What do you mean?" I ask soothingly.

"The clients!" Deb wails. "I'm terrified for them! I'm scared to death when they don't get their restraining orders, when they come in to file motions for dismissal before the abuser has even attended the first batterer's intervention, and when they refuse my help, and I don't have anyone to talk to! It's not like the shelter, where there's community. At the courthouse, it's only me and the clerks, no other advocates. . . . How do the paid advocates do it?"

"It's hard for them too. A lot of paid advocates leave the field because of these reasons. What you're going through is common. I know it doesn't make it easier." I try to talk Deb down by offering several solutions: sharing her fears with her volunteer supervisors, working on body language and vocal tone to project a more calming persona to the clients, and taking occasional walks around the building to ease off stress. She eventually calms down.

"Most domestic violence advocates experience vicarious traumatization," asserts Judy. "We work in an environment of violence, anger, frustration, and trauma every day. So researchers must be ready for risk and even safety issues. We need to be aware and help them learn to cope with trauma, both physical and emotional."

"Elizabeth experienced vicarious traumatization, too," Deb observes and leans toward Elizabeth to invite her to share her story.

"Yes, I marvel at the ways in which the traditional divisions between researcher and those being researched have blurred within this project. My friends, classmates, and even several of my mom's nurses disclosed their abuse to me. But the most emotional day for me was when I learned that one of CASA's advocates had been beaten with a pipe. I cried driving all the way across the bridge. I was crying because she was hurt, and because CASA staff members trusted me enough to tell me about it. They said they wanted me to write the story someday, but I haven't been able to write it yet."

There is a subdued atmosphere in the room. Deb and Elizabeth had both agreed that it would be critical to talk during the colloquium about the challenges and problems of conducting research. They worried that the camaraderie among all of the colloquium participants might be interpreted as "too good to be true," but had decided that it also exemplified the mutual respect and deference necessary for poetic activism to occur in a collaborative context such as this one.

Elizabeth moves the group to the final section of the colloquium. "Our time is almost up," she says, "so we want to mention an event that could have been a showstopper. It could have derailed the project and destroyed our research relationship." The audience sits up with attention. She continues, "Problems and misunderstandings resulted among us as a result of a public performance that we brought to the shelter. It was a dramatic reading of an autoethnographic essay written by a colleague about her experience in a violent relationship. We thought this would be an excellent way to show how stories can be used as research, but we didn't do enough work on preparing ourselves or the staff for such an event."

Clarissa jumps in, "CASA staff saw it in very different ways, such as dramatizing their daily work, exploiting a victim, and promoting erroneous stereotypes of abuse victims. We were trying to be polite and listen, and we kept looking at our coordinator, but it was upsetting. We didn't feel like you were acknowledging our professional expertise. We just couldn't figure out why you would have someone do a story like that because we hear those stories every day."

Deb clarifies, "The misunderstandings among us about what we saw as research and what we were going to do with their stories was so important! When the performance was over, we were all unsettled. Elizabeth was smoking on the porch, and it was hard for us because we wanted to confer with the professors who were there, but we also felt an allegiance to the CASA staff."

As moderator, Elizabeth shifts the discussion. "In the interest of time, I want to focus on how we processed what happened—not just what happened but what it meant to the relationship, how we created the meaning to the event. We talked about it in many meetings with different people who were involved. In talking about the problem, we moved our relationship to stronger levels."

Judy nods and says, "We learned that our way of processing problems is also something that researchers do. Both CASA and academics talk problems through. We were going to discuss it anyway, but then Elizabeth said, 'Let's have pizza and sort things out.' We found out so much that day. But I still don't think we could see exactly what kind of research you were talking about. It wasn't until we read the stories in the book that it all started to make sense."

Elizabeth replies, "And this wasn't the first time we had talked about our talk. We had practiced reflexivity from the beginning, so we could use the same model to process conflict when it did occur. In the end, the performance wasn't a success in the way we anticipated but it was a huge success in that it helped us to identify some messy issues and look at our different perspectives. We learned a lot about each other because we didn't avoid a difficult situation. We were able to clarify our ideas about what constitutes research, and we were able to address other concerns as well. For example, the performance caused CASA staff to question our sensitivity, so it was important to reassure staff of our intentions in staging such a realistic and volatile performance. This incident could have derailed the whole research project, but it strengthened our relationship. It became mutually transformative. It was an example of Gergen's theory of poetic activism because we challenged each other's assumptions and reframed our ideas, yet continued to work together for productive change."

Colloquium Part IV: Discussion

There is a long pause when Elizabeth opens the floor for questions and comments. Finally, Dr. Kenneth Cissna, a faculty member in the Department of Communication, said, "As I listened to the four panelists, I was struck by how you were demonstrating your research relationship while you were talking about it today. I could see the respect and trust you have for each other. I was thinking that perhaps this is an idiosyncratic example, that these four women were just a certain combination that worked. I wonder if this relationship could have developed with four different people involved in the project. Would this work in a similar way in a different organization?" Dr. Cissna pauses and then continues, "But as I thought about it further, I realized that the panelists have shown us a model of a research relationship that we could all develop. This isn't just one specific example; it is a way of building trust, a way of researching and working in the community, and, as such, is an excellent example of applying dialogic communication."

Dr. Doni Loeske, chair of USF's Sociology Department, and one of the CASA project participants, asks the panelists, "Has this research project and the research relationships changed you, and if so, how?"

Judy and Clarissa look to Deb and Elizabeth who glance at each other. Elizabeth hesitates momentarily and then says, "That's an important issue. I hope that our panel today demonstrates the recursive nature of our relationship. Frankly, I didn't want to do this research in the beginning." The audience laughs because the comment is so incongruous with the panel presentation. "I went to a meeting because Dr. Carolyn Ellis, my advisor, invited me. When I heard Linda Osmundson, the CASA executive director speak, I was intrigued because she was charismatic. I'll never forget how she described the victims as courageous women, facing incredible odds. She touched my mind and my heart. I also saw the chance to engage in research that would make a difference. Once I got involved, I continued because I had developed relationships. I was also drawn to the tensions of working through the philosophy of empowerment at CASA. It resonated with my personal philosophy, and now it's my dissertation topic."

Deb shares her story. "The meetings with the executive director and CASA staff also inspired me, but I knew immediately that I wanted to work on the CASA project. It fit my interests in studying volunteerism and the construction of volunteer identities. I volunteered in several different departments at CASA and really learned how different each experience could be, and that's what I'm writing my dissertation about."

Clarissa holds up some papers, pats her heart, and says, "No matter what happens, or when Deb or Elizabeth leave CASA, I'll always have part of them in the stories they wrote. Elizabeth wrote *my* story, and I'll always have that as part of our relationship. That booklet of stories has changed us in ways we didn't even expect. Some of us worked together, but we hadn't shared our stories with each other, so the team is tighter now than ever before. We use the booklet for training new staff members, advocates, and volunteers. We take it to all kinds of presentations for those who work in domestic violence, like the Florida Coalition Against Domestic Violence, and even to presentations at community group meetings."

Deb elaborates, "We've also used the booklet to do campus and community outreach, advocating for CASA and against domestic violence with our sociology and communication classes, with the Victim's Advocacy Office and Panhellenic Council on campus, with the local Creole Club, at professional conferences . . ."

"We sell them at fundraisers for $5 each, and all the money goes to support CASA programs," interjects Clarissa.

"It's even been used as a lobbying tool with state government legislators in Tallahassee to secure greater funding for domestic violence service providers. CASA's legal advocate believes that the booklet of stories was instrumental in getting Florida's first 'date rape' legislation enacted," adds Elizabeth.

Judy nods in agreement, "It is unique to have such interest in our work, in our stories. Most researchers study the victims, and sometimes they don't realize that many of us were victims or had family members victimized before we started this work. I cried when I read the story that Elizabeth wrote about me. I've told that story for almost 15 years whenever I gave presentations about domestic violence. My daughter never really wanted to hear it, or she couldn't hear it, but she could read the story. This project has changed me and my family. In families with domestic violence, you are taught to keep secrets, not to talk about things, but Elizabeth and Deb listen without judging. The whole process of being open to talking about myself and my work has helped me be more open, more confident."

Deb's final remark brings the panel to a close, "In our conversations with staff members, I've heard them say how the booklet of stories and the research process has changed individual staff members, even CASA as an organization. It has changed us all. But I want to close by reminding you that our work is part of CASA's efforts to stop domestic violence, to change society. It's all about achieving social justice for women and children and families who are abused. This work is our poetic activism, in response to the poetic activism that CASA advocates practice each day."

After the colloquium, as Elizabeth and Deb walk down the hall, they overhear several positive comments about the panel from other faculty and students. Deb says, "That really worked! We performed it while we talked! We enacted the measures of success in social action and feminist research projects that Stringer (1999) talks about: pride, dignity, affirmation of identity, sense of personal control, responsibility, unity, and social ties."

Elizabeth stops and faces her colleague, "After all this time, I am still humbled by the power of narratives, for the CASA panelists, the advocates, volunteers, and, even today, for our audience. I'm also humbled by everyone's gracious participation. You know, this project wouldn't have been possible if Doni, Linda, Carolyn, and Marcie hadn't sponsored the grant proposal . . ."

"Or if the CASA participants had refused our research," adds Deb.

"And this colloquium wouldn't have worked without Judy, Clarissa, and all of the other audience members who spoke up and made a contribution," Elizabeth says. "So I guess the panel was an act of poetic activism about poetic activism, with people engaged in poetic activism reframing how people see research relationships, action research, and domestic violence."

REFLECTIONS ON COMMUNICATION ACTIVISM

In this chapter, we presented a narrative representing a university colloquium that focused on the research relationship. We use narrative because it privileges the voices of our co-researchers from CASA, addresses the specific ways our relationship with them developed, and serves as an embodiment of the communication activism this project encompasses. The colloquium became an enactment of our relationship in format, content, and context. We now review the seven categories of challenges and successes within this social action research project: (a) the adoption of an empathetic stance that promotes respect and facilitates collaborative learning; (b) a suspension of assumptions about the "other"; (c) dialogic, active listening; (d) coping with vicarious trauma; (e) metacommunication; (f) cultivating the research relationship; and (g) issues with leaving a research site. We also want to re-examine the specific interventions this project has enabled. Finally, and perhaps most importantly, we want to reiterate our stance that poetic activism—both within our work as academics and CASA staff members' work as advocates—is exemplified within the enactment of these seven categories and can be enabled through feminist, social action research using narrative.

First, this research project demonstrates the development of the empathy, mutual respect, and collaborative learning that occurs among co-researchers. The colloquium narrative exhibits multiple examples of mutual empathy among the participants. From a shared understanding of conflicting professional and emotional demands to a demonstration of mutual concern and caring over distressing events, the colloquium panelists experienced mutual empathy. Empathy does not occur coincidentally, however; it grows from reciprocal respect. As Greenwood and Levin (2000) asserted, in social action research, the expertise of all participants must be valued. We entered the UCI Project eager to learn from our research partners. By obtaining our partners' feedback throughout the research project, inviting their executive director to be a co-principal investigator of the study, structuring our colloquium around their presence and contribution, and demonstrating our willingness to learn from their experiences, we showed our research partners that we respected their work, as well as their contribution to and involvement with the project. Mutual respect allowed empathy to develop so that collaborative learning could then occur in which we learned about their work and they learned about ours. Stringer (1999) identified the key concepts in the development of relationships among partners of action research as being equality, harmony, acceptance, cooperation, and sensitivity. During the UCI Project, in general, and the colloquium panel, specifically, we attempted to enact these qualities and values.

Second, this process of building trust required the suspension of particular assumptions about each other. CASA members had to suspend their assumptions about researchers, and we had to suspend our assumptions about the inviolatibility of the ivory tower. In that sense, we each had to suspend our assumptions about the other. Behar (1992) wondered if there can actually be a "fully feminist ethnography amid the many unresolvable separations between the women doing the research and the women being researched" (p. 108). We wanted to begin to breach these separations. We strove to become "vulnerable observers" (Behar, 1996), seeking to understand and be understood, teach and be taught, transform and, in the process, be transformed. By agreeing to volunteer onsite, actively seeking our partners' feedback about our work, and making that work accessible to this community by creating readable texts that also could appeal to a nonacademic audience, we proved to our co-researchers that we were committed to their cause, their work, and their lives. Consequently, *their* poetic activism resulted in *our* poetic activism. As a result, we began to share a sense of purpose and to care for each other, frequently acknowledging the benefits of the project to all involved and affirming each other's commitment to it—and to each other.

Third, the development of mutual respect and trust and the suspension of assumptions about the "other" rested on the success of dialogic, active-listening processes. We attended to listening in a number of ways. We met frequently with our co-researchers, both formally and informally, to review project progress and obtain their opinions and feedback. We designed the project and chose the methodology specifically in response to our participants' requests, and we quickly made adaptations when some of these choices were not effective, such as when we realized that autoethnographic performance was not as useful for our participants as were written narratives. When these ruptures did occur, we quickly attended to "damage control." We learned to expect and work through conflict: talking, processing, suggesting alternatives, and sharing emotions.

Fourth, sharing emotions and managing conflicting feelings became very important to coping with the vicarious traumatization that invariably occurs in crisis-oriented settings when conducting social action research. Talking through feelings of guilt, resentment, fear, horror, and frustration provided an important outlet for the vicarious traumatization often experienced by advocates, volunteers, and researchers within the field of domestic violence. Empathic listening by the colloquium participants facilitated Deb's sharing of her conflicting feelings about client advocacy, Elizabeth and the CASA advocates' sharing of sorrow for victimized friends, and the advocates' sharing of the story of the baby abandoned at the shelter. This sharing of emotions, coupled with empathic listening, facilitated the assuagement of painful emotion, permitting us to take solace in each other and in the work we were doing. Listening to and writing the stories for the book allowed us to become intimately involved in this crisis-oriented setting. Sharing ourselves with each other in so many ways resulted in enhanced emotionality, safety concerns, senses of loss or misgiving, and a host of other challenges. Not only have we used humor as a coping mechanism for these feelings, such as during the vignette describing lunch with the CASA advocates, but we created other outlets for these emotions, from phone calls to shared lunches to "time-outs" to personal celebrations. In so doing, the research relationship was strengthened.

Fifth, this metacommunication helped us to process and learn from these experiences. The challenge of the autoethnographic performance at CASA, for example, still is being processed today because it involved such critical issues. During the colloquium panel, as we discussed this episode, our voices grew loud, and it was hard not to all talk at the same time. However, we shared the main point with the audience that research often involves a disruption of assumptions, a willingness to explore that disruption, and an acknowledgment of the other within that exploration. Such discourse reflects our commitment to poetic activism within social action research, as we continue to work together to process these events, reach some understanding about them, and continue to learn from them. These steps constitute the process of metacommunication.

Sixth, all of the project's participants—advocates and academics alike— understood that this would be a lengthy, complicated project, and we embraced that challenge. We recognized that it was important to be involved, participate, and not only demonstrate commitment by being prompt and dependable but also by joining the community in other ways, such as by attending CASA fundraisers, grand openings, and thrift store sales. These opportunities for immersion in the site cultivated our research relationship with CASA staff members, as well as demonstrated our commitment to poetic activism through our actions and the products of our actions.

Finally, this intense level of activism poses special challenges when leaving the research site. From the perspective of research as relationship, involvement does not end; it merely lessens and does so gradually. Clear-cut understandings about the level of the research commitment from the beginning of the project are imperative, as are the development of exit strategies for gradually leaving the research site. Despite the funded-grant project ending years ago, we still are immersed in our research site, responding to needs that we continue to recognize, not because we are paid to do so but because we remain activists. We conduct staff development workshops, enrichment activities for the residents of CASA's transitional housing, and arts and crafts for the children involved in CASA's after-school program. We remain committed.

CONCLUSION

The type of communication activism that we have articulated in this chapter is not easy to enact, but if enacted effectively, it can result in great successes. An important component of poetic social action research is the "enactment of a commitment to democratic social transformation through social research" (Greenwood & Levin, 1998, p. 3). The narrative methodology of the UCI Project was designed to support CASA's outreach efforts in conjunction with its social justice mission. The attainment of the UCI Project grant goals also supported this commitment. We established a collaborative community-university relationship, documenting that process as we studied the stories of CASA's staff and volunteers. We developed a successful volunteer program with CASA through the university's communication and sociology departments that has resulted in a formal internship program, an informal honors program, and the hiring of USF volunteers for paid staff positions. We created a booklet of staff stories that has changed some of the perceptions of victims, survivors, advocates, volunteers, funders, donors, judges, and legislators.

We also, however, moved beyond goal attainment to achieve something far more special: We engaged in the process of reshaping our understanding of research relationships, community involvement, and the power of narrative. As Ellis (2002) contended, "The personal is political. We learned that a long time ago. Maybe it's time to rethink what that means and to remember that the reverse is just as true—the political is personal" (403). Poetic activism offers an opportunity to rethink the connections between communication activism and personal narratives because, as Ellis concluded, "ultimately, both approaches are about making a better world" (p. 403).

REFERENCES

Ansley, F., & Gaventa, J. (1997). Researching for democracy and democratizing research. *Change, 29*(1), 46-53.

Baker, P. (1996). Doin' what it takes to survive: Battered women and the consequences of compliance to a cultural script. *Studies in Symbolic Interaction, 20*, 73-90.

Behar, R. (1992). A life story to take across the border: Notes on an exchange. In G. C. Rosenwald & R. L. Ochberg (Eds.), *Storied lives: The cultural politics of self-understanding* (pp. 76-93). New Haven, CT: Yale University Press.

Behar, R. (1996). *The vulnerable observer: Anthropology that breaks your heart.* Boston: Beacon Press.

Cacho-Negrete, M. (2000, October). In the lions' den. *The Sun*, pp. 14-22.

Community Action Stops Abuse. (2000). *Domestic violence: An overview* [Brochure]. St. Petersburg, FL: Author.

Ceglowski, D. (2000). Research as relationship. *Qualitative Inquiry, 6,* 88-103.

Curry, E., & Walker, D. (Eds.). (2002). *Many faces, many voices working against domestic violence: The CASA story of stories.* St. Petersburg, FL: Community Action Stops Abuse.

Dankoski, M. E. (2000). What makes research feminist? *Journal of Feminist Family Therapy, 12,* 1-12.

Ellingson, L. L. (1998). "Then you know how I feel": Empathy, identification, and reflexivity in fieldwork. *Qualitative Inquiry, 4,* 492-511.

Ellis, C. (2002). Being real: Moving inward toward social change. *International Journal of Qualitative Studies in Education, 15,* 399-406.

Ellis, C., & Berger, L. (2002). Their story/my story/our story: Including the researcher's experience in interview research. In J. F. Gubrium & J. A. Holstein (Eds.), *Handbook of interview research: Context and method* (pp. 849-876). Thousand Oaks, CA: Sage.

Ellis, C., & Bochner, A. P. (2000). Autoethnography, personal narrative, reflexivity: Researcher as subject. In N. K. Denzin & Y. S. Lincoln (Eds.), *Handbook of qualitative research* (2nd ed., pp. 733-768). Thousand Oaks, CA: Sage.

Ellis, C., & Flaherty, M. G. (1992). *Investigating subjectivity: Research on lived experiences.* Newbury Park, CA: Sage.

Gatenby, B., & Humphries, M. (2000). Feminist participatory action research: Methodological and ethical issues. *Women's Studies International Forum, 23,* 89-105.

Gergen, K. J. (1994). *Realities and relationships: Soundings in social construction.* Cambridge, MA: Harvard University Press.

Gergen, K. J. (2000). *Invitation to social construction.* Thousand Oaks, CA: Sage.

Gergen, K. J. (2001). *Social construction in context.* Thousand Oaks, CA: Sage.

Gergen, K. J., & Gergen, M. (1999). Toward reflexive methodologies. In F. Steier (Ed.), *Research and reflexivity* (pp. 75-95). Newbury Park, CA: Sage.

Gergen, M. (1992). 7 life stories: Pieces of a dream. In G. Rosenwald & R. Ochberg (Eds.), *Storied lives: The cultural politics of self-understanding* (pp. 127-145). New Haven, CT: Yale University Press.

Glazer, S. (1993). Violence against women. *Congressional Quarterly, 3*(8), 171.

Greenwood, D. J., & Levin, M. (1998). *Introduction to action research: Social research for social change.* Thousand Oaks, CA: Sage.

Greenwood, D. J., & Levin M. (2000). Reconstructing the relationships between universities and society through action research. In N. K. Denzin & Y. S. Lincoln (Eds.), *Handbook of qualitative research* (2nd ed., pp. 85-106). Thousand Oaks, CA: Sage.

Hegde, R. (1996). Narratives of silence: Rethinking gender, agency, and power from the communication experiences of battered women in South India. *Communication Studies, 47,* 303-317.

Jorgenson, J. (1999). Co-constructing the interviewer/co-constructing family. In F. Steier (Ed.), *Research and reflexivity* (pp. 210-225). Newbury Park, CA: Sage.

Lempert, L. (1997). The other side of help: Negative effects in the help-seeking processes of abused women. *Qualitative Sociology, 20,* 289-309.

Loseke, D. (1987). Lived realities and the construction of social problems: The case of wife abuse. *Symbolic Interaction, 102,* 229-243.

Loseke, D. (1992). *The battered woman and shelters: The social construction of wife abuse.* Albany: State University of New York Press.

May, R. A. B., & Pattillo-McCoy, M. (2000). So you see what I see? Examining a collaborative ethnography. *Qualitative Inquiry, 6,* 65-87.

Milburn, T., Wilkins, R. J., & Wilkins, K. W. (2001). Reflexive moments: Negotiating researcher roles in participant observation. *Iowa Journal of Communication, 33,* 107-123.

Murray, S. (1988). The unhappy marriage of theory and practice: An analysis of a battered woman's shelter. *NWSA Journal, 1,* 75-92.

National Coalition Against Domestic Violence. (n.d.). *About NCADV.* Retrieved September 20, 2003, from www.ncadv.org/about.htm

Riley Center. (n.d.). *Domestic violence statistics.* Retrieved June 29, 2004, from www.rileycenter.org/domestic-violence-statistics.html

Steier, F. (Ed.). (1999). *Research and reflexivity.* Newbury Park, CA: Sage.

Stringer, E. T. (1999). *Action research* (2nd ed.). Thousand Oaks, CA: Sage.

Swigonski, M. E. (1993). Feminist standpoint theory and the questions of social work research. *Affilia Journal of Women and Social Work, 8,* 171-184.

Tillmann-Healy, L. M. (2001). *Between gay and straight: Understanding friendship across sexual orientation.* Walnut Creek, CA: AltaMira Press.

Tillmann-Healy, L. M. (2002, October). *Friendship as method.* Speech presented at the Institute for Human Interpretive Studies, University of South Florida, Tampa, FL.

U.S. Bureau of Justice Statistics. (1993). *Highlights from 20 years of surveying crime victims.* Washington, DC: U.S. Department of Justice. Retrieved October 14, 2004, from http://www.ojp.usdoj.gov/bjs /pub/pdf/cvus93.pdf

Weick, K. E. (1995). *Sensemaking in organizations.* Thousand Oaks, CA: Sage.

Weil, M. (1996). Women, community, and organizing. In N. Van Den Bergh & L. B. Cooper (Eds.), *Feminist visions for social work* (pp. 187-210). Silver Spring, MD: National Association of Social Workers.

Women's Rural Advocacy Programs. (n.d.). *Domestic violence statistics.* Retrieved June 29, 2004, from www.letswrap.com/dvinfo/stats.htm

Wood, J.T. (2001). The normalization of violence in heterosexual romantic relationships: Women's narratives of love and violence. *Journal of Social and Personal Relationships, 18,* 239-261.

ABOUT THE EDITORS
AND AUTHORS

ABOUT THE EDITORS

Lawrence R. Frey (PhD, University of Kansas, 1979) is a Professor in the Department of Communication at the University of Colorado at Boulder. His areas of teaching and scholarship include group communication, applied communication (communication and social justice, communication and community studies, and health communication), and communication research methods (quantitative and qualitative). He is the author or editor of 14 books, 3 special journal issues, and more than 60 published journal articles and book chapters. He is the recipient of 11 distinguished scholarship awards, including the 2000 Gerald M. Phillips Award for Distinguished Applied Communication Scholarship from the National Communication Association (NCA); the 2004, 2003, and 2000 Ernest Bormann Research Award from NCA's Group Communication Division, for, respectively, the edited texts, *Group Communication in Context: Studies of Bona Fide Groups* (2nd ed.), *New Directions in Group Communication*, and *The Handbook of Group Communication Theory and Research* (coedited with Dennis S. Gouran and Marshall Scott Poole); a 1999 Special Recognition Award from NCA's Applied Communication Division for an edited special issue of the *Journal of Applied Communication Research* on "Communication and Social Justice Research"; the 1998 National Jesuit Book Award (Professional Studies Category) and the 1998 Distinguished Book Award from NCA's Applied Communication Division for his coauthored text (with Mara B. Adelman), *The Fragile Community: Living Together With AIDS*; and the 1995 Gerald R. Miller Award from NCA's Interpersonal and Small Group Interaction Division and the 1994 Distinguished Book Award from NCA's Applied Communication Division for his edited text, *Group Communication in Context: Studies of Natural Groups*. He is a past president of the Central States Communication Association and a recipient of the Outstanding Young Teacher Award from that organization, as well as a 2003 Master Teacher Award from the Communication and Instruction Interest Group of the Western States Communication Association.

Kevin M. Carragee (PhD, University of Massachusetts at Amherst, 1985) is an Associate Professor at Suffolk University, where he teaches courses in communication theory, mediated communication, and persuasion. His scholarship has focused on news and ideology, the interaction between the news media and social movements, cultural studies, and forms of communication activism. He has edited two books and has published more than 25 journal articles and book chapters. His scholarship has appeared in leading journals in communication and journalism, including the *Journal of Communication*, *Journalism and Mass Communication Monographs*, *Journal of Broadcasting & Electronic Media*, *Critical Studies in Media Communication*, and *Political Communication*. He received a Fulbright Scholarship in 1993 for research and teaching in Poland. Since 1990, he has been a member of the Media Research and Action Project, a group that assists social movement organizations and community groups in framing their messages, influencing news coverage, and securing social and political reforms.

ABOUT THE AUTHORS

Van M. Cagle (PhD, University of Illinois at Urbana, 1988) has taught courses in cultural studies, popular culture, and media studies at Bowling Green State University (Department of Popular Culture), Tulane University

(Department of Communication), and the University of Illinois at Urbana (Department of Speech Communication). His book *Reconstructing Pop/Subculture* examines the ways in which U.S. youth subcultures transformed the media industries of the 1960-1980s. Cagle also has published articles and book chapters on a wide range of topics, including media lifestyles, structural filmmaking, celebrity cultures, niche audiences, and innovative media research methods. From 2000-2004, Cagle served as Director of Research & Analysis at GLAAD's Center for the Study of Media & Society in New York City. He currently acts as a consultant and project director for a diverse range of private and nonprofit media companies, including Nickelodeon, Disney, ABC, NBC, CBS, Lifetime Television, The Lucas Foundation, and WorldLink.

Sue Ellen Christian (MA, University of Michigan, 1990) is an Assistant Professor of Journalism at Western Michigan University. A longtime professional journalist who has written for the *Los Angeles Times* and the *Detroit News*, and was a staff writer for the *Chicago Tribune* for 10 years, she divides her work between continuing to write and report for newspapers and magazines and conducting research on journalism pedagogy, health communication, and the practice and impact of civic and community journalism. Her work has appeared in publications such as *Quill*; *Journal of Intercultural Communication Research*; *Reflections: A Journal of Writing, Service-Learning, and Community Literacy*; and *Journal of Intergroup Relations*. She has produced a video and CD-ROM emphasizing diversity and ethics, featuring working journalists talking about their craft.

Leda Cooks (PhD, Ohio University, 1993) is an Associate Professor in the Department of Communication at the University of Massachusetts, Amherst. Her areas of teaching and research include intercultural communication, interracial communication, critical pedagogy, performance, computer-mediated communication, and conflict and mediation. Her essays and research have appeared in edited books and in journals such as *Communication Education, Communication Theory, Mediation Quarterly, Feminist Media Studies, Women's Studies in Communication, Communication Quarterly, Western Journal of Communication, Electronic Journal of Communication, Frontiers,* and *Michigan Journal of Community Service Learning.* Professor Cooks has been an active proponent of community service learning (CSL) for over 14 years, and has offered CSL and social action research courses on the graduate and undergraduate levels in areas ranging from interpersonal communication to qualitative methods.

Ted M. Coopman (MS, San Jose State University, 1995) is a doctoral candidate in the Department of Communication at the University of Washington,

Seattle. His current research focuses on emergent self-organizing resistance networks that form across new and old media. He also studies the organization and operations of guerrilla media and their role in manifesting dissent in the United States, social movements and collective action, and media law and regulation, with a concentration on the micro radio movement. His work has been published in the *Journal of Broadcasting & Electronic Media*, *Journal of Radio Studies*, *American Communication Journal*, and in the text, *Representing Resistance: Media, Civil Disobedience, and the Global Justice Movement*.

Elizabeth A. Curry (PhD, University of South Florida, 2003) has been involved in community outreach, partnerships, and collaborative projects for over 25 years. Her activities include alternative education, community partnership with the arts, literary events, grant writing, and promoting internet access for senior citizens and minorities. She now teaches leadership development for nonprofit and government agencies. For 5 years, she worked with CASA (Community Action Stops Abuse) as a volunteer and co-researcher. Her dissertation was a "research novel" about CASA workers, community collaboration, empowerment, collegiality, compassion, and using narratives to frame the meaning of work. Curry is currently the Assistant Executive Director of CASA. She also continues her consulting and coaching practice, specializing in leadership development and collaboration seminars.

James S. Ettema (PhD, University of Michigan, 1979) is a Professor and former Chair of Communication Studies at Northwestern University. His teaching focuses on the social and cultural impact of the media and new communication technologies. Among his books is *Custodians of Conscience: Investigative Journalism and Public Virtue* (coauthored with Theodore L. Glasser), which won the Frank Luther Mott-Kappa Tau Alpha Award from the National Journalism and Mass Communication Honor Society, the Bart Richards Award for Media Criticism from Pennsylvania State University, and the Sigma Delta Chi Award for research on journalism from the Society of Professional Journalists.

Lynn M. Harter (PhD, University of Nebraska, 2000) is an Associate Professor in the School of Communication Studies at Ohio University. Her research *praxis* focuses on discourses of organizing and health and healing, narrative theory, and feminist(s) studies. Her work has been published in journals, including *Management Communication Quarterly*, *Journal of Applied Communication Research*, *Communication Studies*, *Health Communication*, *Qualitative Health Research*, and *Journal of Business Communication*. She is coeditor of the text, *Narratives, Health, and Healing: Communication Theory, Research, and Practice*.

Andrew P. Herman (PhD, Northwestern University, 2005) is an Assistant Professor of Communication at the State University of New York at Geneseo. His research has included the interaction of communication and spirituality in the promotion of social activism and the importance of communication in mother-child relationships when a potential for abuse of the child exists. His current research focuses on the role of relational communication in the formation of social capital and the impact of teacher communication on students' perceptions of class assignments. He has contributed a chapter to the text, *Essays on Communication and Spirituality* and is cocontributor to an in *Communication Monographs*.

John P. McHale (PhD, University of Missouri, 2002) is an Assistant Professor in the Communication Department at Illinois State University, Normal. He is the author of the text, *Communicating for Change: Strategies of Social and Political Advocates*; co-author of three other texts on presidential campaigns; and has published a number of academic articles on political discourse. He recently completed *Picture This: A Fight to Save Joe*, his first feature-length documentary; previously directed *Unreasonable Doubt*, a documentary short; and produced and directed several other documentaries.

Eleanor Novek (PhD, University of Pennsylvania, 1994) is an Associate Professor of Communication at Monmouth University. Her research interests include prison journalism, community empowerment, and social justice and feminist methodologies. She also studies the intersection of communication and race in housing segregation and other forms of racial discrimination. Her work has appeared in journals such as *Communication Studies*; *Critical Studies in Media Communication*; *Howard Journal of Communications*; *Women's Studies in Communication*; *Discourse and Society Journalism*; *Media*; *Culture and Society*; *New Jersey Journal of Communication* (now the *Atlantic Journal of Communication*); *Peace Review*; and *Journal of Children and Poverty*.

Saumya Pant (MA, Ohio University, 2000) is a doctoral candidate in the School of Communication Studies at Ohio University. She is from India and her dissertation research investigates the enactment of empowerment by young girls in rural India and the politics of the public and private sphere. Her teaching and research interests center around communication and social change, gender and development, and ethnographic methods. She has coauthored articles in the *Journal of Communication*, *Journal of Development Communication*, and in the book, *Communicating the Environment: Environmental Communication for Sustainable Development*.

Marc D. Rich (PhD, Southern Illinois University, Carbondale, 1997) is an Assistant Professor of Communication Studies/Performance Studies at California State University, Long Beach. Since 1993, he has facilitated hundreds of proactive performance workshops in community and educational settings throughout the United States. Marc's research interests include performance and social change, performance ethnography, and critical race theory. His articles appear in journals such as *Text and Performance Quarterly*; *Journal of Contemporary Ethnography*; *American Communication Journal*; *Race, Ethnicity and Education*; and *Death Studies*; and he has a coauthored chapter in the text, *A Boal Companion: Dialogues on Theatre and Cultural Politics*.

José I. Rodríguez (PhD, Michigan State University, 1995) is an Associate Professor of Communication Studies at California State University, Long Beach. His scholarly interests include proactive performance efficacy, language attitudes, social identity, mindfulness, and empathy. His research has been published in *Communication Research*, *Communication Education*, *Western Journal of Black Studies*, *Intercultural Communication Studies*, and *Journal of Classroom Management*.

Rebecca Sanford (PhD, Temple University, 2004) is an Assistant Professor of Communication at Monmouth University. Her research investigates relationship formation and maintenance and specific contextual influences on relational trajectory. In addition to her university teaching, she also has been working in New Jersey prisons for over 7 years as a college instructor and a programming provider. She is coauthor (with Tricia Jones and Martin Remland) of the forthcoming text, *Interpersonal Communication across the Life Span*, and her work has appeared in *Conflict Resolution Quarterly* and *Sex Roles*.

Erica Scharrer (PhD, Syracuse University, 1998) is an Assistant Professor in the Department of Communication at the University of Massachusetts, Amherst. She studies media content, media effects, and media literacy. She is the coauthor (with George Comstock) of *Television: What's On, Who's Watching, and What it Means*, and her research has appeared in *Communication Research, Journal of Broadcasting & Electronic Media*, and *Media Psychology*. She collaborates with her students every spring to create and offer a media literacy curriculum in local 6th-grade classrooms and is interested in assessment in community service learning.

Devendra Sharma (PhD, Ohio University, 2006) is a folk actor-singer, writer, and director from India. He is creative director of Brij Lok Madhuri, an organization devoted to using folk-performing traditions for social activism. He has created many theatre and musical performances, participatory theatre workshops, and films focusing on contemporary social issues. In 2000, he was a Packard Foundation-Population Communication International Media Leadership Fellow from India at the University of Southern California's cinema school. and Annenberg School of Communication. He currently is an Assistant Professor in the Department of Communication, California State University, Fresno. His research interests center on performance, persuasion and social influence, popular culture, and entertainment-education communication strategies. He has published journal articles and book chapters, and given numerous guest lectures and conference paper presentations on performance and media strategies for social activism and change. A recent essay received a "Top Three Paper" Award from the Performance Studies Division at the 2006 National Communication Association conference.

Yogita Sharma (MA, Ohio University, 1998) is a doctoral student in the Department of Communication at Texas A&M University. Her research focuses on grassroots organizations, zero-history movements, and women's efforts to organize around the discourse of health and human rights.

Arvind Singhal (PhD, University of Southern California, 1990) is a Professor in the School of Communication Studies and Presidential Research Scholar at Ohio University. His teaching and research interests center around the diffusion of innovations, entertainment-education communication strategies, and organizing and mobilizing for social change. He is author of the texts, *Combating AIDS: Communication Strategies in Action* and *Entertainment-Education: A Communication Strategy for Social Change*, and coeditor of the text, *Entertainment-Education and Social Change: History, Research, and Practice*.

Deborah Cunningham Walker (PhD, University of South Florida, 2005) is an Assistant Professor in the Department of English, Communication & Journalism at Coastal Carolina University (CCU). She has been involved in activism, advocacy, and volunteerism most of her life. Her activities include community outreach with the Myrtle Beach Crisis Center Grand Stand Community Against Rape and CCU's Panhellenic Council, as well as her work with CASA (Community Action Stops Abuse). Her research interests center on the creation, maintenance, and fluidity of identity as constructed within discourse.

AUTHOR INDEX

SUBJECT INDEX

Printed in the United States
204221BV00001B/463-471/A